I TATTI STUDIES IN

ITALIAN RENAISSANCE HISTORY

Sponsored by Villa I Tatti
Harvard University Center for Italian Renaissance Studies
Florence, Italy

VENICE'S MOST LOYAL CITY

Civic Identity in Renaissance Brescia

STEPHEN D. BOWD

HARVARD UNIVERSITY PRESS
Cambridge, Massachusetts
London, England
2010

Library of Congress Cataloging-in-Publication Data
Bowd, Stephen D.
Venice's most loyal city : civic identity in Renaissance Brescia / Stephen D. Bowd.
p. cm.
(I Tatti studies in Italian Renaissance history)
Includes bibliographical references and index.
ISBN 978-0-674-05120-1 (alk. paper)
1. Renaissance—Italy—Brescia.   2. City and town life—Italy—Brescia—History.
3. Group identity—Italy—Brescia—History.   4. Political culture—Italy—Brescia—
History.   5. Brescia (Italy)—Relations—Italy—Venice.   6. Venice (Italy)—
Relations—Italy—Brescia.   7. Brescia (Italy)—Social life and customs.
8. Brescia (Italy)—Politics and government.   9. Venice (Italy)—History—697–1508.
10. Venice (Italy)—History—1508–1797.   I. Title.
DG975.B83B69 2010
945'.26105—dc22   2010010601

For Margaret, Robert, Andrew, and Gavin

Contents

Illustrations

Acknowledgments

THE ORIGINS OF THIS BOOK lie in a conversation at a conference in Oxford ten years ago when Donald Cullington first drew my attention to Carlo Valgulio's work on funerals. My subsequent investigation of this fascinating little treatise soon led me to the relatively neglected riches of the Brescian archives. Donald and I have collaborated on a number of Brescian projects since that meeting in Oxford, and I am grateful to him for his guidance as editor and translator. This book could not have been written without his intervention in the first place, and it would be much diminished without the example of his scholarship.

My research for this book has been generously supported by grants from the British Academy (in 2003), the Gladys Krieble Delmas Foundation for Venetian Research (in 2006), and the Carnegie Trust for the Universities of Scotland (in 2007). I was especially fortunate to begin my career in the Department of History and Economic History at Manchester Metropolitan University, which gave me very generous sabbatical leave in order to pursue my research more thoroughly at a critical stage. I am pleased to be able to acknowledge that immense debt here and to thank all my former colleagues for patiently enduring my obsession with Brescia. For happy memories of early morning coffee and conversation I thank Cath Danks, Lesley Ling, Philip Lloyd, and Louise Willmot. Karen Hunt asked some searching questions and encouraged me in many ways. More recently I received financial support from the School of History, Classics and Archaeology at the University of Edinburgh, for which I am also very grateful.

Ennio Ferraglio (of the Biblioteca Queriniana), Mariella Annibale Marchina (at the front desk of the Archivio di Stato), and their efficient and courteous staff made me welcome and helped me through the superbly organized Brescian archives. Many colleagues closer to home have answered my queries or encouraged me in other ways, and I would like to thank them here, especially Monica Azzolini, Alex Bamji, Michael Bury, Sarah Cockram, John Flood, Lucy Grig, Leofranc Holford-Strevens, Paul Kaplan, Catherine Kovesi, Mary Laven, Alex Marr, Robert Mason, Simon Oakes, Noel O'Regan, Diana Robin, David Rundle, James Shaw, Alison A. Smith, Sharon Strocchia, Nick Terpstra, and Emily Wilson. As well as discussing Brescian matters with me, Alex Bayer and Gabriele Neher generously provided me with copies of their unpublished research on Brescian art history and culture. I would also like to mention Tessa Beverley's invaluable thesis on Venetian ambassadors, which she was kind enough to send to me.

I must especially thank Chris Black, Andrew Brown, John Law, and Isabella Lazzarini for reading parts of this book in draft. Jill Burke, Trevor Dean, James Grubb, and Ed Muir read through the entire manuscript. The anonymous reader for Harvard University Press was especially encouraging and provocative. I would like to thank them all for their valuable and incisive comments, while emphasizing that I take full responsibility for the final published version. At the Press Jennifer Snodgrass, Kathleen McDermott, and finally Ian Stevenson answered my many enquiries and oversaw the production process with great efficiency and good sense.

I have presented some of my research at a number of conferences and seminars in Bristol, Edinburgh, Chicago, Oxford, and London, and I would like to thank everyone who invited me to speak on these occasions. I am especially grateful to the delegates attending the "Renaissance Intersections" session of the Association of Art Historians Annual Conference in Manchester in April 2009 for helping me to elucidate the purpose and meaning of the print discussed in Chapter 11.

Chapter 8 is a slightly revised version of my introduction to *Vainglorious Death: A Funerary Fracas in Renaissance Brescia*, trans. J. Donald Cullington, ed. Stephen Bowd (Tempe: Arizona Center for Medieval and Renaissance Studies, 2006). An earlier version of Chapter 10 was published as "'Honeyed Flies' and 'Sugared Rats': Witchcraft, Heresy, and Superstition in the Bresciano, 1454–1535," in *The Religion of Fools? Superstition Past and Present*, ed. S. A. Smith and Alan Knight, Past and Present Supplement 3 (Oxford: Oxford University Press, 2008), 134–156. I am grateful for permission to reprint the material.

Richard Davies, Peter Fry, and Richard Jones have shared their enthusiasm for Italy with me over a number of years, and this has been indispensable to the completion of this book. Finally, I would like to record my love and gratitude for my family, who have provided unconditional support for so many years, not least during the last few difficult years when I was working on Brescia. I dedicate this book with pleasure to them.

Venice's Most Loyal City

PART ONE

MYTH AND HISTORY

CHAPTER ONE

Regional States and Civic Identity

O N 23 MAY 1509 the king of France made his triumphal entry into the city of Brescia at the invitation of its councillors, who had voted to turn their backs on their Venetian governors and submit to the French. King Louis XII, who entered "armed in white" under a ceremonial balda-chin carried by four local citizens, proceeded along streets covered with white cloth and under triumphal arches that had been hastily erected in several parts of the city. As a sign of their victory, the words "veni, vidi, vici" were inscribed by the French on one of the Brescian gates. When the king and his entourage reached the *broletto*, the town hall and centre of political power in the city, they found it adorned with greenery as a sign of triumph and renewal. Brescians lined the royal route and greeted the huge proces-sion of cavalry, infantry, and nobles dressed in cloth of gold with cries of "Franza! Franza!" rather than "Marco! Marco!" as a sign of their new loyalties. Five days of feasting and celebrations followed, and the ritual of subjection and possession reached a climax when a Te Deum was sung in the cathedral by the choristers of the royal chapel in the presence of the local bishop, the most distinguished citizens, and the French court.[1]

The soldiers and cavalrymen who swarmed through the streets of Brescia in their thousands had recently inflicted a humiliating defeat on the repub-lic of Venice at the battle of Agnadello (14 May). Venice was now faced with the prospect of the dismemberment of its northern Italian empire at the hands of the League of Cambrai—comprising France, the Holy Roman

Empire, Spain, Hungary, Savoy, Mantua, Ferrara, and the papacy—which has been called "the most formidable European coalition since the days of the crusades."[2] The gerontocracy that governed the empire from the lagoon city was frozen with shock, and a sharp-eyed patrician who was present when the doge and his councillors received the news of the defeat at Agnadello observed: "Indeed, they were as dead men."[3] Venice had not simply lost a battle but had also been deprived of the most prosperous and populous city in its empire—Venice's "most beloved" and "most loyal." To make matters worse, Brescia had fallen into foreign hands without a shot being fired. Elia Capriolo, a well-born local chronicler who will often reappear in this book, lamented that the Venetians—who held their troops back from a defense of Brescia—had fallen far short of the virtues of their ancestors and that evil astral influences were acting on the most serene republic.[4] In fact, the key cities of Verona, Vicenza, Padua, and Treviso all submitted to the forces of the league in the months that followed the fall of Brescia, and it would be seven years before the Venetians regained complete control of their empire. However, the events in Brescia in the early summer of 1509 were not without precedent: in coming to terms with the French without a struggle, the Brescians repeated the actions of their ancestors who in 1426 had spurned their Visconti overlords in Milan, opened the city gates to the Venetians, and inaugurated over eighty years of uninterrupted rule from the lagoon city.

State-Building and Regional States in Italy, ca. 1300–1454

The exchange of one prince for another in 1509 is no longer an occasion for reflections on Venetian morals or the workings and influence of the heavens. Instead, historians are now more interested in what the loss of Brescia and other cities reveals about the nature of the Venetian mainland empire and more generally about the nature of Italian government and society. Until about forty years ago many historians interpreted the fragmented political history of Italy in the light of eighteenth- and nineteenth-century constitutional conceptions of statehood; that is to say they evaluated the communal, signorial, princely, and republican regimes in terms of the degree to which they exhibited centralized authority, bureaucratic growth, territorial unity, and popular participation. By these criteria the medieval communes might appear to be the precursors of the modern state. In his incisive and elegant *Histoire des républiques italiennes du moyen âge* (1809–18) Jean-Charles-Léonard Simonde de Sismondi presented the communal cities of medieval Italy with their quasi-democratic institutions and independent spirit as early models for modern political liberty. Similarly, Jules Michelet's positive treatment of the "renaissance" in France under the French kings of the sixteenth century in his *Histoire de France* (1835–67) was molded by his belief that this resurgence represented a crucible for the formation of a unified French culture, strong national identity, and democratic instincts. His contemporary the Swiss historian Jacob Burckhardt asserted that one of the Italian Renaissance's main contributions to human history was the "state as a work of art," and he detected in Italy in the period after around 1300 the outlines of the modern state in all its energy and grandeur.

However, Burckhardt's portraits of the decadent, amoral, and plain vicious despots and princes of the Renaissance and even his generally more positive accounts of the republics of Florence and Venice hint at ambivalent feelings about modernity and its discontents.[5] Historical accounts of state-building characterized by political centralization, territorial integration, and authoritarian tendencies have more recently given way to explorations of the "weak state" or the "composite state" made up of a number of different agents.[6] The new political history of the state is founded on an analysis of political organizations and is greatly indebted to social anthropology and sociology, in which the distinction between private and public concerns—a keystone of juridical and historical conceptions of the state—is blurred.[7] In this way the exploration of the plurality of power within each state, the relations between center and periphery, and the formal or informal ties of patronage, or *clientelismo,* that promoted or hindered factions has moved to the fore of many studies of state-building. These discussions have recognized that while princely, signorial, or republican rulers could certainly command large resources and wield great authority, at a local level the dense network of political traditions and social relations that characterized and complicated European society remained strong and pervasive during the Renaissance.

Historians have given particular attention to the internal political dynamics of the "regional state," or "piccolo stato signorile," which formed in Italy in succession to the communes of the late eleventh to fourteenth centuries.[8] Although centralization and bureaucratic development are evident in these states, formal political institutions figured as only one force among the principal mediators of many different groups or opinion-makers. The leading force often sought to impose a unitary or stabilizing framework in order to contain the plurality of powers within a particular region, city, or court. Institutional development was therefore shaped by the struggle to control or harness new social or cultural developments, but the relationship between institutions and society and culture was reciprocal. In this way, princes, nobles, and councils were forced to adapt to the demands of the Church and religious orders, as well as to influential social groups and factions, family ties and relationships, and strong individuals with more personal concerns and ambitions.[9]

Studies of the Visconti dukes during the fourteenth and fifteenth centuries have provided an especially rich source of information for historians interested in the process of regional state formation.[10] During the fourteenth century the Visconti aggressively expanded their power and influence into the territory surrounding Milan by means of feudal grants and other strategies. Like other lords—whether the Gonzaga of Mantua, the Este of Ferrara, or the Carrara of Padua—the Visconti and their Sforza successors were faced with the problem of controlling their vassals and treating them as subjects of a sovereign power.[11] In addition, the Visconti were obliged to deal in Lombardy with urban elites who were fiercely proud of their communal traditions and with established factions tied to local magnates. The Visconti "regional state" was therefore less a central sovereign power exercising homogeneous rule over a defined territory than it was a patchwork of bilateral agreements between central powers and peripheries involving a complex system of compromise and negotiation between dukes and subjects.[12]

The view of the state from its periphery has further underlined the need for a revision of the traditional statist model with its emphasis on central power. Historians writing in English have already devoted attention to centers on the periphery of states such as Pescia, Cortona, Vicenza, Verona, and Padua.[13] These studies have been accompanied or succeeded by a new wave of works in Italian that reconstruct the regional state as it was viewed from the council chambers of Parma, Reggio, and Fontanabuona and from valley or mountain communities.[14] Taken as a whole this body of evidence and microhistorical insight highlights the continuities and common experience in Italian communes even as they passed under a new signorial regime: the predominance of communal law and bureaucracy, the persistence of established factions as a political force, the habits and culture of a communal environment formed in the thirteenth century, and the sense of participating in a civic collectivity through local councils and other forums for debate.[15] One historian, reviewing the continuities in the history of communal life in Italy, has even asserted that it is possible to speak of a "silver age" of civic pride among ruling elites in the fifteenth century in succession to the golden age of communal liberty in the thirteenth and fourteenth centuries.[16] To cite one example, the "separated territories" of the Visconti (and later the Sforza) state centered on Milan often presented themselves in a culturally confident way, demonstrated a vigorous municipal life, and fought a constant battle for their jurisdictional and fiscal autonomy.

This sense of pride and independence was closely tied to the pursuit of honor and nobility. The growing strength of communal offices in its golden age gave rise to an urban patriciate that coalesced and moved to exclude potentially disruptive magnates—often tied to powerful episcopal families or landed estates—from government and to present itself as an urban nobility.[17] However, the contested and equivocal nature of the nobility they assumed complicated their efforts. In the thirteenth century the urban noble had been exemplified by the figure of the *podestà* appointed by communes throughout Italy to govern and render justice for limited terms, and by an order of knights of noble lineage who bore arms, jousted, hunted, and often lived in fortified buildings. The increasingly noble urban patriciate accepted and imitated many of these defining traits but were obliged to face the problem of their lack of suitable ancestry. Therefore, throughout the Middle Ages there were heated discussions about the relationship between nobility of virtue and nobility of blood. The distinguished medieval jurist Bartolus of Sassoferrato distinguished between a natural and a political nobility; the latter could be the creation of a communal body and might be founded on participation in military service (as in Perugia), on wealth and military service (as in Rome), or on a combination of virtue, military service, and membership of a particular clan (as in Venice, at least after ca. 1300).[18]

In the debates about true nobility the claims of *scientia*, in the sense of civic virtue and active involvement in civic governance, were given a boost in the fifteenth century by humanist writers such as Coluccio Salutati, Buonaccorso da Montemagno, and Poggio Bracciolini. Their works gave rise to intense debates about the particular role of investiture, the ties between princes and nobility, the relations between knights, nobility, and *scientia*, and the question of the compatibility of nobility and the exercise of trade or other "vile arts."[19] In general, an aristocratization of Italian society occurred during the fifteenth century, but defining and ranking nobility continued to prove contentious: those invested with nobility by an emperor or doge could claim superiority over other nobles, and while some Ciceronian justification for the nobility of wealthy merchants could be found, a general disdain remained for anyone involved in trade.[20]

In Brescia, as elsewhere in Italy, the nobility and the new patrician elite were far from unified or homogenous. Magnate families rose to prominence in the city under Lombard and then Carolingian rule from the sixth century onward. Some of these families were invested with imperial titles of nobility and established their dominance in the city and surrounding territory, while lesser nobility with feudal bases gradually moved to the city and challenged the citizens of long standing for power. The largely communal era of 1190–1331 and the signorial period of 1332–1426 were strongly marked by fierce hostility between a bewildering range of parties or groupings, labeled Guelph and Ghibelline, whose original loyalties to emperor and pope gradually dissolved. Also apparently, the division between rural and urban families in power was increasingly blurred, and a fairly unified order of the *cives* ("citizens") emerged, with extensive jurisdiction in town and countryside. In fact, in Brescia—as in many other parts of Italy—a number of magnates and *nobiles rurales* became members or associates of urban communes between the mid-twelfth and early thirteenth centuries.[21] At the same time, as a study of Padua has shown, new families regularly rose during the communal period by means of wealth and professional attainment, notably in law, to assume significant administrative and diplomatic roles.[22]

As this discussion of the contested nature of nobility suggests, the intersection of the languages of power and its institutions and agents is a fruitful area for better understanding the nature of regional states in the Renaissance. Microhistorians and structuralists have applied the insights of the social sciences to the surviving evidence of these institutions, groups, and individuals and have provided often startling and unsettling new accounts of social relations, beliefs, and cultural practices in Renaissance Italy.[23] In this way, another of Burckhardt's formulations—"the development of the individual"—has been challenged or nuanced.[24] After around 1300 the autonomous individual was, in Burckhardt's view, conscious of his personal abilities and confident of his place in the wider world. Cultural and gender historians have more recently stressed that the individual was caught in a web of meaning and constrained or fashioned by political, social, and economic structures. However, historians critical of this structuralist approach assert that men or women could employ individual strategies so as to produce communities, collectivities and networks.[25] In this dialectical relationship between individual and community the instruments or strategies of legitimization, definition, communication, and confrontation were varied. For example, for the legal basis of sovereignty to have real meaning, the physical presence and active participation of officials drawn from the territory was required; otherwise, the fragmentation of authority in a composite state could be an obstacle to any consolidation of power.[26] And legitimacy could be forged and communicated not only by means of growing bureaucracies but also through the creation of networks of information and exchange, dynastic alliances, clientage and sponsorship, and linguistic communities sharing myth and history.

In this last respect, historians of state-building have shown how constitutional history may be enriched by considering the transformation of the material assets of a territory while at the same time examining the modes, forms, and ideals through which the "l'universo ideologico" shared by a group of protagonists acted upon that transformation.[27] These ideals were embedded in political languages or discourses and a wide variety of texts but might equally be expressed in architectural and artistic forms.[28] Social and political agents and actors embodied their ideals of coexistence and expressed their ideological universe by means of words, images, and representations. These discursive practices were always embedded in historical conditions of their production and transmission and did not simply form "a closed system of signs."[29]

Humanist panegyrics represented political language in what might be termed a major key and served to legitimate or promote a particular regime: whether Florence (in the case of Leonardo Bruni), Venice, or individual dukes of Milan.[30] Legal texts delineated *iurisdictio* and *territorium* and gave an impression of a shared and homogenous legal framework—an impression that evaporates when the forms and languages of supplications, appeals, and other texts produced by the subject are closely examined. As one historian surveying this field has concluded, while the missives emanating from central authority might contain the language of command (*statim, subito,* etc.) the records of communal or territorial councils were couched in terms that reveal a vigorous defense of civic, of communal, and particularly of local values.[31] To take one Brescian example, what the Brescians called the *capitula* (list of requests) that they presented to Venice as part of the act of dedition were often more dismissively referred to as "concessiones" in Venetian records. These varied expressions of social and political ideals must be read alongside the evidence of action if we are to obtain a fully realized and comprehensive view of the formation of civic identity in Renaissance Italy.[32]

The Formation of the Venetian Mainland State, ca. 1300–1454

The formation of civic identity in a city and surrounding territory that lay within a major Italian regional state in a critical period of state-building, is the subject of this book. The principal actors in this work are not only the inarticulate whose voices have often been lost to history but also the individuals and communities who wielded power on the periphery and who negotiated with the central authority: the most serene republic of Venice. The history of Brescia under Venetian rule is not a narrative of progressive subjection—the history of a community "under siege" or "in the shadow" of a greater power.[33] On the contrary, communal identity flourished in Brescia in ways that reveal the strength of local autonomy and the limits of state-building in what has often been described as the heroic age of regional states in Italy and the triumphal age for Venice. In this way another aspect of the myth of Venice may be challenged and revised.

Venice was praised by some sixteenth-century commentators, notably in Florence and England, as a relatively stable and successful state. As a result of a rare combination of political wisdom and prudence, natural environment and divine favor, Venice seemed to have endured without a major revolution or external threat for over a thousand years since its foundation in an Adriatic lagoon in 421 CE by nobles fleeing invading Huns. Political theorists, Venetian patricians, and foreign visitors were often content to repeat and elaborate mythic claims that the Venetian patriciate was a closed caste of men who had inherited the wisdom of their ancestors and ruled equitably. This quasi-aristocratic gerontocracy maintained an elaborate arrangement of constitutional mechanisms and ensured that the orders who were excluded from formal political power were satisfied with alternative corporate entities tied to the state, were given important religious and social roles, and were celebrated in public ritual and civic culture.[34] Venice's overseas trade, notably in spices, contributed to the republic's great prosperity, which only began to decline in relative terms after around 1630.

It has been argued that from the middle of the seventeenth century French, Dutch, and English commentators were increasingly critical of this Venetian model of good government and social harmony as they stripped away the Venetian veneer of justice, equity, unanimity, and impartiality in order to highlight the repressive powers of a craven and self-serving aristocratic oligarchy.[35] A key witness in the historians' trial of the Venetian state was the Venetian *terraferma*, or mainland empire, which extended as far west as Bergamo by 1428. As the early nineteenth-century nationalist movements gathered strength some critics argued that Venice had extended its repressive power into the *terraferma*. The Venetian patriciate, it was alleged, had failed to organize a centralized unitary state incorporating its mainland empire. Moreover, the Venetian halls of government had been closed to members of the provincial elites of the empire.[36] Some key early studies of the Venetian *terraferma* were marked by the assumption that Venice had encouraged local aristocratization and a general refeudalization as a means of governing the mainland. In this way, the Venetians had hastened the decline of communal life and retarded the emergence of some of the salient characteristics of the modern unitary state.[37]

More recently, scholars pursuing *terraferma* studies, like their counterparts in the field of Milanese history (already mentioned), have moved away from models of the rise and decadence of a unitary modern state and have examined the "plurality of powers within the regional states," the relationship between center and periphery, and the tensions and negotiations between local autonomies and Venetian patricians.[38] It is no longer true to say, as John Law was able to thirty years ago, that historians are still too much "the friends of the Renaissance state" writ large.[39] There is now a flourishing range of subaltern studies in which the careful reconstruction of the provincial setting, in all its private domestic and more monumental public detail, can offer a new perspective on the much-studied republic of Venice by revealing the strength of local political life and the autonomy of local elites.[40] These historians do not view the history of the formation of the *terraferma* as a clear case of consistent and coherent imperial expansion and exploitation by Venice or accept its empire as an example of benign, even neglectful, rule on the part of a Venetian patriciate happy to respect a large degree of local autonomy. Instead, some historians have shown how Venice's acquisition of its empire moved through different stages, with the intensity of its impact on its *entroterra* (hinterland) varying geographically and chronologically.

The extension of Venetian rule beyond its immediate hinterland was at its origins largely a strategic move, as Venice sought to protect its immediate economic interests and lines of communication or trade.[41] Political and economic factors pushed Venice to deepen its involvement with the Italian mainland from the middle of the thirteenth century. Historians of this process agree that Venetian expansion into the Adriatic trade in vital bulk commodities like timber, grain, and salt contributed to a realization that the mainland routes northward needed to be secured. Venice did not turn away from its traditional Levantine trade in spices and luxury goods until the seventeenth century, and throughout this period it maintained its overseas possessions from the Adriatic to the Aegean. However, after around 1330 a significant strand of Venetian foreign policy was shaped by the desire to exploit the mainland economically and to secure the city from attack.

Venetian expansion was initially marked by a system of bilateral commercial pacts concerning commercial privileges, customs posts, and river navigation. Venetian commercial relations with Mantua, Milan, Brescia, and other towns of Lombardy were predicated on the marketing of salt, a Venetian monopoly, in exchange for timber (essential for fuel and for the shipbuilding industry) and the passage of Venetian goods. While Venice's relations with these and other towns in the western Veneto such as Vicenza and Verona hinged on its status as an entrepôt, relations with the towns of the lagoon area—notably Treviso and Padua—were closer. For example, following the demographic crisis of the mid-fourteenth century the inhabitants of the lagoon hinterland were drawn into Venice as textile workers by Venetian offers of citizenship and the benefits that came with that honor.

By the fourteenth century Venice was making episodic armed interventions against those who threatened the city's economic predominance: a brief salt war against Padua (1304) was followed by war with Ferrara (1308–13), and in the 1330s Venice waged a successful battle to check the expansionist ambitions of the della Scala of Verona and acquired a number of towns on the mainland, including Treviso. Venice was also keen to maintain access to the markets of France, Germany, and Flanders and therefore not only maintained good relations with Milan but also concluded separate commercial pacts with Brescia (in 1339), Bergamo, Como, Lodi, and Cremona—although they were all subject to Milan.[42] For much the same reason Venice developed links with the communities of Lake Garda, the Alpine passes, and the Val Camonica that sometimes involved a more formal political presence: for example, a Venetian *podestà* was present in the Riviera del Garda during the 1330s.[43]

The turning of the fourteenth century has often been considered a key moment in the history of the Venetian empire. Venice faced opposition from the ambitious Carrara of Padua (in alliance with the Hungarians) and from the important city-state of Genoa, coalescing in the War of Chioggia (1378–81), when Venice's maritime superiority proved critical to its survival.[44] The costly lesson of the War of Chioggia for many Venetian patricians was the sharp realization of their city's vulnerability to an alliance of hostile powers. By the beginning of the fifteenth century a "terraferma faction" was gaining influence in the city, and it reacted quickly to renewed Carrarese expansion by occupying Verona and Padua in 1405 and Vicenza the following year.[45] However, it is not at all clear that the acquisition of Verona, Padua, and Vicenza was the culmination of a consistent and continuous process of imperial expansion. The Venetian patriciate remained deeply divided about the westward movement, and indeed some attempt was made to scale down military commitments after 1405. A conjunction of immediate circumstances may have been more important in making 1405 a turning point in Venetian history: the coincidence of the crisis of the Visconti regime, after the death of Gian Galeazzo, with the internal weakness of the Ottoman empire allowed Venice to devote unusually large resources to its wars on the mainland. Other short-term conjunctural factors may have played a critical role: Jacopo dal Verme, the captain of the Venetian forces, was a native of the Veronese, and his family were hostile to the Carrara lords. The passage to Venetian dominance may also have been eased in the case of Verona and Vicenza by their previous experience of subjection to an external power.[46]

During the following twenty years Venice's commitment to defending its *terraferma* possessions increased and prompted the development of a larger and more permanent military force and a permanent captain-general.[47] At the same time Venice applied the lessons learned in the governance of its maritime empire and permitted a fairly large degree of autonomy to its subject cities. Viewed from the periphery, the Venetian state was no more than an aggregation of communities in bilateral agreement with Venice: a fluid and "polycentric reality."[48] There was no attempt to impose political centralization or social integration throughout the mainland empire. The formal submission of subject cities was usually followed by their presentation to Venice of requests for privileges, which the Senate discussed and conceded as it saw fit.

Viewed from the center or capital, the Venetian state offered some employment for patricians: as *podestà* or *capitano* (usually known as rectors in English) sent to govern the mainland together or separately.[49] Episcopal nominations were also made from the ranks of the patriciate, and between 1405 and 1550 over three-quarters of episcopal appointments to mainland sees were Venetian patricians rather than local men.[50] The Venetian Senate was initially the body with the most general concern for the mainland, while the *avogaria di comun*—the "juridical conscience of the Venetian state"—oversaw the conduct of Venetian officers.[51] A new range of magistracies was also created to deal with *terraferma* matters: the *auditori novi* in 1410, with competence to oversee appeals from the subject cities against the decisions of the *podestà* in civil matters; the *sindaci*, who travelled through the mainland gathering evidence for appeals against rectorial decisions; and the *savii della terraferma*, who after 1421 prepared material for senatorial discussion. The Quarantia, which was the principal judicial body based in Venice, considered these appeals, and as the volume of business increased was split into bodies separately concerned with civil and criminal matters.[52]

For their part, the inhabitants of the subject cities gained through their privileges the right of trading with Venice by the grant of Venetian citizenship *de intus* and some access to minor offices. Most centers reformed, confirmed, and preserved their local statutes and a large degree of control of the judicial process and, indeed, gained the right of appeal to Venetian bodies like the Quarantia. The Venetians issued ad hoc edicts and instructions to rectors respecting the relationship between local statutes and Venetian laws: the commissions, which grew considerably in length in the course of the period under consideration, stated that rectors were to observe local laws and customs so long as they were in accordance with divine law and justice and did not dishonor Venice.[53] No uniform law was imposed on the *terraferma*, and Venetians preferred a more pragmatic approach in accordance with Venetian myth and tradition.[54] The rectors who were sent to govern in the *terraferma* were patrician members of the Venetian sovereign body—in 1516 the Brescian *podestà* Francesco Falier was described as "the image of God in administering justice"—and in theory this gave them some honor and authority.[55] In practice, it was only in minor centers with a weaker tradition of legal autonomy—lacking their own body of statutes for instance—that rectors seem to have imposed their will with much frequency.[56]

The third and fourth decades of the fifteenth century saw a marked increase in Venetian military and political commitment on the mainland as Venice fought in alliance with Florence against the aggressive expansionism of Filippo Maria Visconti of Milan. The Venetians sought useful allies and were therefore happy to tolerate the regime of the condottiere Pandolfo Malatesta, the general of the Milanese forces who was granted dominion over Brescia in 1404 by Caterina Visconti, so long as their own economic interests were secured and Pandolfo provided an effective buffer to Milanese ambitions. Indeed, in 1412 two Venetian patricians were appointed by the Senate to exhort the Brescians to obey their just lord Pandolfo Malatesta, while the following year the Venetians granted Pandolfo patrician status, a house in Venice, a thousand gold ducats, and the command of their troops in the war against Sigismund of Luxemburg. In 1419 and 1420 the Venetian Senate even rejected Brescian requests, made both unilaterally and in conjunction with Pandolfo Malatesta, for the imposition of Venetian rule over the city.[57]

In 1421 Venice came to an agreement with the Visconti, and Pandolfo Malatesta found himself abandoned by his employer and caught between two powerful forces. Consequently, he opened the gates of the city to Milanese troops led by Francesco Bussone, Count of Carmagnola, in exchange for 34,000 gold florins.[58] In Brescia, the passage to Viscontean domination was marked by the concession of a number of privileges to favored families and the city and the recognition of communes in the territory with exemptions. There were also some attempts to suppress the expression of Guelph and Ghibelline loyalties. In practice, as one historian of this process has concluded, the privileges were largely insignificant in their effects on the Brescians. Until 1426 the duke acted through his *podestà* and captain and their staff in the city to impose taxes and to demand funds for repairs and fortifications in the city without much regard for the protests presented in Milan by Brescians or by representatives of the separated or nominally exempt territories.[59] The chronicler Elia Capriolo later characterized the regime as avaricious and arbitrary and described how one man who spoke openly against the duke was hung from a tree with a notice around his neck declaring: "One who wished to piss into the wind is hanged from the cross."[60]

The reconquest of Brescia by the Visconti and the loss of an important and sympathetic ally on the far side of the River Mincio, which marked the western edge of the Venetian possessions, was a moment of danger for Venice and immediately threatened its economic interests. Consequently, the opportunistic revolt of Brescians led by a leading aristocrat Pietro Avogadro against Visconti rule in 1426 resulted in the occupation of the city by Carmagnola, who returned as an ambitious Venetian captain-general. Under the terms of the Peace of Ferrara (1428) Bergamo and Brescia were formally ceded to Venice. The aim of recovering these strategically important towns led to further Milanese assaults and renewed Venetian military expansion in Lombardy. Brescia was besieged during 1438–40, but the skill and daring of the Venetian military *provveditore* (commissioner), Francesco Barbaro—later named *pater patriae* by some grateful Brescians—and the new Venetian governor-general, Erasmo da Narni, known as Gattamelata (Tabby Cat), helped to secure the city.[61] The sly tabby made a legendary retreat to Verona to spare his forces and later slipped from Brescia and ensured that an armada of eighty war galleys was hauled five miles over Alpine slopes to Lake Garda in order to provide the city with supplies. The long siege, the heroic defense of the city, and these exemplary military tactics were celebrated by Brescians and Venetians alike. For example, the battle on Lake Garda and the siege—as well as a figurative representation of the subjection of the provinces to Venice—featured in the decorative pictorial schemes of the doge's palace in Venice.[62]

At the same time, the designation of Doge Foscari as imperial vicar in 1435 meant that the doge's authority over the *terraferma* was enhanced. In theory the imperial grant gave Venice the power to act like other feudal landlords who might concede privileges and extract obligations.[63] This imperial sanction included the city of Brescia and its territory, and in 1440 the Brescians acknowledged their submission and presented their standard to the Venetians in Piazza San Marco soon after the naval battle on Lake Garda that had helped to break the siege of the city.[64] The standard was gratefully received by Doge Foscari and two hundred patricians dressed "regaliter" in front of a large crowd before the basilica. On the standard were depicted the arms of Brescia with its patron saints, Faustino and Giovita, and above them a scene of the Annunciation of the Virgin.[65] Between her and the archangel Gabriel appeared the lion of Saint Mark worked in gold and above this figure the words "Powerful Brescia bears witness to its loyalty over other cities" ("Brixia magnipotens sue fidei ceteris urbibus testimonium tulit").[66] Brescia was to prove loyal to Venice for almost another seventy years until the city submitted to the French in 1509 and symbols of Venetian rule, like the standards and the bronze lions of Saint Mark placed in the public spaces of the city, were defaced or removed in a careful process of *damnatio memoriae*.[67]

This extension of rule over the *terraferma* during the first half of the fifteenth century was contested by some Venetians who saw it as a distraction from maritime priorities and was castigated by other Italians who feared that Venice now sought to lord it over all of Italy.[68] However, the extension of territory was largely in line with the behavior of most Italian powers during the later Middle Ages. The Venetians, like the Florentines, sought to justify it not only in terms of right of conquest, providence, and self-defense, but also as a means of defending liberty in Italy. Venetians and other pangyricists also claimed that the subject cities came freely under Venetian rule, often in search of peace, justice, and security.[69] In 1517 the Venetian patrician and diarist Marin Sanudo observed that Venetian lawmakers and governors in the Bresciano and other parts of Venetian territory alluded to the rule of law in ancient empires and suggested that the Venetians should try to live up to this model.[70] The patrician Gasparo Contarini, writing a few years later, asserted that Venice in forming its empire was merely reconstituting the Roman province of Venetia, which, "as though it had never beene seperated from the same, returned willingly with a franke and liberall good will."[71] The cities of the *terraferma*, he claimed, were given a large degree of self-rule, and Venetian representatives governed with justice and moderation. To prove his point he noted that Padua and other cities conquered after the battle of Agnadello in 1509 had in fact soon returned very willingly to the peace and security of Venetian rule.[72]

The large degree of autonomy granted in many *privilegia* conceded to subject cities may have formed the basis for Contarini's view, although he was being rather ingenuous in ignoring the divisions within each city that the deeply skeptical Florentine Niccolò Machiavelli claimed Venice fostered so as to weaken opposition.[73] In practice, Venice usually governed with a light hand except when it saw its enemies' interests favored by the behavior of families or cities in the *terraferma*. Most decisions were taken by Venetian representatives on the ground who were all elected by the Venetian Senate. The rectors might serve for up to sixteen months in one posting before returning to Venice, and they were reliant on their legal officers and local advice in their decision-making. In addition, when rectors infringed local statutes or encroached on too many local privileges and traditions, civic representatives could be very quick to complain.[74] In Vicenza, Verona, and Bergamo evidence suggests that the judicial autonomy of the local civic officers even increased "at the expense of the power of the *podestà*" during the fifteenth century.[75]

In Venice, on the other hand, contention over the nature of the central control of the *terraferma* occurred among the different organs of government, notably the Council of Ten, the Senate, and the republic's principal law officers: the *avogadori di comun* (public prosecutors). The Senate shaped the general direction and execution of *terraferma* policy for much of the fifteenth century. For example, it deliberated on the Brescian *capitula* submitted in 1427, 1440, 1448, and 1454 and again in 1517 and granted or withheld them on each occasion as it saw fit. The Senate also secured defenses and considered a wide range of matters relating to the Venice's *terraferma* possessions. A sample of records of senatorial deliberations suggests that they enforced economic restrictions there,[76] responded to Brescian petitions in relation to mercantile disagreements,[77] considered requests for copyright privileges from Brescian printers in Venice,[78] and reviewed fiscal matters or moved to maximize revenues by reviewing exemptions.[79] The Senate was happy to intervene in *terraferma* judicial matters when they seemed directly to affect Venetian citizens or when especially grave crimes such as murder were involved.[80] On occasion, the Senate defined the punishments to be employed by the rectors for the honor of Venice and "the peace and tranquillity of our subjects" ("pro quieto pacifico victu Subditorum nostrorum") as it was phrased.[81] The Senate also intervened in ecclesiastical matters in Brescia, writing to the Venetian cardinals when pressure had to be applied in Rome in favor of the introduction of observance in Brescia,[82] or when it was necessary to ensure the integrity of the diocese of Brescia during an episcopal vacancy.[83]

After the middle of the century the effectiveness of Venetian rule over its mainland possessions was increasingly hampered by internal divisions in the capital. The new magistracies of *auditori novi* and *sindaci* have been judged ineffective by one historian, and the men who held these posts attained important political roles less frequently than the more prestigious *avogadori*.[84] The Senate was also occasionally forced to reprimand or rein in the ambitions of the Council of Ten, which acted with some agility and arrogated to itself a wide variety of powers over the *terraferma* on the pretext of internal security.[85] The Ten markedly increased its influence in military and even diplomatic matters after the War of Ferrara (1482–84), but its power reached a zenith during the War of the League of Cambrai (1509–17) when it helped to engineer a Brescian uprising against French rule in 1512.

The inhabitants of the *terraferma* could take advantage of such divisions in order appeal to the doge, the Senate, or the *avogadori* and *minor con-*

siglio against decisions taken in a variety of fields.[86] Equally, the confusion of authority in the appeals process could result in wearisome delays in the execution of justice.[87] Responding to a Brescian presentation of material against a Venetian who attacked the Brescian official representative or orator to Venice in 1503, the doge could assure the Brescian orators that the case was in the hands of not only the Council of Ten but also the Brescian syndics and the public prosecutors, or *avogadori,* and would proceed to its proper conclusion by all these ways and with respect to the privileges conceded to Brescia by Venice. To all appearances the Brescian petitioners retired satisfied with this response, although it is unlikely to have inspired much confidence as matters dragged on.[88]

Brescia and the Bresciano

The impact of Venetian rule on the *terraferma* has been characterized as "uneven" and related to the size of the subject city and its distance from the center. Historians have sometimes generalized about the nature of Venetian rule in the *terraferma* from the experiences of Padua, which was close to the center and therefore subject to closer scrutiny and relatively heavier exactions.[89] Equally, historians may be tempted to conjure up a fairly relaxed image of Venetian rule in comparison with an exaggerated view of the harsh nature of Florentine treatment of Pisa and its other subject cities in Tuscany.[90] It is important to bear in mind that Brescia was much more distant from Venice than Padua or Treviso and was a larger city than Verona, Vicenza, or Bergamo. Brescia's population has been estimated at around 15,000 in 1440, around 28,000 in 1459 and rising to around 48,500 in 1493. An estimate of the population that includes the inhabitants of the *chiusure,* an area up to three miles from the city subject to urban statutes, suggests a demographic peak for this period of around sixty-five thousand in 1505. At this date a further ninety thousand or so lived in the Alpine valleys and along the western shore of Lake Garda.[91]

The inhabitants of the city itself were largely restricted by the walls built during the thirteenth century and punctuated by five principal gates: delle Pille, San Nazaro, San Giovanni, San Alessandro, and Torlonga. The area within the walls was divided into four quarters that were in turn divided into *quadre.* The quarters were San Faustino, San Alessandro, San Giovanni, and Santo Stefano—subsequently known as the *cittadella.* The *cittadella* was the most important quarter of the city since it coincided with the site of the Roman town and included the major public buildings and many private palaces. During the 1360s the Visconti overlords divided the

cittadella into two parts (*vecchia* and *nuova*) by building a wall and erecting internal gates in order to impede civic conflict. The *cittadella nuova*
incorporated the castle to the north, with the most important classical,
episcopal, signorial, communal, and noble buildings to the castle's south,
and the *cittadella vecchia* to the east. Here the neighboring and connected
churches of San Pietro (the duomo) with its bell tower and the eleventh-
century Romanesque Santa Maria *(rotondo)* together formed the city cathedral. The neighboring *broletto* (town hall), built at the end of the twelfth
century, also had a bell tower, whose bells called the city council to meetings. The interior of the chapel of San Giorgio was decorated between
1414 and 1419 by Gentile da Fabriano when Pandolfo Malatesta held
court in the city.[92] A large market opened in the twelfth century lay to the
east of the *cittadella vecchia*. However, in the course of the fifteenth century the fish, wine, meat, and linen markets once held within the *cittadella*
were relocated in an effort to clean up the city, and for much of this period
they lay in San Giovanni, in the southwest part of the city, close to the
course of the Garza river that ran from north to south through the city.[93]

Venice regarded Brescia as the richest and among the most strategically
important of its subject cities. Brescia and the Bresciano provided one-
quarter of all revenues from the *terraferma* in 1469, and its fiscal income
exceeded that of every other town in 1475–76.[94] In the course of the sixteenth century Venice extracted ever-increasing amounts of money from
Brescia as it increased indirect taxes *(dazi)* and military subsidies *(limitazi-
one)*. The wealth of the city and the Bresciano derived from its natural resources: several lakes and rivers provided food and means of communication,
while the fertile plains to the south provided crops and raw materials for
trade and consumption. The mountainous pre-Alpine region to the north of
the city was wooded on its lower slopes and was mined for the minerals and
metals used in the important local armaments industry. The arms and cloth
trades also benefited from proximity to the Milanese markets and to several important trade routes, including those north to Germany, France, and
Flanders.

A map of the Bresciano that was printed around 1505 to accompany
Elia Capriolo's Brescian history (Figure 1.1) suggests the dominance over
the *contado* of Brescia's urban complex of churches, walls, monasteries,
and towers. In many ways this is an illusion of scale—an imagined political
space serving to magnify and glorify the city.[95] In reality the Bresciano was
large, difficult to unify, and highly varied in its topography and political
relationship with the center. The Bresciano was made up of three distinct
geomorphological zones—to the north of the city of Brescia was a mountainous area, that included three valleys: the Val Camonica, Val Trompia,

and Val Sabbia. The Val Camonica was the most populated and sheltered Lake Iseo in its southern part. In the foothills, or *pedemonte,* which lay north and east of Brescia, was a group of settlements dominated by Nave, Gavardo, and Rezzato. To the south and west of Brescia lay the Francia-corta, where Gussago and Rovato formed the major loci of power, sur-rounded by the fertile plains where most of the settlements in the region were located. The Riviera del Garda, with the town of Salò at its heart, and the town of Asola to the south marked the most eastern outposts of the Bresciano. The Bresciano shared a border with Milanese, Mantuan, and Tridentine lands and stretched from the Bergamasco in the west to the Veronese at Lake Garda in the east. Brescia had jurisdiction over some of this territory, but the Alpine valleys of the Camonica and Sabbia enjoyed a large measure of autonomy, while feudal nobles held sway over towns and lands in the plains. Venice—much to the annoyance of the city of Brescia—was careful to respect the political strength of these areas and to confirm feudal power, and for the whole century under consideration in this book, relations between Brescia and its rural hinterland were as complex and fraught as those between Venice and its subject city.

My aim in this book is to explain the origins and nature of the events of 1509 described at the beginning of this chapter. The relationship between Brescia and Venice and the formation of local identity during the first cen-tury of Venetian rule are the broader themes under consideration. In par-ticular I will consider the strategic importance of the Bresciano which lay at Venice's highly contested border with Milanese territory, and will try to assess how closely and effectively Venice policed the area. I will also con-sider to what degree Brescia was altered by its absorption into the Venetian dominion, and whether it is possible to discern a clash of cultures.[96] How effectively did Brescians make their grievances heard in Venice? To what extent were Brescians and Venetians collaborators in governance? Finally, I will return to consider the more general questions with which this chap-ter began and try to suggest what the answers to these questions reveal about political culture and the role of religion in shaping civic identity and the formation of territorial states.

First of all, the means of the communication of ideas, especially myths about the city, will be outlined in the remainder of Part 1. A reading of texts, objects, and images will introduce some of the basic grammar of the Brescian language of politics, as well as the perceptions of the city held by contemporaries. These myths relate to the foundation of the city, its subse-quent history, and its relationship with Venice and are treated as politically and socially sustaining rather than simply as picturesque falsehoods subse-quently swept away by the rigorous scientific methods of modern histori-cal practice.[97] The urban fabric was also marked by mythic and related

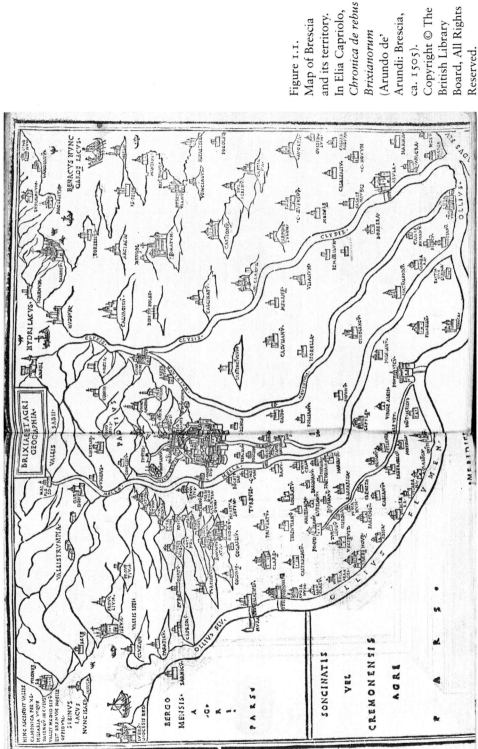

Figure 1.1.
Map of Brescia
and its territory.
In Elia Capriolo,
*Chronica de rebus
Brixianorum*
(Arundo de'
Arundi: Brescia,
ca. 1505).
Copyright © The
British Library
Board, All Rights
Reserved.

antiquarian concerns, and since statues, buildings, fountains and other mythic sites framed political identity, they are also read for answers to some of the questions formulated above.

The examination of political institutions in Brescia and Venice is a necessary foundation for a deeper knowledge of the more formal or more public channels of power. The records of the Brescian councils, decisions taken by the Venetian rectors, instructions from the Venetian doge, Senate, and Council of Ten, and records of their deliberations cast light on political priorities. Accordingly, these form the core of my discussion in Part 2. The focus here is the gradual narrowing of access to membership in the Brescian council that took place from around 1460 onward and the establishment of an urban oligarchy. The tendency of urban elites to form closed or exclusive bodies with the trappings of nobility was common throughout Italy, but it is a process now under close scrutiny by historians. The closure of the Venetian Greater Council after 1297 provided the foundation for the closed patrician caste, which dominated formal political power in the city for centuries.[98] The closure of councils at Verona in 1405 has also been dissected in great detail, and the nature of the emerging oligarchy there has been described with some attention to lifestyle, culture, family ties, and political or dynastic strategies.[99] The Venetian closure was probably more prolonged and less complete a process than previously presented.[100] Moreover, the *cittadini* who were excluded by birth from the patriciate had more access to power, either formal or informal, than previously believed.[101] In the case of Verona less weight is now attached to the abolition of the Council of Five Hundred in 1405, and it has been pointed out that this council had fallen into disuse before the Venetian conquest. There is also now some evidence based on detailed studies of individual cities to challenge the view—expressed by Angelo Ventura half a century ago—that the Venetians themselves encouraged the narrowing and aristocratization of the elites in Venice's subject cities in order to encourage loyalty and strengthen their grip on their new subjects.[102] Similar observations can be made in the case of Brescia. The Brescian council had already contracted from five hundred in 1315 to 120 after the Visconti conquest in 1385 and then fell to seventy-two in 1421. My study of the formation of the Brescian oligarchy reveals a complicated picture in which the closure of the Brescian councils was highly contested and formed part of a long-term struggle to maintain and increase Brescian dominance over the *contado* and to reverse the trend of rural migration and political insinuation into the city.

Civic religion and morality underpinned and shaped the language and behavior of political actors in Renaissance Italy, and these matters are addressed in Part 3. The records of the Brescian council's deliberations are studded with references to donations to religious orders and churches in the city. The Brescian council was also involved in the organization of processions and rituals in which both clergy and laity were supposed to take part, as well as the sponsorship of visiting preachers who attracted large crowds to their sermons. All of these events took place in public spaces that underwent some reconstruction and elaboration after around 1430. The sacred objects that were ritually displayed in these spaces were also embellished during the same period. New sacred spaces associated with miraculous images or the recovered relics of local saints were inaugurated. In sum, the formation of civic identity in Brescia during the Renaissance took place in churches and squares as well as in the halls of government, and a close examination of language, forms, and behavior shows how this took place in a way that was largely independent from Venetian interference.

Although many panegyricists described the ancient origins of Brescian institutions and traditions, Brescians were also obliged to articulate their loyalty to Venice in a public, ritualized manner. Brescians were evidently put out by the Venetian power of appointment to their diocese noted above, and requests for the appointment of local sons were sometimes accompanied by laments about the absenteeism of previous incumbents. The Brescian council was also acutely concerned with the standard of monastic observance in the city and made considerable efforts to eliminate abuses and expel backsliding orders. It is tempting to see the myth of "Brescia beata," the city of thirty sainted bishops, as a driving force behind this process, and indeed one of the striking discoveries in this part of the book is the council's and the clergy's conscious, concerted effort to uncover and centralize these saints' relics. This process of centralization was accompanied by increased efforts to display and honor these relics through decorative schemes and the construction of churches, chapels, and sarcophagi. These often costly efforts were key to the delineation of civic identity in Brescia and played an important role in attempts to bind countryside to city by means of a common "local knowledge."[103]

In Part 4, I turn to three instances of political factions within the city engaging with local religious knowledge and practice. I consider these conflicts in the context of broader Venetian, papal, and humanist concerns. Sumptuary legislation was frequently issued by civic and royal authorities in Renaissance Europe, and its regular appearance can be related to a combustible mix of economics, morals, and social rivalry. The regulation of furs and funerals in Brescia was clearly an expression of the patriciate's unease about the pressures on the social and gender boundaries that they were attempting to police. The explosive nature of these matters is demonstrated by a dispute over funerals in Brescia that broke out at the beginning of the sixteenth century. The fracas drew local councillors, mendicants, and humanists into a pamphlet war about the nature of life and death in a civic setting. In doing so, a number of significant social, political, and religious fault lines in the city are thrown into especially sharp relief. These fissures can help to illuminate some of the broader questions with which this book is concerned. For example, local attitudes toward Jews—said to be encouraging costly funerals by offering loans—were complicated by the Jews' direct subjection to Venice, as well as by the religious prohibitions and strictures reiterated in Brescia's council and squares throughout the fifteenth century. In Chapter 9 I attempt to discern Brescians' shifting attitudes toward the Jewish community in their midst and to trace the way Venice tried to steer a course between satisfying the hostile demands of its subject cities in this matter and its own recognition of the economic advantages of a resident Jewish population in the *terraferma*. The persecution of witches—with whom the Jews were frequently associated in medieval tradition—provides the final case study in this part of the book, and I examine the role of the Bresciano as the center par excellence of mass witch-hunting in Renaissance Italy. A series of religious persecutions that began in 1454 and continued to 1521 provides an insight into the often tense relationship between the Brescians and the Dominicans who conducted a series of inquisitions. This episode also highlights conflicts between Brescia and Venice, and between the Church and the Ten—for the Ten claimed jurisdiction in crimes of this serious and disturbing nature while clerics were unhappy about lay interference in ecclesiastical matters.

All of these episodes can help to answer some of the questions posed above. They also provide an important insight into the world of those standing outside or on the margins of the Brescian and Venetian elite: from the crowds welcoming kings, bishops, and preachers to Brescia to priests and prostitutes affected by sumptuary legislation to Jewish moneylenders treading a fine line between providing a necessary service and provoking the ire of their cloth-worker clients. These lower orders were not merely the victims of impersonal forces, and evidence of words and actions that these men and women directed against the Brescian or Venetian authorities are noted throughout this book. This resistance could take the form of organized and effective rural institutions that stymied the Brescian authorities or of graffiti and jeers directed at local castellans, the Venetian or Brescian rectors, and others that are recorded in outraged official reports. Overt resistance to Venetian rule was generally unknown throughout the Bresciano during the fifteenth century, but the revolt against the Venetians in 1509 was the result of a critical and unusual conjunction of circumstances acting on the structural flaws outlined above.

The year 1509 would seem to provide a natural terminus ad quem for this study, marking as it does the year of Venice's greatest crisis and Brescia's capitulation to the French. However, I consider events beyond that date in this book; whereas the period of foreign occupation and recovery does have distinctive characteristics, it is also remarkable for its continuities with the preceding century. In particular, French rule and the experience of the French troops' devastating sack of the city in 1512, exacerbating existing social, political, and religious divisions, contributed to the agony of these dark years for the city. In recognition of this fact, when Venice recovered the city in 1516 there was some public discussion about the role of the narrow elite in exacerbating civil dissension in the city. Consequently, some of the men excluded from government petitioned Venice for a wider range of privileges. In fact, Venetian governors failed to revise Brescian political structures and continued to work to maintain internal peace and to strengthen Brescia's defensive position. Accordingly, they instituted extensive levellings of outlying churches, monasteries, and other buildings and a subsequent program of military fortifications. And in Brescia itself a reaffirmation of civic myths and a further centralization of holy sites and relics occurred. In tandem with these actions, renewed efforts were made to enforce clerical discipline. These moves were intended to placate God, who had clearly punished the city for its sins for seven unhappy years, but were also consonant with the civic puritanism of earlier decades.

Throughout the period under consideration the Brescian communal authorities produced a substantial volume of records, which form the foundations of the arguments in this book. In particular, the bound volumes of council deliberations, or *provvisioni,* cover the entire period of Venetian rule—as well as some of the years of Visconti domination—and have proved invaluable in reconstructing the values of the Brescian councillors, both the shared and contested, and in following the course of key events in the life of the city government. A range of documents relating to the activities of the Venetian rectors have also been examined: originals and copies of missives from the doge, the proclamations of the Venetian rectors and foreign governors, the records (albeit patchy) of the chancellery that operated in conjunction with the *podestà* and dealt with matters of justice, and the surviving reports and letters that Venetian rectors sent to Venice. In Venice itself the records of the Senate and the Ten have provided material relating to Brescia (on occasion included in general instructions to *terraferma* rectors). These manuscripts have been supplemented by the productions of the very active Brescian press and Brescian authors, as well as the observations of contemporary visitors to the city. Finally, nontextual sources have proved extraordinarily rich in evidence for Renaissance Brescia: architectural language acted as an art of persuasion and expression of power in the city, while artistic and other representations such as frescoes and maps, as noted above, projected individual or group identities in public and private spaces, sacred and profane places.

Despite its place as the largest and most economically prosperous city on the Venetian *terraferma*, Brescia has not generated as rich an array of historical studies as Vicenza, Padua, or Verona, although like those cities it has had its share of local historians—notably Federico Odorici, Agostino Zanelli, Paolo Guerrini, and Carlo Pasero—who wrote on a very wide range of topics and edited, or otherwise brought to light, many important sources.[104] Brescia—like Milan, Cremona, Pavia, and Verona—is the subject of an encyclopedic multivolume history from the earliest times to the mid-twentieth century that attempts to provide a synthetic narrative based on local sources and studies.[105] The essays contained in this set of volumes, now almost fifty years old, provide a valuable means of historical orientation but do so within fairly restricted methodological, geographical, and historiographical bounds.[106] More recently, Joanne Ferraro has analyzed in detail the composition and marriage strategies of the Brescian elite during the century after around 1550; Maurizio Pegrari has explored the development of the Brescian society and economy over eight centuries (1038–1797); and Daniele Montanari has provided an account of Brescian political history during the entire period of Venetian dominance (to 1797) in which he explores the complex relationship between capital and province, city and *contado*.[107] Brescia's place in the wider historiography relating to the Venetian empire and the Italian Renaissance has not been so well served, although there are now some new studies in English that address the artistic history of the city and its region.[108]

This book brings to light an array of new evidence in order to illuminate the formation of civic identity and regional states. My general aim has been to contribute to the revision of the model of the strong or interventionist state that marked earlier studies of Venice. This process of revision encompasses social, religious, and cultural fields of study, as well as politics more narrowly defined. There has also been a conscious effort to synthesize the work of previous historians in these fields and to test the claims of these historians in the light of the Brescian experience. I have tried to avoid an unquestioning acceptance of public over hidden transcripts of power and have been at pains to highlight occasions when political dissent and social rupture occurred. I have also been conscious of the pitfalls of a facile reductionism by which every piece of evidence can be interpreted as part of an elite program for the formation of civic identity.[109] I hope that I have avoided such dangers, as well as the twin temptations of antiquarianism and *campanilismo*, and that, above all, I have been alert to the footprint traces that the historian must track and fashion into history.[110]

CHAPTER TWO

The Myths of Brescia

O N 1 AUGUST 1546 Cardinal Andrea Corner made his ceremonial
entry into Brescia as the city's new bishop "with very great pomp,"
as one local diarist noted.[1] The Brescian council went to great lengths to
greet the distinguished Venetian visitor, who succeeded his uncle Francesco
as the bishop of Brescia and was related to the former queen of Cyprus.[2]
As early as May 1546 the council met to deliberate on the form of welcome to be provided for the new bishop and, as in the case of Louis XII's
entry four decades earlier, ordered the erection of five triumphal arches in
a classical style on which were depicted a complex iconographic program
celebrating the occasion, evoking Christian virtues, and recalling some
of the most cherished myths of Brescia.[3] Corner was conducted to the city
from the border of Brescian territory by a small group of aristocrats and
was then met by the Venetian rectors in the company of one hundred
gentlemen and their grooms ("stafieri . . . palefreneri") together with the
bearers of the episcopal baldachin under which he processed.[4] As he passed
through the first arch, dedicated to public joy ("pubblica letitia") and set
up at the city's San Nazaro gate, the cardinal would have seen on the arch
his arms, flanked by those of the current rectors of the city, and a representation of the city's patron saints, Faustino and Giovita, along with the
lions of the city arms and several epigraphs. The following three arches
were dedicated to the Christian virtues of faith, hope, and charity, and the
last commemorated religion. Despite their overtly religious meaning—

appropriate for the occasion and a timely response to mounting evidence of heresy in the region—each of these four arches also contained scenes ("historie") from classical history and legend that were clearly intended as allegories and as flattering references to both Corner and Brescia.[5]

The dominant theme running through the scenes depicted on the arches was that of self-sacrifice for a greater cause, usually the homeland. The figures included Marcus Atilius Regulus, who voluntarily gave his life as a prisoner to the Carthaginians rather than let Rome make any concession to the enemy; Marcus Curtius, who willingly rode into a great chasm in the Roman Forum in obedience to an oracle; Publius Decius Mus, who rode into the enemy's ranks, destroying both them and himself; and the sons of the priestess of Hera whom the gods rewarded with death for doing their filial duty.[6] This grim litany also included a depiction by the local artist Girolamo Romanino of Gaius Mucius Scaevola, the young Roman famed for placing his right hand voluntarily in the fire as a show of indifference to torture while held prisoner by the Etruscans. The council also employed Romanino to depict an image of the city of Saguntum under siege on the arch dedicated to faith. A preparatory sketch by the artist inscribed "Saguntom obsessom" clearly represents the moment when the inhabitants of Saguntum, besieged by Hannibal, started burning their possessions so that they would not fall into Carthaginian hands. This feat of endurance and act of self-sacrifice earned the praise of Rome, with whom Saguntum was allied. The presence of this scene in the scheme of decoration for Corner's entry was far from casual: Saguntum was recaptured a few years later by Publius Cornelius Scipio, and the image would have flattered Corner, who claimed descent from the Cornelius family. However, it would also have flattered the Brescians, who endured a prolonged siege during 1438–40; indeed, a mysterious image of "a theatre [i.e. public meeting place] within an old one in a state of collapse with the rest of the population at the walls in defense of the city from enemies within" may have recalled the celebrated defense of Brescia's *cittadella* (a fortified area that stood within the city walls) from a critical Visconti assault during the siege.[7]

A reading of this image of a city under siege in conjunction with the allegorical figure of Hope depicted on the next arch under which Corner would have passed makes it clear that the Brescians wished to celebrate both their loyalty to and faith in Venice and their own fortitude. This message would have been fairly clear to the assembled crowds waiting to greet Cardinal Corner and serves as a useful introduction to this chapter, for as I outline below, local governors, writers, and artists had been celebrating Brescian loyalty and explicitly associating the city with Saguntum and classical virtues of loyalty, self-sacrifice, and fortitude for almost a century. The city's artistic self-portrayal of 1546 has been dismissed as "rather confused and generic in its allusions," but in fact the scenes are united both by these themes and by allusions to Rome's struggle with Carthage and Hannibal.[8] The council recognized that Brescia's identification with Rome's loyal allies during the Punic Wars was well established in local tradition, and Cardinal Corner would have accepted the flattering parallel made between Rome and Venice. In addition, the figures of Ceres (goddess of grain and fertility), Flora (goddess of flowers and companion of Hercules), Pomona (goddess of fruit trees, gardens, and orchards), Pales (deity of shepherds, flocks, and livestock), and Iacchus (the son of Ceres) that were included in the scheme were a reference to the Bresciano's natural abundance—another well-worn theme.

The triumphal images employed in conjunction with the ritual entry of Corner therefore served to reflect Brescian values, promote unity, and act as a model for the inhabitants.[9] These images were also ambiguous enough to reflect Venetian concerns and, given the occasion and spatial setting, reinforced the city's position within the Venetian empire.[10] Finally, the fact that the council produced an elaborate written program or ontological narrative that could be realized in image and word over the spring and summer of 1546 for a specific public performance indicates the councillors' faith in the persuasive power of such displays, as well as the persistence during this period of the medieval tradition of writing the commune and its key role in the formation of civic identity.[11]

Writing the Commune

The scribal revolution that took place in medieval Europe was driven by the growth of ecclesiastical and secular bureaucracies and resulted in the marked proliferation of texts. The jurists of the thirteenth and fourteenth centuries provided reams of written material in response to the struggle between papal and imperial authority, and much of this was applied by secular rulers grappling with the problem of expanding states and a multitude of new social problems. Chancelleries attached to the princely and communal states provided employment for men who had attended the new Italian universities and were trained to digest these works and to delineate power on vellum. The chancelleries of Venice, Milan, and the papacy provided models for the expression of good government in this way, and the judges, lawyers, and notaries who proliferated in towns and villages throughout the peninsula helped to found a new secular culture.[12]

The production and preservation of the word was given official attention in Brescia, although at least in the case of its statutes, it was rather slow in participating in the scribal revolution. The civic statutes exist in copies dating back to 1277, and the first redactions may only have been made a century or so before that date. By the fifteenth century the statutes were treated with much greater care and were placed for safekeeping in a box ("capsono") in the duomo with some of the most important religious objects of the city.[13] The chancellor of the city was expected to compile and register the writings held there.[14] Furthermore, the Venetian *podestà*, or his vicar, was obliged to consign the keys to this box to the bishop of Brescia, the captain, the chancellor, and two notables elected by the elders and wise men of the city ("ancianos & sapientes") as well as to retain one for himself.[15] In addition, after the statutes were printed in 1473 at the instigation of the council it was agreed to assign copies to the *podestà* and to the judges.[16]

The privileges Venice granted to the city during this period were preserved on richly illuminated vellum copies, while missives sent to the Brescian rectors in the name of the doge were written on vellum to which the seal of Saint Mark—usually lead, but occasionally in gold as a sign of very special pleasure or favor—was attached.[17] Some of these records—notably concessions made by the council and the economic privileges obtained from Venice by the city, various rural bodies and the leading families— were copied into a richly illuminated and sumptuously bound volume after the middle of the fifteenth century.[18] This volume of over 350 folios included illustrations that served to guide good business relations and provide a warning of the limits of Brescian-Venetian relations. In one illumination (Figure 2.1) Brescians are shown fleecing the winged lion of Saint Mark and saying: "We strip as much as we can in the time we have and as much as will be borne" ("Pelemo tanto che el tempo havemo et che el ne vien supportato"), and "Strip the bird slowly so that it does not cry because it can bear it once but not every time" ("Pelati pian piano che la gazola non crida per che el se supportara uno tempo ma non sempre"). Together with at least one other register this volume was probably drawn up in connection with the revision of the civic statutes, and together they formed an archive or "site of memory" in themselves.[19] A wide variety of public records were added to these in the course of the century: as well as the periodic volumes of tax estimates, the council agreed to a number of ad hoc records, for example a book recording the names of clerics guilty of crimes, of "diabolical deceptions," or of leading immoral or shameful lives.[20] Letters from the doge and other edicts emanating from Venice were probably held in the chancellery, but these were not weeded and edited into indexed volumes until the middle of the sixteenth century.[21] In the meantime a number of documents may have gone astray: some disquiet arose in the city in 1512 when some claimed that Jews had plundered the

Figure 2.1. Brescians fleece Venice figured as the winged lion of Saint Mark, ca. 1472. In "Codici di privilegi concessi alla città, alle famiglie e al territorio di Brescia," Biblioteca Queriniana, Brescia, fol. 64v. Photo: author.

communal archive during the sack by the French troops. It was subsequently agreed to construct an "archivio" in the new *palazzo della loggia* close to the meeting rooms of the College of Judges, and this was in use by 1523 and finally completed a decade later.[22]

The language and form of these texts can suggest how Venice viewed the Brescians and how the Brescians themselves represented, or rather wrote, their own community.[23] The form in which the records of the council meetings were kept did not change as Brescia passed from one ruler to another in the fifteenth century: attendance was minuted, proposals recorded, discussion summarized, and voting numbers noted. Occasionally the missives from the doge to the Brescian rectors were read to the council and incorporated verbatim in the record.[24] Individual contributions to debates were periodically noted, but the summary of business was often terse, and it is sometimes necessary to consult other records to grasp the acrimony that often lay behind apparent expressions of concord. The records of council meetings were recorded in Latin, as were the local statutes, and in 1485 a proposal that the chancellor provide decisions in vernacular for the better understanding of councillors was narrowly rejected by the special council.[25] The titles of councillors were usually given as "Doctor" or "Ser," and as a mark of respect orators from the Val Camonica referred to the "magnifice comunitatis" of Brescia.[26] The Brescian records were concerned to honor the dignity of the Venetian *podestà* and captain, who was addressed as "Magnifico Ser."[27] On several occasions in the first half of the fifteenth century the scribe recording the council deliberations even depicted the rector on a throne of justice holding a staff of office (Figure 2.2). The rector also addressed the Brescians with terms of respect and usually as a collective body, while the records of the Venetian Senate refer to the Brescian "subjects," an appellation the Brescians employed on occasion.[28]

The collective memory was also supported by notaries who produced chronicles that were extensions of their public function, shaped by their training in the *ars dictaminis* (a stylized prose used in legal documents and letters) and often combining local and world events.[29] These chroniclers, who flourished in Italy from the thirteenth century onward and produced some remarkable verse and prose accounts of contemporary and past events, drew on vernacular compilations of Trojan history and world history, including Vincent of Beauvais's encyclopedic *Speculum majus* (ca. 1220–44). These compilations were often made by members of the mendicant orders (especially the Franciscans and Dominicans) and were sometimes recopied with local interventions.[30] Roman historians were also plundered by local historians: Livy's works were fairly easily available in vernacular compilations, while the writings of Suetonius, Sallust, and Lucan were translated

Figure 2.2. Ettore Pasqualigo enters office as Venetian *podestà* in Brescia, 1451. In "provvisioni del Consiglio Cittadino," 5 August 1451, Archivio di Stato, Brescia, ASC 495, fol. 228v. Photo: author. Reproduced by kind permission of Archivio di Stato, Brescia.

into Italian from French editions and used by preachers, writers of fiction, and others looking for *exempla*.[31]

Notary-chroniclers, true to their professional training, followed common and fairly rigid formulations so as to give their texts authority. The use of classical Latin terms and the frequent citation of ancient and medieval texts added further gravitas to their productions. The public and political nature of such chronicle or history writing was often blatant and did not necessarily disappear when new values and stylistic elements were introduced by Renaissance scholars. Far from it: humanists at the Sforza court in Milan in the fifteenth century wrote copiously in praise of a new regime that hoped to shore up its shaky claim to rule.[32] As Eric Cochrane has noted in the case of Venice, the production of more humanist histories of the city after around 1420 did not lead to the abandonment of the republic's most cherished myths; indeed most of them were simply clothed in new classical "garb," and new ones were invented to strengthen basic Venetian "truths."[33] In the case of Brescia, awareness of the classical heritage and origins of the city increased during the fifteenth century and provided useful material for history and myth. The remains of some ancient Roman buildings were visible in the *cittadella* quarter, and in 1480 the council unanimously decided to preserve the engraved Roman stones found during construction work and to incorporate them into the new buildings.[34] The chroniclers, historians, and panegyricists writing about Brescia were generally happy to cite these, as well as to plunder Livy or Justin's epitome of Pompeius Trogus among ancient sources, and to follow the suppositions of medieval chroniclers. Just like the Venetians, the Brescians were content to dress up older myths in a more classical style.

The elaboration of myths that resonate with collective memory, underpin ritual, and serve as a means of self-definition is a common feature of Italian urban history.[35] In Brescia, council members, chancellors, and other officials probably considered it a civic duty to compile chronicles of past and present events that perpetuated and celebrated Brescian myths. Within a few years of the city passing into Venetian hands, the councillor and doctor Giacomo Malvezzi, a relative of the city's chancellor during 1426–56, compiled a chronicle of Brescia from its origins up to 1332.[36] Cristoforo Soldo, the city chancellor, kept a detailed chronicle of events in the city during 1437–69 that several subsequent chroniclers consulted. Soldo's book of the *Custodie notturne* (the night watch) compiled during the siege of the city in 1438–40 provided a vital record of those eligible to be admitted to the council according to the rules drawn up and revised in the course of the fifteenth century.[37] A number of notaries, including Iacopo Melga, recorded contemporary events during the fifteenth century, while the councillor Elia Capriolo wrote a more elaborate account of Brescia's history from its foundation to the opening of the sixteenth century.

Capriolo, described in 1502 as an erudite man of "mild and modest manners," was an active servant of Brescia's civic government and an acute observer of the foibles of his fellow Brescians.[38] Capriolo's chronicle of events up to the year 1500 was published in an authoritative folio format during his lifetime, but a supplement recounting the events of the turbulent first decade of the sixteenth century that he compiled at the urging of his friends the bishop Altobello Averoldi and Giovanni Cavallo, the son of the professor of medicine at Padua, remained in manuscript until the seventeenth century and was not published in full until the eighteenth century.[39] Capriolo drew on a range of classical sources in his work but also relied on earlier chronicles by Malvezzi and Soldo and consulted official records. Capriolo's work, which has been denigrated as "il meno esatto e il più leggiero" of all Brescian histories, clearly betrays the author's prejudices and feelings and, while not uncritical of various aspects of life under Venetian policy, presents a positive picture of Venetian rule and Brescian politics and culture.[40] Equally noble by birth but, in contrast to Capriolo, resolutely hostile to Venice was Pandolfo Nassini, who compiled a frank and copious set of *ricordanze* from around 1520 onward. Nassini's attacks on his fellow Brescians relied on a variety of sources: his father's accounts, his own firsthand experiences, Malvezzi's chronicle, Soldo's book of 1438, and the inscriptions found on public buildings in the city and its suburbs.[41]

Nassini's intended readership was probably fairly limited, given the outrageous libels his work contains, but the Venetian rectors in the city may have encouraged Capriolo and some other humanists to disseminate their work. For example, Capriolo's chronicle was printed under the auspices of the Venetian *podestà* Francesco Bragadin.[42] Panegyrical verses and speeches about the city were written by a wider range of figures—ecclesiastical and lay, humble and well-connected—who were usually attempting to ingratiate themselves with the city or the rectors with a view to securing a teaching post or some other reward: Ubertino Pusculo's 1458 work in praise of Brescia probably falls into this category, and he subsequently set up a school in the city.[43] Soon after the Venetian conquest the commune of Brescia began to import teachers of grammar and logic to educate and instruct the young—in 1432 the council appointed Tommaso Seneca di Camerino, who had taught rhetoric and poetry at the schools of Bologna and Perugia, to a generously remunerated post as public teacher of rhetoric and grammar.[44] His successor in 1435 was of equal caliber: Gabriele Concoreggio, a former pupil of Vittorino da Feltre of Mantua, whom he rejoined during the Venice-Milan clash of 1438–40, only to return to Brescia in 1441 at the request of the humanist *podestà* Francesco Barbaro.[45] Concoreggio's achievement in producing large numbers of learned pupils was posthumously honored in a resolution of the council in 1490.[46]

The commune was keen to foster the learning of Greek, and in 1500 Giovanni Taverio, a leading Hellenist and a close friend of Capriolo, was appointed to teach this language.[47] His successor in 1503, Marino Becichemo, born at Scutari but educated in Brescia, may well have stayed in his adoptive city until he moved to Padua in 1517: his commentaries on Pliny, Cicero, Virgil, Livy, Fabius, and Persius earned him the renewal of an unusually lucrative contract in 1505.[48] The commune rewarded scholars in other ways: it gave 25 gold florins to Pietro Lazzaroni in 1487 for his *Carmen civitatis Brixiae* (lost) and gifts of money to Francesco Arrigoni in 1508 for his *Panegyric of Brescia* (also lost), to Giovanni Britannico in 1482 and 1508 for his commentaries on Persius and Juvenal, respectively, and to the Modenese poet Panfilo Sasso in 1500 for expounding on the literary titans Dante and Petrarch.[49] The council granted citizenship to the humanists Lazzaroni in 1471, Taverio in 1486, and Giovanni Stefano Buzzoni (Vosonius), who wished to return to the city from the Riviera del Garda, two years later.[50]

Unsurprisingly, a major theme these humanist writers and their colleagues in neighboring cities stressed was the flourishing state of scholarship and learning in the city of Brescia. The Paduan Girolamo Campagnola wrote to fellow humanist Cassandra Fedele urging her to move from Padua to Brescia, where she would find an ancient and now booming city with a flourishing society of the learned, artists, philosophers, jurists, and doctors.[51] Giovanni Francesco Boccardo, Elia Capriolo, Laura Cereta, Ubertino Pusculo, and Carlo Valgulio were all drawn from the oldest families in the city and sometimes worked in collaboration under the patronage of local feudal nobility such as Ludovico Martinengo. There is some evidence of semiformal gatherings of these men and women in the city during the latter part of the fifteenth century, although there is no contemporary evidence for the existence of a more formally constituted academy in the city.[52] In general, Campagnola's praise of Brescian learning may be read as a typical piece of humanist flattery, and the city cannot really be placed in the first rank of humanist centres in Renaissance Italy, although some works of striking originality (discussed later) were produced.

Brescia is more important as an early and productive center of printing. After 1472 many Brescian humanists could take advantage of the press to publish their own works or editions and translations of classical authors, notably historians and moralizing poets like Plutarch and Juvenal. At least 327 separate editions were printed in Brescia by fifteen presses between 1472 and 1511. In addition to these a Hebrew press was active at Soncino and Barco—probably under the patronage of the Martinengo—at the end of the fifteenth century. A press was briefly active at Toscolano in 1479–80 and again in 1523, and there was even a press at Collio in the remote Val Trompia to the north of Brescia during the early sixteenth century.[53] The peak decades for the production of books fell either side of 1500, but after the French occupation output slackened considerably, and during 1512–14 when the city was devastated by sack and occupation no printing activity took place, except for the production of the pious engraved print discussed in Chapter 11. After the return of Venetian rule the pace of printing slowed, with 128 editions printed during 1515–50.[54] Taking the figures for the incunable period (to 1501) alone, Brescia's 293 editions places the city among the top eight Italian printing centers in terms of output.[55]

Brescian printers and editors could be innovative and enterprising, and in 1502 the printer-publisher Aldo Manuzio complained to the Venetian Senate that a book had been printed in Brescia falsely under his name and that editions of his letters were being printed with many errors and being exported to Lyons.⁵⁶ Lorenzo Valla's prose translation of the *Iliad*, issued in Brescia in 1474, was the first complete translation printed during the Renaissance, while the "experimental printer" Tommaso Ferrandus, who complained that he was paid in clipped or debased currency for his edition of the Brescian statutes, published the first ever printed edition of Lucretius's *De rerum natura* around the same time.⁵⁷ In 1487 the prolific Bonino de' Bonini printed an edition of Dante's *La Commedia* with lavish woodcuts, some of which were based on Sandro Botticelli's designs for an edition printed in Florence six years earlier. The Hebrew press active in the city for several years also produced one of the earliest complete Hebrew Bibles in Europe. Finally, the presses responded to national events, such as the invasion of the French in 1494, with vernacular verse accounts and issued pamphlets related to more local disputes, such as that between the Dominicans and humanists on the matter of funerals (discussed in Chapter 8).

Origins and Romans

The origins of Brescia were agreed to be very ancient, indeed to predate those of Venice, but there was some variety of opinion about the precise nature and date of the earliest settlement. As one Milanese visitor remarked in 1494: "amongst those who have written about its origin, I find a great variety of opinion, and therefore I leave the subject alone."⁵⁸ By one tradition Hercules, the heroic son of Zeus who had crossed the Alps in Greek myth, had been responsible for the earliest building work in the city after killing the Hydra at nearby Lake d'Idro. The name Hercules was attached to a column, street, fountain, square, and even palace in Brescia.⁵⁹ His association with Brescia was perhaps fitting given the city's prominent role as the headquarters of the captain-general of Venetian forces and as the preeminent center for the making of arms and armor in Italy.⁶⁰ The shield of the city—as represented on a variety of objects, including coinage, the title pages of the 1490 edition of civic statutes, and in Capriolo's chronicle of around 1505—featured a lion in reference to Hercules.⁶¹ Indeed, in 1565 the Brescian council instructed the leading Venetian artist Titian to decorate the ceiling of the communal palace with an allegory of Brescia in which the female figure of Brescia held a lion skin and stood near a club. An accompanying representation of the forge of Vulcan by Titian also included a lion, and in both cases a reference to Herculean origins and strength was intended, for one of the Herculean labors was the slaying and flaying of the Nemean lion.⁶²

In common with the perpetrators of many other European foundation myths, some Brescians claimed that the Trojans had been early settlers in the region. However, although Elia Capriolo mentioned a certain Thracum who supposedly founded the city some 1,280 years before Christ, there was no single figure like Aeneas or Antenor, the legendary founder of Padua, who stood out in these myths, and this theme is not dominant in the surviving texts.[63] The key event in the city's foundation story, like other towns in the *terraferma* including Milan, Bergamo, and Verona, was the settlement in the area of the Cenomani, whose original base was in southern France.[64] Livy, Pliny, Pompeius Trogus, and Ptolemy provided the main sources for this supposition.[65] Giacomo Malvezzi dated the arrival of their king, Brenio, shortly after the reign of Numa Pompilius in Rome (717–673 BCE) and attributed to Brenio the institution of consuls and a senate in the city as well as the establishment of some noble families in Brescia such as the Martinengo, Pallazzo, and Prandoni.[66] The aristocratic nature of this foundation was further emphasized by the chronicler Capriolo, who regarded Brenio as at the very least the restorer of the city and made a comparison between the aristocratic rule and impartial justice of Brescia and Marseilles—another city founded by the Cenomani. He even asserted on the authority of Livy that Brescia had been the chief city of the Cenomani and therefore superior to Bergamo, Crema, Cremona, Verona, and Mantua.[67]

Provincial pride could be further enhanced by reference to Brescia's brush with the glories of ancient Rome. The Romans invaded and took over the rule of Brescia after the creation of the first consul in Rome, and the chroniclers and panegyricists agreed that under the Romans the city flourished.[68] One anonymous Florentine Franciscan even asserted in an oration given in the *piazza della loggia* in 1483 that civic virtues flourished and civil dissent ceased in the city.[69] The importance of Brescia under Roman rule was evident in the splendor of the ancient fabric of the city.[70] Capriolo repeated the assertion of an authority on Roman inscriptions that there was no other city in Italy with so many Roman remains, and he argued that these proved that the city was noble from its inception—indeed a sister to Rome—and that some Brescian families like the Maggi and Calini were descended from these Romans.[71] Similar claims to illustrious Roman lineage were made, as has been noted, by the Corner of Venice and were not uncommon in other humanist texts of the period.[72]

In his chronicle Capriolo cited a Roman inscription that served to support a second theme in the Brescian tradition: the city's association with the celebrated victor of Carthage, Scipio Africanus.[73] Giacomo Malvezzi described how Scipio returned to Brescia after his defeat of Hannibal and founded a family line that culminated with the patron saints of the city, Faustino and Giovita, who were martyred by the emperor Hadrian.[74] The patron saints were also cited in 1488 by the Brescian humanist Laura Cereta, alongside Christian martyrs such as Vincent and Stephen and classical figures such as Ulysses, Scipio, and Hannibal, as exemplars of those who had overcome misfortune.[75] Capriolo was skeptical about the story of the patron saints' descent from Scipio but argued that it was with Scipio's advice that the Brescians set up their magistracies and councils and preserved their liberty in the face of the barbarian incursions of Cimbri and Teutons. He went on to argue, again on the basis of a surviving Roman inscription, that Julius Caesar had a particular affection for Brescia and as a consequence it was given Roman citizenship with special privileges such as the right to choose its consuls, praetors, prefects, vicars, and other officers.[76]

Loyal Subject and Ally

The association of Brescia with Scipio and the Romans generally was noted by writers who sought to highlight the city's constancy, loyalty, and martial valor. According to one tradition, based on Livy, Brescia had participated in the struggles against Hannibal and his Gallic allies in Cisalpine Gaul when all of the other Gallic tribes had deserted Rome.[77] This theme of constant loyalty seems to have emerged only under Venetian rule and was naturally applied to Brescia's relationship with Venice, as has been noted in relation to the entry of Cardinal Corner in 1546. In this way, writers asserted that Brescia had endured the tyranny of Filippo Maria Visconti before enjoying the most just rule of Venice.[78] Even then, Brescia had endured several assaults by the Visconti and Sforza of Milan since it had accepted Venetian rule, and in particular a conflict and siege during 1438–40 when Brescians had once again fought for their liberty under the just rule of the Venetians, whose virtues equalled, if not surpassed, those of the Romans.[79]

Brescia had never wavered in its loyalty to Venice, and as a token of this the city was compared in inscriptions, verses, and chronicles with Saguntum (the city that endured an eight months' siege by Hannibal's forces) and its Venetian defenders with Scipio. Of course, the fact that Saguntum fell to Hannibal's forces because of the failure of Rome to send reinforcements was passed over without comment.[80] The local humanist Ubertino Pusculo composed a verse account of the siege in seven books.[81] Capriolo devoted an entire book of his local chronicle to it.[82] Brescian loyalty to Venice during the siege, as well as the Venetian decision to send boats overland to Lake Garda and the stout defense of the city by its men and women,[83] were probably the events in Brescian history that had the widest resonance in Renaissance Italy until the city endured the sack of 1512 and similar themes reemerged.[84] The events of 1438–40 also shaped Brescian identity concretely, bringing new and more generous concessions to the city, and within two decades participation in the defense of the city became one of the criteria for admission to the ranks of citizens.[85]

In a speech of welcome for the visit of the Venetian cardinal Giovanni Battista Zeno to the city in 1489 the local humanist Giovanni Casato asserted that in general the Brescians fought with loyalty to Venice uppermost in their minds and that no images or sculptures of Saint Mark were needed to inspire them. Venice and Brescia, he declared, were joined as in the rational soul the three essences were mingled.[86] He compared Brescia to a virgin with many lovers, but noted that the city's true love was Venice.[87] Venetians and their Brescian supporters sometimes asserted that Brescia was a "lover," "ally," or "friend" of the lagoon city.[88] Others patronizingly referred to Brescia as the most beloved son or daughter of Venice, and after 1509 this ostensibly warm and familial comparison was imbued with a bitter twist familiar to the parents of rebellious children. In the aftermath of the sack of Brescia in 1512 the Venetian Marco Negro castigated the Brescians for welcoming the French, who were the agents of the city's ruin. He wondered that the Brescians could have betrayed the benign and pleasing rule of the Venetians who had governed them for eighty-four years not as subjects but like their own sons and had lifted them out of misery and servitude (under the Visconti) and replaced their rustic matters with a gilding of urbanity. As he observed sententiously: "After the death of the father the son's vices rise up with a vengeance"[89]

In the aftermath of the Venetian defeat at the battle of Agnadello and the loss of most of its mainland possessions in 1509 the Venetian diarist Girolamo Priuli lamented that Venice had spent millions of ducats to secure the fortifications of its subject cities and to keep the passes secure. Venice had held them as dear as the pupils of its own eyes. Venice had loved Brescia above all and spent a fortune fortifying the city and had given it many benefits, privileges, and exemptions, and indeed all that it had asked the Senate. The people even said that the city was more faithful to the Venetian empire than its own nobles and non-nobles (*popolo*). Given its fidelity during the siege of 1438–40 the Venetians had expected better of the city than such an easy capitulation to the French without a shot being fired. It was now declared a rebel city and enemy of the name of Venice.[90]

Brescia Beata and *Brixia Magnipotens*

One of the most celebrated episodes of the siege of 1438–40 was the moment when the Brescians were fighting off a Visconti attack on the *citta-*

della quarter and the patron saints Faustino and Giovita appeared in armor at the tower of Ravarotto during the assault by the troops led by Niccolò Piccinino.[91] This incident was said to have demoralized the enemy to such an extent that the siege was called off and Brescia preserved for Venetian rule. Tellingly, this episode goes unrecorded in contemporary chronicles and is only mentioned in passing by Capriolo.[92] However, the saints were frequently represented by artists and sculptors under Venetian rule, and this may have given added force to local pride and to the Brescian association with Ancient Rome, for Faustino and Giovita were Romans of aristocratic birth—if not direct descent from Scipio, as some chroniclers asserted.[93] Malvezzi suggested they were of Trojan blood and that the father of one of them was head of the local senate. In any case, Faustino and Giovita were leading men in the city: wise and learned, skilled in war, patriotic, and exemplary civic figures who contributed to the public good by building an aqueduct.[94] Faustino and Giovita, together with Bishop Apollonio, preached and converted many Brescians, including their guard Calimero, who later became bishop of Milan.[95] The story of their martyrdom pitted them against Emperor Hadrian himself and was characterized by their repeated escapes from a variety of means of execution, including drowning and the attack of savage beasts.[96] Capriolo, who called them "nobilissimos cives nostros," cited them as examples of those persons who could endure physical torments with equanimity of soul.[97]

The memory, return, and vestiges of the presence of Faustino and Giovita were celebrated in Brescia in prose and poetry by local humanists, including Laura Cereta's brother Daniele Cereto.[98] Malvezzi noted that a fountain miraculously appeared—almost as a Christian counterpart to their pagan aqueduct—to the east of the city near the hill where Faustino and Giovita preached. The church of San Fiorano was subsequently built there in the Lombard era, while a church was also founded on the location of Faustino's incarceration.[99] The remains of the saints were fortuitously uncovered in 1455, and their images—like those of the civic patrons San Proscodimo, San Zeno, and San Vincenzo of Padua, Verona, and Vicenza, respectively—adorned the important buildings of the city in sculpted and painted form.[100] The full story of Faustino and Giovita was subsequently repeated in vernacular and in Latin versions that were printed in the city.[101]

Many chroniclers, panegyricists, and visitors also noted that Brescia was almost like "another Rome," for it venerated the memory of the thirty-two sainted bishops who followed Apollonio.[102] Among these eminent figures was Anathalon, a companion of the apostle Saint Barnabas, who spread the Christian faith in Milan and Brescia.[103] Toward the end of the fifteenth century the local antiquarian Taddeo Solazio enumerated the sainted bishops and dismissed the poets, historians, orators, and lawyers of other cities who boasted of their leaders in war. As Solazio argued: "Brescia celebrates and exults in so many of its citizens in the heavens and with these immortal companions joins in venerating God."[104] This holy presence in the city was supported in the fifteenth century by the regular clergy, whose churches were the sites for the veneration of these saintly relics. In 1483 it was noted that the Franciscans alone had founded eighteen monasteries in the Bresciano.[105] In 1458 Ubertino Pusculo recorded a comment made about the numbers of men and women enclosed in monasteries in the city: "For not only monks . . . but also the whole population of Brescia itself seems to follow the religious life."[106]

Holy protection for the city came in the form of the holy crosses: a Lombard cross of the field (*del campo*) and the relic of the true cross referred to as the cross of the golden pennant (*orifiamma*). These were celebrated for their beauty and miraculous powers and were key objects in civic ceremonial from around 1260.[107] The holy cross of the field was believed to have been made for the emperor Constantine the Great and was passed to Charlemagne by the Byzantine emperor Constantine VI while Charlemagne was returning to France from a visit to Jerusalem. The relic of the true cross was discovered by Constantine's mother in Jerusalem. Both crosses were subsequently given to the abbot of San Faustino by Namo (or Naimo), a duke of Bavaria who was converted by the sight of the blood of Faustino and Giovita that appeared when their bodies were moved in 843.[108] The crosses were celebrated for their public healing powers and were regularly processed in the large civic processions that marked the liturgical year, responded to severe weather conditions, or preempted divine displeasure with the city on account of its sins.[109]

Panegyricists asserted that Brescia flourished under a new golden age of Venetian rule, and the words "Brixia magnipotens" were regularly cited and celebrated by visitors and locals alike.[110] In 1426 the prayer at the act of fealty to Venice that took place in the duomo included the words "Brixia magnipotens floreat."[111] As noted in Chapter 1, the appellation was also used on the standard presented to Venice in 1440 at the conclusion of the war with the Visconti.[112] In 1458 Ubertino Pusculo celebrated a city of natural fertility and human splendor in which justice reigned supreme and discord between nobility and plebians had ended.[113] Subsequent panegyricists and poets also dwelled at length on Brescia's natural beauty and fertility, and the chronicler Capriolo remarked that its abundant fruit made it seem like "another Corfu."[114] The city's Gaulish name, Brimonia, was said to mean "gentile, legiadra e bella," while its Latin name, Brixia, was understood, rather obscurely, to derive from its Edenic charms.[115] In 1483 a young Marin Sanudo summed up his feelings about Brescia in verse

("Brexa demum zentil e si cortese") and elsewhere commented on the city's opulence and growth since 1440. Brescia, he observed, was full of fountains, bells, and whores ("è fornida di fontane, campane, et putane"), and he noted that despite twenty-four thousand deaths during the plague of 1478 the city was now very populous. He concluded his account with a proud Venetian variation on the usual Brescian motto: "Brixia magni potens Marco dominante triumphat."[116] In a similar fashion, the Milanese pilgrim Pietro Casola concluded his generally complimentary account of the physical appearance of Brescia as follows: "He who called this city 'Brixia Magnipotens' made no mistake, because it is so opulent."[117] Given the importance of the theme of Brescian fertility and abundance it is hardly surprising that the Brescian council's commission to Titian in 1565 also included an allegory of a rather matronly Ceres and a boozy Bacchus to accompany the other figures on the ceiling of the council chamber.[118]

This brief survey of the myths of the city indicates some of the ways Brescians and Venetians resorted to a "metaphoric discourse tending towards conciliation and accommodation" similar to that employed in Verona, Vicenza, Padua, and other subject cities.[119] Brescians adopted familial and paternalistic imagery and presented themselves in a subordinate role as loyal sons or daughters. The Brescian virgin was wooed by many but gave herself only to Venice, in an appropriation of the virginal role more usually assigned to Venice. In return for this act of loyalty the Venetians declared that Brescia was more beloved than any other city. These metaphors contained the seeds of a more negative reading of the relationship between the two cities, and the ungrateful son or daughter could be chastised and deplored.

There is also some hint of Brescian independence and pride in these myths. The emphasis on the city's ancient origins provided an implicit contrast with Venice's more recent foundation and can be found repeated in other towns of the *terraferma* that were proud of their local heritage.[120] Moreover, the semidivine or noble nature of the Brescian founders underscored the pretensions of the city's current elite and contrasted with the mercantile nature of the Venetian patriciate. The social distance between Brescians and Venetians may also have been one reason why the Bresciano's natural wealth was so often mentioned by some Brescian panegyricists, for it reminded audiences of the feudal and noble origins of many of the Brescian families, whose surnames—Capriolo, for example—derived from their country estates.

The noble Brescian families were descended from Gaulish nobility and Roman heroes, and many writers were quick to assert the special place "Brixia" had enjoyed in the Roman republic and empire as a Julian town with the privileges of Roman citizenship. In the same way, an accommodation with Brescia's place in the Venetian empire may have been intended, or it may have flattered Brescians to think of themselves as the most beloved and most loyal of the subject cities of Venice/Rome. As the evidence I will present shows, the public spaces of the city were given a more classical or monumental appearance during the fifteenth century, and the sense of reborn city flourishing under Venetian peace and prosperity was projected in marble and bronze, paint and gilt. Even here, though, local pride could be manifest, and the most overt statements of loyalty must be read alongside the heroic figure of "Brescia armata" placed on the façade of the offices on the south side of the *piazza della loggia* around 1485 and the images of local saints that the council took care to see were put in place around the same square and kept in good order. In reconstructing the history of Brescia's struggle to adjust to Venetian rule after 1426 and in tracing the formation after around 1460 of an urban oligarchy, this sense of local pride and independence must always be borne in mind.

PART TWO

POLITICS

CHAPTER THREE

Privilege, Power, and Politics

THE FOUNDATIONS of the relationship between Brescia and Venice were laid in 1426 when the citizens of Brescia, like their counterparts in every other major city that fell into Venetian hands, submitted "capitula et petitiones" on a range of political, economic, and religious matters to the Venetian doge.[1] These twenty-four *capitula* defined the relationship between the city and Venice, outlined new constitutional arrangements, and sought a range of economic benefits, but like the *capitula* of other subject cities, for example Verona, they should be regarded as petitions to a new lord rather than as preconditions for the acceptance of Venetian rule. Venice asserted the right to modify them while at the same time insisting that rectors observe them.[2]

The Brescian demands were not born ex nihilo. The privileges granted to Brescia by Gian Galeazzo Visconti in 1385 and Filippo Maria Visconti in 1421 represented their accession to Brescian requests for juridical authority over much of the Bresciano, the restitution of stolen goods and creditors' funds, and the reform of other abuses. It is clear that by these grants the Visconti dukes did not sacrifice any power and that they kept open the possibility of making separate concessions (for example, to the Val Camonica) and arbitrary interventions in Brescian affairs.[3] The Brescian councils maintained an appearance of communal autonomy while in practice they became administrative organs devoid of executive power and subject to the direct influence of Milanese appointees resident in the city.

Under this cover the Visconti legitimized their rule in the Bresciano and imposed a range of taxes on the city and *contado* in a manner consonant with a trend toward heavier and more closely controlled fiscal exactions that was observable in other Italian communes under signorial or republican domination after around 1380.[4] Therefore, the Viscontean privileges should not be dismissed lightly, since they provided some of the political structures, notably that of the rectors and the territorial representatives, with which Venice and Brescia would build their relationship.[5]

The privileges granted by the Venetians are marked by a new theme: the denunciation of the precarious state of the city. Brescia had clearly suffered during the disruption of the preceding years of war and was described, perhaps with some exaggeration, as being "until now gutted, suppressed, depopulated, and miserably tortured by tyrants."[6] It is certainly true that after several years of war and socioeconomic distress the population had declined markedly from its level in around 1400.[7] Venice also eschewed the easy promises of the Visconti in favor of considered and pragmatic responses to Brescian requests for aid. For example, Brescia's depopulation would be reversed by granting citizenship to anyone who built or restored a house in the ruined parts of the city. The predominance of commercial privileges earlier in the text than in the grant of 1421 is also significant. The Brescians ask to be brought into the loving embrace of Venice, to be numbered among its faithful subjects, and in so doing to be brought from servitude to liberty.[8] They request the same exemptions and trading rights with Venice as the Paduans, Vicentines, and Veronese, and they ask Venice to send experienced and knowledgeable men ("officiales notabiles et experti") chosen from among the more important and distinguished Venetians to govern the city.[9]

Most important, Venice reserves the right to impose taxes as it sees fit for the maintenance of Brescia, as well as the right to offer exemptions, but agrees to Brescian demands in relation to tax assessments and the granting of citizenship in order to bring the city back into a flourishing state.[10] In 1442 in the teeth of Brescian protests Venice imposed a heavy annual tax of 24,000 ducats on the city in order to cover military expenses and in 1452 demanded further funds in order to meet the new Sforza threat.[11] However, during the century after 1426, and especially after 1440, the Brescians recouped some of the fiscal privileges and exemptions lost under previous overlords, and the economy flourished. At the same time, the urban patriciate enjoyed some of the lowest direct and indirect taxes in the *terraferma,* while the rich and populous *contado,* directly subject to Brescia, shouldered a relatively heavy fiscal burden.[12] During the fifteenth century the balance of power between the city and the *contado* tilted markedly in favor of the former as citizens bought up large areas of land and the economic and legal advantages of urban life drew migrants from the countryside.

The political integrity of Brescia and its *contado* formed a central core of the requests made to the doge, but Venice signally failed to affirm the wide scope of jurisdiction the Brescians demanded. Two rectors—a *podestà* (in charge of civil and judicial matters) and a *capitano* (in control of military affairs and finance)—were appointed by Venice, as well as castellans for key towns in the region. Major policy decisions, for example concerning the forging of alliances with other states, as well as the level of taxes and the ways fiscal income was employed, rested with Venice. Venice also assumed a more decisive and influential role in Brescian domestic politics. In the eighth clause of the "capitula et petitiones" the Brescians invite Venetian intervention, and in response the doge outlines the Venetian rectors' role in the Brescian communal councils: the rectors will draw up a list of local citizens qualified to be chosen for the council of seventy-two and the bimonthly council of twelve elders, by the extraction of ballots *(brevia)* from a sack.[13] However, like other citizens of the *terraferma*, Brescians were denied the right to sit in the Venetian Great Council.

It seems extraordinary that the Brescians invited Venice to control political life in the city in this way. However, such direct intervention was not unusual in the *terraferma*, and comparing the Brescian case with these experiences is instructive. In 1422 the Venetian Senate instituted a Council of One Hundred in Vicenza in response to Vicentine complaints of exclusion from government, and in 1446 an enlargement of the Paduan council from sixty to one hundred was approved by the Senate in order to avoid a similar situation. Finally, in 1462 the Venetian Council of Ten, recognizing that many men loyal to Venice were being excluded from the councils, agreed that the rectors in Verona should have the power to appoint twenty *cives* as councillors, although in practice the Veronese elite maintained its autonomy and control over the composition of the councils.[14] Many Brescians long excluded from power probably welcomed Venetian direction as a way of ending the civil hostility, local vendetta and bloody internecine struggles that had marked the previous century. At the same time they almost certainly expected local statutes to be observed and Venice to govern with a fairly light touch. For its part, Venice probably intended to reward and strengthen the loyalty of its subjects in a way that respected local interests.

In general, there is little evidence that Venice attempted to "centralize" its growing mainland empire, least of all the outlying Bresciano or Bergamasco areas, during the fifteenth century. Law has argued that the survival of the mainland state as a loosely integrated body owes a great deal to Venetian diplomatic skill and to the autonomy and flexibility of regional government. Venice sent rectors into the *terraferma* to direct affairs in the name of Venice, and Law has remarked of the roles of the *podestà* and *capitano* that "the aim of their detailed and steadily elaborated commissions was to achieve honest, conscientious but detached government."[15] However, in practice such governance could be hampered by a lack of local knowledge and conflicting legal advice, or even by a clash of values between landholding or feudal elites and the predominantly commercial ruling class of Venice.[16] In the case of Brescia, the desire for a greater control of the territory—not the arrogation of power by the rectors—was one of the main sources of contention with Venice. The history of the troubled relationship between city and countryside demonstrates how Venice followed a generally pragmatic line in the Bresciano by recognizing and accepting a multiplicity of powers and interests or by imposing direct rule by means of rectors. The Brescians, by contrast, were often hostile toward the fact of growing autonomy of the Bresciano and resented its resistance in fiscal matters. During 1426–1530 the Brescians sought to undermine the independence of the Bresciano and to maintain the city's upper hand in fiscal matters. At the same time, as I will show, the Brescians began to restrict access to power in the city to newly created citizens, especially recent immigrants from the countryside.

Governors and Governed

On 24 September 1501 the Brescian lawyer and humanist Bernardino Bornato addressed the departing *podestà,* Lorenzo Giustiniani, in highly flattering terms as a man with such honesty, humility, and clemency that he had acted not only as a *podestà* in the most noble city of Brescia but also like a father who settled the dissensions of squabbling neighbors and siblings and acted with piety and justice to bring about the highest good: concord and tranquillity. By abhorring crime, honoring offices, and punishing of those who transgressed the statutes, a golden age of justice had flourished under the governance of Giustiniani, who had garnered a great reputation ("ita sub tuo magistratu aurea iusticia florebit tuque iustissimus ab omnibus decantaberis idemque optimus").[17] Bornato's comments echo the contemporary musings on the office of *podestà* set down by the Venetian writer Marcantonio Sabellico and indicate both the high ideals invested in the office and the tremendous challenges faced by each Venetian patrician who assumed the role.[18] In theory, the *podestà* and *capitano* in Brescia had fairly wide-ranging authority over political life, justice, and other matters such as defense, finance, and relations with the territorial bodies. The *podestà* represented the prestige of Venetian authority and brought with him a staff that included a vicar, two judges in civil and criminal laws, two investigating assistants, a constable, and a chancellor. As well as designating the names of those eligible to join the Brescian council, the *podestà* presided over council meetings, mediated between the Council of Ten or the Senate and the Brescian councils, enforced criminal and civil laws, and rendered accounts to Venice each month.[19] The proclamations issued in Brescia in the name of the Venetian rectors during this period were often prompted by decisions of the city council and were largely concerned with the regulation of the grain supply, the conduct of shopkeepers and traders, the protection of the city against plague, and the oblations and processions for important feast days, churches, and other special events.[20]

Under the Malatesta and Visconti regimes the *podestà* and *capitano*, together with their staff, were forced out of their usual residences in the *broletto* and into rented accommodation in the neighbouring *contrada* (neighborhood) of the Bruciata gate. The *podestà* presided over meetings of the special council and executed justice in this new setting. After 1422 a complex of buildings was added to the main residence, which was bought and decorated. In 1426 these buildings were damaged in the course of the Viscontean defense of the *cittadella*, and therefore the *capitano* returned to the *broletto*, while the *podestà* and his court, together with the communal magistracies, met in a rented space on the ground floor of the palace of Count Francesco Martinengo della Motella.[21] The council's decision, prompted by the Venetian *provveditore*, to build an entirely new palace for the *podestà* in the *contrada* of the Bruciata gate was overturned when in 1432, following the execution for treason of Francesco Bussone, Count of Carmagnola and captain-general of the Venetian forces, his palace in the *contrada* of Sant'Agata, a little to the west of the *contrada* of the Bruciata gate, was appropriated for the use of the *podestà*. The *podestà* presided over meetings of the Brescian councils there until 1502–3, when the councillors moved to the newly constructed *palazzo della loggia*. Until 1596 the *podestà* continued to reside and execute justice in the *palazzo vecchio*, as it became known.[22]

Despite their physical proximity to Brescia's center of power and politics, most rectors had little detailed knowledge of the nature of Brescian society and were hindered in deepening their understanding of local affairs by the requirement that they live and dine in the rectors' residence and bring their own vicars rather than appoint local men. This was a deliberate attempt on the part of Venice to shield rectors from local factions and to encourage the fair application of justice. The execution of justice was also constrained by the existence of a codified body of local statutes that the rectors were obliged by their commissions from the doge to respect. In addition, the rectors or their judges and advisors had to deal with an array of legislation emanating from the communal councils that was not usually written into the statute books or even collated from the council records until the sixteenth century. There is some evidence of rectors being ignorant of these local customs or overstepping the bounds of their commissions, but local statutes were generally respected by Venice. The Venetian Senate instructed the Brescian *podestà* to ignore local statutes in order to execute justice only on a few occasions during this period.[23]

If the Venetian rector was to avoid becoming a cipher at the mercy of competing interest groups in the city, he had to act with some prudence, force, and low cunning, as well as with the justice, temperance, and astute diplomacy praised by Bernardino Bornato.[24] The post of rector in the *terraferma* attracted Venetians of generally high caliber and extensive political experience, although a large proportion of rectors were relative novices. Giuseppe del Torre has estimated that only around one-quarter of all rectors appointed by Venice to posts in the *terraferma* during 1506–40 had some previous experience of such a post. Moreover, he has calculated that over two-thirds of those appointed never undertook more than one posting.[25] As far as it is possible to calculate, most of the rectors during the fifteenth century arrived in Brescia in their late forties or early fifties—the usual age of political adulthood for a Venetian patrician—and a few had some previous experience of acting as a *podestà* in the *terraferma*. Andrea Leon, the *podestà* in Brescia in 1460, had taken the same role in Bergamo in 1452.[26] Domenico Trevisan acted as *podestà* in Feltre in 1474 and then took up the same post in Brescia in 1491. Some of these men had served in Brescia in the capacity of *provveditore* (serving as an adjunct to the rectors or directing military matters in the key outposts of the region) before taking up the rectorial role: for example, Ludovico Foscarini served as *provveditore* in Brescia in 1451–52 and was appointed *podestà* to the city in 1453.[27] He had also served as *podestà* in Ravenna, Feltre, Vicenza, and Verona before he took up the ducal commission in Brescia. Other patricians served as *podestà* in Brescia twice and could therefore bring some prior knowledge to bear on the later posting—Leon in 1467, Ettore Pasqualigo (1452 and 1463)—or returned in the capacity of *provveditore*, as did, for example, Marcantonio Morosini (in 1484 and 1499).

It has been suggested that for Venetian patricians there may have been "a strong link between Terraferma experience and a development of humanistic interests."[28] In the case of Brescia, the aforementioned Ludovico

Foscarini was one of a number of rectors with pronounced humanist interests, including Andrea Giuliani (*capitano*, 1435–36), Francesco Barbaro
(*capitano*, 1437–40), Candiano Bollani (*capitano*, 1471), Francesco Diedo
(*capitano*, 1479–80), Girolamo Donà (*podestà*, 1495–97), Marco Sanudo
(*podestà*, 1497–99), the experienced diplomat Marco Dandolo (*capitano*,
1508–9), and Francesco Bragadin (*podestà*, 1504–6).[29] Diedo received the
dedication of Taddeo Solazio's copy of Valerius Maximus's *Memorabilia*
and wrote a life of San Rocco during his tenure in office, and (as already
noted) Bragadin publicly sponsored the publication of Elia Capriolo's chronicle of Brescian affairs while he was *podestà* in the city.[30] There were cases
of able rectors of Brescia, for example Andrea Trevisan, who held a number of posts in the *terraferma* and as *provveditore* took Brescia back in the
name of Venice in 1516 and helped put the city back on its feet after a
traumatic decade.[31] It was said that the lavish welcome Brescia gave to the
former queen of Cyprus in 1497 reflected not only the visitor's status and
the city's wealth but also its inhabitants' happiness with the governance of
the former queen's brother, Giorgio Corner, as *podestà*.[32] In general the
posting was no hindrance to political advancement: for example, Francesco Bragadin subsequently held many of the highest offices in Venice,
and it is worth noting that he often expressed his favor toward the loyal
inhabitants of the *terraferma* in the aftermath of the War of the League of
Cambrai.[33]

Inevitably, there were also cases of disappointing or insensitive rectors
who aroused local displeasure and were usually repudiated or reprimanded
by Venice.[34] The conduct of the *capitano* Vinciguerra Dandolo when he
presided over an inheritance dispute in 1492 was considered especially
outrageous, for in a public forum he questioned the right of anyone in the
city to suspend litigation and thereby usurp the authority of the rectors.
Dandolo was quickly assured that Brescia willingly obeyed Venice and that
the Brescians were good and faithful subjects of Venice ("[b]oni & fideles
subditi essent eiusdem"). Dandolo was not impressed by this argument
and retorted that the city had submitted to Venice only on account of the
depredations of the duke of Milan ("propterea quia male tractabatur per
Ducem mediolani") who hanged three or four Brescians each day and not
because of any love or good will toward Venice. The Brescians were forced
to cite the privileges and offices granted to their most loyal city ("fidelis-
sime comunitate") by Venice in recognition of its good faith and its other
merits, but the *capitano* responded loudly ("alta voce") and publicly that
it was well known how Brescia had acted during the last war and hinted
darkly that the Venetians would take measures in this regard. Dandolo
also seems to have favored the Ghibelline faction in the city. An outraged

Brescian council voted eighty to six to inform the Venetian Council of Ten of Dandolo's false, ignominious, and scandalous words, and he was eventually recalled from duty.[35]

Such partial, undiplomatic behavior must have helped to increase hostility toward the rectors, which was expressed in a variety of strategies of resistance and occasionally broke out into open conflict. For example, in 1439 words attacking the rectors were found on the wall of the Bruciata gate, while in 1442—at a time when the city was faced with especially heavy financial demands from Venice—the following cryptic words were inscribed on the *loggia* recently completed on the west side of one of the city's main squares: "Love of one's overlord is a pox / Wait for something better, to teach you a greater good" ("Amor de segnoria è una vesica. / Anch'altri attende, al myor te aprende"). Six years later a note attacking the rectors and their wives was placed near the same spot, and in 1459 the council noted that contemptuous words had been spoken against the rectors.[36] The following year a horseman (*cavalero*) in the service of the *capitano* was struck on the head with a sword at night by an unknown person.[37] In 1494 certain delinquent persons dared to tear up ("extirpare") a boundary marker that the vicar of the Brescian *podestà* had placed to the north of Brescia.[38] In 1503 notices attacking the rectors—probably in relation to their execution of justice—were posted in the city, and a fine to punish the offenders of extraordinary size was agreed on.[39] However, the Brescians must have had some foundation to their disquiet, since they presented two hundred pages of evidence against the outgoing *podestà*, Pietro Capello, in Venice.[40]

Such resistance was sporadic, but complaints and representations on behalf of the city, like that against Capello, were usually made by an orator, who, like his Venetian counterpart, gave a report *(relazione)* to the Brescian council on the completion of his mission.[41] On several occasions orators from Brescia successfully appealed to the *avogadori di comun* against decisions made in Venice that infringed local statutes.[42] The city also sent richly attired members of the oldest families, often youths, to Venice to acclaim the new doge as an act of loyalty and homage. The council went to considerable time, trouble and expense to organize this legation and to ensure that it was as splendid as those sent by other communities in the *terraferma*.[43] After 1461 a Brescian orator was resident in Venice for six months of the year, rising to a full year and a salary of 15 ducats per month after 1499. Orators probably lodged in the Brescian house in the city that was acquired by the middle of the century.[44]

The orators from the *terraferma* were not always welcome or heard very quickly in the capital. In 1481 it was noted by the Venetian Senate that the

Brescian orators had been in the city for fifteen months without their business being put to a vote.[45] In 1492 the heads of the Ten instructed their rectors in the *terraferma* to limit the number of orators arriving in Venice.[46] In 1517, at a time when many recovered *terraferma* communities were seeking the renewal of their privileges, the Senate attempted to expedite matters, noting that embassies ("nuncij") from different places in the Brescian, Veronese, and Friulian territories were presenting various tiresome petitions ("longo & de gran tedio") to the Senate. It was agreed that in future these petitions could be considered and voted on by the full Collegio (a smaller executive body of around twenty-six men), which might act with the same authority as the Senate.[47]

Without a more detailed examination of the administration of justice in the commune, it is difficult to state with certainty how far each Venetian *podestà* interfered with Brescian deliberations or proved an obstacle or support to Brescian priorities. Established institutions like the mercantile corporation *(mercanzia)*, the colleges of judges, notaries, and doctors, and the ecclesiastical and lay corporations and guilds seem to have enjoyed a large degree of autonomy from the *podestà*, who—to take one example of 1470—complained of clandestine meetings at night of around fifty citizens.[48] Evidence from elsewhere in the *terraferma* suggests that the colleges of judges and notaries in particular, as *consiliatores* responsible for interpreting and reconciling local statutes with Venetian decrees and common law and for dealing with appeals, exercised a near-monopoly in the exercise of justice. The judges were also gatekeepers to communal councils and prerogatives because, as in Brescia, they were often members of the councils and were prepared to ask the doge to ensure that rectors respected local statutes.[49] These bodies wielded great power, which would prove crucial to the narrowing of access to formal channels of power in the city after around 1460.[50] A revealing comment in this regard was made in 1525 by a Venetian *podestà* who argued that the ability of the Brescians—in their councils, colleges, *mercanzia,* and occupational guilds—to meet in different parts of the city without the knowledge of the rectors or their staff had been the source of some difficulty and one reason why the Brescians opened their city gates to the French in 1509.[51]

Commune and Countryside

One of the most complex and significant problems in Venetian-Brescian relations was the governance of the Brescian *contado,* which was perhaps the most politically fragmented part of the Venetian *terraferma* but also one of the richest and most economically significant. The increasing control of the surrounding *contado* by urban agglomerations was especially marked in the history of communal development in Italy after around 1100 as economic demands and demographic growth fueled the need for a secure and productive hinterland and city-dwellers' aspirations to nobility drew them to the land.[52] During the course of the fifteenth and sixteenth centuries the citizens of Brescia, subject to fiscal demands from Venice, acquired an increasingly large proportion of the *contado*. According to one estimate two-thirds of rural possessions were in the hands of *contadini* (rural inhabitants) in 1442, while by 1609 three-quarters were in the possession of urban dwellers.[53] At the same time, the burden of tax fell with increasing pressure on rural areas as city-dwellers underestimated their taxable income and delayed or gerrymandered revisions of the *estimi* (tax assessments), rural migrants acquired urban immunities, and large portions of the Bresciano—notably the valleys—were given exemptions or granted favorable terms by Venice.[54] A struggle for political control and immunity ensued, for each part of the Brescian *contado* had different institutions or mediators of power and varying degrees of independence from Brescia or Venice.[55] The Venetians were inclined to respect local traditions but also to act on local petitions. In sum, the history of communal control of the countryside during this period suggests an unequal struggle in which the urban patriciate were usually the victors.

As noted, the Brescian desire for complete territorial dominion was denied in 1428, in 1454, and on several subsequent occasions in the fifteenth century.[56] The Venetian preference for a mosaic of concessions that it could revoke at will may principally reflect a Venetian strategy of divide and rule, but as Diego Parzani has convincingly argued, the unsettled condition of northern Italy before the peace of Lodi in 1454 also forced the Venetians to respect local autonomy or impose direct rule in many parts of the Bresciano.[57] Thus, Chiari (until 1441) and Orzinuovi (until 1443) each had a Venetian *podestà*, while the Val Camonica was governed by a Venetian *capitano* of the valleys and until 1440 was entirely exempt from Brescian or Bergamasque jurisdiction. This situation, taken together with the fact that the valleys—rich in men and resources—also obtained a large degree of commercial and fiscal autonomy from Venice, helps explain why the valleys did not prove amenable to Brescian exactions.[58]

An examination of the fiscal decisions made in Brescia during the first decade of Venetian domination has revealed that the fiscal immunities promised in the privileges conceded in 1421 and 1428 were, in practice, identical and gave central authority full *arbitrium* and the power to decide when to apply a privilege. Venice requested contributions for military aid

during the military crises of these early years and at other times funds for
fortifications and *cernide* (troops raised locally). These fiscal demands not
only divided the city council, which met to consider how to raise the necessary funds, but also pitted town against countryside. Brescia, like other
cities in the *terraferma*, exercised fiscal discrimination against the countryside, which had the effect of encouraging migration to the town.[59] The
drawing up of *estimi* in the *terraferma* was usually left by Venice to local
councils, and it was on the basis of their estimates for city, district, and
clergy that Venice imposed direct taxes. The Brescian *contado*, like that of
Bergamo, was divided for fiscal purposes into *quadre* made up of a number
of communes. The *quadre* were headed by a vicar drawn from the Brescian
council but also sent deputies to a council of elders of the *contado*. The
territorial *quadre* varied in size; some, for example Gavardo, Iseo, and
Rovato, were made up of a large number of communes, and others, for
example Chiari, Gambara, and Pontevico, consisted of three or four communes. The total amount of taxes was divided between the *quadre* and the
subsidies, or any contributions were shared according to the *estimi* of the
inhabitants of each *quadra* made by the council. The *privilegium civilitatis*
meant that many rural landowners were urbanized and paid taxes on their
land in the city estimate, which gave them eligibility for the city council, to
the detriment of the country, where the fixed estimate was shared by a
smaller group and at a less favorable rate.[60]

In practice, the *Territorio* was a relatively well organized body of around
one-third of the Bresciano, which defended its privileges and concessions,
especially in fiscal matters.[61] The council of the *Territorio* met in Brescia in
the *palazzo della loggia* under the supervision of the Venetian *capitano* or
his representative, but a proclamation of 1492 against the "scandals" provoked by meetings of the "contadini" in their council without the presence
of these Venetians suggests that this council could act with some independence.[62] This developing autonomy of the *Territorio* may have had its origins in the pre-Venetian period when it began to resist Brescian fiscal demands
but reached its apogee only in the decades after around 1530. Giorgio
Chittolini has concluded that the political formation of this Brescian association of rural communities was a case of "singolare precocità" (singular precocity) in the process of the formation of regional states in which a
new relationship between rural areas and cities developed with the crucial
intervention of a dominant power, such as Venice, offering new privileges
and *fora* for appeals.[63]

The *Territorio* benefited fiscally from changes introduced in 1418 and
upheld by Venice until 1440. Under these rules it was agreed that when
land passed to a city-dweller, he must be estimated for tax on it according

to the conditions imposed on the seller—at least until the next revision of the *estimo*—and not according to the more favorable urban estimate. In response to Venetian demands in 1430 the Brescian councillors tried to pass some of the tax burden to the *contado* by proposing a new general *estimo* for both town and countryside that would be drawn up by mixed commissions of citizens and rural inhabitants. These proposals met with rural opposition, and Venice not only quashed the Brescian initiative but also ordered a return to separate *estimi* and a recalculation of the tax burden in a manner that shifted the balance in favor of the *contado*.

The impression of rural clout is again suggested in 1436 when the valleys of the Trompia and Sabbia, together with the towns of Orzinuovi, Orzivecchi, and Chiari, refused to contribute a levy of two centuries' standing to the duomo of Brescia for the eve of the Feast of the Assumption, alleging that they had been given an exemption by Venice.[64] In the course of the sixteenth century the community of Chiari continued to agitate for separation from Brescian jurisdiction.[65] The Val Trompia and Val Sabbia successfully objected to attempts to be included in the Brescian *estimo* in 1492.[66] The Val Camonica, to which Venice conceded separate privileges in 1441, already had its own body of statutes, held its own general council, and appointed local officers.[67] In supporting or accommodating local autonomy in this way Venice seems to have recognized that the valleys and the *Territorio* together formed an organized and politically powerful force. Venice was also highly conscious of the fact that the valleys offered strategic access to the northern passes for both troops and traders.

Venice conceded greater governance of these areas to Brescia only as a reward for its loyalty and resistance to Francesco Sforza during 1438–40, and Brescian statutes were careful to preserve the record of Venetian concessions in this matter along with medieval imperial grants to rule in the territory.[68] Brescians were subsequently faced with a tangled knot of different interests and privileges, complicated by assertions of feudal nobility and continuing direct Venetian interference. After the granting of new privileges to Brescia in 1440, all of the Bresciano, with the exception of some feudal territories, was divided into some twenty-one *podesterie* and vicariates governed by Brescia, and direct Venetian rule ended in most places except for the strategically sensitive border areas of Val Camonica, Orzinuovi, Anfo, Salò, Lonato, and Asola, where Venetian *provveditori* worked alone or alongside Brescian appointees and were usually allowed to make appeals in civil or criminal cases and mercantile matters to Venice via the Brescian rectors.[69] The major *podesterie* in Brescian control in this period were Riviera del Garda (with Salò as its administrative center), Orzinuovi, and Asola. The minor *podesterie* were Lonato, Chiari, and Palazzolo. To the west of Brescia the major vicariates—covering a more restricted area than the *podesterie*—were Iseo and Rovato; to the south of the city they were Quinzano, Pontevico, Calvisano, and Gottolengo; and the final one was Montichiari in the eastern part of the region. The minor vicariates were the smaller communities of Castrezzato, Gavardo, Manerbio, Ghedi, Gambara, Pontoglio, and Pompiano.

The *provveditori* sent by Venice to the towns of the Bresciano, where they usually shared jurisdiction with a Brescian appointee, have not been given much attention by historians, and it is difficult to form a general view of them. Niccolò Bassadonna was *provveditore* in Salò in 1473, and this seems to have been only one of a small handful of official posts he took up (and the only one he seems to have held in the *terraferma*). Leonardo Boldù was appointed to the same post in 1461 at the start of his career, while Cristoforo Duodo took up this role in 1478 as the first such posting in the *terraferma,* but not the last: he was subsequently *capitano* of Verona (1484–85) and *podestà* at Padua (1488). Paolo Trevisan was appointed *provveditore* to Salò and the Riviera del Garda in 1505 after holding the post of *podestà* in Bergamo in 1498 and a number of other government positions and embassies. Pietro Morosini was appointed as the *provveditore* for Asola in 1455 at a fairly young age (around thirty) but after having been entrusted with two ambassadorial posts (one with Marco Donato to the duke of Savoy and the marquis of Monferrato in 1451–52, another to Modena in 1454). In sum, it seems as if the post of *provveditore* in the Bresciano was a fairly minor one although no bar to career advancement.[70]

Brescians of high intellectual aspirations or social standing were involved in the governance of the Bresciano: for example, the humanist Giovanni Stefano Buzzoni edited the statutes for the Riviera del Garda, which were approved by Venice in 1484 and published in 1490 complete with a prefatory verse citing the lawmakers Solomon and Solon. The humanist and chronicler Elia Capriolo was *podestà* at Lonato (population 5,260) and then at Asola (population 9,490) at the beginning of the following decade.[71] The salaries of Brescian vicars, who could administer fines of up to 5 *lire planete* according to local statutes, were stipulated in the ducal letter of 10 February 1440 granting this competence to Brescia.[72] These vicars were supported with a stipend raised wholly or in part by the local commune. A banquet was also to be provided for the incoming vicar, although this was not always forthcoming.[73] There were also sporadic attacks on the arms of the Brescian vicars in the territory, and on one occasion a vicar was run out of town.[74]

The Val Camonica and the major *podesterie* of Salò and Asola were notably hostile to Brescian intervention. The Val Camonica, together with

Rovato, Orzinuovi, Asola, and Soncino, welcomed Sforza representatives in 1448 and made offers of loyalty to Milan rather than Venice.[75] Even after the settlement of Sforza claims at Lodi in 1454, there is evidence of local resistance to the Brescian *podestà* or *capitano* in the Val Camonica.[76] The occupation of Brescia by French and then Spanish troops after 1509 prompted further petitions for separation, which the Brescian council was at pains to see that the occupying powers rejected.[77] From the beginning of the period of Venetian rule the thirty-four communes of the Riviera del Garda obtained the doge's assent to a large degree of autonomy in legal and fiscal matters but the presence of a *podestà* nominated by the Brescian council as well as a Venetian *capitano* provided many occasions for "differentia" (disagreements) between the inhabitants and the Brescians, which the Venetians were expected to resolve by reconciling precedent with privilege.[78] Asola had sought direct Venetian governance in 1440 but was obliged to accept a Brescian *podestà,* who was expected to apply civic statutes as well as observe local "ordines."[79] Asolan displeasure was quickly demonstrated; for example, Asolans provided an oblation for the Brescian duomo at the feast of the Assumption in 1441 only under protest, declaring that it would be subject to no city but Venice. The Brescian rectors urged the Asolans to reconsider their wish to have the duty to make an oblation revoked and noted that the duomo in Brescia was like a mother to the whole territory of the Bresciano.[80] After 1484 a Venetian *provveditore* was sent to Asola to maintain local defenses and was expected to respect the jurisdiction of the Brescian representative.[81] This division of authority did nothing to discourage an Asolan strategy of appealing to Venice for the resolution of disputes with Brescia. Accordingly, in 1492 the Asolans objected to the Venetian Senate about their inclusion in the *estimo* for the Bresciano, and the Brescians were forced to appeal to the Senate, which eventually accepted their case after receiving delegations from Asola and Brescia.[82] In 1497 some of the Asolans even assaulted the residence of the Brescian *podestà* and accused him and his chancellery of employing torture and other malpractices. This premeditated act of aggression provoked an outraged response from the Brescian council, which condemned the arrogance, temerity, and ill-will the Asolans had shown toward Brescia. It was eventually decided to elect no less than ten orators to put the Brescian case against the Asolans before the Venetian governors.[83]

The position of the Venetian representative was therefore a delicate one as he mediated local, territorial, and Venetian concerns. Venice could call its own officers to order on occasion,[84] but the records suggest that Venetian appointees would often place Venetian and local interests first and even ride roughshod over Brescian privileges.[85] Brescia naturally resented this interference or encroachment on the Brescian *podestà*'s jurisdiction, but in practice there was very little they could do about it except direct their protestations to Venice in the hope of some redress or appeal, in vain, for the complete withdrawal of the Venetian representatives.[86] To make matters worse, Venice also cut across Brescian authority by making separate agreements with feudal powers in the same way the Visconti and Sforza dukes had done in the years preceding Venetian rule.[87] Pietro Avogadro, who led the revolt against Visconti rule in 1426, was rewarded with the feudal title to Lumezzane. Francesco Bussone, Count of Carmagnola, who had clinched the victory for the Venetians, was lavishly recompensed, and as Count of Chiari he briefly established a local power base close to Brescia. The loyal branches of the powerful Federici clan, which dominated the Val Camonica, were also well treated with feudal grants.[88] A number of feudal territories were concentrated in the southern half of the region, with the Gambara family appointing vicars with jurisdiction in civil matters to Verola Alghise, Milzano, and Pralboino, although not to Gambara itself. The Martinengo title to the feudal possessions of Urago d'Oglio, Padernello, Barco, and Villachiara was recognized by Venice in 1427. The family appointed vicars to Gabbiano, Pavone, and Urago d'Oglio along the river Oglio, which marked the border with Cremonese territory, and to these Venice added Orzivecchi in 1433.[89] In each case the feudal lands, which admittedly were not vast, were largely excluded from the city and district of Brescia in fiscal terms but were occasionally directly subject to exactions and demands from Venice.

The members of these feudal families often played an important role in Brescian society and projected an image of nobility through their claims of lineage, dynastic alliances, military service, fortified castles or palaces, lifestyle, culture, and sporting prowess. For example, the Martinengo acted as patrons of the arts, commissioning works by artists such as Alessandro Bonvicino, known as Moretto, Lorenzo Lotto, and Bartolomeo Veneto, and promoted their family name by accepting humanist dedications and erecting elaborate funerary monuments in the city.[90] This feudal nobility also maintained very close ties with Venice. In 1497 members of the Martinengo, Avogadro, and Gambara clans turned out in Brescia for the ceremonial welcome and jousts staged for the entry of the former queen of Cyprus. The Venetian queen Caterina Corner was housed in the palace of Ludovico Martinengo (formerly the property of the condottiere Bartolomeo Colleoni) like other prominent visitors to the city.[91] Two members of the Martinengo clan were inscribed in the book of gold of the Venetian patriciate for their feats of arms, and others were members of the patrician "companies of hose" that organized parties, dances, and theatrical events in Venice.[92] Ludovico Martinengo, described as the first and richest man of the city ("la prima testa richa di Brexa"), was called "one of our gentlemen" ("zenthilomo nostro") by a Venetian patrician: Ludovico's first wife had been a member of the patrician Venier clan of Venice.[93] Imperial recognition further enhanced the prestige of this feudal nobility: when Emperor Frederick III visited Venice in 1469 he created a number of knights of the Golden Spur, including members of the Martinengo clan and other families.[94] Military service, culture, and ceremony in this way may have strengthened ties between the feudal nobility and the Venetians, and it is worth noting that Alvise Avogadro, whose company played a part in the processions welcoming Caterina Corner in 1497, was instrumental in plotting with the Council of Ten against the French occupiers and bringing Brescia briefly back under Venetian rule in 1512.[95]

As a result of their wealth and power the feudal nobility could act with a large measure of independence. The *sprezzatura* and refinement of certain nobles was beautifully captured in 1526 in Moretto's full-length study of a member of the Avogadro clan, now in the National Gallery in London (Figure 3.1). However, the arrogance that lay underneath this studied pose occasionally caused trouble for both Brescia and Venice. In 1503 the Brescian orators were driven to complain to the doge about the calumnies of Girolamo Martinengo.[96] Occasionally the Brescian vicars in the territory of the Gambara were hindered in the prosecution of their business, and Brescia appealed to the Venetian Senate to intervene on its behalf.[97] The Gambara also acted in violation of civic privileges or even disobeyed and insulted the Venetian rectors. For example, in December 1503 Giovanni Franceso Gambara encountered the *podestà* Andrea Loredan in the street in Brescia and among other things insolently proclaimed: "Andrea Loredan I am better than you" ("Andrea Loredan son da meglio de ti"). The *podestà* naturally complained to Venice about this insult and mentioned other matters, such as Gambara's refusal to give up his arms, which had been a source of long-standing tensions. The Venetian advocate and patrician Luca Tron was sent to Brescia to investigate the matter, while orators came from Brescia to speak against Gambara, who had dishonored the city in this way and fomented faction.[98]

One of the main sources of the conflict lay in the refusal to give up arms, which were not simply ceremonial indicators of noble status and necessary for serving the state but potentially fatal weapons in the conflict between clans.[99] In January 1505 the new rectors sent to Brescia hopefully informed Venice that peace had been made between Gambara and Ludovico Martinengo. Gambara, it was said, had refused to hand over his arms, "saying that he was a condottiere in the service of our lords" ("dicendo era condu-

Figure 3.1. Moretto da Brescia, *Portrait of a Man*, 1526. Oil on canvas, 201 x 92.2 cm. Image © The National Gallery, London.

tier di la Signoria nostra [i.e. Venice]"), and all Brescia had taken up sides in the matter as Guelphs or Ghibellines until the factions between the great families had been settled.[100] However, when the following year members of the Gambara clan attended mass at the church of San Pietro Oliveto, Vettore Martinengo pushed his way in front of the crowd and walked ahead of Count Niccolò Gambara, who was walking with the castellan. The count responded to this insolence by pulling on the chain hanging from Martinengo's jacket ("lo cularo del zupone"), to the surprise of those present.[101] These enmities resurfaced in a much more serious form during the occupation of 1509–16, when those hostile to Venetian rule and favorable to the French were closely associated with the Gambara.

Brescian politics were therefore marked by a plurality of powers that seems to have been especially pronounced in comparison with the rest of the Venetian *terraferma*. Unlike the Vicentines the Brescians were not granted extensive communal jurisdiction and were unable to wrest control of the patchwork of feudatories from the hands of the large and established clans. In this respect, the Venetians acted as their Visconti predecessors had and preferred a system of bilateral agreements rather than a unitary framework. In following this line of least resistance the Venetians probably recognized that feudal autonomy was fairly well developed although not a threat to Venetian interests. Unlike the case of the Friuli region, where civic control of the *contado* was very weak, the clans were generally not a destabilizing force in the Bresciano, although they were held in great esteem and their actions would prove critical to the events that unfolded after 1509.

The natural wealth celebrated in Brescian myth, as well as the precocious political independence, and remoteness, of the Brescian valleys and other parts of the Bresciano may go some way to explaining why it maintained much of its autonomy in the face of feudal or urban claims. The economic and political weaknesses outlined at the beginning of this chapter may also have imposed on the Brescians the need to struggle sometimes to impose their authority, especially in fiscal matters. The Venetians entertained appeals from the Bresciano for the rest of the century and responded with pragmatism to its orators' demands. However, as peace and prosperity returned to the Bresciano after the middle of the fifteenth century the growth of the city of Brescia and the political ambitions of its patriciate resulted in a concerted attempt to reassert the city's autonomy within its governing councils by wresting political and fiscal control from Venetian hands, excluding recent immigrants and newly created citizens and concentrating power in the hands of the oldest and wealthiest clans.

CHAPTER FOUR

Forming an Urban Oligarchy

D URING the first century of Venetian rule the Brescian social and political elite was not a homogeneous class with roughly similar economic status and sources of wealth. Nor was it a completely closed social
order absolutely defined by lineage and lifestyle—as the Venetian patriciate has sometimes been viewed.[1] It would be more accurate to describe the
Brescian elite as a composite body of different groups with varying degrees
of economic and political power and prestige, which were prone to frag-
ment along a number of different social or political lines. The aristocracy
was made up of *nobiles* (nobles), whose origins lay in the Bresciano countryside, although they had gradually became urbanized: among the prominent families in this group were the Capriolo, Emilii, Fenaroli, Foresti,
Gambara, and Ugoni.[2] Another group consisted of the *cives veteres* (citizens of long standing), who had risen during the communal age and who
took on government posts. Another group consisted of the *cives creati:* the
recipients—many of them immigrants from Bergamo, Como, and Milan—
of the signorial appointments made in the century before Venetian rule, the
benemeriti cittadini who entered the Brescian council between 1426 and
1488, and finally the men who had been given citizenship to meet the city's
economic needs.[3]

The first two of these three major groups merged in the course of the
Middle Ages and concentrated formal political power into their hands,
maintaining their links with the countryside, and fortifying their palaces in

the city, notably in the *cittadella* neighborhood to the east of the duomo and the *broletto*. They ruled with imperial protection during the communal era, and Ghibelline and Guelph labels were still applied to different groups within the city during the fifteenth and sixteenth centuries. These labels recognized the traditional affinities of some families and may have served fairly loosely to delineate parties in different disputes on a local level but could also emerge as rallying points when Brescia's relations with ruling powers such as Milan, Venice, and France were points of political conflict. Thus in 1426 the Guelphs, led by the Avogadro, opened the gates of Brescia to the Venetians, while the Ghibellines of the *cittadella* resisted.[4] Similarly, in 1509–16 the *cittadella* was regarded as the center of anti-Venetian or Ghibelline opinion among the urban patriciate.[5]

Some of these divisions within the old nobility are evident in the comments made by Pandolfo Nassini, a member of one of the most ancient families in Brescia, who drew up a list of noble Brescian families during the second quarter of the sixteenth century.[6] Nassini was especially hostile toward men and women with Venetian (or Guelph) sympathies and to families or individuals with what he believed were low social origins. For example, on one occasion he refers to the Averoldi, an ancient and rich family, as originating in the Bergamasco as cloth-workers.[7] This assertion is somewhat at odds with the decision of the council in 1475 agreeing to instruct the Brescian orators in Venice to seek the election of an Averoldi as bishop due to his nobility of birth and other qualities.[8] Nassini also disparagingly remarked that the Avogadro family arms bore a "scalimpertego" (a peg or tool used in gathering of olives known in Brescian dialect as a *scalempertegh*), that they came from the Val Trompia, and were lowborn ("di bassa conditione.") Nassini also undercut the pretensions of other ancient families such as the Buschi.[9] The progenitors of the ancient clan of the Capriolo were brusquely dismissed as muleteers who had grown wealthy during the lordship of Pandolfo Malatesta by carting his treasure around.[10]

These acerbic private comments aside, there is no doubt that those who claimed nobility ranged from the powerful Martinengo and Gambara clans with their many branches, imperial titles, and rich feudal possessions to much poorer families and individuals who possessed almost nothing besides their noble names. Something of the variety of social origins within the range of noble family names is indicated by a list of nobles in the Brescian city and territory between 1426 and 1498, which contains 570 surnames.[11] The compilers of the list calculated that there were thirty-five hundred "nobili rurali" over the whole period, making up 1 percent of the rural population and perhaps 8 percent of the urban population.[12] Among those included on this list are men who were designated as manual workers or artisans ("meccanici"), pitchers ("pegoloti"), brazers ("brasenti"), cobblers ("caligarii"), textile workers, soldiers, and even shepherds.[13]

One of the other most notable social divisions during this period was that between the older citizens and the newly created citizens, who were often drawn from the countryside and had achieved citizenship under the lordships of the Malatesta, Visconti, or Venice. Like other civic authorities in Italy during the Renaissance, the Brescian council encouraged men of wealth or skill to apply for citizenship in Brescia. The grant of *civilitas* to inhabitants of the valleys and *pedemonte* near Brescia seems to have been part of a strategy of drawing these areas into a closer orbit of the city and repopulating the city after the disasters of 1425–26 and 1438–40. The right of *civitates* to create *cives* was well established in civil law. The creation of citizens in Brescia rested on a property requirement such as the possession of a house in the city or, after 1355, on ten years' residence, but might also depend on the prestige or profession of the individual—doctors, lawyers, and teachers were naturally useful to towns and were often granted citizenship. In practice, citizens were obliged to pay taxes and serve the state and were legally regarded as equal to citizens of the town by birth so long as they obeyed the law. However, jurists were careful to exclude the right of citizenship by birth or by marriage from the poor peasants who were involved in seasonal and base occupations. The jurist Bartolus of Sassoferrato distinguished the *cives civitatis* from *cives comitatenses* (rural immigrants granted citizenship) and gave the latter an inferior status.[14] The sons of the former inherited their fathers' legal status, wherever they were born.

These divisions within the Brescian social order were very clear during the first decade of Venetian rule when the Brescian council had to make fiscal choices under pressure from Venetian demands for military contributions.[15] In response to a request for 2,000 ducats in May 1427 the council placed in question the immunities and exemptions that in 1422 the Visconti—following similar grants in 1385 and 1416—had granted to immigrants, doctors, and school teachers for five years. These immigrants seem to have been targeted as an especially vulnerable group, and evidence from the period of Malatesta rule in 1411–17 suggests that they came in large numbers from the impoverished Bergamasco and that they featured significantly in criminal accusations and condemnations.[16]

A further influx of immigrants from the territory to Brescia during 1440–42 was encouraged by an agreement that they would enjoy not only urban privileges but also the privileges in the territory where they lived and possessed goods. Not surprisingly, Pandolfo Nassini poured scorn on the apparent Venetian policy of encouraging immigration and diluting the social composition of the elite with men of base origins and occupations.

Nassini dismissed the Fasani clan as parvenus and claimed that they were sausage-makers rewarded with citizenship.[17] Similarly, he noted that the Rava clan had originated in the Bergamasco but had been made citizens and given offices in Brescia on account of their goods ("la robba").[18] Another recent arrival to Brescia were the Scanzi, again of the Bergamasco, who achieved citizenship through marriage, although Nassini claimed to have seen them selling pieces of ironmongery, German cloth, and other base items.[19] Of his own family Nassini unsurprisingly claimed origins of great antiquity and an unimpeachable pedigree in the eastern Roman empire ("questa casa fo antiqua et venne de Costantinopoli de Romania").[20]

In the course of the century the requirements for residence in the city were tightened up, and some earlier concessions were revoked, although the group of new residents of *contado* origin was still substantial and the number of *cives creati* peaked during this period—at 431 during 1440–50.[21] After around 1450 the Brescian council moved to restrict the creation of citizens and to change the rules governing admission to the ruling elite, in order to form an urban oligarchy with more independence from Venice and a more restricted social profile. This movement, which encountered both internal and external opposition, was partly a product of the more settled social and economic conditions in the city that replaced the uncertainty of the first two decades of Venetian rule. The changes in the political machinery of the city and in the qualifications for civic participation may also have been prompted by the relatively large number of men from the *contado* who had been awarded *civilitas* since 1440. These men exercised their disdained manual occupations while at the same time claiming the right to be admitted to the councils of the city as urban taxpayers. The patriciate therefore imposed more stringent criteria governing *civilitas* or legitimacy, lifestyle, and reputation and began to make claims of noble status. They made admission to the council more difficult and reformed its structure and procedure in order to concentrate power in a few hands. In sum, by around 1530 the Brescian patriciate was well on the way to completing a process of self-definition as an exclusive governing class with an aristocratic consciousness that mirrored urban aristocratization in other parts of the *terraferma*, for example Verona, and shared in some key elements of Venetian identity and ideology.[22]

Closing the Council

The main formal political assemblies in the city were the great or general council *(gran consiglio),* on which one member from each eligible family could sit—clerics and soldiers excepted—and the special council. The general council was "re-formed" biennially in January when the dead or disgraced were removed from the list and new members were admitted on the advice of the *podestà* and a committee of scrutiny. The syndics deputed to investigate applications presented their findings to the general council, which then voted on admission. The special council included the *consulta* of seven elders, which comprised an "abbot," who was a member of the College of Judges and the most senior representative of the citizens (who changed every two months), an advocate for the commune (who changed every six months), three public deputies for statutes, who were elected for a year, and two syndics who were in place for two years. The membership of the *consulta* for the subsequent two years was also decided at the "re-formation" meeting, along with the designation of the various public deputies charged with overseeing social, moral, religious, and economic needs of the city.

In addition to these bodies, each *quadra* of the city chose elders who acted to communicate the decisions of the general council to each neighborhood, to draw up a local tax census, and to voice local grievances in the civic councils.[23] This arrangement may reflect a strong sense of neighborhood consciousness of the sort common in a larger city such as Florence but absent at this time in a smaller town in the *terraferma* such as Vicenza.[24] Each *quadra* had its own body of statutes, and its role was outlined in the city statutes.[25] Its origins probably lie in the communal period, and unlike the case in Florence, the neighborhood basis of formal political representation did not give way to the domination of the greater guilds or yet to the power of a dominant family like the Medici. An examination of the records of the first *quadra* of San Alessandro has shown that by the beginning of the sixteenth century it consisted of two syndics, a *massaro* (overseer), two legal officers, and other officials, with a general and special council modeled on those of the city as a whole. Every head of family was permitted to sit on the local general council if he had lived in the *quadra* for at least ten years. Each member could vote annually for the new syndic and for the *massaro* who kept a record of any rents and warrants *(bolletini)* due to be paid.[26] In 1439, during the siege of the city, when the Brescian council worked on new *capitula* on account of the evils suffered by the city, there was extensive consultation with each part of the city and with representatives of each of the social orders: three men ("unum de maioribus, unum de medioribus et alterum de parvis") were chosen from each of the sixteen *quadre* to draft the *privilegia* ultimately agreed on and presented to Venice.[27] A similar form of consultation took place in 1517 when five men who represented each of the *quadre* were involved in the process of selecting the new council.[28]

Under the terms of the privileges conceded to Brescia by Venice in 1428 the Brescians lost control in the choice and rotation of civic offices, having invited Venice to propose a method of election. Under Venetian rule there were some changes to the selection and admission of civic councillors, which can be related to an effort to suppress the Guelph and Ghibelline factions whose loyalties were still displayed every year on 1 May by the carnivalesque custom, or "pagan rite," of planting trees bearing arms throughout the city.[29] Venetian rectors attempted to replace loyalty to Guelph or Ghibelline factions with loyalty to Venice. As a result of a pact between the Guelph and Ghibelline factions in the middle of the century—prompted in part by sermons against feuding ("partialitas") and accompanied by rectorial assurances of Venice's wish to promote concord, peace, and love—a number of Ghibelline nobles from the *cittadella* entered the council.[30]

Initially, the Venetian rectors in Brescia controlled membership of the council: they drew up the lists of those who were eligible for admission and annually drew seventy-two names from a sack in order to make up the council for the year. In addition, in 1440 the Venetians decided to make a number of new men eligible for the council on the basis of their participation in the defense of the city against the attack and siege of the Visconti commander Niccolò Piccinino. However, Venetian control of the council may not have been absolute. Between 1452 and 1472 around 150–200 men gathered for admission to the council, and apparently around one hundred regularly participated in its meetings.[31] In addition, it was by no means the case that the council was the preserve of the most wealthy, if the figure of taxable wealth for the later period (when it was supposed to be more exclusive) are anything to go by.[32]

The reform of the civic statutes, notably those that applied to the authority of the Venetian *podestà* and the civic magistracies, was an attempt to narrow others' access to the status of the urban ruling elite. Similar statutory reforms were undertaken in other cities of the *terraferma,* and these revisions were often effected some decades after conquest and underwent a long period of gestation before being promulgated, confirmed by Venice, and finally printed. In the cases of Verona and Vicenza these reforms have also been associated with oligarchic consolidation.[33] The Brescian reforms were certainly not hurried or unexpected: a "reformatione" of statutes was signaled by the Brescians in the privileges granted in 1428 and 1440, and in 1449 the Brescian bishop warned the council against the infringement of ecclesiastical liberty threatened by the reform of statutes.[34] Nor was the reform of statutes isolated from the practice of closure: in 1464 those who did not have the right to do so were banned from attending Brescian council meetings.[35] It was in the following year that a revision

of the statutes was proposed and may have begun, for in 1466 the privileges granted in 1428 were copied into a register with other significant
missives from the doge, probably as part of the process of reform.[36]

This reform initiative quickly stalled. The preamble of the first printed
edition of the Brescian statutes explains that Ludovico Bembo, *podestà*
during 1470–71, recognizing the variety of human nature, the mutability
of times, and the need to correct laws saw a necessity for the "correctione
& reformatione" of the statutes of the city of Brescia. This revision, it is
noted, was first proposed at the time of the *podestà* Leone Diedo in 1465,
but because of the death of many of the fifteen elected to revise the statutes
it was not until 1470 that a committee set about correcting them.[37] In
1471 Venice approved modifications to the Brescian statutes that had been
sought, as the senatorial record put it, "pro maiore robore et firmitudine,"
and the Venetian Senate retained the right to make any further changes
that it saw fit.[38] However, there is no indication in the records that the
initiative came from anywhere but Brescia itself.

In 1470–71 it was proposed that the members of the Brescia general
council would no longer be designated exclusively by the Venetian rectors
but also by the councillors, and that those who were proposed would have
to be scrutinized and their nomination confirmed with a favorable ballot.
Before this date admission to the general council was not based simply on
great wealth but rested on the candidate's ability to show that he had been
listed in a tax census *(estimo)* since at least 1438 and had paid taxes in the
city from at least the same date. Candidates were required to be more than
thirty years of age and to have resided in the city for at least twenty-five
years. Candidates for admission to the great council were now expected to
have lived in Brescia for thirty years and to have been paying taxes for the
same length of time. The election of the abbot followed a similar procedure,[39] and it was agreed that the office of chancellor should be restricted
to citizens who had sustained burdens for thirty years continuously and
were at least twenty-five years of age.[40] Offices were denied to anyone who
had not borne "onera et factiones" (that is to say met fiscal and other
qualifications) for thirty years continuously.[41] This restriction was extended to cover the offices of the *quadra,* although those residents of ten
years' standing who had participated in the defense of the city during
1438–40 were also eligible for office.[42]

Over this period the Brescians also sought to consolidate or reform their
control of legal matters. In 1461 the Brescian council attempted to oversee
the actions of Venetian *provveditori* and its own rectors in the region by
instituting five *provveditori ad utilia* who would defend communal rights
in an array of matters and would ensure that Brescian statutes were re-

spected by all governors. Venice quickly moved to quash this body.[43] The statutes published in 1473 outlined the restrictions placed on the *podestà*, who could not add or change anything without the approval of the council or seek absolution from the statutes in order to rule on his own authority.[44] The elders or consuls of the College of Notaries were also expected to compel notaries in the city to observe the statutes of Brescia.[45] The number of deputies *ad statuta* was increased from two to three, and they were provided with a salary of 1 ducat per month. In 1487 the procedures for discussion at assemblies of the councils were carefully defined in order to provide better order: the abbot would propose an argument, expressing his own opinion, and then the syndics, advocate, and deputies *ad statuta* (that is to say, the *consulta*) examined and discussed the proposal, before they consulted the rest of the councillors. The final decision, if not brought up at subsequent assemblies, was to be agreed with four-fifths of votes in favor.[46] Questions pertaining to the Venetian government or the papal court were to be treated exclusively by the general council.[47]

The decision to abolish the Council of Seventy-Two and to call councils of all those who were eligible under these new stricter conditions has been said to represent a move toward increasing the power of certain factions who might now be able to bypass the control of the Venetian rectors.[48] On the face of it, the power of the special council does not seem to have been notably enhanced, and many of its proposals continued to be defeated by the general council. However, the changes to the criteria for admission to the councils seem to have led to a monopolization of the key offices and some continuity of power: for example, Matteo de Tiberi was elected to different positions in the *consulta* or acted in other's stead almost without interruption between June 1485 and June 1487.[49] Daniele Montanari has questioned the significance of these changes and has suggested that in practice Brescians already formed a "filtro preventivo" for rectorial decisions and that the abolition of the Council of Seventy-Two did not automatically represent a "closure" of the councils but rather a rationalization of an obsolete system ("razionalizzazione del ridondante sistema istituzionale"). However, subsequent restrictions on access did represent a move toward a true closure or "serrata aristocratica."[50]

In September 1488 it was agreed to change once again the criteria for eligibility for admission to council and access to offices in a way that was clearly designed to restrict admission to the ruling elite. The special council observed that offices had been assigned to *cives veteres* and *cives creati* with the possibility of being transferred to sons and without regard for their virtues. It was agreed that in future, Brescian citizens who were not listed in the 1426 *estimo* or who had not participated in the siege of 1438–40 (as recorded in the book of the *Custodie notturne* or night watch drafted by Cristoforo Soldo) would not be eligible for dignities and offices. A biennial reform of the councillors would allow for the admission of new blood with these qualifications. Vicariates and other posts were reserved to these men who, it was initially proposed, would also receive a hereditary title of nobility.[51] The council provisions also stipulated legitimate descent as one of the criteria for council membership. At the end of 1494 the special council agreed by ten to one that whoever had not been born legitimately should not be admitted to offices of the council—for the dignity and good of civic governance and in imitation of Venice.[52] This reiteration of the 1488 provision was prompted in part by the case of Francesco Quarentino, whose nomination and election to the council was blocked because of his illegitimate birth. A proposal to accept him because he had been legitimated by the pope and the emperor was defeated.[53] The proposals of 1488 provoked heated debate and were, unusually, read to the council three times for clarity before being approved by seventy-eight votes to eleven, with a further modification that entry to the council might be allowed to men who could show that they had resided in Brescia for fifty years (including the residence of their ancestors).[54] In December the list of councillors deemed fit was published and consisted of 150 in total.[55]

The ruling of 1488 was not entered into the statutes of the city, and its force derived from the consensus of opinion demonstrated by the majority vote of the general council recorded in the council provisions.[56] As a result this decision, like the one relating to legitimacy, had to be reiterated on 20 November 1495 by the special council.[57] It was recorded on this occasion that many men had been admitted to the council and to the colleges of judges and notaries, contrary to the intention of the council in 1488, and that this had been the cause of much discord. Sons and descendants of those admitted before 1488 were therefore barred. This restriction was intended, as one historian of the process has surmised, "to prevent the fusion of old city councillors with new ones from more modest social backgrounds who had acquired membership" between 1438 and 1488.[58] In December 1496 the general council approved the special council decision in relation to the 1488 ruling by a rather narrow margin, fifty-six votes to forty-six, which suggests some unhappiness with the new arrangements—probably because it represented an abrogation of promises made in 1488 to those who fell foul of the new rules but were already in the council and expected to pass on the status of citizenship to their sons.[59]

Some new lineages entered the council lists after 1488, notably in the abnormal conditions of occupation during 1509–16 and in the years immediately following the restoration of Venetian rule. However, the evidence suggests that the more important offices were monopolized by the oldest and wealthiest families and that a restricted group of almost sixty rich families maintained a constant presence in the councils. In descending order of wealth, these families included names that appear regularly throughout this book: Martinengo, Capriolo, Averoldi, Porcellaga, Calini, Bornati, Fenaroli, Ugoni, Faita, Soldi, Nassini, Malvezzi, and Tiberi. In addition, any move to reverse the closure of the council was effectively rebuffed or quickly reversed, and by the middle of the sixteenth century those employed in mechanical or manual trades were explicitly excluded. By around 1530 an urban oligarchy held sway in Brescia with aristocratic features based on an array of factors, including entry in the city *estimo,* access to the council and to offices, and an assessment of *civilitas* related to wealth, lifestyle, legitimacy, and culture.[60]

Defining the Patriciate

This redrawing of the rules for eligibility for membership of the council was accompanied by a raft of legislation that tightened up access to other centers of power in the city and addressed the common markers of social status. If membership of the council, or eligibility for selection, did not automatically make a Brescian noble, there was a clear—though not uncontested— move to create an urban oligarchy that could be recognized by the more noble lifestyle of its members as well as by their fiscal or legal qualifications. For example, most of the abbots and members of the special council, as well as the advocates for the commune and the deputies for statutes, were members of the influential College of Judges. The college was involved with cases that came before a number of Brescian tribunals, and members of the college brought appeals against the court of *savii* before they turned to the *podestà* or the *auditori nuovi* in Venice.[61] The College of Judges naturally preferred candidates for admission to its own ranks who could also demonstrate original citizenship or who could show that they had been present at the defense of the city in 1438–40. Similarly, the College of Notaries was closed in 1475 to those men who did not fulfil the more stringent requirements for membership of the council.[62] Admission to the colleges was discussed in 1488 and further restricted along the lines already noted.[63] In 1506 the college statutes disbarred entry to anyone who undertook, or whose father or brothers exercised, "artem mecanicam sive manualem," including pharmacists ("aromatarj"), goldsmiths, field workers, tailors, carpenters, and so on.[64]

Given the social prestige and political importance attached to membership of these colleges it is not surprising that those who were refused entry sometimes brought their cases before the Brescian council. Indeed, membership in the college may have been viewed by those who were already in the council but fell foul of the new rules for access to office as a way of securing their position.[65] The council and the colleges considered a number of applications from some well-connected men. For example, Ludovico Gambara sought entry to College of Judges in 1491 and again in 1514 (with a letter of support from the emperor Maximilian). His application was rejected since neither he nor his progeny had ever lived in Brescia.[66] A case of a man prevented from entering the College of Judges by the 1488 provision was considered the following year and he was accepted.[67] In December 1495 the special council heard the case of Ventura di Giorgio Fenaroli, from a noble family, who had attacked Giacomo Feroldi, who was one of the *cives veteres* of mercantile origins and whom Fenaroli held responsible for his failure to enter the College of Judges. Unsurprisingly, in this instance the council was supportive, and the case was eventually resolved in Fenaroli's favor.[68] In 1492 the council heard a supplication from a man who wished to enter the College of Notaries but was impeded by the decision of September 1488 and sought admission on the grounds that his father had taken an active role in the siege of 1438–40. An examination of the *libro d'estimo* for 1430 turned up a reference to his father and led to a successful outcome in this case.[69] The council also showed some flexibility in its dealings with the College of Physicians. In April 1492 the college refused to accept into its ranks those who had not met the requirements under the provision of 5 September 1488, but the council agreed to permit entry to those who could prove their ability—a recognition of the key role doctors played in urban society.[70]

The high social status of the colleges and their members during this period was also reflected by a number of markers of esteem such as precedence in ceremonial. In 1479 an especially heated dispute occurred over processional order in connection with the ceremonial entry of Cardinal Gabriele Rangoni (a native of Chiari who had been promoted the previous year).[71] In a petition read to the council, Gianbattista Soldo asserted his right to take precedence over Bartolomeo de Calzaneliis, who had been placed in front of him in the group of four men organized to greet the cardinal. Soldo asserted that he was of greater birth, had gained his doctorate earlier, and was more senior in the College of Judges. In private and public, he noted, the latter gave way to the former. The council decided to question Soldo in a session that, extraordinarily, was entirely devoted to the matter. After a lengthy debate ("post longas disputationes") it was decided that in this case, and in the future, an order of precedence would be set out: graduates or those otherwise marked with some dignity would be preferred while among graduates precedence would be given in the order usually assigned to the colleges. It was also noted that soldiers would be preferred to doctors and the antiquity of dignity would be taken into account.[72]

Education and lifestyle were therefore important elements in determining patrician status.[73] In 1485 a proposal that the chancellor provide decisions in vernacular for the better understanding of councillors was narrowly rejected by the special council, and it may be supposed that the rejection reflected the oligarchy's educational priorities.[74] However, in 1492 a proposal to exclude blasphemers[75] and concubinists from the council was rejected by the special council by five votes to seven.[76] Two decades later a proposal to bar those who owed money to the commune from public office was also rejected.[77] There were repeated attempts (discussed below) to regulate clothing, dowries, banquets, gambling, prostitution, funerals, and weddings between 1473 and 1508 and again after the recuperation of Brescia by Venice after the War of the League of Cambrai.[78] These sumptuary laws seem to have been aimed at preventing the rise of new men rather than punishing the infractions of the new elite: it was agreed in 1503 that those who infringed sumptuary legislation would lose benefits of *civilitas*.[79] However, this injunction only applied to those in manual occupations.[80]

In May 1495 the general council agreed that *civilitas* would not be valid unless it was confirmed by the general council.[81] An analysis of the 112 applications for *civilitas* considered by the council between 1468 and 1508 suggests that the number of *cives creati* peaked in number in 1486 and declined thereafter.[82] The figure of 112 stands in sharp contrast to the period 1420–70, when 1,221 citizens were created by the council.[83] Moreover, the pattern of admissions after 1488 indicates that royal, noble, or ecclesiastical sponsorship was a key factor in the process, although a dozen or more teachers and doctors were admitted without such support: the humanist and teacher Pietro Lazzaroni (in 1471), Giovanni Britannico, professor of grammar (in 1479, four years after the application), Magistro Francesco de Zobijs, professor of grammar (1485), Marco Picarolo, professor of grammar and rhetoric (1486), Giovanni Stefano Buzzoni, humanist (1488), and the doctor Magistro Cypriani Schalini de Valliscamonica (1480).[84] A professor of grammar was unanimously granted citizenship at the behest of Ludovico Maria Sforza in 1488, and the brother of the king of Hungary's doctor was given citizenship in 1492 with the support of the Venetian doge.[85] Applicants sometimes drew on prestigious family connections, and in 1499 a relation of Pietro Carmeliano, the king of England's Latin secretary, submitted a successful application.[86] The geographical spread shows that Venetians were certainly not among those interested in Brescian citizenship. In fact, 40 percent of all applicants originated in the

Brescian territory or from Soncino just over the border, although the figure may be higher as the origins of 31.25 percent of applicants are unknown or unclear. The applicants came primarily from the Val Camonica, Calvisano, Soncino, Orzinuovi, Iseo, and Ghedi. Just under 10 percent of them came from Bergamo, and a further smaller percentage, each ranging from 2–3 percent of the total sample, originated in the other neighboring towns of Parma or Cremona or from further afield—Pisa and even Rome.[87]

The evidence of the applications and admissions, therefore, rather belies the fulminations of a well-born local humanist Carlo Valgulio, who in 1508 lamented that tax-farmers, "castrators," traitors, and dentists had been honored in various ways. A limited number were admitted in return for immigrating and providing services to the city as civic physicians or teachers in the "communal schools," but the social range of families in the council remained largely unaltered, although the geographical spread of names suggests that the gulf between town and *contado* was not absolutely unbridgeable.[88] Therefore, if the narrowing of the governing oligarchy to the more ancient families and those who had taken part in the siege of 1438–40 was a response to a growth in the population fueled by rural immigrants who sought citizenship, it was very effective in stemming the tide, even when these applicants appealed to Venice for support.[89]

Beyond the criteria based on lineage, residence, and citizenship, membership of the council was increasingly reserved to those men who lived in a "noble" style, and it appears that by 1500 the titles "magnificence" and "excellency" were being used by some Brescians even though they were reserved only for Venetian rectors and their officers.[90] During the first half of the sixteenth century the Brescian patriciate in its aspiration to noble status asserted its pride and authority by building *palazzi*, imposing buildings with multiple specialized rooms and elaborate internal and external decorative schemes, often inspired by Ovid.[91] For example, Floriano Ferramola's frescoes (ca. 1508) for the Calini palace include scenes of the birth of Adonis, Diana and Actaeon, the punishment of Midas, and the sacrifice of Iphigenia. Brescians turned their wealth into furniture such as marriage chests and other objects, for example a set of maiolica plates displaying both the arms of the Calini family and mythological scenes— again derived from Ovid (Figure 4.1).[92] The decoration and control of space also extended to the squares and public buildings of the city. The frescoed façades of Brescia have largely disappeared, but those that remain indicate that mythological tales, hunting scenes, and other feudal or noble activities were depicted. Moreover, gold or silver were used in the façades of houses—on the coats of arms and images of saints that were painted there for passers-by to read and admire.[93]

Figure 4.1. Nicola (di Gabriele Sbarghe) da Urbino, *Neptune Transforming Cygnus into a Swan*, with the arms of the Calini family. Maiolica dish, ca. 1520–30. Image © Trustees of the National Museums Scotland.

The definition and narrowing of the urban patriciate in Brescia after around 1460 is one more example of a process that was occurring in other towns and cities of Italy during the fifteenth century. This process was the culmination of debates about true nobility that had been going on for several centuries. For example, in a dispute over precedence that was published in Brescia in 1497 the Veronese jurist Cristoforo Lanfranchini attacked the claims of *milites* (soldiers) to hold first rank among magistrates when in fact doctors of law possessed a superior claim to nobility—that of the mind. He claimed that these *milites* did not know how to arm themselves, and that they stood about in the city squares and—worst of all—pursued base occupations ("artes . . . viles").[94] The 1479 dispute about ceremonial precedence discussed earlier in this chapter suggests that similar theories about the superiority of lawyers over those bearing arms had the power to provoke debate in Brescia. However, as has been noted, the right to bear arms was fiercely defended by some nobles.

The increasing power of the colleges of judges and notaries that historians have observed in other towns such as Vicenza and Verona was a critical factor in the changes that occurred in Brescia during the fifteenth century. Lawyers and notaries now shaped Brescian political institutions in the face of threats from the new citizens. At the same time, these councillors asserted a more noble lifestyle and outlook, which helped them to put some distance between themselves and people they regarded as mere shopkeepers, dentists, and "castrators." It is likely that a study of the extensive notarial records of Brescia during this period would show that the practice of endogamy confirmed and perpetuated the exclusivity of this new urban patriciate just as it did in the later sixteenth and seventeenth centuries.[95]

Civic and ritual spaces would play a key role in the aristocratization of the Brescian patriciate, but as in the case of the relationships between governor and commune, and commune and countryside, the monumentalization of the city after 1430 was not achieved without some conflict within the patriciate or contention between the city and the territory. In this process, like that of the formation of the urban oligarchy, Venice certainly played an important role, but the new civic space more obviously reflected local traditions. These Brescian traditions and concerns—the city's sustaining myths—were presented in an architectural language of power and incorporated classicizing, pagan, and Christian elements that must have spoken vividly and directly to the Brescians. In the next two chapters I will explore this space and its uses so as to reconstruct, as far as is possible, the parameters of political and social life and what might be described as the texture of the world of Brescians under Venetian rule.

PART THREE

RELIGION, RITUAL, AND CIVIC IDENTITY

CHAPTER FIVE

Space, Ritual, and Identity

I N SEPTEMBER 1497 the Brescian population turned out in force to celebrate the visit of Caterina Corner, who had ruled Cyprus as the widow of King James II of Lusignan from 1474 until 1489, when she was forced to abdicate in favor of Venice. The celebrations that accompanied the visit of Corner, whose brother was the Venetian *podestà* in Brescia at the time, were said to have cost 10,000 ducats, and this amount reflects both her royal status and perhaps also the esteem with which the Venetians held Cyprus. Corner was welcomed at the border of their territory by Brescian nobles, who were later joined by the Venetian *podestà* and his wife. The former queen entered the city along streets covered in cloth under a white damask baldachin carried by eight doctors and was conducted to a pavilion set up on the ravelin of San Nazaro, where she viewed an elaborate procession of around a thousand troops, hundreds of clergy, musicians, and aristocrats from Brescia and Venice. Her visit began and concluded with several days of jousting attended by the duke of Milan Ludovico Sforza, Cardinal Ippolito d'Este, Francesco Gonzaga, Venetian patricians, condottiere in the pay of the duke of Milan, and large crowds of Brescians.[1]

The processions and speeches of welcome for Corner were marked by a distinctly classicized and mythological accent appropriate for the former ruler of an island closely associated with Venus. The entry procession included a triumphal carriage ("caro triomphale") drawn by four horses made up with with horns to resemble unicorns and featuring a representation of Diana. She was accompanied by Cupid (the son of Venus) who was plucked ("tuto spenato") by sweetly singing nymphs.[2] A similar, if less successful, presentation of Diana, Venus, and Cupid, as well as Adam and Eve, was also mounted by the communities of the Val Camonica when the queen continued her journey.[3] On her way to her lodgings in the decorated Martinengo palace in Brescia the queen also attended a sermon in the church of Santa Maria dei Miracoli, which had recently been constructed around a miraculous image.[4]

In an oration subsequently given in her honor Giovanni Battista Appiani claimed that every inhabitant of the city, whether patrician or plebeian, girl or boy, rejoiced to see her.[5] It is clear that the welcome extended to the queen of Cyprus was intended to be fitting for someone of her exalted social status and to reflect well on the nobility of Brescia. The town's learned men and noble families played a prominent public role, and Ludovico Martinengo was praised for acting as host to the queen during her stay. The presence of many Venetians was also indicative of the political dimension of her visit, and one contemporary chronicler noted that the attendance of the Brescians at the three days' of jousting reflected the city's enthusiasm for its Venetian rulers.[6]

As Richard Trexler has argued, jousts were a means of promoting a noble ethos in the communes of Italy, and it is probably the case that the joust in Brescia was symptomatic of the aristocratization of the Brescian ruling oligarchy discussed in the previous chapter.[7] Jousts were not purely local and secular civic events, and they could be shaped by liturgical constraints as well as by the participation of nobles from elsewhere in the peninsula.[8] For example, during the Carnival of 1485 a joust held in the city of Brescia was attended by the bastard son of Ludovico Sforza the powerful regent of Milan.[9] Jousts were also occasionally held to commemorate the ceremonial entry of distinguished visitors: in 1441 there was a joust in honor of Count Francesco Sforza, who had aided the city in its struggle against Milan, and in 1490 the marquis of Mantua Francesco Gonzaga was similarly honored in the year of his marriage. The prizes on these occasions were suitably noble and ranged from a silvered helmet worth 100 Brescian florins to lengths of velvet and brocade.[10]

At the beginning of the sixteenth century the Brescian artist Floriano Ferramola decorated the home of the wealthy Calini family with a number of frescoed scenes of classical and contemporary life that offer a fascinating insight into the world of the Brescian nobility.[11] The Calini were one of the leading clans in Renaissance Brescia, and its members featured among the ranks of those who participated most frequently in the civic councils during this period. The scenes Ferramola or his patron chose were prob-

Figure 5.1. Floriano
Ferramola, *A Joust in
the Piazza Maggiore,
Brescia.* Fresco transferred
to canvas, 454.2 x
273.5 cm., ca. 1508.
V&A Images/Victoria and
Albert Museum.

ably intended to flatter the Calini by representing an especially noble ethos:
well-dressed men and women pose in idyllic landscapes while hunting pro-
ceeds or shepherds serenade them. One of the most important scenes was
that of a joust in the new piazza that had been created in the city during
the first fifty years of Venetian rule (Figure 5.1). This representation probably recalls the visit of Caterina Corner in 1497, and the prominent figures
in the left and right foreground of the fresco may represent Caterina and
her brother the *podestà*.

As the festivities for Caterina Corner and their subsequent representation
demonstrate, civic space in Brescia was key to the projection of civic identity, so the reconstruction and elaboration of urban space is focus of this
chapter. I will study the gates, squares, streets, churches, and more secular
public buildings that Corner visited or passed through in the light of the

rituals and relics that gave them life and form. As the Calini knew well when they commissioned Ferramola to paint his frescoes of the joust, by projecting a sacralized space or an aristocratic style of living, the Brescian nobility offered a controlled and dignified image of themselves and the city to their peers, other Brescians, and the governors in Venice who played an important role in shaping the urban fabric.

Monumental Space

Since one of the main justifications for the conquest of the *terraferma* offered by Venice was a concern for the security and liberty of its subjects and allies, some attention was paid to maintaining and improving defenses in the subject cities. In 1454 the Brescian orators capitalized on this association and opened their list of *capitula* presented to the Venetian Senate by recalling the constancy and loyalty of Brescia and by emphasizing the desirability of fortifying the city.[12] Brescia had an especially important military role in the Venetian empire: it was the center for the manufacture of arms and armor owing to its proximity to areas of metal extraction, and it became one of the main locations for the permanent billeting of frontier troops as well as the preferred residence of the captain-general of Venetian forces. As a consequence the condottiere Bartolomeo Colleoni and Franceco Bussone, Count of Carmagnola, occupied large palaces in the city.[13]

By the middle of the fifteenth century the local council, aided by Venice, was repairing the city walls and reordering or renewing the civic fabric in ways not dissimilar to what was happening in other cities in the *terraferma,* notably Verona, Vicenza, Udine, Belluno, and later Bergamo.[14] The existing fortifications in Brescia were repaired or preserved, and the walls of key outlying towns were also thickened and scarped.[15] The cost of repairing the Brescian walls was shared by the Venetian *signoria,* the city of Brescia, and its territory, though not without some grumbling and resistance on every side.[16] The Venetian Girolamo Priuli later claimed that Venice had poured millions of ducats into fortifying Brescia and pointed out that the Brescians had proved ungrateful recipients of this largesse.[17] Characteristically, the Brescian territory objected to making a contribution to the work that began on the whole circuit of Brescian walls in 1468. This was not simply an occasion for dust and demolition, and the project prompted a high pontifical mass in the duomo in the presence of the Venetian rectors, while the laying of the first stone was marked with a mass and procession from the neighboring church of Sant'Apollonio at the instance of the *podestà.*[18] However, Brescia was subsequently obliged to send orators to Venice in order to secure contributions of 4,000 and 2,000 ducats, respectively, from the Riviera di Salò and the Val Camonica for the construction work.[19]

There was also some disagreement between Venice and Brescia over the future of the walls constructed by the previous regime. Like other cities, including Crema, Lodi, Bergamo, and Bologna, signorial governors had fortified key public buildings and appropriated public space.[20] In the *capitula* drawn up in 1426 the Brescians complained to Venice about the Viscontean fortifications of the *cittadella nuova* that impeded their access to the relics in the cathedral churches and the *broletto*. Accordingly, the Brescians asked Venice to reunite the *cittadella* with the rest of the city.[21] However, Venice refused this request in 1428 and on all subsequent occasions until 1517, because the fortifications of the *cittadella* were valued for their defensive purpose—as was proven during the capture of the city from the Visconti.[22] This refusal was the source of some tension between Brescia and Venice in subsequent years, but—perhaps mindful of this fact—a new space was proposed in 1433 by the *podestà* Marco Foscari.[23] Foscari, whose brother was the reigning doge, declared that a celebrated and magnificent city ("multum famosa et magnifica civitas") like Brescia required a decorous square in place of the existing disorder. A radical project of demolition and building followed, and the new *platea magna* or *piazza della loggia* became the center of civic life in the city during the fifteenth and sixteenth centuries. Magnificent events such as the joust for Caterina Corner's entry were held in this square, and the council worked hard to keep it in a fit and dignified condition: for example, in 1526 a proclamation was issued against persons urinating and defecating beneath the staircase of the treasury and chancellery of the new *palazzo della loggia*.[24]

The new piazza opened up in the heart of the city was embellished with new buildings—notably a small arcade or *loggetta* (planned in 1434 and finished the following year) and clock tower on the east side (projected in 1437 and completed by 1447); salt offices and subsequently headquarters for the public bank or *monte di pietà* to the south (ca. 1485–89); and a new meeting place for the council—the imposing *palazzo della loggia* (ca. 1492–1575) on the western edge of the piazza.[25] The decision taken in 1484 to replace the existing public *palazzo* with an entirely new building on a monumental classical scale was an eloquent expression of good government. The scheme can also be read as a sign of the determination of the new urban elite to project a more grandiose image of itself to the rest of the city and the *terraferma*, and similar motives have been identified in the Veronese oligarchy's restructuring and embellishment of urban space after around 1450.[26]

There is no evidence that these Brescian schemes were boosted financially by Venice, although the Venetian Senate had supported the reconstruction of the Palazzo della Ragione in Padua after it was damaged by fire in 1420 and had granted 5,000 ducats to Vicenza in 1444 for the reconstruction of the *palazzo communis*.[27] More modest and economical symbols of Venetian rule were erected in prominent public spaces throughout the *terraferma* during the fifteenth and sixteenth centuries.[28] Venetian interventions of this nature in Brescian public space ensured that the more obvious signs of political subjection were on prominent display. The arms of the Venetian rectors were painted on the walls of the halls of government and other prominent walls and buildings of the city, alongside the sculptures or images of the city's patron saints and Saint Mark, the apostolic patron of Venice.[29] Loyalty to Venice was ostensibly indicated in 1447 by the council's decision to erect a mast with the standards of Saint Mark, the *podestà*, and the city flying from its top, although it was almost a decade passed before the proposal was realized.[30] In a similar fashion, in 1533 it was proposed to fly the standard of Saint Mark between statues of the local patron saints, Faustino and Giovita, placed on columns in front of the new *palazzo della loggia*, but these public monuments were never built.[31] The *piazza della loggia* also figured in the ceremonial route taken by Venetian rectors and other important Venetian visitors to Brescia. The young Venetian patrician Marin Sanudo accompanied the Venetian *sindaci inquisitori*—who heard appeals against rectors' decisions in the *terraferma*— on a visit to the city in 1483. Sanudo recorded how they were greeted in Brescia with music and elaborate gifts; he was particularly struck by the *piazza della loggia* and the new buildings that surrounded it.[32]

The new urban spaces also had a more local resonance with the myths and traditions of the city: notably Brescia's importance under the Romans and its role as the site of the relics of early sainted bishops and martyrs. Like other Italians from around 1420 onward, Brescians, Venetians, and visitors to the city responded enthusiastically to the abundance of Roman inscriptions that were visible in stone in the medieval walls under repair.[33] The council unanimously decided in 1480 to preserve the engraved stones ("lapides laborati") found during the excavation of the salt offices and to incorporate them into the new buildings.[34] The demolition of the tower of the Paganora gate and excavations behind the prisons on the south side of the *piazza della loggia* uncovered more Roman inscriptions.[35] These discoveries were made at a time when the wooden shops that had burned down in the piazza were being replaced by the new *palazzo della loggia* and offices for the *monte di pietà*. While the insertion of Roman inscriptions in the former building was fairly minimal and unobtrusive, the architectonic statement made by the stones incorporated into the *monte* offices and adjoining prison was far more visible and far from obscure in meaning. The new foundations of the prison were dedicated to Marcantonio Morosini, the *podestà* during 1484–85, and at the base of the arch that later marked the passageway between the two offices of the *monte* were placed *all'antica* (classically styled) inscriptions commemorating the loyalty of the Brescians during the siege of 1438–40 and making an explicit historical comparison with Saguntine loyalty to Rome: "Brixianorum et Saguntinorum miranda constantia." (The constancy of the Brescians and Saguntines is worthy of admiration.)[36]

The style of engraving on these offices is in harmony with the Bramantine and Mantegnesque decoration appearing on a number of tombs, palaces, and churches throughout Brescia after around 1466 (when the choir of Santa Giulia was constructed). The construction and decoration of the palace of Bartolomeo Colleoni in the city after around 1455 was one important channel of artistic innovation, but the appearance of *all'antica* motifs and style also reflects an interest in antiquities taken by local humanists such as Ubertino Pusculo, Taddeo Solazio, and Giovanni Stefano Buzzoni.[37] These men had connections with other antiquarians in Italy, including Michele Ferrarino, the Carmelite whose edition of an ancient guide to inscriptions was published in Brescia in 1486,[38] and Felice Feliciano of Verona, who led an archaeological expedition with Andrea Mantegna on Lake Garda in 1464 that included Buzzoni.[39] In 1475 the local humanist Carlo Valgulio wrote to the Florentine Angelo Poliziano and described a rather disappointing visit to view ancient ruins in Arezzo.[40] A similar expedition was undertaken to Aquileia in 1483 by the Brescian humanist Giovanni Francesco Boccardo (known as Pylades) in the company of his friend the ever-inquisitive and observant Venetian Marin Sanudo.[41]

The arrangement of inscribed stones was not simply an aesthetic or antiquarian exercise, and the use of inscriptions recording emperors, public works, associations of masters, and ancient Brescian families was one aspect of a confident and nobly monumental style in the city.[42] The amalgam of local and more broadly classical traditions has been noted elsewhere in Italy—notably in Venice and Siena—and has been identified with the promotion or consolidation of a ruling oligarchy intent on asserting its authority but also demonstrating its sensitivity to local history.[43] The recovery of Roman remains was also a pious act: Taddeo Solazio's introduction to the Roman inscriptions found in the city and surrounding countryside married the pagan and the Christian: he included in his guide an account of the Christian martyrs of the Roman period, including Anathalon, the first bishop in the city.[44] Solazio also described the holy cross employed in local ritual, praising its beauty, miraculous powers, and imperial provenance. In Solazio's view all of the ancient inscriptions and remains testified that from its foundation Brescia had been powerful and influential ("ab initio potens pollensque Brixia nata conditaque").[45]

The themes of *Romanitas*, piety, and political virtue were also apparent when the Brescian council decided to decorate the clock tower loggia in around 1489. The Cremonese painter Gian Giacomo Moretti provided images of Saint Mark and the local patron saints, Faustino and Giovita, and the local artist Vincenzo Foppa painted a scene that glorified imperial Roman justice.[46] The clock tower loggia was destroyed in the middle of the sixteenth century, but a sketch attributed to Foppa of one part of the original fresco survives and shows that he, or the Brescian councillors appointed to oversee the project, decided that an episode from the life of the Roman emperor Trajan would be a suitable subject for such a prominent public place. In Foppa's sketch Trajan is seated on a horse in imperial pomp surrounded by a well-dressed entourage, and a woman kneels before him holding the lifeless body of a young man. The key to Foppa's image lies in the emperor's awkward backward glance, which is directed to another younger man on a horse. This young man in armor may be identified as the emperor's son, and the sketch may be taken to represent the justice of Trajan, for according to one story known from the *Golden Legend,* "one of Trajan's sons was galloping his horse recklessly through the city and ran down the son of a widow, killing him." The emperor proceeded to exact justice by handing over his own son "to the widow, to replace the son she had lost, and endowed her liberally besides."[47] Trajan appeared as "a model of civic virtue" and a representative of patriotism and military expertise in the defense of the state in Dominican sermons in Siena in 1478.[48] Moreover, in a sermon given in Brescia in 1494 the Franciscan Bernardino da Feltre reminded Brescians of the story of Trajan's justice and the spiritual rewards that accrued to him for this act: Pope Gregory's prayers led to Trajan's resuscitation and baptism and thus his pagan soul was saved.[49] Both incidents were depicted in a 1502 print by the local Carmelite artist and engraver Giovanni Maria da Brescia.[50] The justice of Trajan was therefore a highly suitable subject for such a prominent civic location and may also have served to flatter the Venetian rulers, who were often praised for ruling with justice over their subjects.

Sacred Space

The retelling of the tale of Trajan's justice in sermons and in public frescoes is indicative of the way public virtue and piety were closely intertwined in civic identity and ideology during the Renaissance. The figure of Trajan made an ideal example of virtue in a city where Roman remains were relatively common. These ancient traces could also evoke troubling memories of the earliest religious activity of its inhabitants, for the duomo was identified as the original temple dedicated to Mars or the Sun, while the *rotondo* of Santa Maria was said to have been constructed on the site of the ancient temple of Diana, and the churches of San Pietro in Oliveto and of San Salvatore on the sites of the temples of Jove and Saturn, respectively.[51] There were some fears that elements of paganism might survive in Brescia: in their discussions of the temple and the ancient cult of Diana, the local chroniclers Giacomo Malvezzi and Elia Capriolo noted that the Brescians continued to swear by Diana, and observed that at the feast of the Assumption a bull was still offered in her name.[52] Capriolo also recalled that the early Christian bishops had some difficulty suppressing these and other pagan rites; indeed, he later noted the reappearance of such carnivalesque or pagan rites in his own day among a sect of men and women living together on Lake Garda.[53] The supposed pagan remnants of the past in the duomo were the targets of religious reformers: in 1456 ancient and idolatrous sculptures of rams on the walls of the nave of San Pietro were destroyed by a crowd after a mendicant sermon and the council subsequently agreed to whitewash the walls and to supply new sculptures in stone or wood.[54]

The movement to cleanse and renew the sacred spaces of Brescia often revolved around the architecture of a building but was also connected with the holy objects within that protected the faithful of the city. For example, the fabric of the cathedral church in Brescia seems to have been in a generally poor or vulnerable state during this period: in 1485 the local humanist Laura Cereta wrote to the bishop deploring the fact that the host had been left unprotected in the crumbling church, and it seems to have been attacked on at least two occasions.[55] The silver left by the previous bishop for the construction of the duomo may have been diverted to fund the construction of the tabernacle for the holy cross.[56] It was later claimed that the administration of the oblations for the feast of the Assumption was taken out of episcopal control, and this may have been the source of dissensions in the cathedral reported in 1478.[57] Some enlargement of the Marian chapel was proposed in 1489 in order to lay it out in a Greek cross plan, and it was subsequently decorated by the artist Vincenzo Civerchio.[58] Further repairs and the installation of seats in the large chapel were proposed in 1511 after an earthquake damaged the building, and in 1520 the construction of a "templum magnum" was proposed. However, it would be almost a century before work on the new and more fitting cathedral— which now graces the city—finally began.[59]

A crucial factor in the reinvigoration of sacred spaces in Brescia after around 1450 was the discovery and display of the relics associated with local saints. The promotion of sainthood in Europe until around 1300 had often reflected popular enthusiasm for local holy men and women as much as the initiatives of princes and the Church.[60] Local cults of *beati*, or uncanonized saints, proliferated, and until around 1400 the distinction between canonized and uncanonized saints was generally ignored. The papacy increasingly tried to regulate the process of canonization, but episcopal involvement often lent weight to local cults regardless of decisions taken at Rome or Avignon. By the fifteenth century the mendicant orders were achieving notable success in promoting the sanctity of their members, and leading mendicant preachers were sometimes treated like living saints. In general, a gulf seems to have opened up between official sainthood and local devotions that grew without the benefit of recognition by the Church. For example (as we shall see in Chapter 9), the cult of the boy martyr "Saint" Simon spread throughout the Bresciano with mendicant support, despite Roman hostility toward it.

The assertive communes of medieval Italy were particularly keen to promote a civic cult that might focus on a broad range of patrons and defenders. This civic pantheon usually included local sainted bishops, whose relics often lay in the cathedral, as well as a range of great saints, such as the apostles. Civic cults often began locally with *inventiones* (discoveries) and *translationes* (transferrals) of relics, which, as "embodiments of the holy . . . emerged into the urban space and sacralized it."[61] The image of the leading local saint was placed on coins minted by the commune, while civic statutes usually record the patron saints honored with vacations of the law courts and with more general public holidays that fell on their feast days. Local governors were expected to honor local patrons, and guilds and parishes honored their own saints. The guilds, the parishes, and the surrounding *contado* were expected to honor the patron saint of a commune in public rituals with offerings, usually of wax, participation in processions, and attendance at the cathedral church. Historians have been divided about the significance of the growth of this civic pantheon, with André Vauchez suggesting that the gulf between the ascetic and mystical saints approved by Rome and the persistence of semiofficial civic cults of bishops, children, and the poor was a symptom of local political impotence and Gary Dickson arguing that the pantheon was a sign of an invigorating local enthusiasm.[62]

The civic pantheon of saints in Brescia was fairly typical of other Italian communes: the coins minted in Brescia from around 1254 until 1421 usually depicted the local patrons Faustino, Giovita, and Apollonio together or separately. After that date Brescia had to accept coins minted in Venice, including small denominations intended for Brescia that merely bore the initials of the doge, a cross, and the winged lion of Saint Mark.[63] The Venetian rectors were required to observe Brescian statutes and to honor both Venice and a range of Venetian, local, and more universally popular saints. After God and the Virgin Mary, these saints were Saint Mark, the apostles Peter, Paul, and John, and the holy martyrs, as well as Faustino and Giovita, the blessed bishops of Brescia Apollonio and Philaster, and the more recent intercessor Francis.[64] In 1473 statutory legal holidays fell on the great feasts of the church calendar but also on the feast days of forty-two individual saints, seven of whom can be considered local. The few additions made to this roster by 1490 consisted entirely of great saints, members of the holy family, or mendicants.[65] Guilds and colleges processed with their banners to make customary offerings on the feast days of great saints, such as Sebastian, Bernardino of Siena, Bartolomeo, and Lucy and of established local saints, including Faustino and Giovita, Apollonio, Cipriano, and Savino.[66] These saints were expected to protect the city, and the ritual of procession must have offered a reassuring sense of continuity for the local population, although it is clear that the Brescian *contado*, like rural areas elsewhere, resented and ocasionally resisted such civic and saintly demands.[67]

Although few new saints were admitted to the Brescian civic pantheon, some changes occurred that shed light on local religion.[68] It is especially clear that the promotion of more local saints, notably the city patrons, Faustino and Giovita, and the city's third bishop, San Apollonio, was undertaken with increasing urgency after around 1440 and that much of this was inspired or facilitated by the observant orders. The promotion of local cults was accompanied by the discovery of relics and their placement in new churches and chapels or in new caskets and sarcophagi in existing churches. Like other city councils in the *terraferma*, the Brescian council ensured that holy sites and relics were protected and made available for veneration by pilgrims.[69] Therefore, the location of holy sites in the suburban areas of cities, outside the walls, or next to the city gates was not simply a result of the pressures on space in the growing urban nucleus but also a means of facilitating protection and intercession. However, after around 1440 a significant number of relics were moved into the sacred space of the city, and there seems to have been an "expansion and filling up of liturgical space" in Brescia similar to that taking place throughout Italy as urban populations recovered their pre–Black Death levels and many new institutions were founded.[70]

The local chronicler Giacomo Malvezzi noted that the churches built on the sites where Faustino and Giovita had carried out their conversions of many Brescians and where Faustino had been incarcerated before his martyrdom at the hands of the Emperor Hadrian were in ruins in Malvezzi's own time, and the latter was unfortunately situated next to a brothel.[71] In 1455 there was much excitement when the bodies of Faustino and Giovita were discovered in a lead-lined marble sarcophagus under the altar of the church of San Faustino Maggiore by happy chance just a few days before the anniversary of their appearance to Brescians defending the city in 1438.[72] In recognition of the importance of the event, fourteen prominent citizens were elected to act with the episcopal vicar and the abbot of San Faustino to provide for the *solemnitates* (religious rites) to accompany the opening of the sarcophagus and its ornamentation. The opening of the sarcophagus on 11 December was attended by all of these men as well as the *podestà* and *capitano* of Brescia, the communal chancellor and two syndics, and a crowd of canons and other religious. As the cover was lifted off a loud cry went up: "Hic sunt, hic sunt!" The bodies of both saints were revealed, and any doubts about the identity of the two bodies were quashed, it was said, by the discovery of a lead tablet ("tabella") inscribed with their names. Finally, a major procession was organized at the end of December involving the bishop, all of the clergy, the Brescian rectors, and the others who had been present. An offering was to be made in the square before the duomo in the presence of the relic of the true cross which was processed through the city.[73]

The cult of the patron saint Apollonio was also commemorated and promoted by the council, which paid for his image to be painted below the loggia on the *piazza della loggia*.[74] The ritual procession for Apollonio was an established tradition in Brescia by the middle of the fifteenth century: the clergy gathered in the duomo on the morning of Holy Wednesday, removed the arm of Apollonio from its unlocked casket, and processed to the church of Sant'Apollonio in the hills to the east of the city walls.[75] The history of the storage, migration, and display of the relics of Sant'Apollonio is indicative of their importance. By one tradition Sant'Appollonio's body was placed under the altar of Peter and Paul in the duomo by the bishop Landulph in the tenth century; by the fifteenth century his relics were set in silver and placed in a new casket held in the same chest as the relic of the true cross (*orifiamma*) and cross of the field.[76] At the beginning of the sixteenth century the relics were held in a stone sarcophagus covered with a marble lid and were held in a chapel dedicated to Sant'Apollonio in the duomo, but by 1503 they had been transferred from an old and deteriorated wooden casket to a case in the chapel of the holy crosses.[77] Finally, an impressive new sarcophagus showing the sculpted figure of Sant'Apollonio flanked by his converts Faustino and Giovita was constructed in 1510 at the expense of the College of Notaries and was placed in the new titulary chapel.[78] On the saint's feast day in July 1510 the relics were finally moved from the chapel of the holy crosses to the new marble resting place in a procession led by Mattia Ugoni, the bishop of Famagusta, together with the clergy and laity of the city, representatives of the occupying French, three deputies representing Brescia, the cathedral treasurer, and a deputy from the College of Notaries.[79]

At the same time, Brescia was well known as a city blessed with more than thirty sainted bishops, and the discovery of the remains of Faustino and Giovita was just one of many made in the city around this time. In February 1456 the body of San Philaster, a fourth-century Brescian bishop, was discovered in the crypt of Santa Maria, where it had been placed in the ninth century.[80] When the chapel of San Philaster, which had been set up at the beginning of the fifteenth century by an earlier lord Pandolfo Malatesta, was flooded in 1945, the body was submerged and the bones dislodged. Nine citizens, including the chancellor Francesco Malvezzi, were elected to help the suffragan bishop Dolcino Paganino to excavate under the altar of the chapel, collect the bones, and return them to the sarcophagus. A marble sarcophagus was found under the altar containing a silver ring and inscribed with the letters "E" and "B," which were taken to signify "Episcopus Brixiensis." It was agreed to place the fragments of this sarcophagus in a lead box ("una capseta plumbea") made for the purpose, which in turn was to be placed in a chest ("cassono") in the duomo, where the cross of the *orifiamma* was kept. It was finally proposed that an altar, illuminated by new windows, would be built in the crypt and on this would stand a marble sarcophagus in which the lead box of relics would rest. The relics of Paolo and Cipriano were also provided with sealed and lead lined *sarcophagi* in the church of San Pietro Oliveto at the same time.[81]

The Brescian humanist Ubertino Pusculo noted in the middle of the century that the recently discovered bones of San Calimero, fourth bishop of Milan were being visited by the devout of the city.[82] These relics, which had been discovered on the altar of Sant' Anathlon in the oratory beneath the church of San Fiorano in December 1458 were moved to the main altar of the church in a solemn and well-attended procession led by Bishop Bartolomeo Malipiero.[83] The relics of the Brescian bishop-saints Ottaziano and Vigilio were moved to the new altar in the church of San Lorenzo at the end of the fifteenth century, probably when the church as rebuilt. In the case of Vigilio his head and other relics were brought from the neighbouring community of Iseo.[84]

In 1464 the body of San Latino in the church of Ss Faustino and Giovita *ad sanguinem* was placed for better safe keeping in a new sarcophagus with a plaque and sculpted bust.[85] Relics of the martyred saints Crisanto and Daria were found in the *duomo* in 1470.[86] It is likely that the reconstruction and building work in the city that reached a new pitch around the middle of the century helps to explain some of these discoveries. For example, the relics of a fifth-century bishop Gaudioso were found in 1453 when the great chapel of the church of Sant'Alessandro was renovated at the expense of the Venetian general Gentile da Leonessa.[87] However, the initiative behind this Christian archaeology may also have rested in part with the learned bishop Pietro del Monte, who brought the relics of the fifth-century saints Savino and Cipriano—natives of the city martyred in France—to the city in 1449 and ordered the construction of a decorated chapel in their honor in the cathedral.[88]

After around 1470 the pace of discovery in the city slackened, but the traffic in relics increased and was largely one-way, as bones were discovered and translated from the territory to the city. In 1472 the body of Anathalon was translated from the church of San Fiorano (outside the city walls) to the cathedral.[89] Six years later the council unanimously agreed— in a meeting held on his feast day—to concede permission to the Benedictines of the monastery of Sant'Eufemia to move the body of San Paterio (a bishop of Brescia who died in 606) from their wartorn lands outside the city walls to their monastery in the city. They granted a fairly generous sum from the communal treasury for the transportation of the relics in a sealed casket ("in capsula sigillatis"), and the relics were to be transported on the day of Saint Matthew the Apostle with clergy and disciples.[90] On 24 February the transfer took place with great pomp, and it was probably at this time that a sculpted sarcophagus with the heads of Saints Benedict, Paterio, and Eufemia was provided.[91]

In 1497 the relics of San Paolino were transferred "cum grandissima solemnità" from the church of Sant'Eusebio, outside the city walls, and placed in San Pietro Oliveto in a chapel dedicated to the saint.[92] The relics of San Silvino, a ninth-century bishop of Brescia, were initially translated from the Benedictine monastery of San Pietro in Monte, near Serle in the mountains northeast of Brescia, to the duomo.[93] However, in the course of rebuilding the church of San Pietro Oliveto in the city in 1508, members of the order of canons regular of San Giorgio in Alga arranged for the relics to be transferred in solemn procession from the chapel of Mary Magdalene in the duomo to a new marble sarcophagus in the reconstructed church of San Pietro Oliveto, where they would join the relics of four other sainted bishops, Paolo, Cipriano, Evasio, and Deusdedit, and allow for greater devotion.[94] In a similar fashion, an impressive marble sarcophagus in Lombard Renaissance style was erected in 1505 in the church of Saints Cosmas and Damian to hold the relics of Tiziano, a fifth-century Brescian bishop, whose relics had been moved there by Bishop Zane at some point during the previous decade.[95] The centripetal movement of relics to Brescia continued after the War of the League of Cambrai, and the relics of San Calimero, who was martyred in Milan and brought to Brescia by Sant' Apollonio, were moved from the now ruined Dominican convent of San Fiorano in 1521 to San Clemente in the city.[96] Just over ten years later the relics of San Silvino were brought from the ruined church of Sant' Apollonio outside the city walls to the new church of San Giuseppe in the heart of the city.[97]

The loss of such relics, which might serve to attract pilgrims and offerings, was naturally resented by some communities. During the third quarter of the century Bishop Johannes Hinderbach of Trent noted the contest between Trent and Brescia for relics of the martyr Vigilio, who may have been confused with a bishop and patron of Trent.[98] Closer to home, on 16 September 1481 the body of Saint Constance was translated from the church of Santa Maria in Conche, just outside the city, where it had been found by the Dominican brothers, and was placed in part in the church of Santa Caterina in Brescia and in part in the parish church of San Giovanni de Foris.[99] The bones of one of the arms were taken to the main Dominican convent (San Domenico) and to the duomo in a great procession. The communes of Nave, Caino, and Mesane, where the body had been found, aided by some Brescian citizens, including Count Alvise Avogadro and his followers, armed themselves with sticks and attacked the Church in the hope of recovering the body. Learning of this, the prior of San Domenico, Tommaso Donà, hid the body in the bell tower of the church of Santa Maria, but it was discovered and spirited away to Nave, sealed in a box, while Donà escaped the angry mob with his life.[100] Brescia and the Riviera di Salò sought to hold onto the remains of the fourth-century Brescian hermit and former bishop San Herculano, but eventually, "concorditer et unanimiter," the body was transported by boat to Maderno on Lake Garda and buried there.[101]

Ritual

Like other Renaissance Italian cities Brescia marked the periodic discovery and transfer of holy relics with processions. The Brescian calendar was also, more regularly, marked by a round of religious ritual that can be interpreted as evidence of the nature of civic identity and ideology: while these rituals were driven by the Christian calendar, they were also shaped by the local social and political concerns.[102] In his survey of ritual in Florence in around 1300–1530, Trexler has suggested that ritual behavior there was a function of the need to assert the legitimacy of the political and social order, to encourage trust and honorable behavior, and to bolster confidence in a new republican and mercantile order.[103] The definitions of lay and sacred spaces and time were key to Renaissance ritual and public life but were far from uncontested or unambiguous in meaning. As Edward Muir has argued, each city was made up of a mosaic of overlapping sacred spaces that might imbue objects and rituals with special meaning. The sacred space of the parish church was complemented by the street-corner Madonna or miraculous image and by the meetings and processions of neighborhood confraternities. Muir has also argued that a tension could exist between these sacred spaces as the local and neighborhood spaces felt the tug of the charismatic, sacred, or more secular political center. In Venice, Muir suggests, the parish lost out to a more distinctively corporate ritual involving the confraternities, which were closely regulated by the state.[104] The triumph of the public over the private spaces was marked in Venice, and patricians did not ordinarily glorify individuals or their lineage publicly unless some very close identification could be made between private achievement and the welfare of the state.

Public rituals in Brescia centred on the city's cathedrals, the square in front of them, and the *piazza della loggia*. Although envisaged as essentially a secular space from the 1430s onward, the *piazza della loggia* was the scene of key religious as well as more secular ceremonies sponsored by the council.[105] The processions for the feasts of Faustino and Giovita and other saints, sermons, episcopal entries, and public executions all took place at or passed through the piazza.[106] These rituals were designed to incorporate the quarters of the city and to unify the population, but there is evidence of local initiatives that are indicative of the strength of parish loyalties and competition between groups over sacred spaces. Moreover, despite the nominal involvement of corporate bodies—for example professional colleges, trade guilds, and religious confraternities such as the flagellants—there is evidence that these groups occasionally failed to fulfil their roles in public ritual. And the attempt to incorporate the surrounding territory into Brescian ritual sometimes met with indifference or hostility. Just as images of Saint Mark signified and sacralized Venetian rule, the processions that wound through Brescia were designed to strengthen, cleanse, and protect it. In reality, just as their feelings about Venice were ambivalent, Brescians were not always successfully united in ritual.

Corpus Christi processions throughout Europe are especially well known as having been designed to serve the purpose of incorporation by means of an annual procession of the social orders in a hierarchical arrangement expressed by their relative proximity to the consecrated body of Christ. In

Vicenza at the end of the fourteenth century the involvement of all citizens was promoted by the Viscontean regime as a way of symbolizing the liberation of the city from the Carrara and similarly was promoted in Padua in 1434 by the Venetian rector as a way of unifying the city.[107] It has been argued that in reality the procession was not an exact reflection of the community and that "by laying hierarchy bare it could incite the conflict of difference."[108] The rituals of Corpus Christi in Brescia were hardly well adapted to incoporate the whole city: the host was paraded in a tight, anticlockwise circle only along the perimeter of the city walls established by the end of the twelfth century and now superseded by urban expansion.[109]

As far as the civic records are concerned the preeminent feast in Brescia was that of the Assumption of the Virgin and, like the feast of Corpus Christi, was originally designed to unite the community. The feast of the Assumption was established in Brescia in the thirteenth century when the city was riven with faction, and accounts of its preparation appear in the local civic records, while the Virgin and her Assumption were celebrated by local poets.[110] The rituals surrounding this commemoration demarcated and linked the civic spaces with the social orders in order to promote civic harmony.[111] Letters were sent to the surrounding towns and to Milan, Bologna, Ferrara, Mantua, and other cities giving notice of the Assumption *palio* (race) to be held on the holiday, which was paid for out of the cathedral funds.[112] The decision to hold these races was made by the local council, who were probably mindful of the fact that they, like the nobility with their jousts, could dignify the city by offering an occasion for noble participation.[113] The importance attached to nobles' attendance at the Brescian festivities is indicated by the willingness of the Venetian rectors to comply with the Marquis of Mantua's request in 1490 to postpone the *palio* for eight days because it clashed with the Mantuan counterpart.[114] Five years later, the presence of the marquis at the Brescian *palio* was the occasion for the presentation to him of a scepter and a standard by orators from Venice in recognition of his role as commander of the forces of the Holy League, which had defeated the French at Fornovo a month earlier.[115]

The significance of the feast for urban identity was complicated by more profane or unruly elements, which sometimes led the council to decide to suspend the races. On the eve of the feast of the Assumption, butchers ran a race in the piazza in front of the duomo, and a bull ran at the Bruciata gate, apparently accompanied by young men on either or both occasions.[116] On the day of the feast itself after none (3:00 pm) there were races of young men, asses, horses, and prostitutes.[117] The rectors accompanied the runners to the gate of San Giovanni and then left a vicar to officiate there. The prostitutes were obliged by proclamation to all turn up and run from taverns close to the gate; the asses came from the river outside the gate; the horses departed from the church of San Jacopo della Mella. As with jousts the winners of these races received lengths of cloth, which were displayed on poles: for example, "panno verde" was given to the winning prostitute.[118]

Races of prostitutes were quite common in Italian towns and were a form of public ritual that could serve to reinforce princely or communal authority—especially in terms of social and gender relations. Like the topsy-turvy world of Carnival, the prostitutes' race temporarily overturned the established hierarchy, which placed prostitutes in a firmly subordinate position in society, in order to reaffirm that very hierarchy. The fact that prostitutes were forced to race in front of besieged towns in order to humiliate and demoralize their inhabitants is an indication of the negative social meaning of the act. However, this form of stigmatization lay on the limits of acceptable behavior, and in Brescia the races, especially that of the prostitutes, frequently provoked discussion during the first three decades of Venetian rule, as they seem to have been used as an excuse for rites of violence that the authorities regarded as dangerously uncontrolled. It is probably significant in this respect that criminals, especially adulteresses, prostitutes, and procurers, were sometimes required to run through a town naked or partially dressed as objects thrown by onlookers rained down on them.[119]

In Brescia a prohibition on the throwing of flour into the faces of those racing was introduced in 1433, and both the bull run and the prostitutes' race were prohibited at the instance of the *podestà,* who argued that they both amounted to an insult to the Virgin and had caused deaths and injuries.[120] He argued that such bestial and vain indulgences were not fit for reasonable men and were moreover prohibited by civil and canon laws. One Brescian lawyer declared the *podestà's* advice more precious than gold or silver since it concerned the well-being of the city, which ought to be ruled according to spiritual, not carnal, concerns ("secundum spiritum et non secundum carnem seu sensualitatem"). Human and divine laws, he added, clearly prohibited such diversions ("ludos"). Others in the council chamber got to their feet and argued that these races were useful diversions for the people and that the local statutes did not prohibit them. A compromise was agreed: in future a race would be held on the day of loyalty to Venice on 17 March (the date in 1426 when the Visconti troops were driven out of Brescia). The *podestà* proposed one race of horsemen in place of the existing races and offered a rich crimson cloth that would attract the great men of Italy to the event.[121]

Subsequent injunctions against races of bulls and prostitutes indicate that this reforming proposal was not put into effect. In 1442 preachers inveighed against these customs as a useless spectacle from which many evils arose.[122] Two years later the races were again attacked as a bestial custom, and as one that served as an affront to the current regime because it had been introduced by the "former enemy."[123] However, there is no straightforward narrative of a reform of the races—as in Siena—even though they were described in council records as a pagan rite comparable to the curing of epileptics at the church of San Bartolomeo on the feast day of that saint.[124] The races were suspended on subsequent occasions when there was a threat of plague but proved to be a popular and durable diversion for the rest of the century.[125] The authorities even recognized that they could reinforce the social order by example, and in 1463 it was agreed that the races should be held in perpetuity, since they had been instituted by the wise men of former times to serve as an example to good women.[126]

As the example of the races for the feast of Assumption suggests, ritual was an imperfect and often contentious tool in the formation of civic identity. It is clear that some members of the city councils disapproved of the more carnivalesque and profane elements evident at these events, which threatened to get out of hand and bring dishonor on the city before distinguished guests. The ritual subordination and integration of the communities of the *contado* as well as the offering of oblations was also a point of dispute and conflict, and in this respect Brescia's experience is similar to that of other towns in northern Italy.[127] In 1446 a certain Pachenus was one of the representatives of the *contado* who came to Brescia for the Assumption races. Pachenus was described in the council records as a farm laborer ("bobulus") and was said to have shown disloyalty to the city by offering the judges a rug ("copertanis abobj" or "copertam abolj") in place of the usual cloth of velvet with the rectors' arms on it.[128] In 1436 the representatives of the Val Trompia, Val Sabbia, and the towns of Orzinuovi, Orzivecchi, and Chiari refused to make the usual offering on the eve of the feast.[129] There were other occasions when the *contado* showed its displeasure in like fashion, especially when loyalty was at stake or Brescia was attempting to extract money and other services from these communities.[130]

A concern for the protection of the entire community lay behind the presentation and manipulation of the holy crosses by the civic council. In 1474 the council commissioned a tabernacle so that the cross of the *orifiamma*, might be moved around and venerated in a secure and fitting way.[131] There was some delay in the construction of the tabernacle that may be attributable to disputes between the council and the cathedral canons, but after a decade or so it was built, and both the cross of *orifiamma* and the cross of the field were displayed in the cathedral sacristy and subsequently in a new chapel lit by twelve lamps.[132] The council also ensured that the tabernacle was given additional worked metal ornamentation in

1517, when the rest of the treasury and the chapel were ornamented.[133] The cross of the *orifiamma* was often carried around the district in times of extreme weather—drought, floods, and frost, with the clergy would imploring God for rain, or calmer weather, over three days of processions, sometimes in the company of the heads of households.[134] It seems as if the amount of water appearing in the fountain that had miraculously appeared where Faustino and Giovita had preached and converted their fellow Brescians was the cue to undertake these processions.[135] This cross also featured in the processions for the feast of the Assumption, the rogation days,[136] the feast of Corpus Christi,[137] and on special civic occasions such as the transfer of Faustino and Giovita in 1455.[138] Just like the tabernacle constructed at communal expense in Padua between 1434 and 1453, the cross of *orifiamma* was a venerated communal object offering protective power for the whole city and was frequently on show at times of particular anxiety.[139] For example, in 1524 the cross was paraded for three days with the body of Christ and all the fraternities and clergy after a "messa granda" in the duomo. This procession, ordered by the bishop, was an extension of the cross's traditional role in weather processions, for it was hoped that it would placate God who was widely expected to bring down a great flood in that year. The whole community of Brescia fasted for three days, alms were distributed, and the bishop gave communion to a mass of families in a show of popular devotion that impressed the Venetian *podestà*.[140]

The organization of ritual was not effected entirely from a central authority, and the mosaic of overlapping sacred spaces that Muir has suggested for Venice is evident in Brescia. In an effort to placate God during the devastating plague of 1478–79, some inhabitants of the parish of Sant'Alessandro, together with some brothers from the convent of the Servi, carried through the city an image ("una anchona") of the Virgin that usually stood on an altar dedicated to her in the parish church. As they processed through the city the parishioners and clerics recited the litany and cried out "Misericordia, misericordia."[141] Around the same time, the council agreed to support with 5 gold ducats a certain Joanne de Corzano and his "socijs" who wished to make an image of San Rocco ("quandam dignam et devotum representationem ad laudem & honorem Sanctam rochi").[142] The veneration of San Rocco, a plague saint, was increasing in popularity during this period and received mendicant and conciliar support as a means of promoting local autonomy and civic identity.[143]

Local parish initiatives may have arisen when civic ritual and procession failed. During an unusually dry season in May and June 1483 the holy crosses were processed as usual. As the drought wore on, the flagellant confraternities ("battudi") with their priests and parish priests processed daily around their parishes with men and women singing litanies and chanting prayers. Finally, squads of fifty or a hundred children spontaneously formed processions and went from church to church with little books of offices in their hands or singing the litanies. Each child carried holy images ("una maistade, chi de charta, chi depenti su tavolette, chi una devotione, chi una altra") and prayed to God to send rain, crying "Misericordia, misericordia." It finally rained on the night of 21 June.[144] The usual processions organized by the council followed a month later.[145]

The council appropriated or sponsored processions associated with miraculous images that appeared in the city. An image of the Madonna at the church of Santa Maria delle Grazie, to the north of the city, which was a focal point of veneration during the plague of 1452, was honored on the feast of the Purification of the Virgin and the council invited the Hieronymites to install themselves in the church.[146] In 1486 the special council elected two citizens to work with the owner of a house whose wall bore the miraculous image of the Virgin in order to found a chapel; construction work was funded with money left in front of the image by the devout and with 300 ducats donated by the council.[147] The church of the Miracoli, as this chapel became known, soon became a focal point for offerings and processions during Pentecost, as well as a key point in some public processions, for example that of the former queen of Cyprus in 1497, for it stood on the main route into the city taken by distinguished visitors arriving at the gate of San Nazaro.[148] The civic sponsorship of devotion to the Virgin was hardly a new phenomenon in Italy, but it may be no coincidence that this church was built at a time when the Franciscan campaign for the recognition of the immaculate conception of the Virgin was gaining ground in Rome.[149]

The civic and sacred spaces of Brescia, like political and religious ritual and procession, are not always easy to distinguish clearly, and a modern temptation to do so should perhaps be avoided. In Renaissance cities political life was deeply imbued with religious symbolism, imagery, and language. The images of protecting saints appeared on the city walls and were represented in many other public places. The feast days of these saints were marked by the closure of shops and the suspension of business in the courts and councils. The councillors were seemingly content to devote time and resources to the promotion of ritual that involved the city's clergy, corporations, and rectors. These processions provided a way of ensuring holy protection for the city, of projecting an honorable, pious, and dignified image of its inhabitants, and of ensuring that social order was confirmed and enforced. However, it seems that councillors were sometimes divided in their opinions about the meaning and utility of some ceremonies

or traditions. It is also apparent that the power of the charismatic or political center was not always sufficient to satisfy all parts of the city, and
rituals and processions based around the parish, confraternity, or guild
continued to be significant features of the urban landscape. Both the
strength and the limits of civic religion and identity are even more apparent when the activities of the episcopacy and the secular and regular clergy
in Brescia are examined.

CHAPTER SIX

Civic Religion and Reform

L IKE OTHER CITIES in the *terraferma* Brescia regularly expressed a
desire for the appointment of native sons to local benefices; this was a
wish Venice just as regularly failed to meet. In fact, Venice repeatedly appointed Venetian patricians to these positions and interfered in many local
ecclesiastical matters. In this chapter I will first assess the impact of these
appointments on civic identity in Brescia and will then show how the Brescians were not simply passive recipients of Venetian initiatives. It is clear
that while Venice arrogated formal powers of appointment, the Brescian
council, in alliance with the mendicant orders, worked hard to promote
local civic and religious concerns. Civic control of religion in Brescia operated in a number of ways—some subtle, others much less so. Roman authority, feudal powers, and Venetian patrician-bishops could act to weaken
local control while humanism may have induced some anticlerical senti-
ment (as I will show in Chapter 8), but there seems to be little justification
to speak of a "civil religion," with the accompanying implications of secu-
larization, in Brescia at this time. The myth of the blessed Brescia strengthened the core of civil life and animated many local concerns, occasionally
with some violence, throughout this period.[1]

The study of religious belief and practice must pay due attention not
only to the presence of official Venetian appointees and aspects of a distinctly Roman Catholic religion in the provinces but also to the civic or
religious ceremonies and structures that were entrenched in local tradition

and formed "local knowledge."[2] The reciprocal relationship between Venice and Brescia in religious matters traced here varied in intensity, and while in some cases Venetian priorities took precedence, in other respects more local initiatives and traditions—such as the civic pantheon of saints discussed in the previous chapter—seem to have been tolerated or even encouraged. As I will show later, the civic puritanism that was one of the striking facets of this process also reinforced the Brescian social order and had dire consequences for some marginal groups in the city such as Jews and prostitutes.[3]

The development of local knowledge in Renaissance Italy was a key element of a regionalization of ecclesiastical matters as princes and magnates usurped episcopal autonomy and sought to control lucrative benefices, restrict the sale of land and alienation of secular property to the church, and find places for family and clients. Episcopal nomination under political pressure was especially marked in northern Italy, and the proliferation of benefices there provided many opportunities for the ambitious and well-connected as well as for the more spiritually inclined. Moreover, during the Middle Ages the sale or leasing of land by churches and monasteries increased in pace and enriched large numbers of laymen.[4] Accordingly, as the Venetian *terraferma* empire expanded in the course of the fifteenth century, new monasteries, churches, lands, and benefices tumbled into Venetian hands and were shared among the patriciate or with favored local families. Venice succeeded in controlling the appointment of secular clergy in its new dominions, and it was affirmed in 1488 that all the benefices of the *terraferma* were in the hands of the patriciate. This state of affairs is in line with the aristocratization of benefices that occurred throughout Italy at this time and was especially noticeable in Florence.[5]

The return of the papacy as a political power on the Italian peninsula after around 1440 complicated the relationship between center and periphery in the territorial states and had a direct impact on the formation of Brescian local knowledge. Venice seized papal lands and fell under papal interdict in the course of the fifteenth century. The papacy asserted its right of nomination and appointment, and successive popes worked to regain lost territory by diplomatic and military means, notably with the formation of the League of Cambrai and its armed assault on the Venetian empire in 1509. The growth of the papal bureaucracy during the fifteenth century provided employment and opportunities for travel and enrichment for some Venetians and Brescians.[6] However, the loyalties of Venetian ecclesiastics were sometimes considered highly suspect in Venice. To complicate matters further, members of the Venetian patriciate or the *terraferma* elite often appealed directly to Rome for benefices or on a range of other matters and attempted to avoid state interference.[7]

This tangled intersection of Brescian, Venetian, and Roman axes of power in religious matters requires careful elucidation. The records of the Venetian Senate provide some indication of the different ways Venetian patricians could monitor and control clergy, the sale of ecclesiastical land, and the distribution of benefices in the Bresciano. For example, the bishop of Brescia occasionally would nominate a candidate—often, but not invariably, a Venetian patrician—for a vacant benefice, and the Senate would consider his suitability.[8] The bishop might also punish or dismiss a misbehaving cleric as a matter of normal episcopal discipline, but the Senate could also impose further penalties for especially grave crimes.[9] The senatorial records also provide evidence of the enforcement of the Venetian right to control the sale of ecclesiastical land and to hinder the alienation of secular goods and land to the Church. To take only one example: in 1482 the observant Franciscan friars at Iseo, near Brescia, successfully requested permission from the Senate to sell or alienate some of their lands in a public auction. Many similar cases can be found in the records of senatorial deliberations, and it may be presumed that high-ranking ecclesiastics of Venetian origin were in a good position to lobby senators connected to them by birth and of similar social standing.[10]

The clash of Brescian and Venetian priorities could appear most clearly when, as already indicated, the question of episcopal appointments arose. Venice invariably imposed its choice of bishop on Brescia, and while the city council could express a preference for a native son, the Brescians usually found themselves welcoming a Venetian patrician to the diocese. In the *capitula* granted in 1428 Venice reserved its right to intercede with the pope in the nomination of the Brescian bishop. At the same time Brescians had asked for benefices to be given to men of "pura conscientia" and not to foreigners unless they had been resident in the city for ten years and had a good reputation; the Brescians asserted that such men cared little for improving their benefices.[11]

Once again, in one of the *capitula* addressed to Venice in 1440, the Brescians complained about their titular bishop and requested the designation of a *Brescian* bishop, adding that such an appointment would be pleasing to clergy and laity alike.[12] Bishop Francesco Marerio had absented himself from the city during the recent siege, and with Venetian approval (but papal opposition) the council had appointed four citizens to administer episcopal income.[13] In addition, the council decided to petition Venice and Rome for the appointment of a local cleric in Marerio's place. The Venetian Senate was in favor of this proposal, but the pope decided to appoint the Venetian Pietro del Monte.[14] The Brescian council noted, with evident disappointment, that del Monte was not a noble Venetian but merely a citizen. The recalcitrant Brescians were threatened with an interdict and left without a spiritual head after the pope recalled the episcopal vicar. The Brescians petitioned Venice for a noble appointee but, after much wrangling, were forced to accept del Monte.[15]

The ceremonial entry into the city of the resented Bishop del Monte in 1445 provoked a scuffle in which certain members of the crowd ("vulgo") tore the ceremonial baldachin and injured a horse. The incident may be interpreted as a rite of passage confirming popular possession of the bishop; it may also be understood in the medieval tradition of the ritualized riot during which the episcopal or papal baldachin and horse were seized by those eager to gain some spiritual benefit.[16] However, whatever its motives, the incident was so violent that soldiers in the retinue of the captain-general, who was accompanying the bishop, were obliged to step in and defend him. The bishop, "trepidans," was forced to complete his journey to his palace on foot.[17]

After this somewhat inauspicious start, relations between the bishop and his flock were never very smooth. For example, del Monte clashed with the Brescian council over the question of ecclesiastical liberty, which he felt might be infringed by the proposed reform of the Brescian statutes. He threatened the city with excommunication, and his vicar read two decrees to the council on the matter. The council responded by sending five ambassadors to reassure the absent bishop, who never revisited the city despite repeated invitations from the council.[18]

There is little evidence that successive Venetian appointees, who were often absent from the city for long periods, provided any kind of bridge between Brescian and Venetian concerns or anything more than temporary spiritual leadership in the city.[19] Del Monte helped promote a new monastery following the rules of Saint Clare. He also commissioned a tabernacle for the sacrament and induced the council to buy vestments decorated with gold brocade for the cathedral sacristy. He made repeated attempts to suppress the races of women and bulls at the feast of the Assumption and opposed the construction of a *lazaretto* (hospital for infectious diseases) and the residence of Jews in the city. The reform of monasteries in the city seems to owe more to the efforts of the council than to the bishop.[20]

Rather more encouraging was the appointment of the theologian and humanist Domenico de' Domenichi. Bishop Domenichi made his ceremonial entry into the city in August 1466, a full two years after his appointment.[21] He made some attempt to exercise episcopal authority, and in preparation for a proposed pastoral visitation he rapidly issued *capitula* concerned with the state of the churches (including the condition of robes and instruments, relics and treasures) and the faults of the local clergy (which included gambling, blasphemy, quarreling, usury, and consorting with concubines).[22] He also delivered a tactful and flattering Latin oration in praise of the city that touched on the traditional themes of the beauty of its natural setting as well as the public service, martial virtue, riches, charity, constancy, faith, and piety of its nobility. The bishop declared that Brescia had withstood war and tyranny and added that the heroic struggle of its priests, women, and children during the siege of 1438–40 was worthy of praise.[23] He returned to Brescia from Rome in March 1470 and, after a pontifical mass was celebrated, made a number of gifts of ecclesiastical apparatus to the cathedral and issued edicts regulating the dress worn by clerics in church.[24] His brief and sporadic visits to Brescia have been associated with the periods when he was out of favor in Rome or "in reduced demand" there, and his real interests, whether humanist or political, seem to have lain far from Brescia—just like those of del Monte earlier in the century.[25]

In 1474 the Brescian council once again agreed to send orators to Venice to promote the election of local son Bartolomeo Averoldi as bishop of Brescia in succession to Domenico de' Domenichi, who had mistakenly been reported dead. The Brescian orator was instructed to proclaim to the Venetians that first among Averoldi's qualifications was his ancient and noble name and then to praise his intelligence, character, and other virtues.[26] In the event, on the death of Domenichi in 1478, another Venetian patrician, Lorenzo Zane, was appointed to the see.[27] His tenure soon came to an abrupt and ignominious end when he was exiled from Brescia and all other Venetian territories as a result of his condemnation for betraying state secrets to the pope.

The disgraced Lorenzo Zane's successor as bishop was his twenty-year-old nephew Paolo, whose absenteeism resulted in some of the ceremonies for Holy Week in 1482 being neglected while a mysterious effusion of blood in the duomo seems to have disrupted the occasion as well.[28] There may also be some hint of the resentment of the appointment of Paolo in the violence committed by "nonullos incognitos" in 1487 against a member of the bishop's household.[29] A few years later it was reported that "verbis et terminis calumniosis, et inhonestis" had been uttered—presumably shouted—under the windows of the bishop's palace at night.[30] On another occasion the episcopal chancellor informed the Brescian council of unspecified objections ("oppositionibus") to the episcopal vicar, and the council accordingly decided to elect five men to investigate the causes of this opposition.[31]

It is unrealistic to judge Brescian bishops by the standards of episcopal residence and pastoral care promoted by the Catholic reformers of the sixteenth century. Indeed, episcopal absenteeism may even have gone some way to satisfy local concerns, for the role of the absentee bishop could be taken by a local man acting as suffragan bishop; the Brescian nobles Alto-bello Averoldi and Mattia Ugoni seem to have acted as energetic and rela-tively efficient local suffragan bishops during the first three decades of the sixteenth century. However, it is clear that the Brescian council and those who assaulted the bishop or his household with weapons and words were not entirely content with Venetian appointees. As the examples of the ad-ministration of Marerio's income and the appointment of his successor suggest, the Venetians were not averse to respecting local aspirations. Nev-ertheless, repeated affronts to local pride probably led the council to spon-sor the processions and rituals discussed in the previous chapter and may also have encouraged the spread and reform of the mendicant and regular clergy.

Observant Reform

The civic religion of Brescia was strongly marked by the presence of men-dicants and regular clergy—indeed, the proliferation of religious houses was one of the aspects of the myth of Brescia explored earlier in this book. These orders formed significant channels for the flow of power, wealth, and cultural practices during the Renaissance.[32] This movement was com-plicated by the tug between Rome and provincial headquarters and by new or strengthening currents of reform within established orders that attracted the attention of local lay powers. In Italy there was often a close connec-tion between the patronage of secular rulers and the spread of mendicant observance. Mendicant observance was principally a movement of spirit-ual or observant Franciscans and Dominicans who renewed their vows of apostolic poverty and reliance on public charity as part of a return to the purity of their orders' original rules. The dukes of Milan were notably keen to foster movements like the observant Lombard Congregation of Domin-icans, and in this duchy there were numerous examples of the supporters of observance succeeding with ducal intervention.[33] It has therefore been suggested that this amounted to a regionalization of the regular clergy in which the establishment of observant centers played an important role.[34]

Venice also encouraged observant initiatives: for example, observant clergy were exempt from clerical taxation in the city after 1430, and Vene-tian patricians welcomed and promoted new observant groups who made their headquarters there. The reformed regular canons of San Giorgio in Alga and the Benedictines of Santa Giustina both established their head-quarters in or near the lagoon.[35] The Camaldolese congregation of San Michele di Murano was established in 1474 on an island in the lagoon and attracted many Venetian patricians, some of whom chose to live and med-itate in its cloisters.[36] In the following year the reformed Franciscans of San Francesco della Vigna in Venice absorbed the vicariates of Sant'Antonio in both Padua and Brescia, while the observant Augustinians of the Marca Trevigiana were constituted as the congregation of Monte Ortona in 1436 and absorbed convents in Venice, Padua, and elsewhere on the *terraferma*. Some Carmelites established a provincial organization with its headquar-ters in Venice in 1473, although they continued to obey the authority of the general of the observant Mantuan congregation.

In the absence of strong episcopal authority, local civic authorities within larger regional states like the duchy of Milan or the republic of Venice of-ten stepped in to support new religious institutions or devotions and to promote mendicant observance. The observant movement was backed by many Italian civic authorities who regarded it as good for the spiritual health of the commune as well as a means of consolidating their power.[37] Italian city councils often invited mendicant preachers to address large crowds in churches and squares and make a case against luxury, or attack Jews, prostitutes, sodomites, and other marginal groups and activities. A number of popular and influential preachers emerged in fifteenth-century Italy: the Franciscan preachers Bernardino of Siena and Giacomo della Marca, the observant friar Bernardino da Feltre, and the Dominican preacher and prophet Fra Girolamo Savonarola, who all criticized excesses in public expenditure, fashion, and behavior.[38] Savonarola's prophetic vision led him to urge his Florentine audience to arm itself morally for the final judgment and to destroy lascivious or luxurious clothes, books, and pictures. On the basis of this eschatological outlook and a successful diplomatic effort to deflect a French invasion of Florence, Savonarola in-creased his political influence in the city until he was excommunicated and burned at the stake in 1498.[39]

The Bresciano was the setting for some striking examples of local initia-tives that served to bolster civic image, spiritual health, and territorial unity. For example, the council invited Franciscan or Dominican preachers to the city throughout the fifteenth century, and these visits often had a huge public impact: they filled up the sacred and lay spaces of the city with crowds drawn from both the city and countryside.[40] The Franciscan Ber-nardino da Siena preached in the city in 1422, and his presence seems to have helped bring about the foundation of the observant monastery of Sant'Apollonio, although he was less successful in his attempt to abolish the Assumption Day races or to reconcile the persistent Guelph and Ghi-belline factions. In 1444 the Franciscan friar and renowned preacher Al-berto da Sarteano attacked a range of vices in Brescia, notably usury and civil discord, encouraged the formation of the monastery of Santa Chiara, and reformed the places of pious aid in the city into a hospital.[41] Alberto was supported by the Venetian *podestà,* who called for the end of faction in the council on Easter 1445, and by Bishop del Monte, who laid the foundation stone of the hospital.[42]

Giovanni da Capistrano, whose miraculous cures in Padua, Vicenza, Verona, and Rome were widely reported, was given a triumphant welcome when he came to preach in Brescia in 1451. The rectors met him with three hundred Brescian nobility on horseback at Sant'Eufemia. He was followed into the city by women on foot and a long line of people that was augmented when he reached San Salvatore. The rectors with knights on horseback accompanied the preacher from Sant'Apollonio to the piazza, where he preached before ten thousand people. Despite this armed guard his clothes were torn to shreds by relic hunters. Due to the large crowds he preached, flanked by a tribunal of rectors and gentlemen, on a pergola in the more capacious market in the *cittadella* quarter for three days, including the feast day of Faustino and Giovita.[43] The city was filled with men and women from the *contado* and from neighboring states, and the council claimed that there were between eighty and one hundred thousand people in total, many of whom were drawn by the public display of a Franciscan relic: the beretta of Bernardino da Siena.[44]

Visiting preachers were sometimes adept at flattering local sensibilities with references to local history and tradition. For example, on 19 May 1483 a Florentine friar addressed an oration in the *piazza della loggia* in the presence of Francesco Sanson, the energetic and cultivated Brescian general of the Franciscan order.[45] The friar ran through Brescian history and highlighted the historical occasions when the virtues of friendship and loyalty had been evident among the Brescians. The friar also asserted that eighteen Franciscan monasteries had been established in the Bresciano.[46] The Brescians could also respond in kind with orations of welcome and praise: the Franciscan Bernardino da Feltre arrived in the city at the end of 1493 and was welcomed with a speech by the precocious teenager Bartolomeo Mercando.[47] Bernardino's Advent and Lenten sermons in the city attracted the bishop and the local civic officers, and he seems to have encouraged the institution of a confraternity devoted to the worship of the Sacrament in four parishes as well as the promotion of the new *monte di pietà* that had been established as a Christian alternative to Jewish moneylending in the city.[48] Bernardino's preaching also prompted a spasm of moral reform, and just as in Savonarola's Florence the council organized a bonfire of harmful reading matter or images and luxurious female adornments in the square in front of the cathedral.[49]

There is some evidence that the themes of moral reform and renewal that Bernardino and these other preachers explored struck a popular chord with the local population. The bull run at the feast of the Assumption, with its pagan associations, was regarded by some as an affront to the Virgin, and Bernardino da Feltre helped to suppress it once again in favor of a general oblation.[50] One local poet lambasted feminine fashions, dissensions among the citizens, and other themes touched on by the mendicant preachers.[51] Elia Capriolo also condemned—while also describing in extravagant detail—the luxurious festivities that took place on the occasion of a papal visit to Brescia in 1502.[52] Many of these views were probably shared by the large and enthusiastic crowds that gathered to experience the charismatic presence of preachers in the city throughout this period.

The council frequently supported the reform of older monastic centers as well as new observant convents and monasteries established in the city—often under the auspices of these famous preachers. The council was aware that some orders, like the Humiliati and the Benedictine monastery of Sant'Eufemia, were still recovering from the effects of the war in the middle of the century.[53] Alms were regularly granted to these monasteries to fund repairs and were also given to observant monasteries with the expectation that they would offer up prayers for rain in times of drought or encourage divine mercy when plague threatened the city.[54]

The council was also concerned with the branches of orders that displayed signs of moral decay. In 1440 the Dominicans of San Barnabà were criticized by the Brescian council for their lack of observance and disorderly behavior, while the nuns of Santa Chiara were said to be living wicked lives.[55] Accordingly, observant Franciscan vicars were established in Brescia with the support of the city council in 1447, and a more thoroughgoing promotion of observance was undertaken in the city.[56] Having brought the aristocratic convent of Santa Giulia into observance, the council agreed to elect twelve councillors to undertake monastic reform and to encourage observance, with the result that the convents of San Domenico and San Francesco were soon brought into line.[57] The observant Carmelites also received support from the council later in the fifteenth century when the conventuals tried to oust them from the city.[58] In 1503 the council supported the inspection of Franciscan monasteries in the city by Franciscan clergy and elected three citizens to act as procurators for the monastery for the conservation and growth of religion, for the good and peace of the monastery, and for the good of the community.[59] Local feudal powers could also play an important role. For example, the condottiere Bartolomeo Colleoni founded the convent of Santa Chiara for twelve nuns on land at Martinengo granted to him by Venice.[60] Franciscans received support from feudal powers in the region in a similar way.[61] The lay congregation of Jesuates was established in the city during the last quarter of the fifteenth century with the help of the noble family of Martinengo della Pallata.[62]

Some of the civic support that has been outlined here may have been given with the intention of attaching the clergy more closely to local concerns and undermining outside control—whether from Milan or Mantua, Venice or Rome. The cases of the Amadeites and the Capriolanti are particularly instructive in this regard. The Capriolanti were a reforming movement within the Franciscans that absorbed the monastery at Ghedi (at Lake Garda) and that of Sant'Apollonio in Brescia. Established by the Brescian friar Pietro Capriolo, the Capriolanti had strong support in his native city, in Venice, and less overtly from Francesco Sanson, the Brescian general of the Franciscan order. The Amadeites were a group of Franciscan spirituals led by the Portuguese João Mendes de Silva, who was based in Milan and founded a number of convents in the Val Camonica after 1460.[63] After a period of subjection to Milanese vicars, the Capriolanti and the Amadeites were both absorbed by the observant Franciscans of San Francesco della Vigna in Venice. This union provoked opposition from the Duke of Milan, who complained about Capriolo's expulsion of Milanese friars from the Brescian monastery in 1471, and internal squabbles were noted three years later.[64] In a similar way, the observant Dominicans at the churches of San Fiorano and San Domenico in the city were part of the Congregation of Lombardy, which had its headquarters in Milan. This congregation was sometimes regarded with suspicion by the Venetians due to the role the dukes of Milan played in its promotion, and during the fifteenth century Venice and Brescia worked to ensure that its ties to Milan were broken. The Augustinian monks who were established at San Barnabà in 1456 in place of the disorderly hermits there were also part of the Congregation of Lombardy.[65]

The desire of the Brescian council to detach the local Franciscans from subjection to the Milanese observants may also help explain their support for the new cult of the French plague saint Roch (Rocco in Italian), with which the local observant Franciscans were closely associated.[66] In June 1469, at a time when plague threatened Brescia, the general council agreed, with only one dissenting vote, to build a chapel or church in honor of San Rocco near the gate of San Giovanni.[67] The council subsequently agreed to an annual and general oblation on the feast of San Rocco until the church was finished.[68] The popularity of the cult of Rocco was probably boosted locally in 1478 when a devastating plague began to rage throughout the city and the council granted 12 ducats for mass to be celebrated in the chapel of San Rocco every day by the friars of San Bernardino.[69] The following year, as deaths from the plague declined, the council agreed that the chapel of San Rocco could be completed with the ex-votos and legacies left to the chapel.[70] According to the local chronicler Iacopo Melga, on 13 March 1479 the community held a procession of all laymen and clergy with "trombe et piferi" and other musical instruments, and the first stone was put into place for the church of San Rocco outside the gate of San Giovanni.[71]

After a slow start, the erection of this church ran into further difficulties. Initially, the site was moved to a location outside the city walls near where the church of San Bernardino was already rising.[72] San Rocco was still under construction in 1484 when it was agreed to use part of its site as a burial place for plague victims.[73] On the solemn feast of San Rocco two years later the chapter of the canons of the duomo celebrated divine offices in the church of San Rocco, but it was evidently still incomplete or in poor order.[74] The special council granted funds for its repair of and the following January appointed a chaplain to say mass there daily.[75]

The Venetians and their rectors seem to have responded to local initiatives rather than rolling out a program of regionalization of observance, and care must be taken to avoid painting a crude picture of conflict or competition to the exclusion of cooperation. Indeed, the cult of San Rocco received a boost from the Venetian patrician Francesco Diedo, the Venetian *capitano* in Brescia, who assembled a life of the saint in which he promoted the salutary example of San Rocco's "austerità" and noted that when a vow had been taken to erect a chapel to the saint, the recent plague had passed.[76] The Venetian senatorial records also provide an impression of responsiveness rather than authoritarianism. In 1455 the Senate recorded the desire of the Brescian commune to write to the pope to request that the monastery of Sant'Eufemia in Brescia be united with the monks of Santa Giustina in observance.[77] At the beginning of the following year the Brescian rectors wrote of the poor conduct of the hermits of the church of San Barnabà and asked the Senate to obtain some reform. The Senate decided to write to the Venetian ambassador in Rome to instruct him to intervene with the pope. It was expected that the authority to bring about reform might be given to "optimi religiosi," namely Bernardo Marcello, abbot of San Faustino, and the prior of San Pietro Oliveto (a house of the regular canons of San Giorgio in Alga) in Brescia.[78] In 1457 the Senate confirmed the *capitula* submitted by the monastery of Santa Giulia, which was being brought with some difficulty into observance of the rule of Saint Benedict.[79] Two decades later the Senate asked the Venetian cardinals to intervene with the pope on behalf of "fidelissima communitas nostra Brixie," which sought the introduction of observance to the monasteries of Saints Gervaise and Protasius and of Saint Benedict.[80] Finally, in 1489 the Brescian orators asked the Senate to intervene with the pope in favor of the union of the monastery of Faustino and Giovita with the congregation of Santa Giustina in Padua. The Venetian ambassador in Rome was to be informed that the execution of this request would be to the general satisfaction of the population ("pro universali contentamento et satisfactione totius ipsius populi.")[81]

Fine Venetian words were sometimes matched by constructive Venetian actions, but Brescian piety was established and promoted with greatest vigor by the civic councils in alliance with the mendicants, especially the new observant preachers. The reform of lax regulars by episcopal or conciliar means and the encouragement of pious building works or associations were part of a drive to restore civic pride and piety. In this chapter I have not only suggested how local priorities shaped local religion but also how ideas and practices from outside the territory informed the renewal of the regular clergy. In subsequent chapters I will show how deeply and broadly these ideas and practices of reform and renewal spread and contributed to the strength (or weakness) of local society. Preachers visiting Brescia urged the population to abandon its squabbles—notably the Guelph and Ghibelline divisions that had plagued the city for centuries—and to give up immoral pursuits. The Brescian councils were periodically stung into action by these calls, but the councils' investigation and surveillance of morals does not seem to have been especially effective. In particular, the Brescian council attempted to enforce sumptuary legislation on a number of different occasions. An assessment of the success or failure of these attempts is less important than the fact that the councillors apparently used such legislation as a means to reinforce the new social and political order. In the next chapter I will therefore consider the regulation of lay moral order in this way.

CHAPTER SEVEN

Puritanism and the Social Order

THE CONNECTION between observant preaching and the promotion of what might be termed civic puritanism in Renaissance Italian towns, especially by means of sumptuary legislation, has often been remarked on.[1] The persistent drive to control dress and behavior—especially in towns during the years following the demographic and social disruption of the Black Death of 1347–49—is unsurprising, given Italy's economic prosperity, the cosmopolitanism of its towns, and the close links that existed between public behavior, images, clothing, honor, and social identity.[2] In the morally tense atmosphere of Venice, Brescia, or Florence, seemingly trivial matters such as furs and funerals could become the flash points for intense social and political conflict. Such civic puritanism or purification was often fueled by a mixture of observant Franciscan spirituality, Christian humanism, and millenarianism. However, for all its spiritual motives, such sumptuary legislation also aimed to reinforce the social order by differentiating between men and women and among royalty, titled nobility, patricians, citizens, and artisans.[3] Therefore, it is worth exploring the ways the civic elite of Brescia adopted a restrictive attitude toward dress and other matters through sumptuary legislation, since this further illuminates how the new Brescian oligarchy was defining and restricting social status and constructing a civic identity under Venetian rule.

In general, there was strong disapproval of earthly or carnal concerns in Christianity: many early Christian writers such as Tertullian, Cyprian, Jerome, and Augustine criticized luxury and excess, and medieval church synods and councils repeatedly condemned clerics who indulged in them and supported secular moves against malefactors by means of excommunication.[4] Moralists often linked feminine extravagance and display to prostitution and to the spread of Jews across Italy, for Jews were assumed to supply money at interest to women to enable them to purchase costly goods. The same critics also made the association between prostitutes and Jews explicit by encouraging the adoption of distinguishing signs. In many cities edicts against excessive finery or prostitution were issued at the same time as calls for the restriction, marking, or expulsion of Jews. These movements, however, ran up against the mercantile nature of Italian society during this period: finery, including earrings, was increasingly permitted as a sign of aristocratic status in civic society. As a corollary of the noble appropriation of certain signs and sumptuous apparel, the Jews and prostitutes apparently were more anxiously expelled or contained.[5]

Brescia was occasionally convulsed by public displays of civic puritanism, especially after the visits from mendicant preachers sponsored by the city council noted in the previous chapter. In a sermon given in Brescia on the feast of Saint Stephen in 1493, Bernardino da Feltre condemned dancing, playfulness, "inhoneste conversantes," mercantile activity, and quarrels on feast days. Bernardino argued that these were undignified, diabolical, and bestial actions on a holy day. In particular, he attacked dancing as encouraging lasciviousness through physical contact and pointed out that the sight, sound, and smell of dancing was also dangerous, since perfumed women danced with their breasts uncovered while young men practically showed their private parts, and the dance of Salomé (Mark 6:22) served to underline this point.[6] In the same series of Brescian sermons Bernardino deplored the pride, pomp, and vanity that went with the desire to appear grand. He lamented that such vices led men and women into avarice, usury, illicit contracts, extortion, and the oppression of others, and he praised holy poverty.[7]

Bernardino expanded on this theme in his sermon on vanities and pomp ("De vanitatibus et pompis") given for the feast of Saint Lucy. He recalled the example of Saint John the Baptist, who went barefoot and wore animal skins, a man ill-dressed but dearly loved by God. In answer to those who asked if it was not licit to dress according to one's estate—whether doctor, noble, or respectable citizen (of "bona casa")—Bernardino answered that such people should consider the source of their wealth and whether it was acquired through fraud or other illicit means. He went on to point out that the clergy who wore sacral robes appropriate to their status were nearest to Christ and therefore of highest estate, followed by emperors, who should therefore dress more humbly than the priests, kings more humbly still, as should dukes, soldiers and knights, doctors, noble citizens, artisans, and so on down to the humblest persons ("zente minuti"). Women should avoid a superfluity of clothes, which was nothing more than a form of a fornication ("fornicatio") or encouragement to lust that exceeded the dress of prostitutes. Bernardino also condemned the large dowries that bled a family dry. In general, he viewed the prodigality of so many jewels, precious stones, pearls, clothes, and superfluous necklaces as a grave sin when relatives were dying of hunger and the poor needed alms.[8] Elsewhere he noted that even children demanded new shoes ("scarpette . . . zoccolini, stringetti") while women wore rings on their fingers and sleeves richly adorned with gold brocade.[9]

The highly rhetorical constructs of preachers should be treated with caution, but they clearly found a receptive audience in Brescia among those who yearned for a return to the purity of the early church.[10] The chronicler Giacomo Malvezzi praised the restraint and dignity of ancient pagan religion in the city.[11] In 1501 the lawyer and humanist Bernardino Bornato inveighed against luxury in a decidedly providential vein.[12] In 1504 the Dominican Francesco Codognelli warned the Brescians about their vices.[13] At around the same time Elia Capriolo, who recognized that scents, gems, and clothes gave pleasure to both men and women, deplored the predilection of Brescian youth for carnival masquerades and dancing, condemned artisans and *contadini* for adopting the dress of their betters, and attacked prostitutes who wore loose maternity dresses from Naples.[14] Almost a decade later Marco Negro, who had just witnessed the terrible sack of the city by French troops, pointedly recalled the sermons of Bernardino da Feltre in 1493–94 in which he had foretold the calamities and miseries that would be the result of the great sins committed in the city.[15]

Many of Bernardino's points were also echoed, or anticipated, in a series of interesting letters written by the humanist Laura Cereta that circulated among a group of men and women who met at the Franciscan monastery of Santa Chiara in Brescia. In a letter written around 1486 Cereta described her nocturnal studies and early-morning needlework and observed that although the latter task wasted much of her precious time, nevertheless "the demand by women for luxury items and their fascination with the exotic . . . has increased to such an extent in our society that there is no end today to the public display of such merchandise. An aversion to moderation is characteristic of women everywhere—and by their own doing." Cereta wondered: "What is it about our desires and our era that has caused us to reject the Oppian law, in which garments embellished with this kind of artfulness were characterized as 'wantonly painted,' as though those garments might, in all their proliferation of color—their golds, silver, and blazing purples—run amuck under the weight of so much useless erudition?"[16] Cereta returned to this subject a year later when she asserted: "Today our city has become a disciple in the passions of women, indeed the city has become a pillager of the orient. In no age has there been a more wasteful tolerance for vanity." She described perfumed women attending weddings or strolling boldly through the city streets with artificially smoothed and whitened faces and adorned with "various and diverse ornaments." Women wore necklaces that drew attention to their breasts, rings sparkling with gems, and earrings. Some women wore tight sashes to accentuate their breasts, others loosened their belts to increase what she euphemistically termed their "popularity." Cereta added to the list of feminine faults "Arabian veils" and fashionable footwear. Finally, she noted that some women wore their hair piled up with false additions, fashionably curling over the brow or lasciviously tied back to reveal the neck. In sum, women were pursuing "the enticements of whores."[17]

Cereta's attack on excessive luxury owed much to classical satire in form, but its main thrust and choice of targets seem to have been rooted in especially contemporary concerns. Cereta was appalled at the way women were associating themselves with whores (who were normally allowed fine garments as distinguishing signs in fifteenth-century cities) or even with Jews (who normally wore earrings, which were associated with their supposed vainglory and concupiscence) and degrading themselves for the sake of their own vanity or for men's pleasure: "Some wind strings of pearls around their throats, as though they were captives proud of being owned by free men."[18] Acutely conscious of female vulnerability to the sharp criticism of men, which she had experienced firsthand, Cereta wanted women to be on their guard and to strive for chastity, humility, and true inner virtue rather than the outward show that was more often than not a prop to social position. As she wrote to her sister, the nun Deodata di Leno: "[L]et society women, whose counterfeit finery exposes their notorious lack of modesty, pet themselves and bask, to the extent that they can, in their own vanity. But we women, since we are the objects of contempt, should be conscious with the humility of our chastity that these fragile, small bodies of ours are chaff for fire and filth."[19]

The virtues Cereta invoked were preeminently Christian ones, although she clearly found Stoic self-restraint an appealing philosophy.[20] Cereta contrasted the use of ruby and emerald earrings "to imitate nobility" and the "corrupt devotion" to the image of one's face in a mirror with Christian virtue and a natural simplicity: "[H]ave we Christian women refused ostentatiousness at our baptismal ceremonies so that we could make ourselves up like Jewish or pagan women?"[21] In a letter to Barbara Alberti she wrote that the "veils of desire" that are driven by carnal impulses and the source of mental anguish should be peeled away to reveal true virtue, which abhors luxury, "glistens with its own light," and is the "right road of innocence to God." Cereta had earlier acknowledged that her own passion lay in her love of studies, but she asserted that such study caused her mind "to grow and expand" and that she was content to "molder away at home" in pursuit of virtue by this means and with the example of her father before her.[22]

Cereta's preference for frugality and simplicity was sometimes associated with the rural leisure that afforded her time for study. In a letter to her mother she evoked the natural environment of the family's country retreat near Lake Iseo, to the north of the city. She described the country people who greeted them with songs, music, and dancing. She concluded: "Thus, with charm and freshness, the sensations aroused by the land filled our city-bred minds."[23] In a letter modeled on Francesco Petrarch's famous account of his ascent of Mont Ventoux, she gave an account of an expedition into the mountains above Lake Iseo in which Epicurean, Stoic, and Christian reflections on the pursuit of pleasure were intertwined with natural observations: from the country people's "faces full of friendship and yet kindly deference as well" to meadows filled with wild strawberries, vines, and apple trees; crags; and gushing streams. Sensual pleasures are described: Cereta gobbles grapes, drinks great flagons of milk, washes in icy mountain streams, and finally dines on plain country food—chestnuts, polenta, turnip, barley bread, wine, and hazelnuts. As she says: "The sage is content with plain foods: he asks for that which nourishes rather than that which delights. For his frugal lifestyle and his moderation brought Socrates more glory than the enjoyment of luxury brought to [King] Sardanapalus." She concluded this letter by emphasizing the transitory nature of life and its pleasures and by affirming her desire to live a secluded life in contemplation of the eternal and divine.[24]

Laura Cereta and Bernardino da Feltre also shared a providential view of the world in which excessive luxury might provoke divine wrath and retribution or internally weaken society. A contemporary warning, or *cominatione,* in verse described the luxurious living rampant in the city, the squabbles that arose from it, the new fashions, and the sexual incontinence of the young and widowed. The poet urged Brescia to repent.[25] In her letters, which were certainly in circulation around the time of her early death in 1499, Cereta concluded that those women who had rebelled against God in their lascivious, arrogant, and ambitious behavior ought not to be surprised by the current Turkish onslaught.[26] She also described the portents of war—glittering fires and bloody stars in the sky—that she herself had witnessed, and she condemned the inhumane behavior of men during war.[27] Bernardino referred to Brescia when he discussed the signs of divine anger ("flagellum Dei et que sunt signa") in his Lenten sermon in Pavia in 1493: he recalled the Brescians dying "like flies" in the devastating pestilence of 1478–79—at table with the bread in their hands, or in bed with babies still clutched to the breast. At the sound of the bell, sons brought out the bodies of fathers to the plague cart, as well as fathers their sons, mothers their daughters, and even daughters their mothers. Thirty thousand people had died, and their corpses were placed ignominiously in mass graves.[28]

Like Bernardino, Cereta was also concerned with the protection of the Holy Sacrament, and a few years before Bernardino instituted a confraternity of the Holy Sacrament in Brescia she wrote to the bishop complaining about the host lying unprotected and "freely accessible to the impious," including magicians and "night-wandering sages" in the crumbling cathedral church.[29] Cereta may have had recent events in Brescia and the Val Camonica in mind here: the desecration of the host was one of the main accusations made against a new sect of witches that was uncovered and investigated by the Dominican inquisitor in the Bresciano.

Sumptuary Legislation and Social Order

The city did not match Florence or Venice in absolute numbers of sumptuary laws passed between 1200 and 1500 (sixty-one and forty-three, respectively), but it ranks quite highly in comparison with other cities in Italy, with eleven known acts.[30] Sumptuary legislation was enacted or proposed by the Brescian council at fairly regular intervals every ten years or so around 1440–1530. These initiatives seem to have originated with the city council, and there is no clear evidence, for example, that the institution of a Venetian magistracy to impose sumptuary law in 1476 prompted the array of legislation proposed in Brescia soon afterward.[31] However, the Brescians certainly sought approval for their sumptuary legislation in Venice.[32] Moreover, Venetian edicts on matters like gambling were also transmitted to Brescia and the rest of the *terraferma,* while rectors acted to suppress gamblers ("zochatori & barrj") who formed clubs ("conventicule") in 1501, and in 1534–35 the Council of Ten moved to increase the penalties usually imposed on blasphemers in the *terraferma.*[33]

Sumptuary legislation was more explicitly linked to local events and preoccupations. In 1442 the advocate for the commune of Brescia explained to the special council that seven outstanding preachers had been

present in the city exhorting people to give up vain and superfluous clothing ("vana & superflua Indumenta") since these satisfied nothing other
than Satanic pride ("luciferianam superbiam").[34] The advocate suggested
to the council that they put the city in some order; consequently two citizens were chosen to draw up ordinances, which would apply to both sexes.
There is no evidence that anything was done in this matter. In 1497 the
special council unanimously agreed that unwonted ("inconsuetos") clothes
be extirpated from the city, since various items of clothing—probably, they
thought, too revealing, or imported and thus harmful to the local economy—had been worn to the detriment of public morals and to the igno-
miny of the Brescian name.[35]

The council also related sumptuary legislation to fears of divine wrath.
In 1505 the general council proposed and voted on seventeen clauses relating to clothing and ornamentation, in order, it was said, to placate God in
a time of growing illness in the city, which was attributed to the city's sins.
Two officials in each *quadra* would be elected to look after the poor there,
giving alms for their support. Moreover, beginning at the feast of the Ascension and for three successive days there was to be a procession of the
entire population, both men and women, along with the clergy, the holy
crosses, and any other holy relics that could be carried. Fasting over two
Sundays was stipulated for everyone of legitimate age so that God might
show his mercy.[36]

Of course, moral concerns of this nature were more troubling at times
of acute socioeconomic distress or when it was feared that excessive expenditure on clothing, ornamentation, "accessories," feasts, and funerals
would exacerbate economic problems or social conflict. In 1477 and again
in 1495, 1499, and 1503 it was noted that there had been great expenditure on feasts to the detriment of the inhabitants of the city. The multiplication of expensive meat dishes or confectionary was prohibited, as was
the use of some spices and of gold and silver dishes.[37] Similarly, it was
stated that no citizen of any condition might use gold or silver in painting
the façade of his house, except in the coats of arms and images of saints
there.[38] In 1503 it was explained in the council *provvisioni* that the unsettled conditions of the period ("la difficultà di tempi") should teach
people to avoid superfluous expenditure, especially in clothing. The council hoped in this way to mitigate the worst domestic disputes that arose
from such excess and to avoid bringing the city into disrepute.[39] In 1505
old legislation relating to funerals was revived and promoted, at a time of
relatively high mortality when Brescians were competing to lay on lavish
funerals and money was pouring, or so it seemed to the council, into the
hands of the *scuole* of mendicants.[40]

Moral and medical concerns are sometimes indistinguishable in the debates and legislation of the Brescian councils: at a time when the spread of plague was feared in the city in July 1457 it was decreed that nobody in Brescia or its *chiusure* would be allowed to play flutes, bagpipes, or other chanting instruments, in order to prevent gatherings of people for public dances.[41] In 1495 the prohibitions relating to feasts stipulated that hands must be washed before and after the meal in pure fountain- or well-water.[42] In the sumptuary legislation of 1503 it was stipulated that no man might wear a beard unless ill ("corotto") and only for six months in mourning the death of a father, mother, wife, or child and two months for the death of other relatives.[43] This last injunction relates to a passage in Saint Paul's letter to the Corinthians in which he states that nature teaches that long hair is shameful for men but a glory for women (1 Cor. 11:14–15). In the sixth century Cyprian criticized "corrupt beards in men" ("corrupta barba"), and beards and hair were therefore supposed to be kept tidy and short. Long beards were a sign of mourning, punishment, penitence, or illness. There was also a medical tradition that viewed beards and hair as bodily "excrement" that needed to be periodically removed.[44]

Sumptuary legislation was also linked, as I have shown, to fears that the social order would be undermined by excessive expenditure and display. These concerns touched both men and women, but whereas men might justify their own fine clothing on the grounds of their public civic role—indeed the new noble style of the patrician oligarchy made such dress indispensable (see Figure 3.1)—women's clothing could bring shame on a family if it exceeded certain bounds. However, dynastic alliances might be cemented with a large dowry, including jewels and clothing. It is therefore no surprise to find that the council rejected moves to limit the size of dowries in 1496 or that a decade later it elected four men to congratulate Niccolò Orsini, the Count of Pitigliano and captain-general of Venetian forces on the marriage of his son to the daughter of Pietro Martinengo, despite the fact that the marriage festivities almost certainly broke the sumptuary laws.[45]

The council was most careful to monitor female clothing when it was thought to reflect a desire for upward social mobility on the part of manual workers. The influx of new citizens, as noted earlier, was particularly acute in the troubled years after the siege of 1438–40 when repopulation of the city relied on immigration from the surrounding territory. On 2 March 1440 an entry in the council *provvisioni* recorded the prices of basic foodstuff and noted that "those dying of hunger or weakness are eating horses and mules, dogs and cats, wolves and mice and every sort of unknown weed; and some die of hunger; while others, as the good priest of [the church of] Sant'Agata asserts, decide to poison half their sons because of the complete lack of food and overwhelming poverty. Alas, *Brixia tam magnipotens* above all other cities, so rich in food, to what have you been reduced?" The cause of the current poverty was attributed to the overwhelming luxury of lower-class women: "Metal workers, pastrymen, cobblers, and weavers dress their wives in crimson velvet, silk, damask, and the finest scarlet, while their sleeves are like the largest banners and are lined with squirrel or martin fur, which are only meant for kings; on their heads shine pearls and the richest crowns crammed with gems; I myself have seen cobblers' wives wearing veils of cloth of gold, and clothes laced with pearls and interwoven with wonderful art with gold, silver, and silk. Alas, *pudor judicia . . .*"[46]

Similar fears were expressed in 1503 at a relatively more propitious socioeconomic juncture when the council proposed in one clause of the current raft of sumptuary legislation that nobody who worked manually ("che in la propria persona exerciti arte mecaniche") be allowed to wear any clothing of silk, scarlet, jewels, or gold. Women should be permitted to wear one pair of silk sleeves so long as they were not of crimson velvet and to wear one pin ("vergetta") so long as it was not worth more than 3 ducats. It was explained that by "persone mecaniche" the council intended to refer to those who were unfit for "le dignità nostre," though it made an exception for soldiers and some others.[47] Interestingly enough, this clause referring to manual workers was solidly rejected by the special council by ten votes to three and did not appear among similar clauses proposed two years later—perhaps because it was some felt that access to the councils and to the urban patriciate was fairly secure after twenty years of oligarchical consolidation.[48]

The privileges of this new oligarchy are indicated in the 1503 proposals that provided very detailed guidelines about clothing and other household goods. The council stipulated that the wives of knights, counts, and those with jurisdiction in the territory—presumably the *podestà* and other officials—could wear a string of pearls of double the value allowed to other women (100 ducats) and a gold necklace, so long as it did not exceed 200 ducats in value, as well as a piece of clothing of gold or silver.[49] Considering this group of clauses a few weeks later, the special council decided to add a clause stating that nobody would be allowed to use bed-covers, or bolsters, or decorative motifs in silk, except for a single bed-cover of sarcenet, which might not be ornamented. On the same occasion the council forbade anyone to own vessels of silver, knives, forks, spoons, salt-cellars, plates, bonbonnières, bronze basins, or table carpets longer than six *braza*, except for knights, counts, and those with jurisdiction in the Bresciano for whom the use of such objects was licit.[50] Venetians, knights, and doctors ("Zentilhomeni di Venesia [*sic*]: cavalieri . . . doctori") as well were exempted from the sumptuary legislation of 1477, and it was stipulated that others who were caught would not only lose the goods and pay a fine of 100 ducats but also be deprived of any public office they held and taxed at twice the normal rate.[51]

These strictures extended beyond the council chambers and into the important colleges: at the end of 1499 regulations concerning banquets it was stated that members of the council or officers or members of the College of Physicians could not be chosen for any office, or accept cases, judge cases, or enter the council until they had paid any fine levied for infringements of the law, and the same applied to members of the College of Notaries.[52] There is a hint of the Guelph and Ghibelline divisions in the city in the final two clauses of 1477, which outlawed the wearing of clothes or devices belonging to another person, of whatever "status, gradus et preheminentia," and not to one's own family, except in the case of soldiers.[53] In 1503 a fine of 100 *lire planete* was to apply to malefactors, as well as the usual exclusion from colleges, offices, and *mercanzia*. Three citizens were to be elected each January to prosecute those who broke the rules; their names would be inscribed in the book of debtors; and a pardon would only be given by a vote of three-quarters of the council.

Prostitution and Sexual Order

Cereta was alarmed by the way her contemporaries were dressing like prostitutes, and as noted, the young Venetian Marin Sanudo commented on the prevalence of prostitutes in the city when he visited in 1483.[54] The distinction between "honest" and "dishonest" women was also a concern for both the Brescian council and the *quadra* organizations, which moved to mark prostitutes out by their dress and to control their movements in the city.[55] In navigating a course between expulsion and toleration the Brescian councillors were following in the footsteps of many other civic governments. Historians of prostitution have traced a distinct evolution in secular and ecclesiastical authorities' policies toward prostitution during the Middle Ages. As Leah Lydia Otis has observed of the French treatment of prostitution: "A primitive attitude of tolerance had evolved into a policy of institutionalization in the late Middle Ages, only to be replaced in the sixteenth century by . . . active repression."[56] It is apparent from the records of the Brescian council that identification, stigmatization, and control of prostitutes gave way by around 1520 to a policy of expulsion or physical marginalization. The motives behind this evolution in policy are sometimes hard to determine but probably lay in local concerns for the dignity of the city and drew on more universal assumptions about the role of prostitution in society.

Roman law defined prostitution as promiscuous intercourse in exchange for money, and this formulation was incorporated into Gratian's *Decretum*. Medieval canonists added notoriety and deception to the legal definition of prostitution.[57] Although it was bluntly condemned in scripture, Augustine provided some basis for the tolerance of prostitution as a lesser evil: "If you expel prostitutes from society, prostitution will spread everywhere . . . the prostitutes in town are like sewers in the palace. If you take away the sewers, the whole palace will be filthy."[58] Thomas Aquinas paraphrased this view and asserted that the elimination of prostitution would result in the pullulation of sexual passions and abuses.[59] It was also recognized that women were sometimes driven to prostitution by necessity and not simply by lust and that their earnings were as legitimate as those of other professions so long as they were acquired without trickery or artifice. Medieval civic authorities often applied a taboo on those who worked in unclean conditions or in morally suspect ways. However, the expanding urban economies of Italy provoked scholastic distinctions between trades condemned "ex natura" or by their very nature and those condemned "ex occasione," or according to case. The trades in the former group were sometimes justified by new ideas of the state as a body with the trades forming its constituent parts. Therefore, in order to serve the public good, professional taboos receded until groups such as usurers and prostitutes were integrated into society, given patron saints like other corporate bodies (Mary Magadalene, Mary of Egypt, or Afra), and confined to certain neighborhoods.[60]

The new system of values that put a premium on sexual obedience could place the prostitute in a wholly new place in society. Legal and intellectual reasoning traded on the idea of the prostitute's "natural" debauchery to develop the concept of "simple" fornication: sex outside marriage could be justifiable so long as it was for male gratification and with women sunk so low in status that they were outside the normal safeguards of chastity and respectability. According to Aquinas, a sin was less grave if it was committed with someone who was not close to God in virtue or function.[61] This approach to prostitution implicitly affirmed men's superiority as spiritual beings and placed natural law in a superior position to positive law with its definitions of mortal sins and subjection to custom.

The "sewer pit" of public women was as necessary to the home as to the wider world in directing the aggression of youth and protecting "good" or "honest" women. By around 1450 the sewer pit was well supplied with female rural migrants excluded from corporations and guilds, denied apprenticeships, and forced into marginal occupations. Prostitutes in Brescia included women from as far afield as Germany.⁶² The public brothel (and associated sumptuary legislation) represented therefore a civic assertion of legal principles, a practical means of controlling poor migrant women, and a useful channel for male sexuality. Accordingly, a brothel was established in Venice in 1358 and was policed by the republic in order to control public order and to prevent men turning to sodomy for sexual outlet. In 1403 the government of Florence instituted its Office of Honesty with the aim of turning men from sodomy by setting up a brothel and recruiting foreign prostitutes (to protect Florentine women).⁶³

It seems that civic concern that men remained unmarried may have led the Brescian council to focus on prostitutes both as sources of temptation and as civic figures who had to be housed in a public brothel. The council noted in 1471 that although there were many young men and young women ("virgines nubiles") in the city, few or none of them were married—behavior that seemed to suggest that there was no worthy person ("persone digne") for them.⁶⁴ This problem was probably a consequence of the rise in the size of dowries that affected much of Italy during the latter part of the fifteenth century and was thought to discourage fathers from putting their daughters on the marriage market and to encourage men to remain at sexual liberty. In May 1477 the council recognized the inconveniences that were said to arise when the arrangement of a marriage was in the hands of marriage-brokers ("messeti"), and it was therefore agreed that a fit citizen be elected by each *quadra* of the city to arrange marriages "cum ogni solicitudine e inzegno." Those elected would swear to work diligently to arrange marriages, with their renumeration set at a maximum of 1 ducat per 200 ducats of the dowry agreed on, under pain of deprivation of office and of restituting four times the amount in excess of the pay they would have received.⁶⁵

Prostitutes in Brescia were neither completely marginal like criminals and beggars nor an entirely integrated socioeconomic group with guild recognition.⁶⁶ They often participated in religious rituals and processions: as noted, a race for prostitutes was held in Brescia on the eve of the feast of the Assumption for the humiliation of these women and for the edification and warning of "honest" women. Some customs prohibited prostitutes from touching food on sale in the market and from entering baths except on certain days. Prostitutes were generally required to wear distinctive signs, to stay off the streets during Holy Week, and to repent. An examination of the Brescian council records reveals sporadic efforts to define and control prostitutes in this way during the first century of Venetian rule.

The prohibition on masks occasionally proposed in Brescia was related to prostitution and the immoral behavior that relative anonymity permitted or encouraged.[67] In 1466 the special council discussed the corruption ("coruptella") introduced into the city now that women went around with their faces covered like respectable women so that nobody could recognize them, and as a result many evils arose daily since not only honest but also dishonest women (i.e. prostitutes), and many men, went into houses they wished to (but could not openly) enter, and this led to many evils. It was therefore agreed that both men and women would be forbidden to cover their faces with any piece of cloth so that they could not be recognized in the street or any other public place, under pain of a fine of 50 *lire planete* for men and 10 *lire planete* for women (honest or dishonest), payable by the woman's father or husband.[68] Fifteen years later the special council agreed (by ten votes to one) to extinguish the damnable rite ("damnatum & pessimum ritum") of carnival masks, which it asserted were of such great inconvenience and offense to God, against good customs, and both a public and private danger. A person caught wearing a mask would be fined 25 *lire planete* or sentenced to six months' imprisonment. It was also stated, rather unusually, that it would not be possible to revoke this unless the special council were unanimous in favor of doing so and four-fifths of the general council voted the same way.[69]

The concern with prostitution that lies behind the prohibition on masks and veils is clear from legislation proposed to identify prostitutes more explicitly and thereby affirm a set of shared moral values.[70] In 1476 prostitutes were prohibited from wearing veils and were obligated wear a cloak, under pain of a fine of 10 *lire planete*.[71] In 1478 the special council unanimously agreed that prostitutes ought not to step outside of the brothel without the sign by which they could be readily recognized by all. The sign, it was agreed, ought to be a yellow stripe three fingers in breadth, surrounded with a red fringe or with red cloth within the stripe. It should run across the shoulder and over the bodice or be tied under the bodice. The sign should be worn clearly and firmly tied or attached, and prostitutes should go uncovered without veils ("senza panicelli ne vello sopra la testa") when they left the brothel, under pain of a fine of 40 *soldi* for each case. The measure was written in Italian and published on 1 April 1479 in the brothel and square at Faustino, with the understanding that it would take effect within three days.[72] In a similar fashion, at the end of the sumptuary legislation passed in 1503 it was stated that each prostitute or woman of "mala conditione e fama" might wear any of the prohibited garments and jewels, necklaces, and other ornaments without any penalty and that by this means honest and dishonest women might be distinguished.[73]

The city was also concerned to control the space through which prostitutes moved and to prevent them showing themselves in public in a disruptive fashion.[74] In 1449 the Brescian council responded to local concerns about public morals and decorum being threatened by the locations of prostitutes.[75] Statutes published in 1473 included a clause allowing for the expulsion of prostitutes from the city and district on petition from neighbors.[76] The elder of the local *quadra* organization was obliged to keep the streets literally and morally clean by denouncing prostitutes living in his *quadra* or frequenting the streets.[77] In 1476 the special council proposed a range of measures to control the movements of prostitutes. The council unanimously agreed that a brothel ("prostibulum") should not be located in the house in the city owned by the abbey of San Gervasio and that the prostitutes must return to the curia dei fabi on the north side of the *piazza della loggia* where the public brothel stood surrounded by public baths and taverns. The council may have been concerned that the property occupied by the prostitutes lay on the decorous civic center, and it may also have had the state of the *curia* in mind. The council decreed that prostitutes should not stand, sit, or in any other way loiter on the public streets or in hostelries ("super hostijs hospitum"), under a fine of 10 *soldi planete* (half to be paid to the commune, half to the informer), and on pain of being beaten. They were also prohibited from standing in windows overlooking the street of San Giorgio or in houses close by, on pain of the same fine; honest women were not supposed to appear in public in this way.[78] In reality, as many visual representations of street life in urban Italy suggest, the window was considered a female space.[79]

The innkeepers whose hostelries or inns overlooked the brothel should lower the blinds or hang cloth over any windows and balconies that overlooked the street of San Giorgio or the neighboring houses and were enjoined to use cloth to ensure that guests were not seen by passersby, under pain of 5 *lire planete*. The council also thought it fitting that a cloth be placed by day in the street, or little alley ("calesella"), that went toward the mill and by there to the brothel, so that the brothel might not be seen by passersby or by those washing laundry nearby. A cloth should also be hung up to obscure the entrance hall of the brothel facing onto the street. Indicative of the strategies of resistance and evasion used by these working women is the council decree against guests at inns who kept prostitutes under the pretext that they were maids and the condemnation of prostitutes who owned little houses or other constructions ("casellas sive materiatios") near the street of San Giorgio—those that were discovered would be destroyed and the prostitutes returned to their accustomed place.[80]

The council tried to move the prostitutes out of the center of town at least as early as 1428, probably spurred on by the feeling that the juxtaposition of sacred and profane was undignified. As the urban space was rebuilt and embellished after around 1430, the city fathers would have regarded the removal of the public brothel as in line with the other improvements to the space around the *piazza della loggia*. In fact, the public brothel was turned over to housing the poor who had fled from the countryside, notably the Val Camonica, to escape plague during 1478–79. It was hoped that their confinement in the building—which accordingly must have been easily secured—would prevent the spread of disease.[81] The prostitutes thus displaced seem to have erected small huts ("casalenge") along the city walls; in 1483 in a more general attempt to bring nocturnal calm to the city the rectors proclaimed that these should be removed and the prostitutes should return to the public place designated for their activities or leave the city entirely.[82]

It seems unlikely that any of these laws were especially effective, given the fact that they had to be repeated or revised at frequent intervals.[83] However, in at least one respect the council succeeded in displacing prostitution from its traditional center. The *spianata* or demolition of churches and monasteries outside the city walls ordered by Venice after 1516 led to the church of San Giuseppe being built on the site of the public brothel. The problem of finding a new location for the "meretrices publicae" exercised the Brescian council in 1519 and 1520, and wishing to avoid the scandals and disease spread by these women, the council sought a new brothel where the Venetian rector could force the prostitutes to live.[84] The council seems to have managed to move the prostitutes to the poorer northwestern part of the city—dominated by manual workers—in the *contrada* of Cirondella and to an area between the churches of Sant'Andrea or Sant'Apollonio in the hills to the east of the city walls.[85]

The problem of lavish dress, banquets, masks, and other problematic objects and forms of behavior was not solved to the council's satisfaction during this period, and such markers of status in no way diminished in significance. As for funerals and the council's attempt to control their scale, it appears that these ceremonies were growing ever more elaborate in Renaissance Brescia. Social competition and upward mobility in the city seem to have increased during the fifteenth century, and some Brescians evidently disapproved of this trend on a number of grounds. In particular, the blurring of social distinctions and the rise of parvenus challenging the patrician elite prompted the raft of statutes discussed in this chapter and resulted in some very elaborate arguments flowing from the pens of the humanistically educated and articulate citizens of Brescia—to be discussed in the next chapter.

PART FOUR

COOPERATION
AND CONFLICT

CHAPTER EIGHT

A Funerary Fracas

AT THE BEGINNING of the sixteenth century the Brescian humanist and priest Carlo Valgulio and an anonymous writer, sometimes identified with the humanist Elia Capriolo, wrote in defense of a statute that was proposed and enacted by the council so as to avoid the "ruinous costs and useless customs" of many funerals. This statute laid down rules for the use of mourning clothes, regulated the number of clergy, candles, crosses, and masses for the dead, and prohibited public displays of grief. The statute might have remained an object of purely local historical interest were it not for the fact that the Dominicans, who often played roles in these funerals, complained about the statute and argued that it infringed on ecclesiastical liberty.[1] The humanists replied with skillful treatises that rose above the narrow confines of a local fracas to address much broader political and philosophical questions.

The rituals of death and burial have always been imbued with significant meaning in human society, and a flourishing genre of *ars moriendi* literature in late medieval and Renaissance Italy testifies to acute concerns about the final stages of death, when the soul of the dying man or woman was thought to be subject to demonic attacks.[2] Before around 1350 the funeral procession itself was "an unobtrusive and secular act in which the honouring of the deceased prevailed over the expression of regret." However, by the late Middle Ages the small group of relatives and friends escorting the body to its place of burial had swollen to "a solemn ecclesiastical procession" comprising priests, monks, the poor, orphaned children, and members of the four mendicant orders: Carmelites, Augustinians, Franciscans, and Dominicans.[3]

This proliferation of pomp reflects the growing wealth of Italy and also the fact that the funeral was not simply an occasion for easing the passage of the soul with intercessory gestures and expressions of grief but was also a public ritual designed to reflect prevalent civic mores and to reinforce the social status and solidarity of the family of the deceased. Funerals offered noble or ruling families the opportunity to enhance their prestige through the richness of their mourning clothes or palls and the numbers of mourners hired to attend. In the same way, costly and showy funerals allowed parvenus the chance to secure a place for themselves among the social elite and to buy "social respectability."[4]

The increasing size of funerals during the later Middle Ages may have also been due to the fact that the death disbursements made by the testator and his or her family toward the cost of a funeral were a form of alms vital to provide for prayers and other forms of intercession in order to reduce the time the soul of the deceased spent in purgatory. These payments formed a key part of the income of the poor, the confraternities, and the mendicant orders. Originally these orders had forbidden the common ownership of property, and members had relied on begging or work for their living. However, by the end of the Middle Ages they had grown rich on the basis of numerous legacies.[5] This disparity between mendicant ideals of poverty and the reality of Dominican or Franciscan wealth was widely resented and encouraged the spread of the new observant groups. Many felt that the Dominicans were too worldly and no longer as interested in receiving charity as in exacting fees for their services at funerals as mourners or torchbearers.

Ostentatious displays of grief were considered shameful and unmanly, and the display of costly garments was often criticized.[6] Therefore, the elaboration of funerary procedures became a target for moralists and legislators. Sumptuary legislation not only regulated costly clothing (especially for women), as noted, but also targeted the conduct of men and women at weddings and funerals. Funerals featured high on the list of concerns of Italian legislators between 1200 and 1500.[7] In part, statutes prohibited uncontrolled weeping at funerals, the tolling of bells, the carrying of excessive numbers of torches or candles, and the misuse of shrouds. It has been suggested that these limitations on the numbers, behavior, and dress of those attending weddings and funerals in medieval Italy were also closely connected to attempts to control gatherings of nobles and to defuse various groups' potentially disruptive political, social, or economic ambitions.

Such limits were promulgated in the context of relatively rapid economic changes and the consequent upward mobility of the wealthy families who were muscling in on communal government during the thirteenth century.[8]

Sumptuary legislation was often an important feature of the relationship between episcopal and communal authority. City governments and bishops could work together to enforce laws, as in Perugia in 1485, when women who broke the sumptuary legislation were made liable to excommunication and other penalties. However, the potential for conflicts between the Church and the state was great in the case of funerary legislation, where "the line of demarcation [between lay and ecclesiastical matters] became more obscure." Milanese funeral regulations adopted by Bergamo in the middle of the fourteenth century determined the number of clergy who could assist at funerals depending on the proximity of the burial to a mendicant convent. Similar restrictions on numbers of clergy were made in Pisa, Aquila, Padua, and Faenza in the fourteenth and fifteenth centuries. Despite this, there is very little evidence of clerical protests against the infringement of ecclesiastical liberty. Besides Brescia, it seems that the only other Italian dispute along these lines occurred at Parma in 1421 in response to a statute prohibiting excessive funeral expenditure. This statute was examined by the College of Judges and approved in its amended form by the ruler of Parma, Filippo Maria Visconti. The statute noted that many laypeople had spent inordinate amounts on funerals—some willingly but others through a sense of duty or in order to avoid embarrassment and not to appear greedy. Henceforth the bier was to be accompanied through the street and adorned in the church with no more than four candles of less than three pounds in weight, and only parish clergy with one cross could attend while the bell of the parish church, and no others, rang out.[9]

In Brescia, by contrast, the strength of local mendicants meant that a battle raged over the perceived assault on clerical prerogatives. Carlo Valgulio and the anonymous author who responded to their protests accused the Dominicans of demanding a "fee" for their services at funerals rather than humbly accepting alms that were freely given. In turn, the Dominicans argued that the statute interfered with the Christian duty to make intercessions for the dead and therefore threatened their souls. The humanists were stung by such Dominican greed and pride and alarmed by the competitiveness between laypeople; the humanist pamphlets to be discussed here are full of moral censure and hostility toward excessive or false outward displays of piety and wealth. Valgulio and the anonymous author portray themselves as Brescian patriots who wish to strengthen the bonds of civil society and prevent the corrosive spread of vice, avarice, and ambition. While their hope for the purification and renewal of society is based on medieval traditions, notably Augustinianism and the preaching of the spiritual Franciscans (who are praised in the pamphlets), the writers' outlook is also infused with a distinctly humanist emphasis on private and public virtues married to faith in the service of the Ciceronian res publica. While the Dominicans have encouraged laypeople to concentrate on externals only, Valgulio and his fellow writer want the Brescians to return to true inner virtue. Valgulio explains why this is so important to civic identity: "we are striving for moderation, integrity, virtue, and fairness—the sources of true honor and of public and private welfare, and the bonds of civil association and fellowship."[10]

Carlo Valgulio and Elia Capriolo—if he was indeed the anonymous author of one of the pamphlets—were descended from the most ancient and noble families in the Bresciano. They were also among the most prominent of the Brescian humanists, and they composed their squibs against the Dominicans as privileged players in the intellectual and political life of Brescia. The pamphlets that were hammered into shape in the heat of the funerary controversy and arguments with the Dominicans in Brescia therefore reflect some of the preoccupations and assumptions of the new urban oligarchy, the ecclesiastical hierarchy appointed by Venice, and the popular and powerful mendicant orders. The council may have been happy to encourage and sponsor the mendicants in their midst, but it is apparent that for some Brescians, there were limits to the mendicants' reliance on public wealth.

The Dispute

The immediate origins of the Brescian dispute lay in a proposal made by the special council on 28 June 1505 to limit the people's superfluous funereal expenses by making people observe the existing statute restricting expenditure and behavior and adding clauses prohibiting anyone dressed as the poor or any member of a religious confraternity, apart from that of the deceased, from attending a funeral.[11] The city's first surviving sumptuary legislation, passed sometime between 1200 and 1276, concerned funeral ceremonies. These laws limited the number of candles permitted at funerals to two and the number of crosses to one and condemned the useless expenses incurred for mourning clothes. Subsequent legislation restricted expenditure on mourning clothes, the number of large crosses, and the number of clerics and religious attending funerals; and in 1477 and again in 1495 the council condemned the custom of hanging black cloth on the houses of those in mourning.[12] The anonymous author was well aware that there had been previous attempts to limit funeral expenditure in Brescia:

> And the fact that the bishop of Brescia (either del Monte or De Domenichi) writes that by his own influence he got the Brescians to reject the same statute has little bearing on the case. They yielded (assuming that what people say was true) to the influence of an outstanding bishop who brings great benefits to the people, and I think that perhaps (as is very likely) the bishop promised to use the same influence to ensure that religious would voluntarily accept the city's forthcoming limit on funeral expenses, not by reducing the number of funeral attendants, but by agreeing to be satisfied with less than the usual fee. The hoped-for result was that, with the expenditure supposedly determined by the statute's intention being weighed against whatever the number of religious might be, due account would be taken of the Brescians' intention and of the churchmen's honor and dignity.[13]

It appears that an almost identical statute had been enacted in 1473 but had remained a dead letter until the devastating epidemics of influenza and plague in 1477–79.[14]

Like those of its predecessor, the origins of the new statute lay in the fear that an inflation of funerary expenditure could ruin many Brescians.[15] This inflation in donations and other expenditure was said to be caused by three local factors: a sharp peak in mortality linked to an epidemic of influenza ("mazzucho" or "mal di mazucho"); the ambition and competitiveness of Brescians; and the greed of the mendicant orders, especially the Dominicans. As the anonymous author explained:

> At a time when the Brescian people were beset by two disastrous and deplorable calamities—an unbearably protracted famine, and a fatally virulent fever which no medical treatment could alleviate—and when funerals were so frequent that wherever in the city you looked you could see funerals, grief, and mourning regardless of sex and age, with lamentation partly for the deceased, partly for those almost starved to death: then it was that, exhausted and afflicted by such calamities, people were seized by an inordinate passion for obsequies. With the competition for funerals growing so increasingly heated that some citizens borrowed money at interest from the Jews and ran up huge debts, because of some custom or other—due to rivalry for a supposed honor—large squads of brothers and the other type of clergy were summoned to these obsequies: a breed so uncompromising that amid the tears and groans of the deceased's relatives, and amid people's deaths, they would sometimes fight with each other. (*Defensio*, sig. Aiir)

He later specifies that the costs of handing alms (or "fees" as he calls them) to the funeral escort of mendicant "brothers" led many people into debt:

That fee was handed over even by unwilling donors, but owing to a sort of respect for the custom no one wanted to be seen as the prime mover in abolishing it—or rather, no one looked to his own interests, lest he seem less honorable or respectable than someone else to whom he considered himself equal or superior, and day by day rivalry, coupled with expenditure, grew so great that many people ran up a huge debt because of funerals. That this is so is proved by the joy and acclamation with which all orders greeted the decree's proclamation. (sig. Aivv)

It is therefore not surprising that the Dominicans objected to this apparent attack on their ecclesiastical liberty and a lucrative source of their income, and they refused absolution to anyone who observed the law. In April 1506 the Dominicans stated their case in a pamphlet entitled *Inquiry as to Whether the Statutes about Death Disbursements Quoted Below Go against Church Freedom.*[16] They also appealed for support to Pope Julius II at the beginning of February 1507.[17] A few days later the pope granted the bishop of Brescia and his vicar-general, Marco Saraco, powers to investigate the matter.[18] The commune had already responded to the Dominican objections by appointing five "wise and honest citizens" to determine whether the statute infringed ecclesiastical liberty.[19] These five wise men rapidly, and not very surprisingly, came to the conclusion that the statute was good and valid and did not infringe ecclesiastical liberty, and they were granted powers to defend it.[20] Consequently, the amended statute was confirmed by substantial majorities of the general council.[21] The episcopal commission, which moved with "leaden foot" ("pede plumbo"), as the final report put it, took the syndics' decision into account and held meetings with Fra Girolamo, the Dominican representative. Finally, the archbishop confirmed the statute's validity, declaring that it merely concerned funeral ceremony and not spiritual affairs per se.[22]

Matters should have rested there, but the Dominican appeal to the pope was found to contain words insulting to the archbishop and to the honor and dignity of the city.[23] The prior of the convent of San Domenico, Don Agostino de Moris, was therefore ordered to appear before the Venetians, who supported the decision of the syndics, and was forced to concede in October 1508 that his fraternity and all the other religious orders in the city would conform to the decree in its final form.[24] The special council seems to have aimed a final dig against the Dominicans two weeks later when it agreed that the names of anyone tonsured or in holy orders who committed crimes, including "diabolical deceptions," or led immoral or shameful lives should be entered in a special book.[25]

The anonymous author may be making an oblique reference to the Dominicans' appeal and their impolitic insults when he begins his pamphlet

with an ironic reference to the "shining example" the Dominicans have set
by their writings and actions:

> They have not, however, done this with the idea and intention of laying bare
> their own diseased minds, which they take exceptionally great care to conceal
> by every possible device: rather, they did it in order to accuse the city of Bre-
> scia, most moderate, economical, and devotedly supportive of true religion as
> it is, of an impious and despicable crime, to render it hateful to the apostolic
> see, and to stir up the whole of Christendom against it. (*Defensio*, sig. Aiir)

Furthermore, he describes the Dominicans' pamphlet, containing these insults, as being "sent to every nation" (sig. Aivr). This pamphlet, as noted,
written by an anonymous author (or authors), summarizes the Dominican
position, quotes the clauses of the statute that outline the penalties for the
use of more than twenty-four clergy at funerals and place limits on the
number of crosses to be carried.[26] The pamphlet argues that the statute
was prompted by a desire to "cheat" or "bind" the clergy.[27] In fact, the
author argues, laypeople do not have power over churches or any right to
alienate ecclesiastical property in this way, and he outlines the grounds for
the excommunication of anyone who has drafted, supported, or attempted
to enforce the statute. The penalties the statute imposes will prevent the
employment of the "balm" of almsgiving—one method for laypeople to
make some provision for their souls. The statute also bars clergy from receiving the benefit of charity and interferes with their rightful duty to attend funerals. Finally, and perhaps most outrageously, it permits laypeople
to judge their superiors and to second-guess the motives of clerics:

> [G]iven that the extravagance which exists in regard to funerals did exist, and
> that it nevertheless existed in regard to spiritual matters or spiritual adjuncts,
> still laypeople would by no means be able to deal with funerals. Otherwise it
> would follow that in everything they could be the judges of clergy and of the
> supreme pontiff, since they could easily interpret everything as evil and ex-
> travagant; and they would become judges of secret thoughts which derive
> from the mind alone.[28]

The Dominican arguments rest on scripture, which encourages and even
enjoins almsgiving,[29] and—most important—on canon law and the interpretations of an array of eminent medieval canon and civil lawyers such as
Panormitanus (Niccolò de' Tudeschis), Hostiensis (Henricus de Segusio),
and Alberico da Rosciate of Bergamo. Parts of three papal decretals are
fundamental to the Dominican case: Innocent III's decretal *On Ordinances;*[30] the final chapter of the decretal issued at the Fourth Lateran
Council *On Not Alienating the Church's Property;*[31] and the decretal de-

fining the four ways of releasing the souls of the departed: by the offerings of priests, by the prayers of saints, by the alms of loved ones, or by the fasting of relatives.[32] The Dominican case revolves around these pronouncements and the supporting scholastic glosses.

The Dominicans' pamphlet argues that "death disbursements" for a number of clergy, candles, money, and other matters related to funerals are a form of Aristotelian "munificence" (as in *Nicomachean Ethics* 4.2.1–19) and should be made freely by each testator without the despotic and unlawful interference of the government. The pamphlet rebuts the argument that the statute prohibits one and not all types of almsgiving by affirming that the statute is nevertheless an infringement of the general principles laid down by divine, papal, and imperial law and by pointing out that an inferior power can never legislate against a superior such as the Church. Following Saint Augustine, the pamphlet's author admits that extravagant funerals do give more comfort to the living than the dead, but such extravagance, which includes the wearing of black mourning clothes, must be distinguished from the things "conducive to the relief of souls" listed in the decretal. Such "solaces for the living" are discountenanced by the Church and are not, in any case, the main focus of the Dominicans' attack.[33]

The Dominicans' rejection of the funerary statute was probably made with some confidence of success, since the alienation of church property by the laity was clearly proscribed by canon law and the bishop of Brescia himself had rejected the enforcement of a similar earlier statute. The Dominicans' intemperate language and their decision to use the printing press as a weapon in the war of words may also be indicative of their sense of self-righteous indignation. However, their excommunication of any Brescian who proposed or implemented the 1505 statute provoked rage among some inhabitants of the city, and the council was forced to take into account this popular reaction. Moreover, the Dominicans' pamphlet may have misjudged its intended audience, for it is a typical piece of scholastic commentary and often punctuated with pomposity. In short, it is just the type of inelegant, unlettered text that angered humanists trained to express their thoughts in the Ciceronian rhetorical tradition.[34] The two Brescian humanists rose to the defense of the statute and the reputation of the city did so with considerable style and panache.

The Pamphlet War

The anonymous pamphlet on the funerary dispute is an ironic, mocking, and occasionally rambling rebuttal of the Dominicans' specific arguments.

It bears an official-sounding imprimatur that seems to indicate that its contents were commissioned and approved by the communal council and the episcopal vicar.[35] After an introduction in which the author describes the miseries endured by the Brescians and sets the tone of high moral outrage at their mistreatment by the Dominicans, the first section considers the Dominicans' claim that the banning of one method of almsgiving effectively abolishes divine law and subverts the injunction to give alms. In the second section the writer examines human law and the argument that the statute overturns an imperial indult allowing Christians to bequeath money and property to the Church, holy men, and the needy. In the third and longest section he considers the relationship between the religious and the secular worlds and their respective claims over property.

A clear thread running through the entire text is a belief that the true Christian way of life embraces virtues such as humility, tenderness, humanity, pity, charity, modesty, meekness, piety *(pietas)*, and compassion *(misericordia)* (*Defensio*, sigs. Aiiir, Aivv–Avr, Avr). The Dominicans, by their attack on the Brescians, their poor conduct at funerals, and their self-serving definition of alms (amounting to little more than a "fee"), have shown themselves to have no claim to these Christian virtues. Indeed, the author even goes so far as to argue that the Dominicans are harmful to both the human body and the body politic. He notes that during the recent famine they had "full granaries" when everyone else in Brescia was starving, yet they refused to help the people who had already given them so much by way of alms. For this injustice, greed and lack of civic duty, the Dominicans should be driven into exile (sigs. Aiiir–v; compare sigs. Aiir–v and Aivr). Moreover, he alleges that the Dominicans tortured and terrorized old women in their inquisitorial activities against witchcraft in the Val Camonica (discussed later) and that in fact they themselves "may plead and pray for frequent funerals and our deaths, and may achieve them forcibly by means of certain magical prayers!" (sig. Avr).

The basis for the central argument of the pamphlet is set out in the first section, where the author explains that the statute does indeed ban one method of almsgiving. However, he argues that the gift of alms should be made freely and without expectation of anything in return, and bestowed on those who need them: "Alms must be free and gratis, not paid for" (*Defensio*, sig. Aiiv).[36] In this way, the money given to the religious orders, who escort a layperson's body to the grave, ought to be considered a fee, as it is given in return for work carried out—work the Dominicans would not undertake without payment. If the Dominicans deny this, he pointedly asks: "Why do you never escort a pauper's corpse to burial?" (sig. Aiiv). Moreover, the order is hardly worthy to receive alms, since they have acquired great wealth through confessions, the "lucrative poaching of wills," and "trapping widowers and widows."[37] In any case, the statute does not prohibit other ways of giving alms: anyone who has some tenderness, humanity, charity, and pity in their heart will be able to act with true piety and compassion toward those in need. By contrast, the Dominicans want to offer their prayers for the deceased in public places and with due care taken to extract the maximum profit. They are the ones, therefore, who most militate against almsgiving by not practicing it.

In the second section the anonymous writer goes on to refute the argument that the Brescian statute infringes an imperial indult made by the sixth-century emperor Justinian that permitted people to leave any goods they wished to the Church. He explains that by this indult the emperor indulged testators in allowing them to leave their possessions to the Church, especially to "upright, holy men." However, it is contrary to human and divine law for a person to leave money to the Dominicans or some other order and thereby leave his wife and children to starve. Besides, the Brescians are very generous to the poor, as the existence of the *monte di pietà* (which lent money to the poor at low, or no, interest) demonstrates. In short, the law should agree with divine reason, but it may also be revised to meet new political circumstances. New laws are permitted by the Venetians, so long as they are just, and many valid historical precedents may be found for a law regulating funeral expenditure.

The third section of the argument covers a wide range of matters and contains many digressions and repetitions. The author asserts that the Dominican doctors' definition of "death disbursements" as candle wax, cash, and a group of clergy is far too narrow. It is clear to him that such disbursements consist of *any* bequest to the Church, as the pope intended by his canon prohibiting the use of church property for secular purposes. Therefore, the statute does not prohibit any of the many ways of releasing souls from purgatory, especially as it has been shown that the statute does not prevent *true* almsgiving. An attack follows on those who argue that all property connected with sacred matters, such as a funeral, should be appropriated by the Church. In this way, he says, the supposedly learned Dominican doctors ignore the examples of Christ and the apostles, who gave away their property. He points out that by the following of this logic, "the whole world will be under your jurisdiction—nothing will be ours" (*Defensio*, sig. Avir) and the Dominicans would turn themselves into latter-day Midases. In fact, laypeople can arrange funerals and decide on the number of candles and priests escorting the corpse without destroying the Church's freedom or breaking the papal canon. Consequently, this statute affects only the layperson and does not impinge on religious freedom.

Finally, the pampleteer asserts that the statute is in the Brescians' best interests. The Dominicans argued in their pamphlet that the government should not intervene to deprive private citizens and ordinary people of the power to decide on their own affairs as they wish:

> [A]lthough Titius[38] can prescribe in his *will* that only twenty-four clergy be invited to his funeral, yet a city in general cannot make a *statute* to this effect, because the first diminishes no one's freedom, as the second does. For power in a city is not the despotic type where masters rule over *slaves*, but the statesmanlike type where masters rule over *citizens*, who in many ways are free as regards nearly all their own affairs.[39]

The anonymous writer brushes this legal finagling aside and retorts: "No doubt this is to enable you too to say what Florentine money-lenders usually say when they have financial dealings with some simple, coarse-featured fellow whom in his ignorance they defraud: 'If only there were plenty like you!' He, however, goes away happy, thinking that the moneylender considers him wise" (*Defensio*, sig. Avv). It is true, he concludes, that the bishop of Brescia persuaded the Brescian people that it was in their best interests to reject a comparable statute. However, it is probable that he did this with the understanding that the religious would voluntarily accept a lower fee, which is clearly not the case in this instance.

The anonymous author is an effective and devastating satirist, and his emotions are never allowed to get in the way of his reasonable and accurately aimed intellectual blows. However, his attack is surpassed in cool and calculated intellectual firepower by that of Carlo Valgulio. Valgulio was born in Brescia in around 1434 into an ancient and powerful Guelph family. His father Stefano was a prominent lawyer fluent in both Latin and Greek, and this background no doubt helped Carlo to become expert in both languages.[40] He spent time in Florence and Rome mixing with the humanist elites in those cities and serving in the papal bureaucracy. When he returned to Brescia, he was appointed priest for the parishes of Sant'Andrea in Iseo and Santo Stefano in Salis, and his translations of Greek works were published in the city.[41] He withdrew from public life in 1506 and devoted his remaining years to philosophical contemplation—he was described as despising the rewards of fortune—and to further work of translation and essay writing.[42] His literary output during his retirement was undiminished, and his essays *De sumptibus funerum* and *Contra vituperatorem musicae* were published together in 1509. Valgulio was murdered on 7 January 1517 by the notorious gangster Filipino de' Salis, whose depredations he is said to have criticized.[43] Valgulio may have been the victim of Brescia's acrid politics: he was associated with the Guelph party, and he seems to have been among those who supported—if indeed he was not in fact the author of—a contentious proposal to broaden the social range of the council that was presented to Venice early in 1517 (discussed later).[44] His work on funerals is an eloquent argument in favor of the nobility of virtue, which might also have encouraged hostility from fellow Brescians who valued the nobility of their blood lines.

Valgulio's pamphlet, which was written several years after the publication of the Dominicans' pamphlet and probably just before they finally gave up the struggle in October 1508, is less concerned with replying to the specific arguments of their pamphlet and therefore complements the earlier anonymous pamphlet. Valgulio turns his attention to those who are "battling for a silly, false notion of honor" (*Statutum*, sig. Ar) by arguing that rich and poor should not be buried in the same way and at the same expense. In doing so Valgulio aims many shafts against the Dominicans, whom he accuses of "giving weight to their cause by a religious manner, title, and appearance" only and "deceitfully indoctrinating the ignorant crowd and some simple-minded, superstitious citizens" (sig. Ar). Later in his treatise, Valgulio refers to the "devout scorner of the world" (sig. Aiiiv), those "encased in the shell of religion's outer clothing" but lacking an inner religious sense (sigs Aiiiiv–Avr), and in a similar fashion to "false brothers," and especially one man whose "name and garb [alone] are religious" (sig. Aviv). These attacks should not be understood simply as anticlerical statements but must be interpreted as an introduction to the principal theme of his pamphlet: the uselessness of external honor in comparison with inner virtue. Valgulio asks the reader to consider whether the expense of funerals bears any relation to the true virtue of the deceased. To make his point, he contrasts the corpse, which is merely "food for worms" (sig. Avir), with the lavish spending on prayers, priests, and other ornaments at its burial. He argues that no honor or virtue can be acquired simply by purchasing multiple masses.

Valgulio outlines in three distinct sections the Christian, natural, and legal bases for his view that there is no rank or distinction among the dead. In the first section he attacks wealth and describes how the will of Christ was opposed to worldly honor. In his view, therefore, funeral expenditure is "more truly commerce and usury than alms, since it demands and expects things greater than itself: it demands honor and praise, as being greater" (*Statutum*, sig. Av). In the second section he explains that all men are equal by nature, and the proof of this lies in the fact that men are all physically alike, mortal, and endowed with reason and speech. Therefore, no one is allowed "what another is not" (sig. A2r), and no one should take precedence over anyone else. In the third section Valgulio traces the development of civil laws under the pressure of human evil. He argues that while all men are endowed with reason, this quality is not evenly distributed among men, and there are some who cannot achieve virtue by the free development of their reason. Laws are necessary to check these men who rebel or do not otherwise follow reason and nature. All force for good in human affairs arises from the use of reason—from the "mental virtues which are willed and natural" (sig. A2v). By contrast, external elements, such as the expenditure at issue, are not good or evil in themselves but should only be appraised according to the extent that they are used for good or evil. Therefore, wealth, possessions, "knightly gold," countships, kingdoms, and therefore funeral expenditure cannot "confer praise or censure on their owners and masters: for nothing gives what it does not have" (sig. A2v).

Finally, Valgulio elaborates on his concept of honor and its relationship with virtue. Virtue—which includes loyalty *(pietas)*, faith, hope, charity, justice, temperance, and compassion—is its own reward and does not seek honor. Men may choose to exercise virtue or vice; and honor will be bestowed on a virtuous man by others when they observe him acting in a virtuous way. In a Stoic or Augustinian fashion Valgulio explains that many things such as wealth or poverty are not within men's control and therefore should not be praised or blamed. In fact, there is no "bliss during life" (*Statutum,* sig. Aiiir), according to Christ's principles, so externals should not be honored, except perhaps when performed for the benefit of others, especially the needy (sig. Aiiir–v).

The remainder of the treatise is a fairly consistent variation on these principal themes. Valgulio contrasts emptiness in prayers, masses, and the outward show of funerals with true inner virtue and the honor it incidentally brings.[45] The climax of his discourse, which most clearly reflects the debates in council about the nature of nobility and "civilitas," is reached when he lists the absurd figures on whom empty outward honors have been showered. Some citizens have done what neither God nor nature can and have made the "unlearned learned and bastards legitimate" (*Statutum,* sig. Avr). To make matters worse, honors have been conferred on such lowlifes as tax farmers, castrators, dentists, trumpeters, flautists, and traitors.[46] Valgulio believes it would be better to scorn those "who have virtue's sign on display but lack virtue" (sig. Avv), particularly because such false distinctions lead to social disruption—as the case of costly funerals has demonstrated (sigs Avv–Avir).

Solidarity between the Living and the Dead

The general questions about honor, the proper use of wealth, and the relationship between the living and the dead emerge and interlink in the two humanists' pamphlets. The relationships at stake in this dispute—between the laity and the clergy, and the living and the dead—were based on traditional Christian notions of reciprocity and gift-giving (particularly alms). Like most Renaissance Italians, Valgulio and his fellow writer accepted that the living owed the dead a service and that a proper funeral and prayers of intercession were good works that would also gain spiritual benefits for those left behind. Charity was one of the cardinal Christian virtues and consisted especially of the seven corporal acts of mercy, which included burying the dead. Such acts were supposed to be made freely to those most in need and with no thought of any immediate benefit to the donor except in terms of the contribution the act made to one's salvation. Such charity was often linked with—or indistinguishable from—noble generosity, liberality, and magnificence or public splendor.[47]

As these two pamphlet authors recognize, solidarity between the living and the dead was strengthened in a variety of ways in early modern Europe. For example, confraternities or lay religious companies made some provision for the burial of members, especially those too poor to afford a decent funeral. Such confraternal solaces were canonically approved and were animated by a strong sense of charity.[48] Confraternities received many bequests and donations in return for their presence at funerals, and it appears that an increasing amount of their income was spent on commemorative masses. This phenomenon forms part of a general trend in northern Italy after the Black Death toward more elaborate funerals and forms of memorialization such as tombs, humanist speeches and consolatory works, and printed epitaphs.[49] Testamentary evidence suggests that the number of religious stipulated to attend the body on its way to burial could vary from one or two, to forty Franciscan friars and forty Dominicans or even an entire monastery.[50] By around 1370 Florentine funerals had become comparatively more elaborate affairs, and a century later the number of clergy involved in funerals had markedly increased as observant Franciscans and Dominicans were drawn in from across the city rather than simply from the local parish. By the early sixteenth century it was not uncommon for hundreds of clergy to be involved in the public rites of notable Florentines, and elaborate tombs of the sort condemned by the anonymous pamphleteer—who points out that even pictures and statues of Christ were hardly permitted in churches by the early ecclesiastical authorities (*Defensio*, sig. Avv)—grace almost every northern Italian church.[51]

Some Florentines viewed the brigades of friars as a form of mere earthly glory ("gloria mundana"); others saw their presence as an indicator of great piety. In 1508 the Florentine archbishop Cosimo de' Pazzi denounced clerics who deliberately flocked to burials in search of alms.[52] In 1526 the

Dutch humanist Erasmus satirized a pompous and elaborate funeral in which the body was accompanied by forty-five mendicants, thirty torch-bearers, and twelve professional mourners. In addition, the deceased's horse was draped in black, his arms were on display, and his body was placed in an imposing marble tomb.[53] Funerals probably reached their grandest scale in Italy, and indeed Spain, during the Counter-Reformation, and few were more spectacular than that of Giovanni Battista Borghese in 1610, which was attended by more than twenty cardinals and comprised some extremely elaborate and costly decorations and processions.[54]

It was probably the growing disparity between the funerals of rich and poor, and the marked growth of clerical income from these rites, that led Valgulio to argue that while the dead should not simply be forgotten, the rituals associated with death may nevertheless be of more use to the living than the dead, especially as the living seem very keen to dispose of the corpse underground as quickly as possible. If the dead were really as much revered as the multiplication of priests and prayers indicates, surely the Brescians would lay the bodies out in their houses (*Statutum*, sig. Avir) as the ancient Persians and Egyptians did (sig. Aiiiiv). Characteristically, Valgulio argues that nature does not want such public obsequies, for "rot and decay" set in to all corpses almost immediately (sig. Aiiiiv). Of course, for all his anticlericalism, Valgulio does not go so far as to call for the abolition of all organized religious ceremony. Although he dismisses much almsgiving, he is careful to distinguish the money spent on self-glorification from alms given freely and without thought of personal honor (sigs Av, Aiiir–v). Similarly, he raises the question whether saying a prayer is any good for "purging the souls of the deceased" (sig. Aiiiir). In an echo of the mystical writings of the Neoplatonist Pseudo-Dionysius the Areopagite (ca. 500 CE), Valgulio asserts that prayers "are no good for the dead," although he does accept that "such charity and compassion is good for the living, and very pleasing to God." He objects to prayers said in public by hired priests with "lips and words" alone. This does not mean that priestly intercession should be abolished, for priests might still come to escort corpses for burial, as long as both clerics and laypeople remember their duty to the needy. While such Stoic conceptions could appear cold, rigid, or legalistic, equally they could encourage personal contemplation and inner development. Like Epictetus (fl. 100 CE), whose work he probably knew, Valgulio deprecated the "honors" bestowed on men by others or by external conditions and therefore emphasized the action of inner virtue. As he wrote: "Virtue is reason that is perfect in itself and taken to its peak; from it always flow each person's just, brave, controlled, and generous actions, due respect shown to God, to country, to parents, in short to all mankind (observing the proper priorities) and, of course, towards themselves" (sig. A2v).

However, within fifteen years of the Brescian dispute, Protestant reformers north of the Alps had largely disrupted the power of gift relations in the economy of salvation and the notions of divine obligation and reciprocity that were embodied in the mass, the concept of purgatory, and payments to clergy and confraternal brothers for funeral duties.[55] Martin Luther argued that masses for the dead had simply become opportunities for making money and contrasted the "true Christian work" of serving one's neighbor with the useless endowment of masses encouraged by the "pope's pseudo-priesthood."[56] Luther and other early reformers in Germany, Switzerland, and England accused the Catholic clergy of *Totenfresserei* (feeding on the dead) and argued that endowing intercessions for the dead impoverished widows and children, as well as the poor. In Nikolaus Manuel's satirical play *Die Totenfresser,* which was performed in Bern during Lent in 1523, one of the devourers of the dead is identified as the pope, who exclaims: "Church offerings, weekly, monthly, and annual masses for the dead / Bring us more than enough. / Pity the hardship it inflicts upon the children of the givers!" while a sacristan declares: "I like dead people better than fighting and screwing / They are our food and pay."[57] As part of their assault on purgatory in England in the 1530s evangelicals such as John Bale deplored priests, canons, and monks who "do but fyll their bely / With my swett and labour for ther popych purgatory."[58] A recent study has shown that the funeral, and especially ducal attempts to enforce burial outside the city walls rather than in the crowded and unhealthy mendicant churches, became a flash point for anticlericalism and subsequently conflict between Catholics and Protestants in Leipzig in 1536. Similar disputes arose in other parts of the German empire at the beginning of the sixteenth century. However, even in Protestant Germany or England the evidence that a simplification or purification of funeral rites actually occurred is mixed. Upper-class funerals in England were certainly scaled down after around 1580, and the Puritans were critical of any wasteful extravagance, but in Germany and England the desire for an "honorable" burial meant that bells, palls, candles, crosses, and processions including paupers and guild members persisted with some variations according to social status. Protestants emphasized that such rites were now considered to be solely for the benefit of the living community—not the dead.[59]

It would be wrong to depict Valgulio and the anonymous author simply as Lutherans *avant la lettre*, although it is clear that within a decade or so of this dispute both Erasmian and Lutheran ideas were spreading in Brescia and the surrounding region among patricians and artisans.[60] While the two humanist pamphleteers shared many of the same concerns about the exploitation of popular fears about death and the afterlife, they never rejected the existence of purgatory, as Luther did by 1522, or the right of members of the mendicant orders to be present at funerals. However, like many Lutherans, they emphasized that the solaces associated with funerals were most important as a form of charity toward the living needy rather than as a form of intercession for the dead. In this way, they were in agreement with Augustine that funeral ceremonies "are more for the comfort of the survivors than to assist the dead."[61] They would have despised the assertion made by one Spanish writer in 1536 that the size of a funeral procession was directly related to the time the soul of the deceased spent in purgatory.[62] Above all, they sought to preserve and strengthen the reciprocal relationship between God and men through simpler and more pious devotions and less grasping and public priestly intercessions. The two men wrote in defense of Brescia and outlined the ways the loyal Brescian citizen could ensure a fitting and decent Christian burial for himself. Their arguments in favor of streamlining or simplifying the ceremony and their emphasis on inner virtue and loyalty are made with the examples of Christ, the apostles, and the primitive Church in mind. However, to modern eyes, the most striking and obvious support for their Christianity and their sense of civic solidarity is their humanism.

Christian Humanism and Civic Piety

The possession and use of wealth and sacramentals was a key point of debate for Christians and humanists concerned with renewing and reforming the Church and popular piety throughout the Middle Ages. The anonymous pamphleteer's comment about Christians being forced to borrow from the Jews reveals that the material burden placed on the living by the dead could be intolerable—especially at times of increased mortality such as 1478 or 1505. At the heart of the Christian humanism expressed by Valgulio and his colleague is the fear that laypeople, and indeed the clergy, have been distracted from true and simple faith by such outward observances and trappings. In the fourth book of his *Convivio* (ca. 1304) the poet Dante had argued that nobility was a virtue planted by God in the souls of men and attacked the idea that wealth imbued a man with any kind of nobility. This notion was based on a reading of the ancient philosophers but, like other early humanist ideas about the philosopher's independence from the blows of fortune, may have been influenced by the Franciscan ideal of voluntary poverty and ascetic renunciation of worldly goods.

As Hans Baron has argued, the presiding figure of the early Renaissance, Francesco Petrarch, was "in many respects an ally of the Franciscan spirit" who epitomized this sense of pessimism and despair about worldly matters and dwelled on the philosophical and spiritual. Petrarch was initially attracted to "poverty in honor and moderation," but his Christian asceticism was gradually tempered by the recognition that such poverty and endurance of unsatisfied needs were only suitable for a few and that wealth could actually aid the wise man.[63] However, Petrarch believed that an attitude of indifference to external fortune was the best course to take, since death *had* dominion: it entirely vitiated earthly affairs. At the end of his life he wrote: "Death does not know *imperium,* does not recognize princes, and is the greatest leveler of all."[64] Therefore, he wrote in his dialogue *Insepultus abiiciar* ("Dying in fear of being cast away unburied"), "all rites of burial are designed for the sake of the living."[65] The virtue and good name of a man established through his wise and just actions will be a sufficient memorial.[66]

Hans Baron also argued that the ascetic ideals of Franciscan and Stoic poverty that permeated society after around 1250 and strongly influenced humanist thought in the fourteenth century were challenged by a new justification and praise of civic wealth in the fifteenth century. In 1420 Leonardo Bruni, chancellor of Florence, translated the *Economics* attributed to Aristotle and in this way helped to bolster arguments in favor of the moral and intellectual value of wealth and worldly affairs. Poggio Bracciolini asserted in his work *De vera nobilitate* (ca. 1440) that the Stoic virtue of the wise man was "naked" *(nuda)* and "partial" or "lacking" *(egens)* since "it does not permeate the civic community, it appears deserted, hermit-like."[67] Many humanists subsequently agreed that the well-rounded human being and active citizen could not live by strict Stoic principles, and fifteenth-century civic funeral orations in Florence began to include praise of the deceased on account of his acquisition and use of wealth rather than for his renunciation of "vain worldly goods."[68] It is worth noting that professional humanists and preachers in Brescia provided frequently printed accounts of classical funeral oratory and ideal speeches adapted to different social groups or genders.[69]

Art historians have identified a parallel change of outlook in funerary sculpture: there was "a rejection of Christian concern for the future in favor of pagan glorification of the past." The Renaissance sanctioned "the principle of individual commemoration" and extended such commemoration to the humanist and the bishop as well as the soldier.[70] Indeed, Leonardo Bruni's wish for a simple tomb was ignored by a grateful city, and his tomb in the Franciscan church of Santa Croce has young cherubs holding garlands of vines and fruit over a triumphal arch, with Bruni himself in his chancellor's robes holding a copy of his history of Florence. In a similar fashion, the 1503 tomb of the Bergamasque humanist Giovanni Calfurnio in Padua, exhibiting the iconographic innovations symptomatic of this "international rage" for monumental glory, includes personal biographical elements (an open bookcase, indicating Calfurnio's humanist achievements) and roundels depicting the seven virtues as "character witnesses."[71] The tomb of the Brescian bishop Domenico De' Domenichi in the duomo, sculpted around 1478, bore many classical stylistic elements such as the profiles of Roman emperors. The Martinengo mausoleum that was sculpted and placed in a Brescian church between 1503 and 1516 also incorporated the profiles of Roman emperors, scenes from Roman history and mythology, and depictions of the triumphs of Faith, Fortitude, and Justice. This mausoleum was on an even grander scale than that of the bishop, and the accent of the decoration was on personal virtue, military courage, and strength, as befitted the tomb of a member of the leading feudal and military nobility in the Bresciano.[72]

Humanists in early sixteenth-century Italy were sharply divided over the spiritual and philosophical benefits of wealth and worldly concerns. In Paolo Cortesi's reform treatise *De Cardinalatu* of 1510, this humanist Roman writer prescribed a large household and palace for the average cardinal. For Cortesi, liberality, magnificence, and charity were virtues in that they led to the employment of learned men, the promotion of study, and the relief of the poor through the building of hospitals and monasteries.[73] However, contempt for the world and for worldliness in a civic or ecclesiastical setting could also be compatible with cinquecento humanism. For example, the Venetian humanists and hermits Vincenzo Querini (Fra Pietro) and Tommaso Giustiniani (Fra Paolo) took a tougher line than Cortesi toward church wealth in their reform treatise of 1513, the so-called *Libellus ad Leonem Decem*. The hermits wanted the papal household to provide an example of good conduct for Rome and indeed for the whole world.[74] Querini asserted that ecclesiastical reform should begin with the papal household, which was the largest of the Roman courts, comprising some seven hundred people by this time (it had doubled in size since Pius III's reign ten years previously).[75] The members of Leo's household who were not performing necessary occupations, particularly women, should return home, and his entire household be reduced to one-third its present size. Leo should also remove all gold and silk hangings from private and public rooms and his own bed and give them up for holy purposes.

The common inheritance of Christian humanists such as Petrarch, Bruni, and Valgulio was the body of writing left by the ancient Stoic philosophers.

Valgulio's pamphlet contains many Stoic elements, such as disdain for external fortune; the idea of virtue as its own reward; and the assumption that the divinely ordered universe is accessible to human understanding, so that man's perception of the rational order of the universe tells him a good deal about the nature and will of God, and consequently that man's reason forms the main link between himself and God. It is notable, then, that Valgulio does not write in the guise of a puritanical preacher, a new Isaiah or Ezekiel, or even in the strict tradition of Augustine. The tone and substance of his pamphlet is more humanist and Stoic than Augustinian: thus, the reference to God's hatred of sin, especially pride, that Valgulio makes at the end of his treatise is uncharacteristic and reads more like an afterthought than the coda to an exhortatory sermon (*Statutum*, sig. Avir).

Rather, writing as a humanist and a Brescian patriot Valgulio seeks to bond civil society together in recognition of the preeminence of virtue, which is the perfection of reason. Valgulio's debt to Cicero is clear here: he argues that the exercise of virtue must encourage fellowship among men, as well as brave, controlled, and generous actions, and the due respect shown to God, to country, to parents, and to all humanity (*Statutum*, sigs. Av–A2v). For Valgulio, loyalty heads the list of virtues, and such societal obligations or "considered action" in a civic setting was considered by Cicero superior to "prudent reflection" (sig. Aiiir). In a similar fashion, the anonymous writer echoes Cicero's discussion of Solon's tough funerary laws and emphasizes the beneficial effects of such just and reasonable laws on society (*Defensio*, sig. Aivr). The anonymous author and Valgulio agree that the Dominicans and the ambitious Brescians have become prey to vice and that there is a danger that this will lead to civil dissolution. As Valgulio says: "For what is an unwillingness to live on equal terms with the rest, and according to the same decrees and ordinances of the city whose parts and members you are—what else is it but a rupturing of civic association, a rending of parts from their whole, and of members from their body, and a desire to lord it over others as wild beasts do, relying on brute strength?" (*Statutum*, sig. Avv).

As their contributions to the funerary fracas demonstrate, Valgulio and his fellow pamphleteer abhorred the way the demands of a conventionally good burial could lead to clerical exploitation, the commemoration of false virtues, and the spread of vice. The anonymous author argued that the Dominicans employed "tunnels of guile and trickery, and catapults of hell-fear" (*Defensio*, sig. Aiiv) and were encouraging corrosive ambition and competition for false honors among the Brescians: in short, they had fallen far from the original intentions of Saint Dominic and were threatening both the city of man and the city of God. In contrast, this writer promoted the true Christian virtues of humility, tenderness, humanity, pity, charity, modesty, meekness, piety, and compassion and punningly praised the observant Franciscans for their "angelic" way of life (sig. Aiiiv).

These Christian virtues were also supported by humanist studies: in particular Stoic philosophy and the concept of a Ciceronian res publica in which virtuous men, loyal toward Brescia and Venice, could live well and achieve happiness in public life. The anonymous author therefore praised the Brescians for their good public works such as the foundation of the *monte di pietà* and the hospital, and Valgulio offered more obviously Ciceronian virtues such as loyalty, faith, justice, and magnanimity in support of the funerary statute and its aims. Both men agreed that these virtues could be expressed through a moderate attachment to the solaces of prayer and almsgiving at funerals and that in this way civil society would remain well-ordered, pious, and secure. The image of integration, balance, and order that was promoted, for example, by the severe architectonic order of the Renaissance tomb also masked deeper anxieties about social disorder.[76] In this way, such Christian humanist concerns with loyalty, civic duty, and purity were also compatible with the normative drive of sumptuary legislation and civic puritanism discussed in the previous chapter. Legislators and preachers prohibited social practices that led to luxury and other vices and in a few dramatic instances such as Savonarolan Florence tried to realize a theocratic vision of government that was highly inimical to conflict or change.

Valgulio's strong sense of civic duty and the nobility of virtue, or *scientia,* may have led him to make his critique of the oligarchic and increasingly self-styled noble government of Brescia seven years after he published his pamphlet on funerals. In 1509 he attacked the "disloyal, unjust, proud, grasping, greedy, cruel, insolent, and ignorant" man, whether knight, count, or king, and scorned those who handed out the "badges" of virtue (*Statutum*, sig. Avr). Both authors ridiculed the rigidity of social conventions in funerary practice, while Valgulio also lambasted the tax-farmers, dentists, musicians, and traitors on whom empty badges of honor had been conferred. It seems highly probable that the concepts of duty, piety, and honor lauded by Valgulio may have been outlined with educated and well-born men at the heart of the Brescian council in mind. However, it is also possible that the emphasis on the ennobling qualities of virtue subsequently led Valgulio to write in favor of the widening of the council to men of true merit, even if they were artisans, and the exclusion of those who ministered to men's pleasure, such as butchers, tailors, dancers, perfumiers, and gamers. It is surely a tragic irony that it may well have been his identification with these ideals that brought about Valgulio's own violent death and funeral.[77]

These pamphlets do not simply open a window onto a forgotten funerary fracas; they also reveal a great deal about Renaissance funerary practices, the relationship between clergy and laity on the eve of the Reformation, and the nature of elite political, social, and religious attitudes during the Renaissance. They also hint at the considerable tensions that existed within the social and political body of Brescia as it struggled to defend its ideology and identity and maintain some degree of regional autonomy in the shadow of Venice on the eve of war: in short, they tell us a great deal about the meaning of death and life in a Renaissance city.[78] The evidence brought to light in this chapter is also a testimony to the relative strength and independence of Brescian cultural life and its reforming piety.[79] Such social rigidity—in theory and practice—may have helped the city to weather a potentially destabilizing, if relatively minor, conflict over funerals; but the "constitutional pact" with Venice that was founded on trust in Venetian virtues and Brescian loyalty was evidently weakened by serious internal social conflicts and was subsequently blown apart by the guns of France.[80]

In the next chapter I delve further into the debilitating religious, social, and political fault lines that ran through Brescia and clearly emerged with the French occupation in 1509. The Jews were a tolerated minority in Brescian society, but their presence often provoked contention, fear, even violence. As noted, groups like prostitutes and Jews were contained and stigmatized in Brescia, as elsewhere in Italy, during the Middle Ages and Renaissance. However, the treatment of Jews in Brescia was complicated by the fact that they were subjects of Venice and it afforded them some toleration. Furthermore, the monetary and fiscal subjection that Brescia experienced under Venetian rule placed huge pressures on the local economy, in which Jews played a vital role. The disputes about the Jewish presence that punctuated the council's discussions during this period were therefore brought to the very doors of the Venetian halls of government and often strained relations between the two cities.

CHAPTER NINE

Jewish Life

I N THE COURSE of the funerary fracas discussed in the previous chapter, one of the accusations made against the Dominicans was that their greed brought them into an unholy alliance with the Jews of the city. The anonymous humanist writer described the initial Dominican reaction to the statute passed by the council with scorn:

> When the decree was published these brothers, seeing their profit somewhat diminished (as though pigs were to lose some portion of their usual acorns), first began to grunt and grumble, then made common cause with the wise men of the synagogue and compiled a book which they published, the work of many months and of all the brothers of that order who had any reputation among them for learning.[1]

The suggestion that the Jews were involved in defending the Dominicans' exploitation of good Brescian citizens, especially the poor, reflects a common stereotype of Jewish avarice but is also indicative of another major fracture running through Brescian society that affected the formation of civic identity. In this chapter I reconstruct the struggle between Venice and Brescia to define and control the Jews in their midst on the basis of detailed and revealing documentation. Just like the witches (discussed in the next chapter), the Jews were subject to clashing jursidictions and vulnerable to persecution fueled by mendicant preaching and tales of gruesome and dramatic events just beyond the Alps. Christians defined themselves and their faith through the vilification of Jews in order to create a unified Christian social body. This vilification encompassed images, texts, and other forms of ritual or symbolic violence but could also erupt into physical attacks.

The history of the Jews in Renaissance Brescia should not be read entirely through the Christian records of limited toleration and persecution; a more nuanced and balanced view of the Jewish contribution to Brescian civic identity can also be reached by noting the strength and persistence of their community. Accordingly, the findings I present in this chapter go some way toward supporting Robert Bonfil's view that Jews and Christians in Renaissance Italy lived in a sort of creative tension with one another, with difference rather than integration or acculturation the dominant cultural force in their lives. The Brescian evidence suggests that Jews were an important "Other" in local society and that Jewish life was highly precarious and uncertain throughout this period as Venetian and Brescian desires, prejudices, and priorities clashed.[2]

Toleration and Persecution

Renaissance Italy was peppered with small Jewish communities that were tolerated by princes or other local powers in return for the Jews' payment of special taxes, provision of specialist services, and acceptance of a variety of forms of stigmatization. The marginalization of Jews was a function of a toleration such that their presence in Christian society served to highlight and offer a critique of Christian spiritual and material wealth. Toleration was also extended to the Jews in recognition of the fact that, as Saint Augustine had observed, they had preserved the original laws and prophecies announcing Christ, and that it was thought that they would be converted at the end of time. Spiritual toleration also had economic benefits for Christian rulers, since Jews had long acted as moneylenders in place of Christians, for whom usury, or the lending of money at interest, was considered a sin and had been condemned by canon law since the thirteenth century.[3]

In the course of the fifteenth century the citizens of Verona, Padua, and Mantua who were in need of usurious services consulted their bishops or sought assurances from Rome that the presence of Jews in their communities would not lead to excommunication. However, the excommunication of the Marquis of Mantua for tolerating Jews in Mantuan territory suggests that the papal attitude toward Jewish moneylenders and Jewish-Christian contact could take a hard line during the fifteenth century. Moroever, the warnings issued by mendicant preachers like Bernardino da Siena, Alberto da Sarteano, Roberto Caracciolo, and Giovanni da Capistrano were consonant with papal pronouncements on the subject and helped to shape debates in many town halls and squares.[4] For example, in rejecting a proposal by the special council of Brescia to allow the admission of Jews to help relieve poverty in the mid-fifteenth century, the general council cited the anti-Semitic preaching of Bernardino of Siena and Alberto Sarteano and described Jews as a public disease and waste matter best kept far from the city and from any contact with Christians.[5]

The tension between toleration and economic necessity caused acute problems in Renaissance Italy. However, the cities subject to Venice were in an especially difficult position, for in all the territories conquered by the Venetians a ban on the local production of coins was imposed, the circulation of non-Venetian specie was restricted, and Venetian coinage stamped with the lion of Saint Mark was introduced. Around the middle of the fifteenth century Venice responded to a bullion famine, increased war expenses, and high demand for coinage in the mainland by issuing large amounts of small change and debased coins. In 1447 the Senate ordered almost half a million coins in small value ("piccoli") from the Venetian mint for Brescia and explicitly stated that this should be done in a way that would not drain the resources of the capital. Brescia was obliged to send gold and silver to Venice and received debased coinage in return.[6] Therefore, false and foreign money circulated widely in the *terraferma,* and Venice was eventually forced to recognize foreign currency and to institute monetary reform to meet local demands. It is no surprise to find the Venetian Senate condemning the quantity of false small coins ("quantitas parvulorum falsorum") in circulation in Brescia at around this time.[7] In Brescia the dearth of ready money also seems to have benefited the illicit moneylenders and loan sharks known as "stochizari."

It was in 1441, as Brescia recovered from the depredations of the recent siege by Milanese forces and the interest rate charged by loan sharks soared to 80 percent that the Brescian council considered the admission of Jews into the city or *districtus* (*contado*). The council, just as its counterparts in Verona and Padua had done, agreed to write to the pope with a request for a license to allow Jews into Brescia in order to lend money at the rate of 12–15 percent per annum.[8] Over the next few years, as the interest rate imposed by the loan sharks fell only marginally, the council continued to debate the question, weighing the danger of excommunication for permitting usury against the desirability of expelling the loan sharks. The Brescian special council, prompted by Jewish requests to act as moneylenders in the city, sent an advocate to Rome to seek a license for Jews to lend money in Brescia while a group of four clerics were appointed to consider the matter. However, though the lack of money and the threat of loan sharks was explained to the general council, the proposal to admit Jews to lend money was narrowly rejected, as was a subsequent offer of a loan of 10,000 ducats made to the city by a Jew acting on behalf of Venice.[9]

The fortunes of the Jews in Venetian territory were strongly marked by local discussions of this nature. These debates were complicated not only by the clash of religious priorities but also by the conflict of jurisdiction and political authority. Accordingly, the case of Brescian Jews can illuminate the troubled relationship between center and periphery in the Venetian *terraferma*. It is important to emphasize that the decisions made by the Venetian government, and especially the Council of Ten, were key in determining the degree of tolerance that was extended to Jews throughout the *terraferma*, since Jews here were directly subject to Venice rather than the local authorities.[10] This direct subjection to Venice explains why the Brescian privileges presented to the Senate during the first century of Venetian rule usually contained a clause concerned with the Jews—calling for Jews, characterized in harsh terms as persecutors of the Christian faith and enemies of the city, to be debarred from lending money and living in Brescian territory without license. One of the clauses in the privileges Venice granted in 1428 acceded to a Brescian desire to be protected from alleged Jewish depredations and to be excused from any violent actions against the Jews—presumably in the course of the recent struggle with the Visconti—on account of zeal for the Venetian cause.[11] Therefore, just as Jews were largely tolerated in princely Mantua and Ferrara for the medical and financial services they provided, as well as the taxes they were obliged to pay in return for their privileges of residence and financial operations, Venice followed a relatively tolerant line with regard to the Jewish presence in its mainland empire. As the Brescian humanist and councillor Ubertino Pusculo caustically observed around 1480:

> Since you [i.e., Jews] most savagely persisted in this madness [of denying Christ], and felt no sorrow for your boundless sin, it was right, not that you should hope for a return to a better state, but that, dispersed into all lands, you should live on the proceeds of usury, with princes as your servants. They do not protect you for love, detested as you are by their peoples, whom you torture with usury. Only the money—drawn from usury—that you pay to your masters saves you from an evil doom.[12]

Pusculo was writing in the aftermath of a case of the ritual murder of a small child, Simon, that was blamed on the Jews of Trent, but his sentiments were certainly shared by his fellow Brescians.

A significant moment in the history of Venetian tolerance of its Jewish subjects occurred in 1464, when the Council of Ten, which was claiming increasing authority over the affairs of the mainland empire, confirmed the judgment of the influential papal legate in Venice, Cardinal Bessarion, that Jews ought to be allowed to reside in Venetian territory, have some contact with Christians, and therefore licitly act as bankers.[13] Bessarion hoped that such contact would lead to Jewish conversions, and the Council of Ten doubtless judged Jewish bankers a convenient solution to the problems of financial liquidity and a good source of fiscal income. While this ruling did not lay down the basis for a consistently tolerant attitude on the part of the Venetian authorities in every local dispute (and indeed Venice sometimes acted to appease local concerns), there does seem to have been a desire on Venice's part to protect Jews in its territories from persecution that might drive them elsewhere.

As noted, Venetian desires frequently met with local hostility or obstruction, and the case of the Jews was no exception to this pattern. In general, local opposition to the Jews and many *terraferma* towns' calls for restrictions to be placed on them after the middle of the fifteenth century have been interpreted as an assertion of local civic prerogatives against a group that was directly subject to Venice rather than to local communal councils.[14] The surviving archival record in Brescia permits a detailed reconstruction of the battle of wills between the city and Venice that seems to support this contention. At regular intervals throughout this period the council called for a tightening of the restrictions placed on Jews or for their complete expulsion. These demands were often made to Venice by Brescian orators there after observant Franciscans had preached in Brescia at the council's invitation.[15] In turn, Venice regularly issued instructions to its rectors in Brescia to try to mitigate the worst effects of sermons hostile to Jews.[16] Venetian antagonism toward these preachers may have stemmed less from a sympathy for Jews than from the republic's strong tradition of ecclesiastical independence, which made it suspicious of Roman interference and intolerant of some manifestations of clerical autonomy.[17]

Brescia's calls for the expulsion of Jews were initially ignored by Venice or questioned by the upper clergy. At the beginning of 1462 the Brescian council unanimously called for the expulsion of Jews from both the city and *districtus* noting that they were "against divine law, the honor of the name of Christians, and good governance."[18] Just over a year later the council in effect resisted the doge's decision on Jewish moneylending, and in 1466 renewed calls came for the expulsion of Jews from the city and territory.[19] Finally, in 1469 the special council of Brescia unanimously agreed to mandate the Brescian orator to ask Venice that Jews be prohibited from acting as moneylenders in the city and *districtus* of Brescia, since they were exhausting and devouring the whole substance of the poor.[20] It was later noted in the general council that this orator had been in Venice for four months with no result, and seven citizens were elected to undertake the task of expelling the Jews.[21] The cause of the delay was soon revealed: the Brescian orator to Venice had discovered that Francesco Frigerio, vicar-general in the diocese of Brescia in the absence of the bishop Domenico De Domenichi, had heard of this matter and had warned the Venetian *avogadori* that this move would raise serious clerical issues, since it would result in Christian usury and would harm the poor laity as well as indigent clergy who might be forced into hands of loan sharks. In what was clearly intended as a robust response to this complication, the Brescian council elected no less than thirteen good citizens to supplicate the pope directly on this matter, with permission to spend up to 1,000 ducats.[22]

The council records for the subsequent decade suggest that the papacy either ignored these petitions or accepted that some Jews were in licit occupations and should be permitted to live among Christians in the Bresciano. In any case, in 1473 the Brescian council decided to take the rather more bureaucratic line of expelling Jews to whom Venice had not formally conceded the privilege of moneylending. Therefore, in October of that year the special council agreed to exhort the *podestà* to mandate the Jews to present their privileges to him for inspection so that he could make provisions against those who ought not to be lending money in the city and district.[23] Venice may have accepted this legalistic approach to the question, and the *podestà* may have been sympathetic to local concerns, for in December the general council, on the advice of the *podestà,* voted overwhelmingly in favor of electing two orators to supplicate Venice for the expulsion of all moneylenders in city and *districtus*.[24] In tandem with this move the council targeted Jewish moneylenders in the outlying towns of Gottolengo and Gavardo, where they might have expected to work more easily without the necessary paperwork.[25]

Brescian resistance and Venetian responses during the 1470s hinged on arguments about jurisdiction and political authority and seem to have transcended consideration of specific cases. Delegations of Brescians and Jews petitioned the Venetian doge, who ignored them and then reaffirmed the Bessarion decision of 1464 with the argument that it had been approved by the Council of Ten and therefore could only be overturned by a two-thirds majority of that council.[26] However, following yet another petition from the Brescian orators in Venice in which they cited an earlier ruling in favor of any commune that did not wish Jews to lend money in its territory, the doge decided to revoke his earlier decision so as not to displease the commune.[27] This decision had immediate consequences for at least one Jewish family, since their earlier concessions were revoked: in execution of the commandment the rectors of Brescia forbade the Jews Rizzardo and Leone or their families to lend money in the city or *districtus* under pain of fine of 10 ducats for every ducat lent.[28] By the end of July 1480 Leone was awarded 50 *lire* by the special council because he wished to convert to Christianity and the council wished to encourage others to follow suit.[29]

In fact, within a decade the council rewarded a number of other Jews who subsequently chose to convert and provided dowries for converted Jewish women who married Christians.[30] For example, in 1491 the baptism of such a convert was attended by the wife of the *podestà* and other prominent citizens in a public display of approval.[31] In a sermon given in 1503 on the occasion of the marriage of the Jewish convert Margaret to the Brescian merchant Filippo Arigone, the Dominican preacher noted that Margaret had been only ten years old when she realized the obstinacy and pertinacity of her fellow Jews in denying Christ and asserted that she demonstrated a girlish wisdom that should put Jewish men to shame. The preacher also took the opportunity to lavish praise on the wise and just governance of the Brescian *podestà*, Pietro Donà, and the virtues of his wife, Laura. They had welcomed Margaret after she fled her home and guided Margaret to her new-found faith—although not before a tussle with Girolamo Campagnola of Padua, who also wished to support her cause.[32] Probably related to these moves to convince the Jews of the error of their ways was the publication in Brescia in 1508 of an account by a tenth-century Byzantine scholar of an exhortation to the Jew Theodosius to embrace Christianity on the basis of contemporary evidence of Christ's divinity.[33]

Toward the end of the fifteenth century the council, in addition to these conversions and exhortations, supported moves to stigmatize or confine Jews in the community. On several occasions during the fifteenth century the Venetian Great Council reiterated its decision of 1397 to impose a distinctive sign (a yellow O) on the clothing of all Jews in its territories. This vestimentary policy was certainly the cause of some difficulty for the Brescian Jews.[34] They complained to Venice in 1483 about accusations made against them for not wearing the sign and claimed that it had been covered by accident.[35] Indeed, an accusation of this kind was made in 1489 against a certain Jacob, son of Moses, and a servant in the house of Solomon in Brescia.[36] Brescian ordinances and statutes also prohibited the Jews from using Christian butchers to kill their cattle, but by the end of the fifteenth century a rectorial proclamation enjoined butchers who sold meat to Jews to sell the whole animal or at least to place a yellow O on the meat that was left over.[37] Jews were also prohibited by local statutes from sexual intercourse with Christian prostitutes and other Christian women.[38] The Jews, like the prostitutes, may have been concentrated in one area of the city in life and death, since at the end of the fifteenth century a "Jewish fountain," a separate Jewish cemetery, and synagogues were mentioned.[39]

A Tolerated Minority

Despite the limited toleration and sporadic persecution that circumscribed its presence in Renaissance Brescia, one historian has called the ten years either side of 1500 the "golden age" of the Brescian Jewish community, with evidence of a thriving seminary, or *jeshivà*, in the city.[40] As an indication of educational attainment, a Jewish book culture seems to have existed in the Bresciano, and a transcription survives of *Mashal ha-Kadmoni* (Songs of the ancients) made in 1483, as well as another manuscript dating to 1491. Around this time the Jewish printer Gershom Soncino transferred to Brescia; between 1491 and 1495 he published nine Hebrew books, including the second complete printed Hebrew text of the Bible.[41] Soncino subsequently worked at the castle of Barco, presumably under the protection of the local lord Gianfrancesco Martinengo.[42]

Local magnates with a thirst for cash had good reason to employ Jews in their households: for example, the Jew Rizzardo lived in Brescia under the protection of the rich and powerful Venetian captain Bartolomeo Colleoni, who had built a palace in the city. Jewish survival in the face of local opposition is also connected with the status and nature of Jewish communities in Italy. Jews were highly mobile, and Jewish migration and settlement patterns in the late medieval period were dictated by available economic opportunities as well as by legal or moral restrictions on their activities. Thus, in larger cities or in well-established Jewish communities such as Cremona, Milan, Mantua, Ferrara, Pavia, and Florence, the opportunities for Jews were much less abundant, as the resident population moved to preserve their traditional rights and monopolies. As a result, smaller towns in Italy began to receive Jews fleeing persecution in German lands, and this was was the case in the Bresciano. Small towns with few other resources were often forced to rely on Jewish moneylenders, and few rural people had access to local Christian banks before the middle of the sixteenth century.[43] The evidence suggests that by the middle of the fifteenth century Jews were present in Orzinuovi, Chiari, Salò, and the Garda coast, as well as nearby Gavardo and Gottolengo and in the feudal territories of the Gambara family.[44]

The names of individual Jews who moved between Brescia and these smaller towns begin to appear in local records during this period. Rizzardo of Regensburg and his brothers Leone and Jacob established themselves as moneylenders in the Bresciano after around 1464, and another brother, Enselino (or Anselmo), is recorded in the following decade (although he may have arrived at the same time as the rest of the family). These men appear to have been joined by a nephew, Lazzaro, by 1488. Moses, Giuseppe, and Vitale (Jacob's son) are recorded in Brescia in the same period.[45] Rizzardo, Jacob, and Anselmo received pledges in their Brescian homes but held their banks at Gavardo and Gottolengo, while Leone lived in Brescia and lent money at Iseo, a neighboring commercial center.[46] Jacob was also on the move between Soncino (in Mantuan territory) and Brescia in 1467 and is recorded as taking pawns belonging to the inhabitants of Brescia with him.[47]

Such movements could arouse the suspicion of Christian observers. In 1481 the doge instructed his rectors that Jews should not lend money in the city and *districtus* of Brescia in any way unless they obeyed the statutes of Brescia and the decisions of the Senate. He agreed that if Brescia did not want Jews to reside within its walls, it could not be forced to take them. However, he also confirmed that if the inhabitants of the district were agreeable, the presence of Jews could be tolerated there so long as they lent money at a rate of interest of no more than 10 percent per annum.[48] Jews continued to act as moneylenders in both city and countryside throughout the 1480s. A conciliar decision of October 1481 stating that pledges given to Jews should not be sold outside the city reflects a suspicion that Jews were buying unclaimed pledges for low prices at public auctions and selling them on at a profit.[49] There may have been something of the same fear behind the accusation made in 1488 that Jews were not transferring the pledges they had received directly to their banks but were keeping them in their own homes—presumably as a way of trading with them in the Brescian markets.[50]

The rare survival of transcriptions from the accounts of four Jewish moneylenders in Brescia in 1488 indicates the extent of their activities and the nature of their clients.[51] The Jews dealt with sums ranging from a few *soldi* or *lire* for a belt or piece of cloth up to 66 *lire* 5 *soldi* for a bag of satins and other stuff ("sachete de raxi et altre robe") pawned by the tailor Filipin de Ramoligo. In fact, the most common occupation of clients indicated in the records was that of tailor, with dyers next, followed by barbers, goldsmiths, and with unique references to an armorer, soldier, carpenter, and member of the household of Estore Martinengo. Women appear three times in the records, each time pawning cloth or clothing for small amounts. The range of goods pawned is fairly narrow, although the values can vary markedly. For example, a silver belt ("una cintura d'arzento") was pawned for 3 *lire* 10 *soldi* by Perseval de Rosi, but on the same day and with the same moneylender Zuan Matheo pawned his damask belt for 12 *lire*. Gold rings and gems (for example, "una turchina" and "una tur-cha de scarlatto," which was pawned for 12 *lire* 2 *soldi*) appear in the rec-ords, but most pawns were cloaks, caps, jackets, and lengths of linen cloth. Some of these items were connected with the occupation of the borrower, especially in the case of textile workers or tailors. Pietro de Breno bor-rowed 2 *lire* 10 *soldi* on "una caldiera" which may have been used by him in the dying process, while elsewhere there is evidence that soldiers pawned their arms.[52]

The smaller towns in the Bresciano called for the expulsion of the Jews every decade or so, or made accusations of counterfeiting or other illicit practices against them.[53] Representatives from the *territorio* appealed to the Brescian council to seek the doge's support for the expulsion of Jews. These calls for expulsion can sometimes be related directly to preaching undertaken in a town by Franciscans or others.[54] They often met with a favorable hearing in Brescia and sometimes received the doge's support, as was the case with Salò on Lake Garda in 1468 and 1471.[55] However, the scattered and mobile nature of the Jewish communities in Italy again worked to their advantage: when Jews were expelled from Padua in 1455 they simply moved to the villages in the Padovano, where they continued to act as moneylenders for locals as well as for Paduans who travelled out of the city to transact business.[56]

The Jews in Brescia and its outlying towns, like their Paduan counter-parts, were also protected by the Venetian authorities and their rectors. In 1473 Venice moved to banish the four inhabitants of Gavardo who had falsely accused the Jews there of counterfeiting money.[57] In 1488 the Vene-tian *podestà* absolved Moses, Lazzaro, Vitale, and Giuseppe of accusa-tions of receiving pawns and not transferring them to their banks.[58] In 1494 letters from the doge confirmed Rizzardo's privileges and his right to reside in Brescia with his family in the face of local decrees to the con-trary.[59] In the following year the *podestà* stepped in to override local at-tempts to assume judicial competence in matters pertaining to Raffaele and Lazzaro.[60] The Venetian Senate also modified a petition presented by the Brescian orators against Jews living and lending money in Brescia and its *districtus* so that the Jews could continue to lend money within defined limits.[61] There is evidence of episcopal protection and the occasional toler-ance of local vicars.[62] Finally, it seems as if neighboring rulers were willing to protect or recommend individual Jews: in 1476 the Duke of Milan asked the Venetian orator to help Benedicto (Baruch) of Como, whose papers had been stolen when he had stayed with Jacob in Brescia, and in 1492 the Marquis of Mantua wrote to the *podestà* of Brescia in recommendation of a certain Abraham.[63]

Simon of Trent and Violence against Jews

The conflict between Venetian toleration of an economically useful group directly subject to the city in the mainland and popular ambivalence or hostility toward the Jews boosted by mendicant preaching was clearly illustrated in the months and years that followed the supposed torture and murder of Simon of Trent. This case resonated throughout Italy, notably in the Bresciano, as it drew strength from the tales of ritual murder known as the "blood libel": an amalgam of traditional Christian stereotypes of the Jews as Christ-killers, Host-desecrators, and sworn enemies of Christians. The case seems to have resonated most strongly in the Bresciano, which had established economic ties with Trent.[64] It was to Brescia that the earliest Christian tales of Jewish homicide were addressed, and it was in Brescian territory that images of the "martyred" child proliferated.[65]

On Easter Sunday 26 March 1475 the corpse of a twenty-eight-month old child named Simon, son of Master Andreas and his wife Maria, was found floating in a ditch in the city of Trent.[66] Simon had been missing for several days and during that time rumors had begun to circulate implicating the local Jewish community in his disappearance. The confessions extracted by torture from the leading Jews of Trent by the local *podestà* were sensational and revealed a conspiracy to use Christian blood in the ceremonies for Passover. The details provided by these imprisoned Jews in the months before their executions in June 1475 were very similar to historic accusations made against the Jews and comparable to a number of infamous cases of Jewish conspiracy, kidnap, and murder that had been uncovered in German lands during the preceding decade.[67] News of the discovery of the body of Simon and the circumstances of his "martyrdom" spread very quickly.[68] Trent was well placed for communications with the archducal court at Innsbruck to the north via the Alpine passes and to Verona and Venice to the south along established trade routes. Moreover, the death of Simon took place at the end of a Jubilee year when many pilgrims were travelling to and from Rome to visit its churches and receive indulgences.

Johannes Hinderbach, the prince-bishop of Trent, prosecuted the case against the Jews and energetically promoted the cult of Simon. Miracles associated with the body of the child were noted within days of its discovery, and by June the following year almost 130 miracles had been attributed to Simon.[69] Pilgrims flocked to Trent from Italy and the German states to view the corpse and donate money. At the end of April Hinderbach wrote to the Italian poet and humanist Raffaele Zovenzoni about the Brescians "who had come here in large numbers because of this affair."[70] Among these visitors was the Brescian nobleman Gasparo Martinengo, who was cured of a fever and made a donation to Simon in gratitude.[71] Hinderbach went on to explain that in response to this surge of popular interest Giovanni Mattia Tiberino, the Brescian doctor who had examined the body of Simon, had decided to send "the magistrates of the city of Brescia a very lucidly and elegantly phrased letter" in Latin describing the murder of Simon. This letter was rapidly and repeatedly printed in Italy and in the German empire in both Latin, Italian, and German, in a process that reflects the power of the early press and the degree to which Italian humanists were involved in speedily disseminating news of notable events among a growing readership.[72]

Hinderbach wrote poems about Simon and commissioned similar verses from Zovenzoni.[73] Zovenzoni was interested not only in drawing his contemporaries' attention to the case but also in appealing to posterity. As he addressed the printer Gabriele di Pietro: "Print it—you, Gabriele, new glory of our age—print the horrible outrage that the Jews have committed! Print it, I beg you, O I beg you, print it on a thousand sheets, so that all posterity, alas, can learn about it!"[74] The Brescian humanists Giovanni Calfurnio and Ubertino Pusculo also produced works about the case that went into print or circulated in manuscript.[75] The accounts of Simon's murder found in diaries of the period clearly owe much to the tenor and substance of these texts.[76]

Those who could not read could learn in other ways about the Jews' murder of Simon. An early German edition of Tiberino's account printed in Trent was accompanied by twelve woodcuts depicting scenes from the narrative of Simon's "martyrdom"—from the conspiracy of the Jews to find a Christian boy to the execution of the condemned Jews.[77] These images and others appearing on walls and in broadsides were the accoutrements of a developing cult—promoted by Hinderbach but deplored by members of the Roman curia. A papal brief threatening excommunication for anyone who painted or printed accounts about the boy was included in a letter from the doge on 5 November 1475.[78] The Brescian *podestà*, like Venetian rectors throughout the *terraferma*, executed the doge's command and issued an order to the local clergy and laity that was to be posted in the palace and in the usual places throughout the city: "No person, lay and secular of whatever station, is to paint pictures on the walls or elsewhere, nor sell such pictures of the martyr or blessed [child]. Nor is anyone to preach *per zaratani*[79] or in any other form of verse, or write epistles, or sell anything written about that small child called Simon who has died at the hands of Jews in the city of Trent."[80]

These proclamations notwithstanding, images of Simon appeared in Brescia and other parts of the Bresciano. The images ranged from highly portable prints to the semistatic painting in the Carmelite church in Brescia, which was observed weeping, and was said to have prompted one viewer to bear twins three months apart.[81] The martyred Simon appeared rather more statically in dozens of frescoes on the walls of Franciscan churches over the length of the Val Camonica.[82] Miracles associated with Simon continued to occur in large numbers in the Bresciano and elsewhere after the papal bull of 1478, which condemned the cult.[83] In fact, Brescian pilgrims were visiting Simon's corpse as late as 1517.[84] In short, there is every sign that the case resonated widely for decades and the cult spread widely among the communities of northern Italy and the German lands, with terrible consequences for the Jewish communities there.[85]

As early as April 1475 the doge, Pietro Mocenigo, wrote to his rectors in Brescia, Padua, and Friuli about the violent actions and threats against Jews travelling through Venetian territory that had been provoked by the rumors about Trent and stirred up by the sermons of certain preachers. He ordered these rectors to protect the Jews from this violence and to stop these preachers. Similar admonitions followed during the next two years, with the additional injunctions against the spread of imagery of Simon.[86] However, it is clear that violent actions against Jews continued in northern Italy, especially in Lombardy and the Venetian *terraferma*, for at least a decade after Trent as the "blood libel" spread and was fueled by long-standing suspicion of Jewish bankers and moneylenders.

Giovanni Mattia Tiberino made a point of raising suspicions about the Jews in the minds of all Christians, and he probably had his compatriots among the governing elite of Brescia in mind when he addressed Zovenzoni at the beginning of his account of the Trent case in the following terms:

> Listen, you rulers of peoples, to the unheard-of crime, and watch over your peoples as faithful shepherds should! Let earth's denizens awake and see what snakes they are nurturing in their own bosom! The cruel Jews not only eat up Christians' property in their frenzied craving for interest-payments but, conspiring against our lives and for our destruction, they feast on the living blood of our sons, afflicting them with terrible punishment in their synagogues and cruelly slaughtering them in place of Christ.[87]

A number of the confessions extracted during the trials at Trent gave support to Tiberino's claims of a viper in the Brescian nest. Lazzaro, who was caught up in the Trent case, confessed that he sometimes spent time with his uncle Rizzardo in Brescia, while Angelo da Verona, who lived in Gavardo, admitted that this Rizzardo possessed the blood of a Christian infant obtained in his hometown of Regensburg.[88] In the summer of 1474 Israel Wolfgang had visited Rizzardo, who commissioned him to illuminate a Hebrew manuscript. Rizzardo allegedly told Wolfgang that he had obtained the blood of a murdered Christian baby in Regensburg. Wolfgang later alleged that the same Rizzardo also claimed to have taken part in a ritual murder in Padua four or five years earlier. In order to avoid the plague Wolfgang transferred to Gavardo, close to Brescia, and rebound a breviary for a local priest, and there one Enselino (or Anselmo) told Wolfgang that his brother Rizzardo had obtained some of the blood of the murdered Paduan child.[89] In fact, acutely aware that the safety of Jews far beyond Trent was at stake, Jacob of Brescia appeared before the apostolic commissioner in Rovereto and pleaded for the true perpetrators to be made known.[90]

In Brescia itself, the difficult financial conditions occasioned by the Venetian demand for a subsidy at the beginning of 1475 may have strained relations between Christians and Jews.[91] The cult of Simon was given vigorous support by Francesco Sanson, the new general of the Franciscan order, who was based in the city and in touch with Hinderbach. At a meeting of the Venetian province of his order in Brescia in 1476, Sanson urged all Franciscan preachers to promote Simon's cult.[92] The Lenten sermons in Brescia that year included attacks on Jews, which seem to have stirred up some tumults.[93] The following year a Franciscan friar, Michele, was criticized by the Venetian authorities for his anti-Semitic sermons in Brescia.[94] As a result the Jews petitioned Venice, and further warnings were issued by the doge against peddlers ("ciarratani") and preachers who were stirring up trouble among the "plebs" against Jews in the city.[95]

The *Monte di Pietà*

As the case of Simon of Trent indicates, symbolic violence directed against Jews in the form of Franciscan sermons and gentile tales about ritual murder and blood lust could be transformed into action when local authorities stood by or aided persecution. During the final decade of the fifteenth century Franciscan preachers, notably Bernardino da Feltre, who preached in Trent in March 1475, were crucial in the next stage of the Brescian council's attack on the Jewish presence in the city. In 1486 the council complained of a large increase in the numbers of Jews from Cremonese territory that was a cause of scandal and inconvenience Brescia's citizens. As well as a proposal to conduct a census of all of the Jews in the city, the council decided to imitate Vicenza and found a *monte di pietà* or Christian bank.[96] The *monte* was a Franciscan-inspired institution that was established in towns in central and northern Italy, including the Bresciano, from 1462 onward and was floated with donations from Christians.[97] The *monte* was originally designed to lend small amounts of money to the poor at no interest and in return for a pledge in order to mitigate the abuses of loan sharks and to prompt the expulsion of Jews.

In August 1489 the general council of Brescia considered the rules of the *monte* at Vicenza that had been outlined by the chancellor and agreed to commission a draft set of rules for a Brescian *monte*.[98] Two weeks later the general council unanimously approved the erection of the *monte* and set out its rules.[99] The sermons against usury given by the Franciscan preacher Michele da Acqui around this time helped promote the new institution.[100] In a more practical effort the council also promised to donate 500 ducats to the fund, although in the end a local worthy, Bartolomeo Capriolo, stepped in and delivered that sum after the council tried to back out of its commitment.[101] Bartolomeo's kinsman Elia Capriolo was one of the first treasurers of the *monte,* and his appointment demonstrates some engagement with the project on the part of the council, despite a somewhat faltering start.[102] The putative enemy of ruinous funerals would probably have approved when three decades later the council agreed that every citizen, of whatever condition, ought to rent mourning clothes from the *monte di pietà* to save expense and avoid burdening the heirs of the deceased.[103]

In practice the *monte* proved an ineffective alternative to Jewish moneylenders, and the Jews continued to find a living in, or at least around, the city, despite repeated calls for their expulsion throughout the last decade of the fifteenth century.[104] Indeed, in April 1494 the increased number of Jews loudly going about their rites and business in the city was condemned in especially colorful language, and their expulsion was deemed as necessary to the city as the liberation of Brescia from the Duke of Milan.[105] However, this liberation was delayed by the great convenience of the service provided by Jewish moneylenders since applicants to the *monte* were obliged to provide proof of their poverty and were not permitted to cash written bonds, while in contrast, the Jews not only offered a relatively low rate of interest but also imposed fewer restrictions on the borrower, and they accepted both pledges and written bonds.[106]

In an atmosphere of official anti-Semitism, making charitable donations in support of the *monte* was a praiseworthy act. The Franciscan preacher Bernardino da Feltre preached to the Brescians during 1493 and 1494 that such gifts allowed the donor to perform the seven acts of mercy and consequently were true alms. In 1490 he had preached in Padua in favor of the establishment of a *monte di pietà* in the teeth of Jewish protests. Venice granted permission for a *monte* in Padua the following year but soon afterward instructed its rectors in Brescia and Crema to warn Bernardino, who had been invited to preach in Brescia at that time, against stirring up anti-Semitic tumults of the kind that had marked his passage through Padua.[107]

Bernardino's Brescian Advent sermons in 1493 did not contain any specific attacks on the Jews or make reference to the *monte*, but his Lenten sermons of 1494 very likely did so, since this was a traditional time to reflect on the perfidy of the Jews, their role in the Passion, and their supposed ritual reenactments of Christ's death in more recent years.[108] The council noted in July 1494 that Bernardino da Feltre had persuaded many by his sermons to give to the *monte* and agreed that officers should be appointed for each *quadra* of the city to collect offerings in a general oblation on the first Sunday after the important civic feast of the Assumption.[109] Following Bernardino's lead, the council agreed to reform the rules of the *monte* to bring them into line with those of Padua (where an interest rate of 5 percent on all loans was charged) and to forbid Jews from acquiring pledges sold by the *monte*.[110]

In conclusion, the Brescian campaign against the Jews is complex in its detail but simpler in its general outlines. The tension between economic necessity and religious or moral disapproval that drove the council's discussions and the popular outbursts are fairly clear, but the precise relationship between Jewish immigrants and Brescians is harder to assess in a balanced way. The treatment of Jews in other towns in the *terraferma* was similarly ambivalent, but at its heart, as Gian Maria Varanini has suggested in the case of Verona, lay a local desire to impose control over a group directly subject to Venice and in this way to assert authority over the territory.[111] This desire was clearly evident in the repeated Brescian requests made to Venice for territorial control during the fifteenth and sixteenth centuries (outlined in Chapter 3). The Venetians were no more willing to grant such authority to Brescia than they were to concede to the patriarch power over the Jews in Venice itself.[112]

By contrast, the rhetoric of disapproval—marked by a strong Franciscan accent—is much more accessible and clearly shares many characteristics with the proclamations regarding prostitution discussed earlier. On the invitation of Bernardino da Feltre, the general council decided to build a bonfire of the vanities in the piazza, and contemporary choniclers noted this inferno of luxury or lascivious goods, which took place a week after the general oblation for the *monte,* with approval.[113] Bernardino's bonfires were a logical extension of the city's drive against excessive personal expenditure funded by Jewish loans and against the undesirable and supposedly unhealthy elements in society such as prostitutes whose dress and manners were the subject of sumptuary legislation.[114] Jews and prostitutes were associated in the popular imagination as symbols and spreaders of disease. In fact, the expulsion of the Jews from Brescia in April 1494 was presented by the council in this way: "While the Christian church may tolerate the Jews, it has in no way decreed that they have to be tolerated in Brescia; they should be treated as public prostitutes, who because of their filth are tolerated [only] while they live in a bordello, even so should those Jews live their stinking life in some stinking place, separate from Christians."[115]

The language of anti-Semitism was also similar to that used to describe witches in this period. In the next chapter I will show how the representation of diabolical men and women in the Bresciano shared with that of Jewish stereotypes an emphasis on superstitious practices, recalcitrance, and blood sacrifice. At the same time, the prosecution of witches entailed conflict and cooperation between Venice and Brescia, clerics and laymen, that also echoes that of the half century of Brescian toleration and persecution of Jews during the fifteenth century. The witch, like the Jew, formed a growing threat to Brescian society during the same century and had to be burned out of existence like the Jews of Trent who had been held responsible for the supposed torture and murder of the Christian child Simon.

CHAPTER TEN

Witches

THE ALPINE VALLEYS of the Valtellina, Val Chiavenna, and Val Lev-
entina were among the first areas in Europe to witness the prosecution of heretics and witches on a significant scale from the latter half of the
fourteenth century. The neighboring Bresciano was naturally one of the
first regions south of the Alps to follow suit, and in the course of the fifteenth and sixteenth centuries popes, bishops, inquisitors, Brescian councillors, and Venetian governors all sought to impose their authority on the
Val Camonica, where witches were appearing with some frequency.[1] The
Val Camonica is the longest valley in Italy, and runs to the Alpine pass of
Tonale for ninety kilometres to the north of Brescia.[2] During the Renaissance it provided the most important means of communication between
the Bresciano and the Tyrol, and its population rose from just under
twenty-five thousand in 1493 to around fifty thousand in 1520.[3] During
this period the valley gained a reputation for benighted activities. In around
1506 the chronicler Elia Capriolo described it as a "place of foolish men
and always abundant with witches where some say there are those who
swap wives and the one who offers the less [valuable wife] adds to her a
goat. He who receives it appreciates the addition of this animal as much as
the other appreciates the more noble condition of the wife he has received.
Such impiety was removed when the Franciscans were established there."[4]
An educated local observer, giving an account of the witch hunts there in
1518, described the Val Camonica as a

place of mountains more than plains, more sterile than fertile, and inhabited by a people who are largely ignorant, goitrous, and almost entirely deformed and lacking all the finer points of civil society. Their customs are often rustic and wild, and there are few who know, let alone obey, the commandments of God. So these valley dwellers are as different from other Brescians as the Portuguese are from those [inhabitants] of Calicut.[5]

Disdain for country customs is also evident in the letters of Laura Cereta, who otherwise enjoyed rustic solitude. Cereta followed her father into exile at his farmhouse, and in her letters she paints a depressing picture of rural life:

I have already begun to be sated with the common folk in this village, where every street and narrow alley is filled with trash and piles of dung. For here the rush mats next door to us can be seen in plain view. Here are the little houses of shepherds with their wooden shingles, and here some rough farmers herd flocks of sheep while others drive cattle. A cart is being pulled out from this very place; a groom is shouting at the horses. His clothes are caked with dirt, and he stiffens, worn-out and disheveled from toil. Many of the folk here practice rural habits; most use degenerate slang. Our sole means of rest and relaxation in the heat has been the fly-swatter.[6]

The clichés of rustic oafishness, isolation, and backwardness have persisted into modern accounts of the witch hunt. Hugh Trevor-Roper once thought that Brescia was interesting as a prime location for the "witch-craze" as an unassimilable and "continuing social phenomenon" because of its remote mountainous location. However, the isolation assumed by Trevor-Roper was far from complete and was much less critical in the construction, persecution, and execution of the witch than the fact that the Val Camonica formed, in his suggestive phrase, a "sensitive social frontier."[7] Arno Borst has argued that the Alpine "witch-craze" owed a great deal to economic and political change in the valleys and was "an accompanying phenomenon of opening, not of isolation."[8] Certainly, the valley's relative autonomy was recognized by the governments of Milan and Venice. As noted in Chapter 3, they ruled the valley directly, appointing rectors, but initially granted it privileges distinct from those of Brescia. Castellans in the Val Camonica responded to local as much as Brescian or Venetian concerns throughout this period, but whereas Ghibelline factions in the valley, led by the Federici clan, came to the aid of invading Milanese troops during the first half of the fifteenth century and welcomed imperial troops in 1509, Breno, the major administrative center in the valley, remained loyal to Venice and withstood sieges in 1438 and again in 1453–54. Brescia regarded the valley as a source of taxes and aid in the reconstruction of the city and frequently petitioned Venice for administrative control.

However, during the second half of the fifteenth century Venice, mindful of its loyalty and of its relative poverty, often intervened to exclude the valley from Brescian exactions, and it was taxed separately from the rest of the Bresciano.[9]

As Capriolo's comments suggest, the Val Camonica was also open to the spread of newly reformed clerical orders concerned with eradicating superstition and reinvigorating popular faith. For example, Franciscan Spirituals led by the Portuguese João Mendes de Silva founded a number of convents in the Val Camonica after 1460. Mendes was based in Milan, and it is important to note that Milanese and Lombard Franciscans were in the forefront of promoting new measures for poor relief in the region from the 1480s onward, notably the *monte di pietà*, which provided a licit Christian alternative to Jewish moneylenders.[10] As noted, when news of the "martyrdom" of the child Simon at the hands of the Jews in the town of Trent reached Brescia, it was quickly printed and was complemented by a number of edifying frescoes depicting Simon on the walls of Franciscan churches in Brescia and throughout the Val Camonica. It is probably no coincidence that this area of intense anti-Semitism, fuelled by mendicant spirituality, was also the site of fears about "synagogues of Satan," the sabbat (witches' Sabbath), and diabolic, as well as Jewish, desecrators of the Host.[11]

Witchcraft, Heresy, and Superstition

The classic stereotype of the witch, which emerged in Europe after around 1400 and fused inversions of Christian belief and practice with pagan or classical ideas, was disseminated by preaching and printed texts. The immediate source of the idea of the sabbat and many more demonological concerns lay with the Dominican inquisitors, charged by the papacy since the thirteenth century with rooting out heresy. Their activities were directed by the head of the Lombard order from Milan, which was an early center of heresy and witchcraft trials and a base for the composition and dissemination of Dominican tracts on witchcraft and the demonic.[12] Franciscan preachers, including Giacomo della Marca, who visited the Bresciano in the 1460s, also preached against magic and witchcraft.[13] Preachers and investigators detected evidence of the adoration of the devil, the abuse of sacraments and the sacramental, and superstition. Increasingly, they also found evidence of *maleficium* (evil action, usually prompted or aided by demons). These elements, many of which were very old, were accompanied by new and alarming reports and confessions of the attendance of thousands of valley-dwellers at sabbats, feasts and orgies, and demonic pacts.[14]

The demonic aspect of the new heresy of witchcraft, especially the sabbat, has received ample scholarly treatment; the role of superstition in the persecution of witches has received much less attention until recently. Superstition, or "superfluous and vain religion," as the fifteenth-century canon of Pamplona Martín de Arles put it, was regarded in early modern Europe as a less calculated and serious sin than heresy, but as "false" religion it could be dangerous to the untutored Christian and lead him or her into heresy or the suspicion of heresy.[15] As Aquinas pointed out in the thirteenth century, superstitious practices were usually based on false and ill-founded opinions that could be exploited by demons, whether one entered into a demonic pact or not.[16] In its common and nondemonic usage, superstition was an elastic term that could include, or exclude, a large number of beliefs and practices that might be associated with common strategies for protection from harm, as well as learned or clerical magic, and witchcraft.[17] This normative process could vary according to the prejudices and aims of the observer or investigator and was also shaped by local circumstances. From this conceptual elasticity a confusion of *religio* and *superstitio* sometimes arose. However, it can also be argued that this was an ordering confusion: in other words, the definition of superstition was contingent on the delineation of religion, and vice versa.

Critical to both concepts was a similar systemic duality of the natural and the supernatural. Communication between natural and supernatural worlds was a given in the whole spectrum of beliefs and practices from church liturgy to folklorized or magical ritual, but the precise boundary between the natural and the supernatural was contested throughout the medieval and early modern periods, as fierce debates about the Eucharist, miracles, the immaculate conception, and demonic power demonstrate.[18] For example, in 1462 Brescia was the setting for debates about the incarnation of Christ.[19] In these debates a local inquisitor—who had instigated the prosecution of witches in the city a few years before—played a leading role.[20] Robert Scribner has shown how the varied and often colorful or tangible emanations of the sacred in the profane were persistent aspects of "popular religion" before and after the Reformation.[21] A similar spectrum of ritual and belief in early modern Terra d'Otranto, in the heel of Italy, has been called a "system of the sacred" by David Gentilcore, and the role of Catholic clergy in the strictly liturgical, the paraliturgical, and the frankly magical aspects of popular religion has been demonstrated there.[22] Evidence of a similar sacred system in northern Italy has been offered by Carlo Ginzburg and recently by many other historians, especially those who have worked on records of inquisition witchcraft trials.[23]

Superstition was also the target of a number of works produced by edu-

cated clerics and laymen as a part of their efforts to reform and reinvigo-
rate religious belief and practices. For example, speakers at the Fifth
Lateran Council, summoned by Pope Julius II in 1512, outlined the duties
of both clerics and laymen and stressed the need for a reform of morals
and the abolition of superstition.[24] The Venetian noblemen turned hermits
Vincenzo Querini and Tommaso Giustiniani asserted, in a reform document that was drafted on the occasion of the council and aimed at the pope
around 1512–13, that there was scarcely a single household unaffected by
some form of superstition. They alleged that the laity and clergy had been
led into superstitions by the Jews and by books on the interpretation of
dreams and on the divining arts. The authors of these works ought to be
condemned by the pope and the books destroyed. People who practiced
the black arts ought to be burnt alive or sent into perpetual exile if they
were not repentant. Querini and Giustiniani also condemned astrology
and astrologers and wrote that the sick ought be forbidden to go to so-
called doctors who used bogus cures, charms, words, and poems. In short,
the hermits scorned the idea that certain prayers, poems, or magical words
could heal specific parts of the body and ridiculed the idea that miraculous
images and pictures carried in procession or on one's own person could
heal the sick, induce rain, or promote fertility in cows—although such
practices were widespread in Italy.[25]

In a similar fashion, the hermits' friend Gasparo Contarini asserted in
his 1517 treatise on the ideal bishop, written for the new bishop of Bergamo, that the bishop's congregation should be prevented by legal sanc-
tions and episcopal guidance from straying from correct religious practices.
Contarini described how the people were affected by impiety and superstition and seems to have associated the former with educated people and the
latter with uneducated peasants. The former vice arose from the arts of
prediction such as magic and astrology, which were opposed to religion
and went by the name of wisdom although they were, in effect, a form of
idolatry. However, superstition was distinguished as another sin that could
lead to impiety, for it consisted of "too much religion" and the worship by
country folk of "a god of fever and a god of pestilence, a goddess of glau-
coma and of eye disease." The peasants also "set up gods for cows, sheep,
and grains," and in times of need "they all immediately exasperate the
saints, even the statues of the saints, with most of their prayers, just as each
one pleases." This quasi-pagan impiety, he wrote, must be destroyed by
the bishop, using "a certain gentleness" in order to "recall the whole
people to the true worship of the one God and of Jesus Christ." Those who
were in the thrall of superstition accepted prayers for good fortune and
health, and revered apocryphal writings as if they were canonical writings.

Women were particularly singled out for censure: "I pass over women, for whom nothing is without superstition!"[26]

Such superstition could arise from an ignorance that was not confined to laywomen or even the country bumpkins of the Val Camonica: Querini and Giustiniani alleged that there were scarcely two out of one hundred of the clergy who understood Latin, and Contarini thought the Dominican and Franciscans superstitious in their excessive devotion to their founding saints.[27] Fifteenth-century clerical writers on superstition, following Aquinas, noted that it was also bound up with demonism, whose force they defined and extended in their efforts to reform religion and religiosity. Clerical necromancy, which had been one of the principal conduits for demonic power in the human world during the Middle Ages, was increasingly accompanied by a more general demonic threat that was embodied in the new heretical sect of witches.[28] I will show how the inquisitors of the Bresciano elaborated on the nature of this demonic threat, identified the clergy partly responsible for its spread, and extracted confessions that led from admissions of superstitious practices such as medicinal healing to confessions of a much more diabolical kind.

In the 1450s, the decade of the earliest surviving evidence, the local inquisitor presented the problem of the practices and beliefs in the Val Camonica to the pope and to Venice as one predominantly of heresy and clerical superstition. Given the traditional medieval concern with heresy and superstition in clerical necromancy, as expressed for example by the inquisitor Nicolau Eymeric in his well-known 1376 *Directorium Inquisitorum*, this is not entirely unexpected, and clergy appeared in many subsequent cases.[29] However, the documentation also reveals some evidence of *maleficium*. In 1455 at Edolo, a town near the head of the valley, the Dominican inquisitor Antonio found heretics "who refuse the sacraments, sacrifice children, [and] worship the devil," and two years later clerics who practiced superstitious conjurations and invocations or "nefarious arts" likely to encourage the laity to fall into deviations were reprimanded.[30] The Brescian council appealed to the doge and apostolic nuncio in Venice in 1494 against the "multa maleficia" committed daily by ordinary clerics and in 1508 condemned clerics who led shameful lives and committed crimes, including unspecified "diabolica fraude."[31]

Similarly, around 1480 the Dominican inquisitor Fra Antonio de Petosellis revived the case of one Stefano from Bellano (a town on the east side of Lake Como) who had been investigated for heresy by the inquisition in 1467 and again in 1476. The inquisitor acted on "new and extremely serious" depositions made by witnesses against Stefano, who was found to have relapsed into his previously abjured heresies, and fallen into many that were much worse. On two occasions, as Stefano confessed, he had gone to a house in Brescia where he had invoked and worshipped the devil, denied the faith, and later refused the sacrament. For nine years Stefano had been transported to a sabbat ("ludum") "realiter et corporaliter" while wide awake. There the devil appeared in the form of a "queen," and every week at this place Stefano denied God and the faith, refused the sacraments, and worshipped this queen, who seems to have been attended or associated with a "holy angel" who, Stefano believed, guarded the gates of paradise.[32] Stefano was sentenced in the presence of a large number of people to public decapitation (his head was to be burned) and then handed over to the secular arm in the form of the *podestà* Giovanni Moro for execution.[33]

A similar example of the new demonic witch was displayed by the inquisitor in Brescia around the same time. Maria, "called the doctor," of Vicenza but living in Calcinato, east of Brescia, fulfilled every requirement for the classic stereotype of the witch. Her many "errors and enormities" included attendance of the sabbat, worshipping the devil, and denying the faith. However, the record of her crimes was much fuller and, presumably, more worrying for the authorities than that of Stefano. She had denied God, refused Christ, received cures and "maleficiatis" from the devil, celebrated masses for the devil using the blood of murdered babies, made animal sacrifices, abused the sacrament, and bewitched ("streavit") thirty boys and girls, half of whom subsequently had died.[34]

On this occasion the episcopal and secular authorities were in agreement with the inquisitor, and the sentence of death was executed. However, cases of witchcraft in the Val Camonica during this period were often marked by conflicts of jurisdiction and authority within and between the ecclesiastical and secular authorities concerned. First, I would argue that in respect to these judicial disputes, the dual nature of law in the Venetian republic was key. Venice largely preserved the body of positive law, whether communal or Roman, that it found practiced in the conquered *terraferma*. Instead of wholesale centralization or regularization of law and procedures to suit their city's emphasis on empiricism and divine justice, the Venetians issued ad hoc edicts, entertained appeals in different courts, or left rectors to deal with local disputes. This state of affairs might have given Brescians a free hand to vent their frustrations against the recalcitrant valley communities. However, it also opened the way to Venetian intervention in matters offensive to God and meddling in local affairs and to some jockeying for authority among several different organs of state.[35] The persecution of sodomy in Venice has been interpreted in the light of these judicial and political struggles. Sodomy was regarded as especially dangerous to the spiritual health of the state, and the Council of Ten arrogated the power to prosecute these cases after 1418. In subsequent years the Ten even defined and extended the power of the patriarch in these matters throughout the *terraferma*.[36]

Second, there was doubt about elements of *maleficium* and the classic witch stereotype, which some observers found "scarcely credible." However, while the extirpation of "manifest heresy" remained largely immune from overt criticism (and indeed after ca. 1535 supplanted witchcraft in the inquisition's list of concerns) the opponents of witch persecution among Venetian lawmakers found that the inquisitors' focus on superstition offered a much more attractive opening for attacks on the inquisition. Both the jurisdictional jockeying and the arguments about the demonic and the superstitious in witchcraft will be the focus of the rest of this chapter. An examination of individual Brescian cases will demonstrate the origins, nature, and significance of these disputes and the respective roles of the concepts of the demonic and the superstitious in the defining of the heresy of witchcraft.

Justice and Jurisdiction

In August 1454 Fra Giacomo de Petris stood up in a pulpit in Brescia and proclaimed an inquisition with the support of the papacy and Holy Roman Emperor. In accordance with these privileges, the community was required to provide Fra Giacomo with twelve good and faithful men, two notaries, and some other "servitores." After carefully examining the inquisitor's credentials the general council in Brescia voted, with only two dissenting voices, in favor of paying the salaries of two men of suitable and loyal nature and two good and faithful "servitores" to aid the inquisitor.[37] There may be hints of a crack in this apparently united front in a decision taken by the council a fortnight later, just at the moment when the inquisitor had condemned two female "pythonesses" (a reference to the goddess of the ancient oracle at Delphi) and revealed the existence of other "heretics." Eighteen members of the council were elected to meet with the *podestà*, Nicolò Marcello, and the inquisitor and were enjoined to hold a colloquy ("coloqum") to ensure that there might be honest, fit, and just provision for the office of the inquisition.[38] The outcome of this colloquy is not known, but there was some delay in proceedings, and the two "hereticas et pitonissas," Charina and Guielma, were not burned until five months later—an event followed within three months by the public burning of the bones of Antonio, a barber who had hanged himself.[39] The inquisitor detained further "mulieres maleficas et Incantatrites" whom he absolved or condemned, and the council agreed to provide a suitable prison for one sorceress ("Venefica") who had been condemned to perpetual incarceration.[40] Some time later the special council also agreed, by seven votes to three, to impose an interdict of one hour at vespers on the activities of merchants and councillors in order to hold a religious service in connection with the heresy affecting the city.[41] However, there are hints of local dissension from some of the inquisitor's decisions. The council considered asking him to write to his superior inquisitor in Milan to request absolution from excommunication for one Serzoczum de Venetiis, whom they reputed a good and faithful man. The council also considered it desirable, in connection with inquisitorial activity, to write to Venice to expedite the plea made on behalf of one man by the city advocate, since he was recognized to be a good and faithful servant of Venice and therefore fit to be liberated from "those most cruel prisons."[42] The Venetian Senate noted that many debates and differences of opinion had been provoked on account of the inquisitor's activities in Brescia.[43]

After a period of apparent inactivity in this area the problem of witches resurfaced over a quarter century later. In December 1485 the Dominican friar Antonio, active in the Val Camonica, told the doge in Venice that

> [b]y the goodness and mercy of God many persons leading a heretical life have been discovered in . . . Edolo. Among other things, they renounce the Catholic faith and spurn the sacraments. They choose the devil for their god, spit and trample on the cross of Christ, and continue ceaselessly to sacrifice babies and to cast spells. They grind up the body of Christ in a mortar and exhume the corpses of babies, and with this flesh they make sacrifices to the devil and [do] other detestable things.[44]

The inquisitor saw a danger to the faith in such heresy and so many diabolical tricks and insisted that the rectors intervene to assist in its extirpation. The doge therefore instructed his rectors, who had been reluctant to act, to arrest every person indicated by the inquisitor and conduct them under close escort to Brescia, where they should be thrown into prison. While the doge urged the rectors to use all diligence and zeal and to punish the accused severely according to their crimes, they were nevertheless to act also "with prudence and the circumspection that seems appropriate to you, with the understanding that justice will be followed."

However, justice moved slowly and the matter dragged on through the following year. Apparently, the Brescian council or the bishop attempted to hinder the process. Certainly, higher ecclesiastical authorities, in the shape of the apostolic legate and the patriarch, were called in to investigate

the inquisitorial procedure against several followers of the heretical per-
versity. As the new doge, Agostino Barbarigo, informed the new rectors in
the autumn of 1486, the legate and patriarch had affirmed that the trial
had been properly conducted in law and that the accused ought to be
handed over quickly to the secular arm for sentencing. As a warning of
future problems, the doge's decision was rapidly followed by a papal brief
addressed to the bishop and the inquisitor rejecting the civil officials' wish
to review the process before passing sentence. It was affirmed here that the
crime of heresy was "an entirely ecclesiastical matter," and the officials
were instructed to act in the matter within six days, on pain of excommunication.[45]

Paolo Zane, the bishop of Brescia, went to view matters for himself and
told the doge that no sentence should be passed without his consent.[46]
Blocked by some of the highest local authorities in this way, the inquisitor
turned on the closest and most vulnerable lay representative: the rector's
vicar, the notary Alberto de Albertis. He was denounced from the pulpit of
the Dominican church and accused of providing hostile advice to the rectors in the matter of the "heretical women." Still worse, the inquisitor accused Alberto of heresy and called for *his* trial, possibly in Rome. While
the doge advised the rectors to demand that Alberto be left in peace, in fact
in the spring of 1487 the Dominicans lured another notary, whom they
presumably also identified with the filibustering tactics of the bishop and
the council, into their monastery and held him there.[47]

Inquisitors could also work with Venice and Brescia against the pope.
For example, it was on the recommendation of the inquisitor in 1499 that
the special council of Brescia agreed to imprison for life two more heretics
of the Val Camonica—on this occasion, "two wicked and impious presby-
ters."[48] The sentences against Martino and Hermano, and a third man
who escaped, Don Donato de Buzolo, exhibit the familiar mixture of outrageous crimes, including attendance at a "ludum Sathanae" on Monte
Tonale at the head of the Val Camonica, worship of the devil, denigration
of the cross, misuse of Hosts and holy oil, and copulation on the cross with
women, all over a period of ten to twenty-five years.[49] In this case it was
the inquisitorial vicar who in September 1499 forwarded the confessions
to Venice and complained that the judges appointed by the pope were infamous men locally and asked for the rectors to intervene and suspend
matters for several months. Although the doge was highly incensed ("molto
caldo") in his opposition to this request, causing the letters to be left un-
read in the meeting of the Collegio, he was eventually prevailed on to ask
the rectors in Brescia to insist that the papal judges act in no way otherwise
than strictly instructed.[50]

Venetian hostility toward Roman interference in ecclesiastical matters was well known at this time and occasionally erupted into serious conflict, as in 1483–84 when the republic and the papacy were at war over Ferrara. In more local and particular terms, tensions between clerical and secular priorities resurfaced dramatically during the first decade of the sixteenth century in the dispute over funerals (explored earlier) that prompted the pamphlet war between Dominicans and local humanists.[51] These pamphlets addressed local concerns about the alms or "fees" paid to mendicant mourners but also considered the lay use of ecclesiastical property and debates about the role of religion and the religious in civil society more broadly. One of the pamphleteers made a point of condemning the Dominican inquisitors' treatment of witches in the Val Camonica and accused the Dominicans of using the Church's weapons

> to satisfy your uncontrollable lusts, frightening a people of pure and simple faith, who fear God and the Church, with all the dreadful bogies of excommunication. Your aim is that this terror may shock them into casting themselves and everything they own at the feet of you greedy and haughty people,[52] who give yourselves such airs by using a certain title of the Inquisition—a title weighty in itself, and rightly established by our forebears long ago, but now weak and hollow thanks to you—or rather, lucrative, for according to popular gossip you use it for profit. You use the office (such is your vanity and pride) almost as a kingdom and, lest it lie idle, you seize from the Val Camonica certain old women who are stupid and frozen in a kind of mental daze, and you interrogate them about their faith, the Trinity, and other such topics. You bring in scribes and drag out the proceedings; you conduct examinations under torture so that, by inflicting pain and torment on women who are admittedly little different from brutish beasts, you may appear as guardians of the Christian faith.[53]

At around the time that the pamphleteer was writing, a certain Mora was imprisoned and banned from Brescia for *maleficium,* and the Dominican inquisitor Silvestro Prierias was apparently actively persecuting witches in the Val Camonica.[54]

Bishop Zane and the man who succeeded Prierias as inquisitor initiated an intense phase of witchcraft persecution in the Val Camonica in June 1518 when news reached them of heretics who denied the faith, took the devil as their god, and thereby caused many deaths.[55] This development came after war and disruption caused in the area by seven or eight years of occupation by French, Spanish, and imperial troops, and just as some measure of peace was being restored in the Venetian *terraferma.* These earthly crises seemed to be echoed by supernatural disturbances, and during the winter of 1517–18, there were reports in the Bergamasco, close to the site of the battle of Agnadello, of ghostly armies, headless men, and giants rising from the earth and of quantities of flying pigs, which the clergy attempted to disperse with processions.[56] The following year further "prodigies, portents, and seeming miracles" were reported around Brescia, including a comet that tore up the land and destroyed buildings and a flood that altogether seemed to presage the early arrival of the long-awaited great flood of 1524.[57] The link between such portents and the spread of evil was pointed out by one observer in 1520 after floods had overwhelmed the already famine- and plague-stricken inhabitants of the Val Camonica: "For this reason we cannot but think that there is an evil sect in this diabolical valley." In fact, some friars who were helping the hungry encountered a witch who asked them what they were doing and told them that "until witches and warlocks are left alone it will never be different." As a result of this statement she was investigated by the inquisitor in Edolo.[58]

The bishop and inquisitor went up the valley to eliminate this heresy, accompanied by preachers who exhorted the people to confess their errors against faith. Those who did so were given a light penance and absolved of their sins, but others remained obstinate and told similar alarming stories.[59] Seven women and one man were excommunicated and expelled as heretics from the Church on the eve of the feast of Saint John. They were handed over to the secular authorities for judgment and as a result of their "excessi" were sentenced to be burned alive. Others, for example the priest in Breno Gaspare da Rivedessa, who had renounced his faith and had done harm for the love of a certain Antonia and urged on by Giacomina, were absolved and given a penance. Gaspare does not seem to have learned his lesson and was imprisoned in 1544–45 for using unconsecrated hosts.[60]

The trial record of sixty-year-old Benvegnuda "ditta Pincinella" of Terra di Nave, in the Val Camonica, who was burnt as a witch in August 1518, sheds light on this inquisitorial procedure: having heard of her quarrels in the area, the inquisitor excommunicated the whole of Navi and commanded everyone who knew of Benvegnuda's activities to come before the inquisition in Brescia and give their testimonies. In all, twenty-four testimonies were taken down over four days at the Dominican convent of San Domenico in Brescia or by a public notary in the town of Gussago (west of Brescia). Benvegnuda had already been punished by the inquisition for earlier offenses connected with "medicine superstitiose" as well as "incantamenti et diaboliche superstitiose," which she believed were the reason for her detention in this instance, but over four days of interrogation she gradually revealed details of the demonic orgies on Monte Tonale, storm raising, and harm caused to children. It is worth speculating how far she was prompted by her interrogators and by the application, or threat, of torture: her admissions grew more "diabolical" over time, and on the last day of questioning she was asked if she dreamt of her trips to the Tonale. She is reported to have replied, in a suspiciously flat contradiction of the early medieval Canon *Episcopi* in which the nocturnal flights of the followers of the goddess Diana were attributed to dreaming: "I truly know that I go bodily and not in my dreams."[61]

Outright scepticism of such details emerges in the letter of a certain Giuseppe da Orzinuovi, who gave a friend in Venice a lengthy and learned account—full of classical pagan allusions—of what the bishop and inquisitor had found in the Val Camonica. A plague of witches had spread from Albania (an area commonly associated with the Bogomil heresy) and for many years had been encouraged by demonic priests who refused to baptize many thousands of valley-dwellers and in fact led them into evil with the temptations of pleasure and wealth. These "rebels against God" gave themselves body and soul to the devil, who presided over an "epicurean paradise" in the forest with palaces, parties, and all manner of good things not found in Portugal, Calicut, or Alexandria, such as "honeyed flies" and "sugared rats." At these "zuogi" (sports) on Monte Tonale, the many thousands of disciples of the devil were given magic powders and unguents, which they used to cause harm, transform themselves, and enchant objects of desire. They also subverted the sacramental rituals of the Church when they attended by using secret signs and prayers. Even as they burned alive, the witches—including a chancellor of the valley who had punctiliously kept their "libri ordenari" for thirty years and a courier who had taken their messages into Spain and France—were tricked by the devil into believing they could survive the fires, since he appeared to them in the guise of the Virgin Mary to reassure them. However, as the flames charred their flesh the women cried: "O Devil you have deceived us." As Giuseppe da Orzinuovi exclaimed at the end of his letter, such things had not been heard of since the time of the sorceress Medea and were "scarcely credible." He dismissed outright as "fables" ("fabula") rather than "history" ("istoria") accounts of invisible but noisy armed battles in the Bergamasco.[62]

Similar scepticism was expressed by a number of others. Alessandro Pompeio of Brescia concluded his account of the sabbat on Monte Tonale saying that he would write no more to his patrician correspondent "because your magnificence would not believe it unless you had seen it."[63] The castellan of Breno speculated whether these were simply demonical delusions or were actually experienced "corporaliter" and wondered if the accused should be consigned to the flames alive. In the absence of any other civilized company with whom he could discuss the matter, as he said, he turned to canon law for guidance and discovered several passages that indicated that these were all the delusions of the ignorant.[64]

Pietro Tron, the Venetian *podestà* of Brescia, even attempted to meet some of the witches condemned at Pisogne by the inquisitor's vicar Bernardino de Grossis. Despite inquisitorial resistance, he managed to interview them and to discover that the inquisitor had used undue force and trickery to extract the fatal confessions. Describing the alleged sexual antics of the condemned women, who had been pleasured at once by the anus and the vagina on a cross by the devil with his bifurcated penis, the *podestà* ended a letter to the Council of Ten with baffled resignation: "These all seem rather grave, wondrous, and strange matters to me, which I believe and I don't believe."[65]

In this instance, the pressure to apply the brakes of the inquisitorial process seems to have come from the Council of Ten in Venice, who read the *podestà*'s letter and objected to the confiscation of laypeople's property by ecclesiastical authorty. The Ten instructed the *podestà* to act discreetly with the bishop ("cum ogni secreteza") and to peruse the trial documentation before sending it to Venice. The vicars appointed by the bishop, as well as the inquisitors, notaries, and *capitano* of the valley were to present themselves to the heads of the Ten with a copy of the statute against heresy and the episcopal orders for the execution of the condemned. The *podestà* was also expected to conduct an investigation into the behavior of the ecclesiastical judges regarding the examination of witnesses and the confiscation and dispersal of the goods of the condemned. Several hundred case notes (now lost) were sent to Venice, and the Ten interviewed the offending inquisitor, Bernardino de Grossis, and notified the pope that he ought to be removed. The council referred the matter to two Brescian ecclesiastics: the apostolic nuncio Altobello Averoldi who visited the Val Camonica in the company of the bishop of Famagusta, Mattia Ugoni, an expert in both civil and canon law, in September 1518. The nuncio returned with a learned priest ("uno prete leterato") held by the authorities in Brescia accused of witchcraft who described how his lust for a certain woman had driven him to the sabbat on the Monte Tonale. Questioned by the doge and other patricians, he was reported to have replied that there were demons with horns on their heads and webbed feet like geese.[66]

Matters were then complicated by the inquisitor's zealous vicar, who arrested a person already detained for heresy without consulting the bishop or the rectors. The Brescian *podestà* informed the Ten that when he had sent his secretary to the inquisitorial vicar to protest, the secretary had been insulted. The exasperated *podestà* wrote dismissively of these vicars:

They are, to speak frankly, overdressed peasants, who have devoured their shame as well as their conscience. I say this of the greater part of those who are here, and this because the decent friars don't want to come to this city, knowing that they are looked upon worse than Jews on account of their squabblings and bad behavior . . . [and] on account of their friars' cloaks, they permit themselves every enormous and nefarious crime, I say this of the bad friars, who by their actions disclose the nature of their lives, confident that the laity and the temporal lords, as they claim, have no jurisdiction over them.[67]

The Ten ordered action to be taken against those who were making the arrests. When one of the accused witches was moved to the public prison, it was discovered that the vicar had extorted money from him. The vicar was questioned and then released, but as a result of all of this the Ten advised the rectors to act carefully, especially in the matter of asking the inquisitor how the goods of those who had been burnt were shared out.

The Brescian council voted almost unanimously to ask their orators in Venice to offer support for the patriarch, and the legate in the Val Camonica and to ask Venice to give officials in Brescia every necessary freedom and authority to make opportune provision for the conservation of the Catholic faith and the punishment of witches ("strigas") and other "perfidious and maleficent persons," whether in the Val Camonica or in the city.[68] By February 1520 around sixty women and twenty men had been burnt, but further inquisitorial activity was hindered by the Ten while it examined the paperwork at length—in several obviously stormy meetings in Venice at the beginning of 1521. At one of these meetings the trial records of the bishop who had been sent by Venice to intervene were read and were found to contain words confirming the "truth" about the witches in the Brescian valley. In opposition to this assertion one member of the council, Luca Tron, denied that they contained the truth. Dismissing the inquisitor from a post that he had held so briefly, the Ten then considered a papal complaint about Venetian infractions of canon law and interference in what was an ecclesiastical matter. Tron was once again vehement in his opposition, and the Venetian diarist Marin Sanudo caught Tron's tone when he commented that "these pathetic creatures [*meschini*] died martyrs, and nothing happened on Monte Tonale."[69] As the Ten patronizingly remarked: "These poor creatures of the Val Camonica are simple people with the coarsest understanding, and have no small need of preachers and prudent instruction in the Catholic faith."[70] A new bishop was appointed, with Roman approval, and sent to Brescia to work on the cases in collaboration with several Brescian doctors of laws and the court of the *podestà*. Finally, in July 1521 the Ten abruptly suspended all judicial action—perhaps because the Val Camonica was once again at the front line of the theatre of war.[71]

It is interesting to note that the surviving evidence of the latest cases in Sondrio (in a neighboring Alpine valley) in 1523 indicate that leniency was used in sentencing witches and that in 1534 the apostolic nuncio to Venice found that witchcraft had been largely overtaken by the Lutheran heresy in senatorial concerns.[72] However, it is clear that the Venetian intervention in the Val Camonica during 1520–21 continued to rankle with the patriarch Girolamo Querini for many years. During 1533–34 the apostolic nuncio in Venice, Girolamo Aleandro, had to mediate between Querini and the Venetian government who were in dispute over a number of matters of ecclesiastical jurisdiction. The patriarch had absented himself from the city, to the irritation of the Venetian authorities, and had presented a list of his grievances to the nuncio before he had even reached Venice. The sticking point in reaching a solution and ensuring the return of the patriarch to the city was the matter of Venetian investigation of inquisitorial activity in the Val Camonica. The Venetians asserted that the matter lay outwith the patriarch's jurisdiction but Querini seems to have been especially affronted by the state's meddling in the affairs of his fellow Dominicans and the nuncio thought that he prized his authority over the order more than anything else. The nuncio read the Ten's original decree on the matter and judged it contrary to holy canons but he was sympathetic to the Venetian position since the inquisitorial vicars had acted so badly and Venice had been obliged to impose order in the valley. Moreover, Aleandro's position was weakened, in the view of the Venetians, since his predecessor had lent his support to the Venetians in this affair. It is not clear how the matter was resolved but the nuncio attempted to shed light on the matter and wrote to Rome requesting a copy of Leo X's brief on hunting heretics in the Val Camonica.[73]

This survey of the cases of witchcraft in the Val Camonica after 1454 reveals that worship of the devil and denial of the faith were associated with heresy in the way outlined by medieval authorities such as Eymeric. Heresy was defined as an "error of belief persistently and perniciously held," with apostasy regarded as a "subspecies" of heresy in which a false belief replaced faith, for example, the worship of the devil. In this respect, witchcraft was clearly a heresy and moreover involved apostasy and idolatry.[74] However, the range and nature of the witches' apostasy in the fifteenth-century Val Camonica surpassed or differed from medieval heresy in some striking ways. If the old and the new shared many characteristics, such as the sabbat or an emphasis on carnality, as well as the presence of superstition, other, newer elements complicated the picture, raising doubts in the minds of men such as Luca Tron and Giuseppe of Orzinuovi.

It is likely that the inquisitors, prompted by new demonological speculations, highlighted the demonic in order to support the urgency of their work. It may also be the case that inquisitors and their vicars were genuinely concerned about the spread of superstition in the Val Camonica. Practices considered superstitious, such as the use of herbal remedies and incantations, were much easier to identify and could serve, as in the case of Benvegnuda da Navi, as a starting point for the investigation of more serious crimes. Dominican inquisitors may also have been troubled by the growing presence of the rival Franciscan order in the Val Camonica during this period, and the assertion of their traditional role may have been part of an attempt to establish a position of influence. The rivalry between mendicant orders and their close association with political authorities, a theme already explored in this book, suggests how pervasive was their influence in Renaissance Brescia. It was no coincidence that the anonymous Brescian who denounced Dominican persecution of ignorant women as witches also lavished praise on Franciscan spirituality.[75]

At the same time, notions of female credulity and superstition were certainly used by Brescians, and probably by Venetians like Tron, to *diminish* the claims of the inquisitors in the Val Camonica. The better known charge of *maleficium* was, like that of superstition, a double-edged weapon. It is not mentioned explicitly in all of the cases but was clearly implicit in almost all of them in the harm allegedly caused to children and adults. The use in these cases of *maleficium*—a crime of concern to both secular and ecclesiastical authorities—may in fact have encouraged conflict. It may have been no coincidence that the evidence of the inquisition in Venice in the century after 1550 contains few or no signs of concern with *maleficium* and hardly any references to the main elements of the classic stereotype such as the sabbat and the demonic pact.[76] Ruth Martin, who has studied the cases of witchcraft brought before the Venetian inquisition during the latter period, has concluded that this lack of a concern with *maleficium* and indeed the absence of any Venetian "witch craze" on the scale of northern and central Europe in the later sixteenth and seventeenth centuries can be attributed to the strength and independence of the Venetian inquisition and the secular courts in relation to to the Catholic Church. Stories of the sabbat, the demonic pact, and cannibalism, if mentioned at all, were regarded with scepticism or as elements of backward rural society.[77] Therefore, after 1550 in place of strife we find broad, if uneasy, agreement between inquisitors and Venetian governors on the nature and predominance of superstition in the cases examined and as a result very few executions but many lighter penalties.

In conclusion, the persecution of witches in the Val Camonica drew the attention of the Venetian authorities at the very highest level and placed them on a collision course with the ecclesiastical hierarchy. The Council of

Ten was concerned by reports of a dangerous sect of witches in one of the most remote parts of the *terraferma* and by reports of the abuse of the judicial process. One member of the Ten, Luca Tron, also took the opportunity to assert Venetian prerogatives and disparage ecclesiastical personnel. Tron was a consistent defender of Venetian secular authority against ecclesiastical encroachments; in 1526 he proposed to call the patriarch to account before the Collegio for excommunicating Venetian officers who had imprisoned a priest for theft.[78] The enhanced powers and scope of the Ten to interfere in *terraferma* matters are on display in this case, but it should be noted that Tron represented only one strand of Venetian opinion and that even the Council of Ten relied on local officers and the counsel and investigations of churchmen in the remote frontier of the Bresciano.

The news of mass gatherings of witches in the mountains of the Bresciano may have confirmed some Venetian prejudices about the ignorance and credulity of mountain folk. Brescians like Laura Cereta could be equally dismissive of country life. However, we must be careful not to accept such statements as further examples of the traditional opposition of urbanity and rusticity, and they should not be interpreted in isolation from the more general experience of the Bresciano during the fifteenth and sixteenth centuries. During this period Brescians were obliged to deal with valley communities, which provided immigrants to the city, formed a vital economic asset, and increasingly asserted their rights and privileges in Brescia and in Venice. As noted, Brescian civic identity was shaped by its relationship with the rest of the Bresciano in some contrasting ways, as the council moved to exclude or marginalize immigrants and some councillors celebrated their noble feudal origins. The key strategic role of the Bresciano, and notably the valleys, was highlighted once again after 1508 as the French and their allies pushed through Alpine passes and occupied Venetian territory. In the scramble for survival many rural communities remained loyal to Venice, which had provided a forum for their complaints and protector of their privileges, whereas many towns, including Brescia, opened their gates to the invaders in the hope of enhanced powers. This episode and its aftermath, are therefore an essential basis for understanding the witch-hunting of the sixteenth century.

PART FIVE

CRISIS AND RECOVERY

CHAPTER ELEVEN

Disloyal Brescia

T HE FRENCH DESCENT into Italy in 1494 and the subsequent Italian
wars shattered the political status quo that had been precariously established in Lombardy and throughout much of the Italian peninsula by
the middle of the fifteenth century.[1] The passage and occupation of French
and then German and Spanish troops supported by alliances with the major Italian powers exacerbated long-standing resentments and rivalries and
introduced new ones. The papacy, in the bellicose form of Julius II, asserted its secular authority and hostility toward Venice in 1508 by the
creation of the League of Cambrai with Louis XII of France, the holy Roman emperor Maximilian I, and Ferdinand I of Spain. The aim of the
League was not only the restitution of papal territories seized by Venice in
1503, which had been a cause of papal irritation, but also the complete
conquest of the Venetian *terraferma*. It was agreed that Maximilian, who
had launched an unsuccessful assault on Vicenza, was to seize that city,
along with neighboring Verona, Padua, and the Friuli. Ferdinand would
take Otranto back from the Venetians, who themselves had snatched it
from Aragonese hands at the end of the fifteenth century. Meanwhile,
Louis would use his foothold in Milan as a basis for an attack on Bergamo,
Crema, Cremona, and Brescia. In the event, Louis defeated the forces of
Venice at the battle of Agnadello on 14 May 1509 and within days had
taken Brescia and other Lombard cities, while imperial troops occupied
Verona, Vicenza, and Padua.

Although Padua soon revolted and was brought back into Venetian hands by a contingent brilliantly led by Andrea Gritti, the republic spent a full seven years using military and diplomatic means to regain its lost empire. An early move in the merry-go-round of shifting alliances saw Venice come to terms with the pope and join him in an alliance, and in 1511 the Venetians joined the Holy League formed by the pope in opposition to its erstwhile French allies. The League managed to weaken the French grip on northern Italy, and despite some successes by Louis's nephew Gaston de Foix, both Brescia and Ravenna revolted against French rule. However, when Milan was taken from the French, the members of the League disagreed about who was to rule there. Julius II decided to partition Venetian territory with Maximilian, so Venice turned to the French for support, signing the Treaty of Blois in 1513. During the next three years the fighting strained the republic's resources and even brought about significant casualties among the patriciate—at La Motta, outside Vicenza (7 October 1513)—until Venice's victory over the Swiss forces of the Holy League at Marignano (13–14 September 1515) weakened the league and eventually resulted in imperial recognition of the integrity of the Venetian empire as it had stood in 1508.

The War of the League of Cambrai forced Venice to take some extraordinary measures to ensure its survival—the executive powers of the Council of Ten were enhanced, and many established political safeguards were bypassed or suspended.[2] The war also brought about a reorganization of relations between the center and the periphery of Venetian territory. Local resources of men and matériel were mobilized in the struggle for survival or victory, while the *terraferma* nobility capitalized on their access to local power and troops so as to secure concessions and favors from their traditional overlords or from occupying powers like the French. However, the encroachment of foreign powers or the resurgence of old enemies could also prompt internal civic factions, including Guelph and Ghibelline parties or divisions, to reappear.[3] It was widely noted by contemporary commentators, including Niccolò Machiavelli, that in the cities that fell into foreign hands the *popolo* generally remained most loyal to Venice, whereas the civic oligarchies and aristocracy, so long excluded from the Venetian halls of government and subject to resented fiscal exactions, welcomed a new régime and opportunities for extending their political influence.[4]

Such was the case in Brescia, which opened its gates to the French after the defeat of Venetian forces in 1509. Benedetto Massimo later noted that the occupation of the city by the French had exacerbated divisions and enmities that had originated in the decision of the Brescian ancestors ("maiores") to give public offices to a small group of men.[5] Venetians also lamented the opportunism of the Brescian oligarchy, which had flourished far from their paternalistic protection. A postwar *podestà* sadly recalled Brescia's rebellion and argued that the ability of the Brescians—in their councils, colleges, *mercanzia,* and occupational guilds—to meet in different parts of the city without the knowledge of the rectors or their staff had been the cause of many inconveniences and ultimately one good reason why they gave themselves to the French.[6] Some Brescians viewed the capitulation of their city to the French as a sign of moral weakness, whether Venetian—as Elia Capriolo suggested in his chronicle quoted at the beginning of this book—or Brescian. In the midst of Brescia's devastation following its revolt and sack by French troops in 1512 Marco Negro, the Venetian superintendant of munitions in the city, recalled the sermons of Bernardino da Feltre in 1493–94 in which he had foretold the calamities and miseries that would be the result of the great sins he had observed in the city. These sins, according to Negro, included ingratitude toward Venice, even though the city had been transformed under Venetian rule from a mere "villa" into one of the first cities of Italy. Several specific instances of Brescian impiety seem to have stuck in his mind: the opposition to the *monte di pietà* twenty years earlier, the misappropriation of the oblations made each year on the feast of the Assumption, and finally the funerary fracas of the prewar years. Negro feelingly described the dispute as "that matter of the death disbursements and the decision to set up a statute infringing ecclesiastical liberty, which took the livelihood from the poor religious, and because they objected to it the Dominicans were excommunicated with the hope of chasing them from the territory."[7]

As these comments suggest, an account of Brescia under occupation and after its recovery by Venice can illuminate many of the themes I have explored in the previous chapters. The loss and recovery of its subject territories reveals the strengths and weaknesses of the Venetian *terraferma* empire that Venice assembled and maintained after around 1330. The urban oligarchy that formed in Brescia after around 1460 appeared fairly strong on the eve of war, but the arrival of the French and seven years of occupation quickly brought old hatreds and disagreements to the surface and betrayed the limits of political unity. The Brescian myths of loyalty were similarly tested and then reasserted in the face of overwhelming evidence of Brescian disloyalty. Equally, religious spaces and ritual, which were severely disrupted by occupation and sacking, were adapted and then reformed as the citizens sought explanations for their apparently endless misfortune. Ultimately, the political, religious, and social physiognomy of the city was scarred by the events of 1509–16, but the evidence suggests that as in Bergamo, Verona, Vicenza, Padua, and other cities of the *terra-*

ferma, some minor political adjustments in the short term rather than fundamental adaption in the relationship with Venice were all that was required to avoid revolution and to ensure that the Brescians could once again assert that they inhabited Venice's most loyal city.

The French Occupation

In 1507 and 1508 Brescian rectors sent reports back to Venice describing the buildup of German troops over the border.[8] As political pressure mounted during 1508 the Brescians assured Venice of their traditional loyalty, and the council unanimously decided to provide troops for the defense of the republic.[9] After the formation of the League of Cambrai the city offered to support ten thousand troops for three months, while the Venetian Collegio passed a bill increasing the amount Brescia would have to pay for its defense.[10] In total, some thirty-five thousand Venetian troops were led by the experienced but mutually distrustful condottieri Count Nicolò Orsini di Pitigliano and di Nola, captain-general, and Bartolomeo d'Alviano, governor-general.[11] They were assisted by two Venetian *provveditori:* the seasoned politician and diplomat Andrea Gritti and Giorgio Corner, who had served as *podestà* in Brescia in 1497–98.

By the end of April 1509 these forces had drawn back to Castenedolo, where they awaited the arrival of artillery from Brescia, which now stood perilously close to the front line. The Brescian council voted with a large majority to spend 10,000 ducats on six thousand troops. In addition, sixty of its "zentilomeni" joined the main forces as light cavalry. On 15 May the Venetians received news of the defeat at Agnadello and French routs of Gritti's troops as they headed eastward into Brescian territory. In Brescia news quickly spread of the loss of artillery and the retreat of Gritti to Crema, as well as the poor leadership provided for the infantry by the mounted forces. One writer observed that the troops had done so badly against the French that they were ashamed to be Italian ("si vergogna esser italiani").[12] Brescian fears about the future increased further as the rectors sent their families hurrying to safety in distant Venice.

The conviction in Venice that the Brescians were ready to fight for the city (it was reported that there were seven to eight thousand armed infantry in the city) evaporated during the depressed festival for the feast of the Ascension—usually a moment of Venetian triumphalism when the doge ceremonially "married" the sea and asserted Venetian independence and inviolability. News reached Venice that the Brescians had decided to ignore the advice of the rectors and capitulate to the French.[13] It was reported that the Brescians had "capitulato in libertà, come Zenoa" and wished only to give a quantity of money to the king in return for a peaceful submission and the appointment of a French governor. The extraordinary magistracy of eleven "ad negocia belli" that had been formed to aid the Venetian rectors assumed control of the city and now acted to bar the gates against retreating Venetian troops and to draft a list of forty-eight privileges that was presented to the French king.[14] The group of ambassadors sent to greet Louis was headed by members of the feudal nobility and the most ancient families, with Vittore Martinengo da Barco and Nicolò Gambara at the head. As a reward for their actions some were made knights, while others (for example, Giovanni Battista Appiani and Pietro Porcellaga) entered the Milanese senate as royal senators. Giulio Martinengo, a close friend of Nicolò Gambara, received the ancient French Order of Saint Michel and also became a royal senator.[15] Bishop Paolo Zane swore an oath to the king on the Host at the feast of Corpus Christi—an act of disloyalty to his native city of Venice that may have been revenge for the way his family had been punished in 1478 for revealing state secrets to the pope.[16]

The French king confirmed existing Brescian statutes, increased the size of the general council to two hundred, and revoked most of the provisions associated with the closure of the council during the past three decades. There was joy in Ghibelline quarters at being admitted to government in the city and being elevated to knighthoods by King Louis in gratitude for their aid at Agnadello. Carlo d'Amboise proposed that at least one-quarter of the conciliar members should be nobles of the *cittadella* and that other offices be reserved for them.[17] The nobles of the *cittadella* had long agitated for this action, but their appeals to Venice for the restitution of rectorial authority in the appointment of offices had been ignored.[18] After eighty years of exclusion from the halls of government in Venice, direct royal patronage opened up possibilities of power and its rewards. Some Brescians did find positions in the Milanese senate, and a number of Brescians, for example the Gambara, were granted more extensive control over feudal territories. Rural communities, which on the whole preferred Venetian justice to feudal exactions, resented the extension of feudal power and occasionally attacked or otherwise resisted the new vicars.[19]

The French king solemnly assured the Brescians that no sacred relics would be removed from the city and the *monte di pietà* would be preserved.[20] The Brescians marked the change in authority by pillaging Venetian property in the form of the Jews.[21] Jewish stores of pledges and lists of debtors were opportunistically stolen or destroyed by Brescians and French troops in the looting that accompanied the latter's arrival in 1509.[22] According to the Jews who reached Venice a few days later, they had lost as much as 30,000 ducats.[23] Louis conceded to the Brescian request, "pro veneratione Religionis Christiane," for the prohibition of Jews from living in the city and from lending money in the district.[24] Subsequent attempts by the council and the new royal government to trace the pledges lost in 1509, reconstitute the lists of debtors, and extend some protection to the remaining Jews failed or were rejected. Apparently, they finally gave up on Brescia and, like many other Jews in the *terraferma,* moved to Venice, where the ghetto was established in 1516.[25]

The Venetian diarist Girolamo Priuli lamented the fact that a city that had been so dearly loved by the Venetians and had received millions of gold ducats for its fortifications had capitulated so easily. As he bitterly observed: "So without one sword blow or artillery round and without a single life being taken in an instant they [i.e. the Brescians] have insolently rebelled against their most loving lords."[26] Marco Negro later concluded that the Brescians had been whipped into welcoming the French by a number of leading men of the city well known for their hatred of Venice, but he thought that some Brescians were also moved by ignorance, weakness, and wickedness.[27] Some Brescians were certainly anti-Venetian and more than ready to come to terms with the French. Members of wealthy and powerful families from the Bresciano had served as *condottieri* on the French side, and others were linked by marriage to the Gonzaga of Mantua, the Montefeltro of Urbino, and other princes and non-Venetian patricians.

Venetian exactions of grain and the heavy burden of defense during the previous seven decades may also have irked some Brescians. Venice regarded the city as one of its most lucrative *terraferma* assets and treated it accordingly.[28] Thus, whereas Cremona may have surrendered to the French in 1509 partly through a feeling of isolation from Venice, which had chosen to fortify only a few frontier posts, it may have been the cost to Brescians of maintaining their city's key military position near the Venetian frontier defenses that was the source of some resentment.[29] As a result, some Brescians may have hoped that the French would grant a large degree of autonomy to Brescia. Some merchants also wished to see the nearby Milanese markets opened to them after years of being tied economically to a fairly distant emporium on the Adriatic. (The French granted the Brescians a house in Milan as a replacement for their Venetian residence, but Brescian merchants ultimately failed to derive much economic advantage form the opening up of this new market.)[30] Finally, some members of the council may simply have recognized that resistance was all but impossible— the Brescian walls could not withstand French cannon, and even if they could, a lengthy siege was likely. Given the glowing example of Brescia's resistance in 1438–40 and the legend of the apparition of the city's patron saints Faustino and Giovita on that occasion, it is ironic, but perhaps understandable, that the Brescian oligarchy chose not to test their own or that their saintly protectors' mettle for a second time. The Brescians may have had little faith that the Venetians would, or could, come to their rescue.

The Brescian submission may have been politically astute, given the circumstances, and at first it was popular in some quarters. French customs and cuisine were soon the fashion in the city, and the sumptuary laws were broken in order to hold large banquets.[31] However, French troops, encouraged by the "Gambareschi," raided the city's munitions, opened the prison, and plundered the palace of the *podestà*.[32] The cost and inconvenience of troops stationed in and around the city also provoked resentment.[33] Even as King Louis, accompanied by six thousand Frenchmen, arrived in Brescia at the moment of his greatest triumph to enjoy his first rich Venetian prize, some divisions were apparent. The French jubilantly tore down the symbols of Saint Mark, although they preserved one winged lion in bronze, which was sent back to Milan as a sign of subjection and humiliation.[34] However, a voice in the large crowd cried out to the departing lion: "*Bon voyage* Saint Mark and may you be lord of Milan."[35] The *popolo* was also said to be loyal to Venice, and the returning *podestà* told the Venetians that when the king appeared in the city, only seven or eight persons cried "Franza." The *podestà* also claimed that on his way out of the city, men and women had blessed him from their balconies and showed great sadness, and he placed all the blame for the loss of the city on the "Gambareschi," who hated Venice. Songs and skits ("canzon e polize") on the betrayal of Brescia by the Avogadro, Martinengo, Averoldi, and others were circulating late in 1509. It was said that many nuns were praying for Venetian aid, that the *popolo* was absolutely loyal ("marchescho tutti,") and that the valleys were also loyal to Venice. The Brescian patriciate or "citadini" were reported to be anti-Venetian but were otherwise divided as they faced a large influx of new families into the civic councils.[36]

Government under the French initially consisted of a royal lieutenant, who was soon joined by two rectors (a *regio commissario* and a *governatore*), at least one of whom reported to the senate in Milan. One was a sort of *podestà;* the other was in military control of the city and territory and depended on the king and his lieutenant, Carlo d'Amboise. They acted on existing laws assisted by a court of their own choosing, although a supreme court in Milan heard appeals. The rector in the role of *podestà* was aided by a vicar, two judges (*ragioni* and *malefizio*), a chancellor, a constable, and several others.[37] During the early phase of occupation, it was probably easy for the Brescians to find subtle legal ways of excluding the new men from government—by imposing residency requirements, penalizing those who broke statutes or had received privileges that ran contrary to the civic statutes, and excluding those who were not of legitimate birth even if they had been legitimized. Secret ballotting allowed council members more freely to reject attempts to open up the office of chancellor.[38] Government in the city generally proved arbitrary and divisive, and the splendid *piazza della loggia* now became the location for the public execution of rebels, including Giovanni Maria Martinengo della Motella (in September 1510) and Alvise Avogadro (February 1512).[39]

Jurisdictional disputes in Bresciano multiplied: the inhabitants of Salò at first welcomed the replacement of joint Brescian-Venetian rule by that of Cardinal Giorgio d'Amboise but rebelled when he decided to demolish the fortifications built by the commune.[40] Separatist tendencies flourished throughout the Bresciano: the Federici and their clients increased their power in the Val Camonica, the inhabitants of Chiari tried to extend their jursidiction, and the council for the *Territorio* turned to the senate in Milan for the redress of its grievances. In short, the political divisions and tensions that had marked the previous seventy years of Brescian life under Venetian rule were by no means diminished by the transfer to the French and would explode into terrible violence in 1512.

The Sack of 1512

During 1510, as Pope Julius II turned against his French allies and opened a rapprochement with Venice, the first signs of open discontent with French rule in the city became apparent. In August of that year there were reports of violence between Gascon troops and *contadini*. It was said that Brescia was poorly defended and ready to welcome the Venetians or their allies from Mantua.[41] Old feudal rivalries and divisions had reopened. The Gambara and Martinengo clans were waging a vendetta against the Porcellaga on account of a Martinengo boy having been maltreated by Francesco Porcellaga.[42] Giovanni Maria Martinengo della Motella had welcomed French rule in 1509 but resented the growing power of the Gambara under French occupation and attempted to bring about the return of Venetian rule to the city. On 10 September 1510 he was beheaded for his part in the plot against the French, and the "citadini" were said to be more pro-Venetian than before. The French suspected the loyalties of the *contadini* and fortified the gates leading to the Val Trompia, the Val Sabbia, and the *pedemonte*.[43]

Alvise Avogadro, who also resented the rise of the Gambara, organized another plot in January 1512 to open the key gate of San Nazaro in the city to the Venetian forces. The Val Trompia and Val Sabbia rose up against the French, and the whole territory was said to be crying "Marco, Marco."[44] Thanks to an accord arranged with Venice, Avogadro and Valerio Paitone entered Brescia on the eve of the feast of the Purification with Venetian troops led by the *provveditore* Andrea Gritti, who had been forced into an ignominious retreat almost three years earlier. As the French withdrew to the *cittadella* and then to the castle with their powerful Brescian support-ers—notably Alda Gambara (widow of Giovanni Francesco and mother of the poet Veronica) and Marco Martinengo—the homes of French sympa-thizers were put to the sack. On the evening of 4 February a messenger reached Venice; leaping from the boat bringing the mail, he ran to the doge's palace crying "Brexa è presa." ("Brescia is taken.") The news pro-voked widespread rejoicing in the city and people cried "Brexa, Brexa" through the streets of the city. Pope Julius was so overjoyed with the news that he invited the messenger to sleep in his own bedroom, and bonfires were lit and bells sounded throughout Rome.[45]

In a letter to the Brescians, to which a golden seal was attached, the Venetian Senate acknowledged the hardships the city had endured but commended its fidelity and deplored the barbaric cruelty God had thought fit to send down to punish ("flagellare") miserable Italy. Venice, the letter continued, had ever had love and paternal charity toward Brescia in its heart, and Brescia had "quello instincto fervor et dispositione" in its soul that seemed to be a sort of hereditary law from its very foundation. Venice had deplored the loss of Brescia but had felt that like a stream returning to its natural course or a daughter to its mother's sweetest lap the city would return to Venetian rule. Brescia, it was said, had escaped by God's grace from servitude to return to its previous tranquillity and secure liberty un-der Venice. All of the concessions, immunities, prerogatives, and privileges granted to the city since 1426 would be reinstated. Brescian faith would not only redound to its own eternal glory but would also lead to the lib-eration of all Italy and consequently the Christian religion. In an accompa-nying letter the Senate thanked Alvise Avogadro for his loyalty, describing him as a mirror and exemplar of sincere affection toward Venice. Avogadro was true to paternal virtue and spirit, for just as his father had been the principal means of bringing Brescia over to Venice in 1426, the son had helped to conserve the city for Venice in 1512.[46]

In spite of these fine words and glib comparisons, this Venetian victory was short-lived. In a fatal miscalculation, Andrea Gritti sent home the thou-sands of troops from the valleys and the *pedemonte* who had been instru-mental in assuring initial success. Gritti intended by this measure to ease pressure on scarce urban resources, but in retrospect this decision appeared lamentably shortsighted and confirmed the low view many held of Gritti's leadership.[47] The Brescian Pandolfo Nassini, no fan of the Venetians at the best of times, later concluded laconically: "In that time the city was sacked on account of his [i.e. Gritti's] poor governance and lack of foresight in providing for the return of the French."[48] The Venetian troops in the city faced constant bombardment and skirmishes with the French troops, who holed up in the well-munitioned and fortified castle until their reinforcements arrived. Gaston de Foix, the French governor in Italy, rushed from Bologna to Brescia on 16 February and began to turn events around—he attacked the soldiers from the Val Trompia at the Dominican convent of San Fiorano and he then seized the Franciscan monastery of Sant'Apollonio, both in the strategically important hills outside the city walls.

During 18–19 February the troops of Gaston de Foix finally entered the city and were joined by the French troops, who left the castle and began fighting in the city. During the three days that began on "Fat Thursday" of Carnival, the whole city was turned upside down in an especially bloody version of the battle of Carnival and Lent. Like the participants in the Friulian massacres a few years earlier, the French were "hacking up the bodies of dead aristocrats . . . [as] a way of carving up the body politic."[49] Old enmities were played out, and every area of the city apart from the Ghibelline *cittadella* and some houses of the "Gambareschi," was put to the sack.[50] The Venetian Collegio heard the first news of the dangerous situation in Brescia in silence, and the following morning learnt from dire reports coming in from the city that a mere fortnight after it had been "presa," Brescia was now "persa." The Piazza San Marco and the court-yard of the doge's palace were full of people waiting for news; when rumors circulated that Brescia was not lost, they chanted "Marco, Marco," and many church bells were rung and bonfires lit. In fact, the postbags of the following day brought more details of the desperate last stand of Gritti and accounts of the Ghibellines in the *cittadella* enthusiastically chanting "Franza, Franza."[51]

A few Venetians continued to hope that the city might be held for San Marco, recalling that in 1426 the Milanese had held out in the castle and *cittadella* for several months until Venice finally took the city. When news reached Venice of the full extent of the sack, including reports of fifteen thousand deaths (soon rising to twenty thousand) such hopes were no doubt considerably dampened. The recriminations began immediately, with the *provveditore generale* blaming the loss of the city on Venice's failure to send artillery quickly or to execute its decision to send in the infantry. Two decades later Pietro Bembo, writing his history of these events at the behest of Andrea Gritti, who was now doge, exonerated Gritti and presented Doge Loredan as a weak and dilatory war leader.[52] Others impugned the Brescians' martial vigor, asserting that if they had all fought like their women—who were reported to have thrown rocks and vases from windows down on the French—Brescia might have been saved.[53] As the Florentine historian Francesco Guicciardini later concluded, with some irony: "In this way that city—not inferior in nobility and dignity to any other city in Lombardy but indeed superior to all others in wealth except Milan—fell to utter destruction at the hands of the French from whom the Brescians proudly claimed descent."[54]

Representations of the Sack

The horrific events of "Fat Thursday" and the days and months that followed were recorded in a number of contemporary diaries, summarized and moralized in several vernacular publications lamenting the Italian wars, and turned into mythological allegory. These literary representations have some key themes in common that may reflect individual experiences of the sack as well as the clerical or humanist backgrounds of the authors. The repeated tropes—the barbarism of the French, the bravery of women and children in resistance, and the instances of divine intervention—also represent vestiges or reworkings of the Brescian myths that had been elaborated around the events of 1438–40. These authors also present the sack as a "rite of violence" or a "religious riot" by describing the desecration and looting of churches and the murder of priests in great detail.[55] In the same way, some of these writers accuse the French of a very close association with the Jews and compare the atrocity of the French to that of the Turks; both these devices also serve to enhance the piety of the Brescians. By examining these texts it is possible to show how observers interpreted and presented the sack within a preconceived framework. In sum, the accounts of the sack may be used as historical evidence but are just as interesting as literary conceits that contemporaries could sift, judge, and use as the basis for reflection, prayer, and action.

The chronicle of Marco Negro was contemporary with the events described and was summarized in Marin Sanudo's Venetian diary.[56] Negro's account reached Venice in the form of letters he sent to his cousins Lorenzo and Pietro Capello (*podestà* in Brescia, 1502–3). In these letters Negro explained that he had been at his post as superintendant of munitions near the *piazza del duomo* when the French had attacked. He described how he called on the Venetian troops to "attack these cowards like the brave men you are and kill them like dogs."[57] Negro's hatred of the French was almost limitless: he describes in some detail the robberies, rapes, and attacks committed by the French and their supporters. He calls the French the "enemies of God and of humanity, bloodsuckers, and people without laws or faith, not worthy of being called Christian."[58] Negro even associated the French bloodlust with that of the Jews. The Jews' close connection with the Martinengo tainted them with the suspicion of disloyalty; it was reported that they stole some of the funds of the *monte di pietà* and that this money ended up in the hands of some Milanese Jews, together with the communal archive.[59] Negro went much further than accusing the Brescian Jews of self-enrichment.[60] In fact, in an echo of the blood libel discussed earlier, he described a massacre in the duomo, with Jews filled with lust for Christian blood among the French attackers.[61] Negro alleged that the French commander Gaston de Foix led Jews in cruel raids on regular clergy and friars and looted holy objects. He even likened the French to the Turkish or Moorish pursuit of such sacrilege.[62] He characterized the king of France was as the "most greedy, cruel and unjust supporter of thieves, libertines and Jews."[63] King Louis's military governor, Robert Stewart, who assisted at the sack, Negro dismissed as a "barbarian without laws or civilized habits, like all the Scots."[64] However, Alda Gambara, who received 5,000 ducats in compensation from the French for the sack of her palace by the Venetians, was judged by Negro with grudging admiration to have been an effective enemy, who "has fought as valiantly against the *signoria* as if she had a thousand horsemen by her side even though she has done nothing but write and promote intrigue."[65]

Negro also placed some of the blame for the sack on Brescian sins and failings. He had a record of insulting the Brescians: in 1503 he was thrown in prison for six months by the Council of Ten after an encounter with the Brescian orator in the Piazza San Marco in Venice. On that occasion he spoke insulting words to the orator, gave him a slap in the face, and accused the Brescian territory of lacking loyalty. Negro was probably incensed by the case against his cousin Pietro Cappello, the outgoing *podestà,* that the Brescians presented to Venice at that time.[66] In 1512 Negro had his revenge and noted that Avogadro's band of men from the valleys had offered to take the castle but had been told that it could not be done, even though the prostitutes who serviced the French later suggested that there had been very few French within its walls.[67] Negro added that Brescian greed had led the city's inhabitants to keep their granaries closed rather than open them up to the valley men, who might have launched an assault on the French in the castle. The wealth of the Brescians had therefore proved the foundation for their downfall, and Brescia no longer had the appearance of a city: like flies who find themselves swimming in milk they had brought down destruction on themselves.[68] They had chased out a government that had governed them for eighty-four years not as subjects but as if they were its own sons ("proprii fioli"), and without the Venetians they were little more than bumpkins or depraved children. Negro sententiously concluded: "The sins of the young rise up after the death of their parents."[69]

In comparison with Negro's vivid and breathless chronicle, the account of the sack and its aftermath by the Lateran canon Innocenzo Casari is a much more polished effort. For example, Casari heightened the sense of drama by introducing set-piece speeches in humanist fashion: as a counterpart to Gaston de Foix's speech rallying his troops, Casari reported the Venetian general's opinion that the French were fighting for gain whereas the Brescians were driven by patriotism, love, and the desire to avoid tyranny.[70] Casari reached for classical rather than contemporary examples of cruelty with which to judge the behavior of the French. He suggested that their cruelties had been worse than the Greek's to Troy or the Romans' to Jerusalem and Carthage and were comparable with the Lombard and Gothic invasions.[71] Casari, like Negro, dwelled on the impiety of the French, who had despoiled the churches and ground the Host into the mud with their feet.[72] Priests, Casari reported, prayed to Christ for help, recalling his own suffering. Churches and monasteries were set on fire with clerics and laypeople inside, and more than a hundred people were killed in the cathedral by the "barbarians" and their Jewish comrades. The *monte di pietà* was looted and 100,000 gold ducats taken, as well as gems, gold, worked silver, and clothes. Again like Negro, Casari placed some blame for the traumatic events on the Brescians themselves and delighted in the irony of noble men and women who had once displayed themselves in their finery in the main squares of the city—the women dressed like prostitutes— being stripped bare and robbed of all their jewels.[73] Given Casari's vivid experiences during the sack, it is perhaps unsurprising that the *Murder of the Innocents* (now hanging in situ in the church of San Giovanni Evangelista, Brescia) that he and his brother commissioned from the local artist Alessandro Bonvicino, known as Moretto, around 1530 was recognizably set in the Brescian *piazza della loggia* and was probably meant to recall the frenzied murder of innocent civilians two decades earlier.[74]

The classical and mythological comparisons were taken much further by Ambrogio Aruscone, a Brescian living in Milan, who wrote an elaborate account of the sack—*De pugna Brixiae a diis immortalibus gesta*—that was published in Milan in August 1512. In his extraordinary verses Aruscone reworked the battle into an epic struggle between the gods hostile to Brescia, Juno, Invidia (jealousy), and Discordia (goddess of strife), and the gods who favored the city, Venus, Vulcan, and Mars. Venus, who laments Italy's destruction, may be interpreted as a figuration of Venice: for the goddess was often associated with that city.[75] Vulcan's gift to Brescia was the armaments for which the city was famous and that provided the means of pursuing so much discord.[76] Despite this work's lofty classicism, the more gruesome details of the sack are not overlooked—the streets piled with corpses run with purple blood, the city is filled with cries, mothers see their children killed, fathers see their daughters raped, priests are murdered as they administer the Host, and innumerable cruelties are committed. Among the notable horrors of the sack Aruscone choose to mention was the way the nobility died indiscriminately alongside the poor.[77]

The sack was the subject of printed verses in rhyming stanzas (*ottava rime* or *terzine*) that were also produced in Milan as pieces of anti-Venetian propaganda and in laments that interpreted the sack from a moralistic point of view.[78] Many of the details of the sack recorded by contemporary chroniclers and eyewitnesses like Negro and Casari found their way into these verses: for example, one versifier mentioned the involvement of Jews.[79] The comparison with Troy also featured in these productions: "Never was there such a scene on earth: / bodies in the streets and paths, / only the clamor of looting, fighting, and death, / bringing to mind ancient Troy."[80] The behavior of the French was compared with the Turkish atrocities at Negroponte in 1470, which themselves had been the subject of a number of verses.[81] The valiant actions of the women of Brescia were woven into several accounts: "boiling water tipped from balconies / by the women of Brescia, and stones rain down / on the backs of those who cry 'France, France!'"[82] One account recognized that some unpatriotic Brescians ("non hano ala patria amor e zelo") joined the French, and another specifically mentioned the pro-French feelings in the *cittadella*.[83] Even the Venetian failure to send artillery was mentioned, surprisingly, in a lament placed in the mouth of Gritti in verses published in Venice in 1522.[84]

Brescian misfortune was transmuted into a symptom of Venetian hubris and held up as a mirror for all of Italy.[85] Having enjoyed the spectacle of Venice's defeat at Agnadello and the loss of its mainland possessions, Venice's enemies imagined Venice personified as the Virgin and lamenting over a ravished Brescia.[86] Many writers used the example of the atrocities at Brescia, like those committed at Ravenna and Bologna, when comparing Italy to a ravished woman and called on the Italians to unite and expel the barbarians who were responsible for the Italians' misfortunes.[87] Most famously, at the end of *The Prince* (ca. 1513) Machiavelli exhorted the ruling Medici family in Florence to seize Fortuna—personified as female—and unite Italy. Egidio of Viterbo, the general of the Augustinian Hermits, also cited the sack of Brescia as a portent and a disaster for the whole of Italy, in a speech calling for the reform of Christendom that he made at the opening of the first session of the Fifth Lateran Council in 1512.[88]

Like Egidio of Viterbo, Negro, Casari, or Aruscone writing in Latin, the authors of vernacular texts also presented the French occupation and the sack of Brescia as an example of divine punishment preceded and followed by ominous, portentous, or otherwise supernatural events.[89] In 1510 a friar from the Val Trompia described an incident in Brescia when a child ("uno puto") was hung up by Frenchmen after it cried "Marco! Marco!" The French held the child by the feet and threatened to kill it unless it cried "Franza," but it refused.[90] In the same year a strange light was observed above the city, and a wooden Madonna in Manerbio cried.[91] One witness later described a vapor ("un vapor afogado") emanating from the moon that obscured it for half an hour. The vapor subsequently divided into two parts: one part went toward Germany, the other hung in the sky before dispersing completely.[92] This event, along with other prodigies and ghostly apparitions, was commemorated in printed verses in Italian and could be given a variety of interpretations depending on the political circumstances, context of publication, and prejudices of the reader.[93] Like the tales of sabbats in the Val Camonica, these stories seem to be the nightmares of men and women disturbed by real violence and "certain uncertainty."[94]

In the same apocalyptical vein Marco Negro in Crema witnessed stones raining from the sky that damaged houses and hurtled into the earth and were of such hardness that they could not be broken with any metal.[95] In 1512 two paintings of the Virgin and a crucifix in a church in or near Castelazo were venerated as miraculous objects after having cried and sweated ("pianto e sudato") at the time of the sack of Brescia and the battle of Ravenna.[96] It was alleged that two Jews had tried to take the holy crosses during the sack but had been struck down by divine displeasure as they tried to enter the chapel of the holy crosses in the Brescia duomo.[97] Other instances of divine intervention were recorded or embroidered in the stories about female mystics or pious nuns in the city.[98] A Dominican friar thrown from a bell tower was saved by making a vow to Mary mother of Jesus on the way down.[99]

The hope of divine protection for Brescia in 1512 seems to be the theme of the only known surviving artistic production of that year—an engraved print of *Five Saints with a Vision of the Virgin and Child in Glory* dated 1512 and signed by the Carmelite silversmith, engraver, and artist Giovanni Maria da Brescia (Figure 11.1).[100] The engraving by the Carmelite friar, who frescoed part of the church of Santa Maria del Carmine in Brescia, depicts the most important figures and scenes from Carmelite tradition, including (at upper left) the putative founder of the order, Elijah (2 Kings 2:11–14), throwing down to his appointed successor, Elisha, the white scapular or cloak adopted by the Carmelites in 1287.

Figure 11.1. Giovanni Maria da Brescia, *Five Saints with a Vision of the Virgin and Child in Glory*, Engraved print, 334 x 232 mm, 1512. Image © The Trustees of the British Museum.

The print carries a dated dedication to Elia Capriolo, who seems to have had many ties with the Carmelites in Brescia: his brother Angelo was elected prior of the Church of Santa Maria del Carmine several times.[101] He was especially interested in signs of divine intervention in human affairs, and his history of Brescia is studded with such incidents.[102] In part, this may derive from Roman models of history, but he also published works that testify to his more Christian and providential interests. For example, in his *De confirmatione fidei* (1497) he was concerned to establish the veracity of the apostles' eyewitness accounts of the life of Christ and, rather unusually, did so by comparing them favorably with the famously wise philosopher Socrates.[103]

Giovanni Maria da Brescia and Elia Capriolo shared an interest in classical antiquity, and both men seem to have held an eschatological view of history. Giovanni Maria's print *The Justice of Trajan*, dating to 1502, reflects both interests: the classical scene and Mantegnesque motifs on the one hand and on the other the anachronistic presence of Pope Gregory the Great, who is shown uttering his prayer for the salvation of the pagan emperor.[104] The subject of this print may have been suggested by Capriolo: the initials "EC" are visible in one corner, and he was one of the councillors elected to choose the original image, painted by Vincenzo Foppa on the clock tower *loggetta* in Brescia around 1490.[105] Like *The Justice of Trajan*, and like Carmelite history generally, the 1512 *Five Saints* elided the distance between the events described or viewed and the describer or viewer, and the viewer engaged in shaping the events.[106] In other words, the print provided a cue for devotion, prayer, and meditation in a way that was not uncommon for other prints produced in Renaissance Italy. This devotion was made more urgent by means of the unusual inclusion at the upper right of Enoch, who was translated to heaven by God (Heb. 11:5). In a visual and narrative sense, Enoch stands as the logical conclusion of the viewer's reading of the print, for the apocryphal Book of Enoch included an account of the final judgment of God on Earth, and Enoch was thought to be one of the witnesses mentioned by Saint John in his dream or revelation (Rev. 11:3). These themes of judgment and apocalypse had a particular resonance in Brescia in the political circumstances of 1512.

It is possible to construct a hypothesis about the purpose of the commission. Very little is known about the Carmelites' experience during the sack. The elderly Capriolo, like so many other Brescians, found himself directly and very personally affected by the French occupation and sack. His son Bartolomeo, who had written verses against the French, left the city in 1510 to join the Venetian forces, which were then gathering to retake the city.[107] Consequently, Bartolomeo was declared a rebel by the French, and a reward was placed on his head, which Elia was obliged to pay if his son did not return to the city.[108] In April 1512 Elia was forced to pay a ransom to the soldiers of Captain Lionardo Napolitano for the return of his goods and the liberation of his remaining family.[109] It is therefore likely that Capriolo witnessed the devastation of the sack firsthand and deplored its effects on the city.

Just as Capriolo had attributed previous disasters in the Bresciano, both natural and manmade, to divine displeasure, he would have agreed with the lamentations about the war and the sack emanating from Italian presses that attributed these misfortunes to divine anger at the spectacle of human sin. Capriolo may have commissioned the print from his friend as an act of penitence or as an ex-voto following his survival from the sack under the protection of the Virgin and Carmelite saints. The link between the tribulations of 1512 and the engraving is reinforced by the inscription on the tablet held by the figure of Saint Cyril of Constantinople, in which the figures—showing a total of 2,264, the number of years from the foundation of Rome—date the print to somewhere between 20 April 1511 and 20 April 1512.[110] Given the inscription "1512" in Arabic numerals elsewhere on the print, the period of engraving can be narrowed down to the first four months of 1512. According to the Carmelites, Cyril was a twelfth-century Greek visionary who received an angelic gift of silver tablets on which the future tribulations of the Church were inscribed in unintelligible laguage and who communicated these to the prophet Joachim of Fiore.[111] The implication would seem to be that during these months Brescia, or the Brescian Carmelites, were suffering in a similar fashion.

Finally, this hypothesis about the circumstances and purpose of the engraving may be supported by the image of the Virgin and Child. The Virgin was accorded special veneration by the Carmelites for her role in instituting their order and accordingly has a prominent position in the print. It should also be recalled that the preeminent feast in the Brescian civic calendar was that of the Assumption. Her pose in the print is striking: shown as the Madonna of humility, after an engraving by Andrea Mantegna, she bends down toward the Christ child and holds him close to her breasts, her arms locked around him.[112] Her eyes are closed, and the Christ child gazes out at the viewer in a way that encourages emotional intimacy and devotion. Earlier medieval versions of the Madonna of humility showed her suckling Christ and sitting on the ground; here she is both a celestial vision—a Madonna of the Apocalypse with the moon displayed at her feet (Rev. 12:1)—and a nursing mother. Her motherhood gave her a special power and character as *Maria Mediatrix,* the compassionate intercessor for humanity before the impartial justice of Christ or God the father. As the inscription asserts, the Virgin is the "bearer of God" *(theotokos)* and as such naturally had a privileged place among the ranks of intercessors, which included saints such as Cyril, Jerome, Albert, and so on who can be seen in the foreground of the 1512 print. Mary was also the mother of all mankind as well as of Christ.[113] Her low posture symbolized her concern with all souls, even the sinful. Therefore, the Virgin in this print is essentially an intercessory image, and given the date, (presumed) location, and dedicatee, it seems likely that the print invited Capriolo and any other viewer to pray to the Virgin for aid in Brescia's time of troubles or to give thanks to her for protecting him or her from harm.[114]

CHAPTER TWELVE

Venice and the Recovery of Power

THOSE BRESCIANS who had not died in the sack and had not fled to the countryside or been expelled by the French as "gente inutile" faced an unpleasant summer in 1512. The French confiscated the goods of those who had rebelled against them and inflicted public humiliations on some of the rebels: the body of Ventura Fenaroli, who stabbed himself to death in French custody, was displayed in one of the city squares.[1] The water supply was periodically cut off by the besieging Venetian forces, and it was said that there were only two wells available throughout the whole city. By July forty people were dying every day from disease. It was also reported that there was nothing being sold in the squares.[2] However, as a sign of hope for future liberation, the leading Brescian exiles based at Iseo managed to put aside their differences and form a provisional council under the leadership of Vittore Martinengo da Barco.

Venetian plans for the reconquest of Brescia with the aid of their new Spanish allies were set back when the ambitious and duplicitous Spanish general, Ramòn Folch de Cardona, came to an accord with the French governor and sent in his troops to occupy the city. The period of Spanish rule of the city after October 1512 saw some attempts to restore normal life: sixteen Guelphs and Ghibellines were installed to govern in the name of the Holy League and under the supervision of the military government.[3] In order to augment the population and meet emergency needs the governor reopened the city gates, and the council of sixteen made an increasing number of concessions of citizenship to those who had land or were doctors and surgeons, as well as those who had lived in the city for some time and were willing to pay 50 gold ducats. Few applications were refused by the council, although Giorgio Francesco Cappi's letter of recommendation from the emperor Maximilian was not enough to overcome a poor reputation earned by his violent attack on a woman.[4] Brescians who had fled the city were ordered to return to help repair buildings and walls and maintain the fortifications as well as to combat the spread of disease.[5] Clearly, few thought fit to return, and many stayed in the *pedemonte,* where at least they did not have to pay the usual levies to pay for plague measures in the city or offer labor services to the state in lieu of taxation ("angarie"). As a result, there were said to be only two hundred people in the city in June 1513.[6] The usual religious processions were suspended on account of the fear of disease but also because of a lack of money.[7]

As the threat of a renewed Venetian assault receded, political and spiritual order was gradually restored and power returned to Brescian hands: Girolamo Peschiera, Francesco Castelli, and Giovanni Antonio Monti were appointed to deal with civil and criminal cases in 1513.[8] Cardona repulsed an attack by troops led by Bartolomeo Martinengo di Villachiara in October 1514, and in an effort to maintain internal security a general council of ninety and a special council of twelve were restored, with the participation of many newly created citizens chosen by the governor. There followed some attempt to revise the *estimo* and to appoint officals to administer the duomo treasury and the communal funds of the church of the Miracoli. Arrangements were also made for the use of offerings to San Rocco in propitiatory processions, the ornamentation of the church of San Rocco, and the repair of the clock tower.[9] New seats were made for the council members' meeting in the palace on the west side of the *piazza della loggia,* although these new arrangements provoked dissensions in the College of Notaries.[10] Repairs were made to the organs, bells, glass, clock, and tower of the duomo, which had been damaged by earthquake and by looting.[11]

The Venetian siege of the city that followed the successful outcome of the battle of Marignano put a further stranglehold on the city from the autumn of 1515 onward.[12] Accordingly, the advance of imperial troops under the command of Maximilian at the beginning of the following year was welcomed by Ghibellines in the city, hoping for an end to the siege. However, the French troops and Venetian forces led by Andrea Gritti skilfully fought off this imperial advance. With the hope of imperial aid gone and dissent breaking out among the occupying Spanish and German troops, the governor decided to capitulate, and Gritti finally reentered the city on 26 May 1516. The Venetian Senate wrote to congratulate him and immediately communicated the news to Venice's representatives at the courts of the allied powers of France, England, and Rome.[13] The recapture of Brescia prompted the illumination of the campanile, the ringing of bells, and the setting of bonfires in Venice, although some argued against these measures—perhaps reflecting on Gritti's short-lived success in 1512.[14] The Spanish headed east from Brescia toward Trent, with a baggage train that included more than sixty prostitutes, many in carriages or on horseback holding children in their arms. "There was never a more beautiful sight," observed one Brescian wryly.[15] In this rather ignominious fashion the seven years' occupation came to an end.

Political Reform

The return of the Venetians was ostensibly a cause for celebration and renewed patriotic fervor in Brescia: it was agreed that a sculpted and gilded image of Saint Mark would be placed in its traditional location in the *piazza della loggia* "in order to demonstrate the unassailed and most constant faith and most earnest devotion" the city held toward Venice.[16] The council later agreed that the entry of Venice into the city on 26 May, having liberated it from innumerable evils and restored to it the happy protection of Venice and its most just and illustrious prince, should therefore be celebrated each year.[17] In fact, the return to Venetian rule was marked by uncertainty, fear, and contention.

In June 1516 the *provveditore* Andrea Trevisan wrote to the heads of the Ten explaining his desire to make some provision for the returning interim council of the city so that no complaints would arise that the council members had returned without reason and so that they could proceed without delay in electing a new council following traditional form ("secondo la usanza"). Trevisan understood that only 100 remained alive of the 140–150 members who had met in the last year of Venetian rule and added that around 25 of these men were reportedly in "bon odor" (good standing) as a result of their actions in the intervening years. Trevisan had reliable information about most of these men and cautiously accepted the judgment of Taddeo della Motella and Vittore Martinengo on the rest, since no Guelph names figured among those in poor standing and the list included relatives of Taddeo and Martinengo. However, Trevisan wanted the advice of the Ten before proceeding: he did not wish to provoke resentment by including a number regarded in poor standing.[18] The heads of the Ten quickly advised Trevisan to delay the formation of the council until further information could be gathered. At the same time Trevisan noted that the Brescians were alarmed by the dismissal of the artillery and were nervously expecting the enemy's return.[19] Many citizens remained in their villas in the countryside and held wheat and wine there to the disadvantage of the city; sometimes those poorly disposed toward Venice even sold their provisions to the enemy.[20]

When the Brescian council finally met, it proved resistant to Venetian demands for money and to the desire the border towns Asola and Salò expressed for jurisdictional separation.[21] These points were brought up when four Brescian orators arrived in Venice on 12 February 1517, resplendent in crimson and black velvet, gold chains, and damask, to offer formal and public thanks for the return of the city to Venetian control. Mattia Avogadro, doctor and Venetian knight, made an oration in which he made the best of the Brescian defection almost eight years earlier, offering praise of Venice and its prince, speaking of Brescian loyalty, and lamely excusing its capitulation to the French. Having recalled the horrors of the sack in all its gruesome violence, he then asserted that Brescia would have difficulty paying the 20,000 ducats Venice had demanded in compensation for the expenses of the city's recovery.[22] He went on to offer instead true and perpetual loyalty and requested that Venice confirm the Brescian privileges of 1428. In reply Doge Loredan affirmed that Brescia had always been Venice's most loyal and most loved city and he preferred to dwell on the providential rather than political causes of the sufferings experienced by both cities in the recent past.[23]

The petitions Avogadro and three other ambassadors read to the Senate in April 1517 were the most extensive of their kind that the Brescians had presented since their city had first passed into Venetian hands.[24] As usual, the Brescians' sensitivities with regard to taxes and the control of Bresciano were acute, and in one of the clauses they requested a return to the status quo of 1509 in jurisdictional matters, "especially in the *podesterie* of Salò and Asola."[25] In fact, Venice was faced with conflicting fiscal and jurisdictional demands from the Bresciano: for soon after the Brescian orators arrived in Venice, an orator from the Bresciano arrived and asked that it be placed under Venetian rule and given some fiscal relief.[26] To complicate matters further, orators from the outlying valleys also arrived in Venice wishing to be heard. And later the same year Salò requested complete separation from Brescian jurisdiction.[27]

Of forty-five articles (*capitula*), the Venetian *savii* initially responded to only eight judged "molti disformi" in April 1517.[28] They confirmed the privileges granted in 1428 but added that they wished to see Asola separated from Brescia and returned to its pre-1484 state when it had enjoyed *civilitas* and the right to appeal to Venice in both civil and criminal cases.[29]

The Brescians were also granted a house in the capital, and the Venetians agreed to write to Rome about the assignment of minor benefices.[30] However, the suggestion that appeals against civil judgments should in future be dealt with by the Brescian College of Judges was met with disapproval in Venice, and one of the *avogadori* asserted that such appeals should only be considered by the Venetian *auditori novi*.[31]

The Venetian response to the articles provoked disquiet among the Brescians. The orators were reportedly "tutti malcontenti"—probably as a result of these debates and the Venetian failure to consider most of the remaining Brescian demands. In May one hundred Brescian youths appeared at the doors of the council demanding that the orators repudiate the Venetian responses to the *capitula*, which the youths deemed unworthy of a city that had been loyal and suffered a sack. They were especially displeased with the separation of Asola.[32] The council, having read the orators' accounts of the Venetian response, unanimously agreed to write to Venice explaining that the course taken in Venice was not pleasing, just, or fair to this most faithful city. In addition, the orators were instructed not to accept the way matters were proceeding in Venice.[33] However, the orators put their case in vain, and in June the Senate provided a summary response that demonstrated some sensitivity to local statutes but reaffirmed the concessions made to the *Territorio* in fiscal matters. In addition, the Senate made demands to the *terraferma* for men and arms for its galleys and imposed a tax on the city to pay for building works there.[34] The orators spent three hours in the Venetian council trying to persuade the councillors to accept this disappointing outcome.[35]

A further source of disagreement and conflict in the city at this time lay in attempts to persuade Venice to revise the restrictions on entry to Brescia's council that had been reinstated with the return of Venetian rule. The first rumblings of discontent were evident when the Ten sent two extraordinary *avogadori di comun* to Brescia on 11 May 1517 to effect the election and reformation of the Brescian council and to examine the extraordinary taxes imposed at the time of the Spanish occupation. In a letter to the Ten the *avogadori* described the difficulties the rectors had encountered when they had sought the election of five men who were to represent each *quadra*. The *avogadori* and the rectors then called a general council, that is to say a traditional council of seventy-two, and the *quadra* representatives deliberated with the rectors, the *avogadori*, and an interim council of nineteen on the election of forty-four. The *avogadori*, who attended this meeting on 12 May, described the suspicions aroused by their arrival and the problems that emerged at the beginning of this deliberation process: "[the] many difficulties provoked by these citizens with endless altercations by different factions and raging disagreements between them." In fact, the *avogadori* were forced to bring order by means of a written prorogation of proceedings and so, with dexterity and the use of other methods, "by the grace of the lord God we sufficiently calmed the spirits of these citizens," and those elected were sworn in. The new councillors were drawn in equal measure from the Guelphs and those of the Ghibellines who were loyal to Venice, but the election proceeded very slowly; by 24 May only half of the necessary supplement had been elected. The *avogadori* wrote that they expected to complete the process within several days and judged their presence very useful, especially as their magistracy was held in very high regard. They observed that there were three factions in the city—those elected to the council since 1438 formed a distinct group alongside the Guelphs and Ghibellines—but concluded that the proceedings had been accomplished to everyone's satisfaction.[36]

The complacency of the visiting *avogadori* appears misplaced in the light of other evidence. Several hundred Brescians supported a memorial, probably drafted at the end of 1516, that was offered to the doge and the Senate in the first months of 1517. This memorial argued that the restrictions imposed in 1488 should be relaxed in order to allow an influx of men from a broader range of occupations and backgrounds to enter the council. This attempt to broaden the political base of the city was probably prompted by the animosities that the recent occupation had aroused and by a desire to see loyalty to Venice rewarded and scores settled. Benedetto Massimo, who was ostensibly the prime mover in this affair, outlined these proposals in a pamphlet he addressed to the doge; the captain-general, Andrea Gritti; the new *podestà* for the city, Francesco Falier; and the new *capitano*, Pietro Marcello.[37]

In his pamphlet Massimo compared himself with his ancient Roman ancestor, Quintus Fabius Maximus, who had supposedly reconciled the four divided Roman tribes. The modern Massimo deplored the ancient history of civil strife in the city of Brescia, which was unparalleled in Italy, and noted the divisions and enmities that the French occupation had exacerbated. In Massimo's view the decision of the Brescians to give public offices to a small group of men was the source of this discord; accordingly, he proposed the opening up of this restricted group. He justified this broadening of the governing class in a number of ways: first of all he remarked that just as a meal to which many people contribute is better, the laws elaborated by a council of many men are more sacred, as they are the product of many minds. Massimo also pursued a more flattering line of argument praising the advantages of the Venetian constitutional model, which tempered the best form of monarchical authority (the doge) with that of the aristocracy (the patriciate) for the public good to produce mixed government.[38] However, as Angelo Ventura has pointed out, Massimo's proposal for Brescia was more popular and practical than an emulation of this model would have been.[39]

Massimo argued that the restricted number of wealthy men in the Brescian councils set up by Venice had acted for personal advantage rather than public utility and were bound together by self-serving familial ties, friendships, and other associations.[40] Careful to present himself as a conservative reformer, he dismissed the idea of all citizens being admitted to the council, for this would produce confusion and besides, there was no hall big enough to house them. Nor should all working men ("artifices") be admitted but only those whose art involved "ingenium et honestas . . . et utilitas communis," such as merchants, pharmacists, bankers, and the like. He would exclude those who ministered to men's pleasure such as butchers, tailors, dancers, perfumers, and gamers. He assured the Venetians that he certainly would not want to admit well-fed cattle-drivers who stank of the country and wandered the city with drunken faces pursuing pointless legal disputes.[41] Furthermore, admission should be permitted to men over thirty who had resided in the city for at least thirty years—for why should men of learning and prudence be excluded at a time when the city was in such great need of them? He concluded that although divine providence ruled most affairs on Earth, men had the power and will to govern their own opinions and actions for good or for ill.

Massimo and four hundred "gentiluomini" met to discuss their proposal and chose a delegation that went to Venice to present their request for its implementation. Massimo's lavish praise of the republic, the doge, and his rectors may not have had the desired effect; Pandolfo Nassini said the delegation was given a hostile reception, although Venice might reasonably have been expected to intervene in favor of its most loyal Brescian subjects as it had done in 1428.[42] Indeed, in 1517 the Venetians marked the return of Verona to its empire by enforcing an enlargement of Verona's city councils in order to admit those who had been loyal to Venice during the war. The Venetians also hoped to widen the social range of those participating in the Veronese council by securing the admission of men with mercantile origins or interests.[43] The proposals of Massimo were not as fundamentally subversive as Angelo Ventura has suggested, but they remained a dead letter.[44] The influx of new citizens ceased after around 1520, and the council moved to exclude the sons of citizens involved in base occupations.[45]

In June 1517 Brescia's special and general councils condemned the temerity of those who wished to subvert the ancient order and set up a new one. Three citizens were elected to look into the affair.[46] Their report, which was read to the general council just over a week later, alleged that for some time Massimo had been working with some citizens, including "[a]rtifices," for a new regime and intended to go to Venice to seek the aforementioned changes. The council voted with only one dissenting to seek punishment for Massimo and his (unnamed) followers from the rectors or the heads of the Council of Ten in Venice.[47] Massimo's supporters included Carlo Valgulio, who had written with such eloquence about the true badges of honor and nobility in his pamphlet on funerals of the previous decade; Massimo singled Valgulio out for special praise as a Brescian patriot at the conclusion of his pamphlet. It has even been suggested that the humanist Valgulio, rather than Massimo, who was a "modest wool merchant" was the true author of the pamphlet published under Massimo's name.[48] In 1509, as noted, Valgulio had expressed his contempt for the honors bestowed on lowlifes such as tax farmers, castrators, dentists, trumpeters, flautists, and traitors. He may very well have written in favor of the widening of the council to men of true merit and the exclusion of those who ministered to men's pleasure such as butchers, tailors, dancers, perfumiers, and gamers. Valgulio's involvement in what has been called, with some exaggeration, the "true manifesto of the anti-aristocratic party" could explain his murder at the hands of the Brescian aristocrat Filippino de' Salis at the beginning of 1517.[49]

The fiscal settlement reflected the recuperation and consolidation of power by the urban oligarchy. In the wake of the War of the League of Cambrai, Venice was faced with calls from the *terraferma* for a revision of the *estimi* because many inhabitants had become impoverished through warfare and many towns had a pressing need for increased income to support their defenses. In Brescia the revision began on 27 December 1516 and was completed very quickly in a fashion that Angelo Ventura and Giuseppe del Torre characterize as oligarchic because it specified the incomes of the popular and nonnoble classes to be assessed but remained vague about typically aristocratic sources of income.[50] Moreover, in the spring of 1517 the Brescian council requested from Venice an exemption from *contado* taxes for citizens with property there, and the *contadini* in turn demanded that such citizens who had been made *cives silvestres* be taxed along with the *contadini* in order to prevent the further erosion of the tax base of the *contado*.[51] Venice responded by agreeing to abrogate the Brescian citizenship of those who had been made *cives silvestres* before the war against the rules, as well as all those made since 1509.[52] Accordingly, a large number of recent entrants were excluded from the Brescian council.[53] In future all goods acquired by citizens would not remain in the *estimo* for the *contado* but would be included in the city *estimo*.[54]

Moral Reform

In the privileges granted by Venice in 1517 Brescia was finally allowed to sell off or rent the land that lay within the Viscontean *cittadella* in the heart of the city. This decision marked an important new phase in the urban development of Brescia, since it coincided with a reordering of public and ecclesiastical buildings in the city as a result of the work of demolition *(spianata)* under the supervision of Andrea Trevisan, the *provveditore* in Brescia, and the general guidance of Andrea Gritti.[55] Five churches outside the city walls (San Rocco, San Fiorano, Santa Maria delle Grazie, and two others) that had provided crucial protection to Venetian and enemy forces were to be demolished as part of an improvement to the fortifications.[56] These churches may have been in a poor state as a result of bombardments and had counterparts elsewhere in the *terraferma,* including Padua, Treviso, Crema, and Verona, where a similar *spianata* took place.[57]

The *spianata* reflected Venetian military priorities but also offered a chance for Venetians to reassert their ecclesiastical objectives. For example, the demolition work was cited in a discussion in Venice about the complaints of the friars of San Giorgio. In the course of the debate the patrician Luca Tron, whose stout defense of secular authority and scepticism about the records of episcopal witch trials has been noted earlier, asked rhetorically: "Do we ask the pope permission to fortify our lands? We have demolished churches in Padua, Treviso, and Brescia without asking for papal agreement."[58] The project of demolition and rebuilding also provided the Brescians with the opportunity to promote their own projects for the city and to assert their autonomy, for on several occasions they reminded Venice of the privileges granted in 1517 in this respect.[59] At the same time the Brescian council sought to restore the funds of the *monte di pietà* and restitute the *monte*'s debts to the treasury of the duomo and the church of the Miracoli through processions and oblations and by imposing a limited tax.[60]

As a result of the *spianata* in Brescia, an area of gardens and monasteries and churches was destroyed. Some smaller communities disappeared entirely or were subsumed into larger congregations along with their relics and venerated images. San Paolino's relics were brought from Sant'Eusebio outside the walls to San Pietro Oliveto by the castle. San Calimero's relics were also moved from the observant Dominican house of San Fiorano to San Clemente within the city walls. The Franciscan observants of Sant'Apollonio and San Rocco built an entirely new church, San Giuseppe, close to the *piazza della loggia* in the city; this move may have suited the order, which had strong ties with the governing elite and benefited from many bequests, alms, and tax exemptions during this period.[61] Their great new church symbolically replaced the brothel that had stood in that place and was close to the new main axis of power in the city.[62] This church was the location of chapels of prominent families like the Calini, Capriolo, Ugoni, and Avogadro and was endowed by Bishop Mattia Ugoni (who was buried there in 1537). As Andrea Bayer has observed, the simple design and unadorned quality of this church may owe something to Ugoni's desire for a "simpler, more righteous" church or to observants' disdain for overelaborate decoration.[63]

Santa Maria delle Grazie, which was built around a venerated image of the Madonna that had come to prominence during the plague of 1452, was also moved into the city and a new church built on the site of a former Humiliati church to the west of the city. This rebuilding was funded partly by donations elicited by the processions on the feast of the Nativity of the Virgin (replacing the communally sponsored processions on the Feast of the Purification of the Virgin) after 1524 and partly by the commune. Many architectural elements in the new building owed more to Venetian than Milanese models, and the paintings commissioned for the altarpieces are said to reflect a new spirit of lay piety and active charity in the city from around 1520 onward.[64] For example, Angela Merici, who was active in the city from 1516 until her death in 1540, impressed many during this time with her personal asceticism and spiritual leadership. She was sought out as a mystic and "living saint" who could act as an intercessor with God and was active in civic affairs, trying to settle marriage disputes and other social disagreements, including the feud between the ever troublesome Filippino de' Salis and Francesco Martinengo. Merici also provided an influential example of a virgin of Christ living a holy life outside the cloister walls and during the last decade of her life gathered around her a company of virgins who dedicated themselves to Christ but continued to live at home. As her most recent biographer has argued, the Company of Saint Ursula (as it was known from 1535) was less an institution channeling charitable activity, as has traditionally been thought, than it was an exemplary expression of female mysticism. The Company attracted most of its recruits from the families of artisans, who may have been unable to afford the dowries demanded by the local convents and were probably impressed by the Company's distinctive lack of social hierarchy. As Brescia's economic and political extremes became increasingly polarized during these years, Merici's organization offered one way of bridging the gap.[65] A branch of the Roman Oratory of Divine Love was also founded in the city around 1520 by Bartolomeo Stella after he came into contact with one of its founders Gaetano da Thiene. In addition to their personal and more private devotions, his followers were obliged to work in the new hospital for the *incurabili* that Stella founded and built, with the support of the council and a legacy from Mattia Ugoni, to replace a hospital destroyed in the *spianata*.[66]

These new personalities, projects, and activities seem to have thrived in an ambience of renewed civic piety, fostered by the town council. The close relationship between politics and piety in the formation of civic identity is again clear here. Brescians were especially keen to revive their involvement in ecclesiastical affairs in the city and to renew spiritual life after a period when God seemed to have abandoned them. Between 1509 and 1516 religious ceremonial faltered but did not die out completely. The larger processions and rituals were temporarily abandoned or altered: the usual offering of gloves at the feast of the Assumption was replaced by one of wax in 1511, and the customary offering for the feast of the Assumption in 1513 was deferred until the following Easter due to public and private poverty.[67] Given the spread of disease in the city, it is perhaps not surprising that an offering and procession was organized in 1513 to honor the new wooden altarpiece in San Rocco with a statue of the saint sculpted by Stefano Lamberti.[68] The council also agreed to support an anonymous request for twelve virgins to be clothed in white in honor of God and Saint Vincent, in fulfilment of an unusual vow made in return for the end of plague in the city.[69]

The procession with the holy crosses, like the veneration of San Rocco, had in fact become more urgent during the difficult conditions of the occupation. At the end of April 1509, a month after the arm of Sant' Apollonio had been processed to preserve the city from all adversity ("ab omni adversitate"), money was given by the council to the observant orders to process for three days with the crosses in order to preserve the city from harm, and this procession was ordered repeated a few weeks later.[70] The customary processions with the cross of *orifiamma* imploring God to send rain seem to have been interrupted between 1509 and 1517, although this impression may be due to the disorder in the civic documents.[71] On the restoration of Venetian rule the cross of *orifiamma* received special attention: in April 1517 the council agreed to ornament the tabernacle on which the cross stood when it was carried in procession.[72] The council also agreed to decorate the chapel of the cross of *orifiamma* and to add ornamentation to the box in which it was held. Moreover, the cross was to be venerated with a daily mass, and a chaplain was employed to say mass in its chapel. A procession with the cross on the feast of the Holy Cross on September 14 each year was also agreed on, with each corporation making an offering of 3 *lire planete* for the use and ornamentation of the chapel.[73] In 1520 the confraternity of the Holy Cross was established, and structural alterations were made to the chapel, possibly to accommodate their meetings.[74]

The young Brescian artist Alessandro Bonvicino, called Moretto, may have provided the image of the exaltation of the cross of *orifiamma* for a banner in the chapel. This image shows the city's patron saints, Faustino and Giovita, holding an ornamented gold or gilded reliquary and cross up at which gaze male and female figures in contemporary dress, including bishops Ugoni, Zane, and Averoldi. The relic of the true cross known as the cross of *orifiamma* had originally been given to the original church of Faustino and Giovita by Duke Namo of Bavaria, who was possibly depicted kneeling before it on the reverse of Moretto's image (now lost) with a large crowd of onlookers and the inscription commemorating the role of the cross in weather processions.[75] The cross was in fact processed to the church of San Faustino and Giovita with the clergy and corporations in March 1520 and 1521 in order to ensure good weather and to placate God.[76]

The patron saints of Brescia, who had appeared at a crucial moment during the siege of the city in 1438–40, now reappeared in more secular guise as patriotic symbols in the "civic iconography."[77] At the feast of the Assumption in 1518 the organ shutters in the duomo that had been commissioned in 1515 were finally unveiled. Floriano Ferramola's image of the Annunciation could be seen on their exterior, and on their interior Moretto's Faustino and Giovita appeared as mounted knights in shining armor. These figures have been interpreted as "vivid statements of the city's renewed strength and civic pride": in contrast with some earlier depictions of these saints in ecclesiastical robes (for example, in the marble tomb frontal, ca. 1470, in the Averoldi chapel in the church of Santa Maria del Carmine) the organ shutters "shifted the emphasis to this secular aspect of their biographies."[78] The iconography of the saints had long reflected both their military and sacerdotal roles—indeed, they appear in both guises on the sarcophagus holding the relics of Sant'Apollonio that was placed in the duomo in 1510—but it is interesting that a shift toward their military role may date from the years around the beginning of the War of the League of Cambrai.[79] This change in iconography can be detected in the contrasting title-page images in these saints' biographies printed in Brescia in 1490 and 1511. In the first, the saints are shown in noble contemporary dress; in the second appropriately enough for a Latin edition, they are depicted in Roman cuirasses—though not, it must be said, in especially martial poses.[80] In Girolamo Romanino's *Coronation of the Virgin with Ss. Dominic, Faustino, and Giovita* the saints also wear armor over their aristocratic silk and damask outfits. However, armed figures were prominent in Brescian civic iconography before 1509: the nude female figure of "Brescia armata" was placed on the façade of the *monte*'s offices (around 1484–89), and around the same time Faustino and Giovita may have been depicted in antique dress or armor nearby on the *loggetta* of the clock tower on the east side of the *piazza della loggia* (see Figure 5.1), and certainly were in the portico vault keystones of the *loggia* itself (ca. 1497).

Along with the revival of ritual procession and the recovery or promotion of the local protective saints, the communal council also revived the promotion of religious observance in the city and undertook to improve monastic behavior as part of a campaign of moral and spiritual improvement. The protection and promotion of the regular clergy was viewed by most civic authorities as a good use of public funds, as the prayers of monks and nuns were felt to be especially gratifying to God. Accordingly, monastic behavior was increasingly monitored in Venice and the *terraferma*, and after the crisis of 1509 the Venetian Senate increased penalties on those who desecrated monasteries.[81] The Brescian council continued to give alms to monastic orders, including the observant Carmelites, throughout the period of occupation. The presence in the city of especially holy figures, often drawn from the ranks of the aristocracy, could also attract noble sponsorship and civic patronage. The nuns of the convent of Santa Croce, especially the prioress Francesca Capriolo and Laura Mignani, attracted the attentions of spiritually inclined aristocrats at home and farther afield, including the Duchess of Ferrara, Lucrezia Borgia, the Duchess of Urbino, Elisabetta Gonzaga, and the Countess of Gambara, Lucrezia Gonzaga.[82]

The Brescian council took steps to restore monastic life to better order soon after the end of foreign occupation and the simultaneous timing of those actions and those of Venice, where a new magistracy concerned with convent affairs was set up in 1519–21, may not be a coincidence.[83] At the end of 1516 two citizens were chosen from among the better sort of the city ("ex praestantioribus istius Civitatis") and assigned to each monastery in order to ensure that its inhabitants were living honestly and chastely.[84] The surveillance of monasteries was a point to which the council soon returned; in July 1517 it unanimously agreed to choose five honest citizens to look into the behavior of the religious, especially monastics who committed terrible sins. Three years later the behavior of the nuns of the socially select Santa Maria di Pace scandalized the council with their behavior, their behavior and some "reformatione" and "correctione" of the convent was sought.[85] The council was prepared to take strong measures against those monastics who displeased it: in 1520 it was proposed that the fountains that served the religious who refused to take part in the Corpus Christi processions should be shut off.[86]

At the same time, and even before the end of the occupation, the council targeted the moral failings of lay citizens. A sermon given at the church of Sant'Agata in 1515 prompted the council to elect seven men to act to stamp out a number of vices in the city ranging from civil discord, blasphemy, and familiarity and intercourse with nuns to superfluous clothing and harmful games. Brescians were invited to denounce those who blasphemed and who played the games by placing their names in a locked box placed in different parts of the city and *contado,* including the chapel of Sant'Apollonio in the duomo. The council also condemned the fact that prostitutes were living in the city alongside "honestis et pudicis mulieribus" rather than outside the city or in some less frequented spot.[87] The poorer northwest part of the city and a spot between Sant'Andrea and Sant'Apollonio in the hills outside the city became the resorts of prostitutes.[88] The decision was reiterated by the council after the return of Venetian rule, and it was observed that after many calamities, troubles, and other evident signs of divine displeasure the Brescian council should also elicit alms from the population, restore the *monte di pietà,* and prosecute loan sharks to avoid the danger of Jews in the city, as well as concubinists and others who broke divine injunctions. Two men from the more worthy ("ex notabilioribus") of each *quadra* would investigate crimes and report them to the rectors so that they might proceed against them sharply ("acriter").[89]

On the face of it, prosperity returned to the city quite quickly after the end of the occupation. As early as June 1517 the "avogador extraordinario" Marco Foscari was praising the city on his return to Venice, saying that it seemed to him to like a rich and loyal "regno" that had never been sacked.[90] Pietro Tron, the returning *podestà* in 1520, claimed that the population of Brescia was fifty thousand and described it as "an extremely wealthy city where everyone wears silk, including the women. The city is full of shops, and there is no sign that it has ever been sacked."[91] Tron's very optimistic picture is belied by other records that provide a much grimmer picture of the economy and society. Brescia emerged from seven years of occupation with an urban population of around twenty thousand, around one-third of that in 1505. The city's recovery was checked by the famine and plague during the third decade of the century: Marin Sanudo noted starving Brescian peasants begging outside churches in Venice in 1528.[92] By the middle of the century the population reached around forty thousand, roughly what it had been a century earlier.[93]

Luca Tron noted in 1520 that the region was "licentiosa" and he had had to deal with several cases of murder.[94] Hostility toward the Venetian rectors was evident in the postwar era, and notices with "scandalous and diffamatory words" directed toward the *podestà* and his court were found posted in the city in 1521.[95] There is also some evidence that heretical ideas were beginning to circulate in the city, and even the veneration of the cross of *orifiamma* came under attack.[96] The rivalries and disputes between the leading families also continued as usual;[97] Guelph and Ghibelline divisions were maintained in the valleys; and Venice was obliged to step in to settle continuing jurisdictional squabbles, for example between the Brescian and Bergamasque parts of the Val Camonica.[98] Finally, the feudal nobility—whose privileges were confirmed by Venice after the war—continued to arrogate power in the territory.[99]

In general terms, Venice acted pragmatically and with some sensitivity to local concerns. In 1521, in the course of a debate about a dispute between Brescia and Chiari that was dragging through the Venetian tribunals, Luca Tron described Brescia as "un regno" that was contributing 100,000 ducats to state revenues and praised its loyalty ("è sta fidelissima"). He suggested that this dispute be heard before no less an authority than the heads of the Ten, while the ducal councillor Antonio Giustiniani argued that this was more properly a matter for the Quarantia.[100] The Venetians confirmed or respected most local privileges in the immediate postwar era. Indeed, the fear of renewed hostilities and a second Agnadello to be followed by revolution may have led Venice to turn to the *terraferma* with greater attention after around 1520.[101] However, the balance of relations in the Bresciano was not static, and as Alessandra Rossini has shown it was strengthened by Venetian concessions so that in the course of the sixteenth century *territorio* succeeded in mitigating some of the inequities that favored the city in fiscal terms.[102]

The Venetians were motivated by practical concerns of defense and reconstruction: forced subsidies became a regular imposition on Brescia and other towns after 1529, and indirect taxes continued their seemingly inexorable rise upward.[103] These two factors probably help to explain why Brescians were apt to emphasize their economic troubles to Venice despite the great wealth successive rectors reported. In a memorial of 1534, prompted by the demand for the forced subsidy of 10,000 ducats, the Brescian ambassadors reminded Venice of the costs Brescia had incurred since 1487 in wars and subsidies by the occupation and recovery of the city.[104] At the same time the Brescians were exploring ways of meeting the demanded sum through credit, reduction of spending, or the sale of goods. They reminded the *savii* in the first part of the memorial that the increased subsidy demanded went against the privileges conceded in 1511 and 1517 and was the cause of discord with neighboring cities. The petitioners asserted that Venice must take into account the troubles endured by Brescia since 1426 and although the other subject cities thought Brescia rich, profits were low and the cost of flooding and river defenses was high. Other communities were turning to silk, cloth, and other merchandise whereas Brescia remained largely agricultural and subject to periodic seasonal absences in the duchy of Milan of workers, beasts, and tools necessary for the local economy. In an echo of the accusations made earlier in the century against greedy mendicants, the petitioners also argued that a greater burden should fall on the clergy who had done well from lay bequests. The outcome of the petition was not in favor of Brescia, and Venice continued to make regular demands for subsidies for the rest of the century.

The population of Brescia only gradually recovered from the losses of the war years, and the demography of the city followed the peaks and troughs generally experienced in Italy during the rest of the sixteenth century. By the end of the century the demographic balance between city and countryside may have tilted even further in favor of the latter as ironworks and textile production developed in rural centers. At the same time the Brescians extended their control over the feudal territories, and many such pockets of immunity were disappearing after around 1550.[105] By around 1630 there was a decline in the urban inhabitants' incomes under the combined influence of global economic trends, falling grain prices in the wake of plague and demographic collapse, and Venetian taxation.[106] Brescian patricians, reluctant to adapt to new conditions, were increasingly unhappy with the political status quo. Open conflict broke out in 1644—a "revolution of the discontents" that embraced, among other things, a concerted attempt to reverse the closure of 1488.[107]

Conclusion

THE AFFAIRS of Brescia during the first century of Venetian rule ended, as they had begun, somewhat inauspiciously. When Brescia submitted to the Venetians in 1426, the city was depopulated and in economically straitened circumstances. A century later it was slowly recovering from further demographic losses caused by the displacement or death of much of the population by war and occupation. Brescia's fortunes reached their nadir in 1512 when the French sacked it and old divisions flared up with renewed vigor. Between those dates the city had experienced the violence of the assault and siege of 1438–40 and the devastation of the influenza and plague of four decades later. Despite these setbacks, Brescia maintained its position as the richest of the cities and regions of the *terraferma* even if its reputation as the most loyal of Venice's subjects had proved largely illusory.

On the whole during this period, the relationship between Brescia and Venice was presented with some fine rhetorical flourishes but when viewed through the lens of the official records in both cities does not seem to have been marked by any genuine warmth or much sense of rapprochement. The Venetians regarded Brescia above all in the cold light of of fiscal policy, military strategy, and judicial responsibility. The republic's promises to relieve the city of the burden of direct taxation were very quickly forgotten as direct subsidies were imposed to finance military expenditure. The Venetian patricians recognized that Brescia and its *contado* formed a key part of the strategic defenses of the *terraferma,* especially while Visconti or Sforza dukes were pursuing expansionist ambitions in northern Italy; accordingly, the city was the headquarters for the Venetian captain-general, and troops were permanently stationed there or in the surrounding fortified towns of Asola, Orzinuovi, Anfo, and Pontevico. If Venetian demands for direct subsidies declined in the second half of the fifteenth century, it was as a result of the relative peace that prevailed on the peninsula after 1454 or of Venetian preoccupation with its eastern frontier, not as a reward for Brescian fortitude in resisting the renewed assaults of the Visconti during the first half of the century.

The Venetians were content to send rectors to the city who respected local statutes, customs, and traditions, so long as these were not seen to offend God or the dignity of the most serene republic. In practice the rectors and their officers were hedged around by local lawyers and notaries, and on a number of occasions the rectors' advice of was ignored or rejected; the Brescians, like their counterparts elsewhere on the mainland, were adept at making appeals over the heads of their local Venetian representatives to a range of bodies with responsibilities for the affairs of the *terraferma.* At the same time the Brescian case could be made directly to Venice by orators who temporarily or permanently resided there, although it does appear that their access to the executive and deliberative bodies of Venice was restricted. The Venetian government could respond with sensitivity to Brescian complaints and demands, and rebukes could be issued to rectors who overstepped the bounds of their authority. The Venetians left the Brescians a free hand to grant *civilitas* and also some latitude in drawing up the *estimo,* although this most contentious area was the occasion for direct Venetian intervention—often in favor of the *contado* rather than the city. Venetian pragmatism was clearly displayed in the government's approach to the resolution of a number of areas of potential conflict, for example over the presence of Jews in Brescia. The evidence suggests that Venice tried to balance the the economic desirability of the Jews' presence with the hostility this presence aroused in local communities. In this sense, the seemingly random tergiversations amounted to a consistent Venetian policy.

The strength and continuity of Brescian identity during this first century of Venetian rule is striking. The terms of the Brescian submission to Venice in 1426 were in many respects similar to those drawn up under Visconti domination; they contained little that was essentially new, except perhaps for a further refinement of communal political structures that gave the Venetian rectors enhanced power in the selection of those eligible to sit on the council, probably as a way of ending years of debilitating dissensions.

Even in this regard the Brescians were on familiar ground, having experienced the contraction of their communal council and an influx of new men under the previous *signori*. This change under Venetian rule does not appear to have been imposed by the capital or to have aroused any opposition until the Venetians began to encourage a dilution of the established conciliar clans with new members. Like other cities—notably Treviso and Verona—the Brescian council, or at least a significant section within it, then moved to claw back control.

The process of closure, albeit partial and contentious, and the construction of an oligarchic urban patriciate was largely driven by lawyers and notaries; the exploration of Brescia's past and the writing of the commune in records and chronicles were expressions of this group's formation of identity. Brescian councillors shared an understanding of the nobility of office and now added an emphasis on ancient and rural origins, martial valor, wisdom, and piety. Accordingly, Brescia's citizens looked to their family histories and to those of their ambitious neighbors for support and reassurance of their status. They placed great emphasis on service to the city during time of war—notably participation in the city's defense during the siege of 1438–40, which they made a benchmark for admission to the council. The citizens also distanced themselves from the shopkeepers and merchants around them who exercised manual or supposedly vile crafts, and they embraced a costly style of dress that they tried to deny to the same men and their wives. The architectural language of the city could also express these concerns: public buildings and spaces were given a monumental and classicized appearance fitting to their use by the descendants of Scipio living in a city founded by Hercules or, at the very least, by the noble Cenomani. The staging of jousts and the acquisition of rural property were further expressions of these noble ambitions and perhaps reflect a greater admiration for neighboring princely Mantua than for republican Venice.[1]

Brescian pretensions to communal autonomy and authority were limited under Venetian rule, although once again the continuity between the signorial and the Venetian regimes is striking. In particular, the Brescians were unable to realize their wish to govern and tax the *contado* without hindrance. The Venetians, like their Visconti predecessors as lords of Brescia, preferred to make a series of bilateral agreements with local feudal powers and with a number of key towns in the region. For example, the Martinengo and the Federici, to name two powerful clans, were treated with the same respect they had received from the Visconti. In a number of towns, notably lakeside Salò and Asola in the southern plains bordering Mantuan territory, or in the valley communities, Brescian authority was largely bypassed or subsumed and complicated by the involvement of officials appointed by Venice. For much of the first decade of Venetian rule the republic respected the statutes of these towns, and even after 1440 some places continued to exercise a right of appeal directly to Venice in criminal, civil, or fiscal matters.

The precocious autonomy of the territorial organization known as the *Territorio* was especially problematic for Brescia. The city faced a determined resistance to any attempt to spread the overall region's burden of taxation from the city into the *contado*. Orators from the *Territorio* presented appeals to Venetian rectors or appeared in Venice to argue their case. The development of a direct relationship between Venice and the Bresciano in this way foreshadows the similar relationships that were forged in other parts of the *terraferma,* notably the Vicentine, during the sixteenth century.[2] In the case of Brescia the strength of the territorial institutions probably was as important to this development as the weakness of the Brescian mediators of power, who were sometimes bombarded with insults or physical violence.

Venice lay some two hundred miles and several days' travel away from Brescia. Viewed from this distance, the city on the lagoon must have seemed a remote, unthreatening, and perhaps irrelevant force.[3] Brescia, unlike Padua, was never at risk of being called "uno deli principali borgi dela citade veneta."[4] The Venetian patriciate did not invest heavily in the Brescian lands during this period and was generally content to let the oligarchy of Brescian patricians accumulate landed wealth, fiscal exemptions, and political power during the first century of rule. After 1509 the Venetians seem to have turned to the *terraferma* with renewed, even sentimental, interest, and an extensive program of fortification was undertaken in the course of the sixteenth century.[5] However, for the period with which this book has been concerned, the haughty disdain of Marco Negro for Brescian manners may capture something of the true nature of Venetian feelings about far-flung Brescia. Equally, the tetchy comments of Pandolfo Nassini, the proud scion of a noble house, about the misconduct of Andrea Gritti and other Venetian failings probably represent a significant strand of Brescian opinion. Others represented the relationship between Brescia and Venice as one fraught with potential difficulties, as is demonstrated by the manuscript illumination of around 1472 that shows the Brescians literally fleecing the winged lion of Saint Mark (see Figure 2.1). By these lights, it is perhaps all the more remarkable that Venetian rule in Brescia recovered after 1517 and that the capital was able to impose ever greater burdens on the city and its region without granting even greater political autonomy. Indeed, in 1553 the returning Venetian rector could complacently assert before the Senate that "Bressa naturalmente è fidelissima" as a result of the justice, honors, and benefits it enjoyed under Venetian rule.[6] A conjunction of circumstances may have helped Venice to acquire its hinterland beyond the Mincio, but it seems clear that the structure that allowed some latitude for local autonomy, fostered loyalty among its subjects, and contributed to this success. A light governing hand, reasonable and engaged rectors, a periodically responsive system of courts and official bodies that helped to develop a "common political language," and some mythmaking were also key.[7]

During the Renaissance the Brescian oligarchy was in a constant process of negotiation with the Venetian center. In a wide range of matters the Venetians recognized the limits of their practical authority and accepted the local power of a range of mediators. This balancing act was achieved at a fairly minimal cost to the Venetian polity and without imposing an authoritarian or unitary governing system on the *terraferma*. Brescians did not seriously challenge their place as Venetian subjects and allies until 1509, when divisions predating the era of Venetian rule broke the consensus of the ruling patrician oligarchy and (as in Padua) led to revolt. This consensus was quickly restored and managed to stifle open and effective resistance for another century and a half, until a "revolution of the discontents" threatened to destroy the civic identity that had formed between 1426 and 1530. In the final analysis, the survival of this patrician oligarchy owed a great deal to the strength of that identity, to the adaptibility that oligarchy, and to the nimble and pragmatic management of the Venetian republic.

Finally, the evidence of the relationship between Venice and Brescia during the period examined in this book supports the view that in most periods of history the formation of a state, even a regional state, is a two-way process in which centre and periphery interact.[8] The early modern state was often unable to delineate jurisdictional boundaries clearly, and such boundaries that were established could fluctuate from decade to decade. Conversely, the inhabitants of frontier zones where the state might hope to claim jurisdictional power, or have some real influence themselves acted to confirm or collude in governance and to settle boundaries. In the case of Venice's empire, it seems that the formation of local identity could involve the appropriation of some Venetian values and even claims to being Venice's most loyal city, but well-established feudal and communal customs persisted and remained dominant; even though Venetian territorial jurisdiction survived until 1797, there is little evidence in the Bresciano that any sort of unified Venetian national identity or imagined community ever emerged. I would argue that this does not represeent the failure of imagination or of political modernization but rather the triumph of a provincial life that was far from parochial.

Notes

Bibliography

Index

Notes

The notes are given in short form throughout, and a full bibliography is provided at the end of the book.

In transcribing primary source material in Italian and Latin I have generally preserved original spelling, capitalization, and usage (e.g. "&" for "et" or "e"), except in cases where the meaning would be obscure without some modernization—especially in respect of the use of periods and colons.

Citations to the Brescian council *provvisioni* provide the Archivio di Stato's register number followed by date of meeting and folio number(s) (e.g., ASC 509, 9 June 1486, fol. 75r). Since foliation begins anew with the entry of each new *podestà*, sometimes two or even three sets of foliation are joined in a single register. In order to avoid cluttered and confusing citations, I have omitted mention of these different sets; the date of the meeting and the folio number will suffice to locate the correct folio.

Abbreviations Used in the Notes and Bibliography

ASB	Archivio di Stato, Brescia.
ASC	Archivio Storico Civico (in ASB).
ASMa	Archivio di Stato, Mantua.
ASV	Archivio di Stato, Venice.
b./bb.	busta/buste.
BL	British Library, London.
BQB	Biblioteca Queriniana, Brescia.
BS	*Bibliotheca sanctorum,* 12 vols. (Rome: Città nuova editrice, 1961–1970).
DBI	*Dizionario biografico degli Italiani* (Rome: Istituto della enciclopedia italiana, 1960–).
m.v.	*modo veneziano*/*more veneto*—indicates a date given according to the Venetian calendar; the Venetian new year began on 1 March.
Sanudo	Marin Sanudo, *I diarii di Marino Sanuto,* ed. Rinaldo Fulin, Federico Stefani, Nicolò Barozzi, Guglielmo Berchet, and Marco Allegri. 58 vols. (Venice: Fratelli Visentini, 1879–1903. Facsimile, Bologna: Forni, 1969–1970). Cited by volume and column number.

1. Regional States and Civic Identity

1. On Louis's triumphal entry see Mitchell, *Majesty of State*, 101; Capriolo, *Chronicorum de rebus Brixianorum,* col. 139; "Cronaca di anonimo autore," 141–143. On the words inscribed on the Brescian gate see Priuli, *Diarii*, 4:117.

2. Finlay, "Venice, the Po Expedition," 38.

3. Sanudo, 8:248; English tanslation in Sanudo, *Venice,* 174.

4. "Quod faustum, felixque sit semper, & procul a *Venetorum* lapsu, qui si maiorum suorum virtutem, justitiam, benignitatem, & fidem in omnes continuo prosequuti essent, praesentem status sui cladem cum tanta subditorum inopinata mutatione forte non sentirent. Uti enim virtutibus ipsis regna surgunt, crescunt, & servantur; ita etiam contra cadunt, ruunt, & funditus evertuntur; eo praecipue quod principum gesta tempore pacis, subditorum documenta sunt tempore belli. Quare tanti *Venetorum* interitus sola causa fuisse videretur eorum a parentibus, & maioribus suis degeneratio: quamquam ea omnia caelorum influxu contigisse aliqui arbitrentur; cum praecipue Mars in revolutione in angulo contentiones, & bella significaverit, & Luna Virgine hora oppositionis luminorum ante solis adventum in Arietem in domo inimicorum inventa, sanguinis effusionem, & oppidorum, villarumque depopulationem portenderit. Quum autem *Gallorum* maximum facinus prope futurum esse, duodecimo Chronicorum nostrorum libro, annis jam novem vaticinati sumus." Capriolo, *Chronicorum de rebus Brixianorum,* cols. 139–140.

5. Burckhardt, *Civilization of the Renaissance,* title of pt. 1. On Burckhardt's conservative cultural outlook see Gossman, *Basel in the Age of Burckhardt.*

6. On composite states see Elliott, "Europe of Composite Monarchies."

7. Chittolini, "'Privato,' il 'pubblico,' lo Stato."

8. There is now a vast literature on this topic, but see Lazzarini, *Italia degli stati territoriali;* Kirshner, *Origins of the State;* Chittolini, *Città, comunità e feudi;* idem, *Crisi degli ordinamenti comunali;* idem, *Formazione dello stato regionale;* and idem, "Alcune considerazioni"; and Fasano Guarini, *Potere e società.*

9. This paragraph is indebted to Lazzarini, *Italia degli stati territoriali,* 160–179.

10. On the territorial dynamics of Milanese expansion see Somaini, "Processi costitutivi."

11. Chittolini, "Terre separate," 115–128.

12. Varanini, "Aristocrazie e poteri," 153. See also Cengarle, *Immagine di potere.*

13. Brown, *In the Shadow of Florence;* Grubb, *Firstborn of Venice;* idem, *Provincial Families of the Renaissance;* Law, *Venice and the Veneto.*

14. Gentile, *Terra e poteri;* Della Misericordia, *La disciplina contrattata;* Gamberini, *Città assediata.* For the later sixteenth and seventeenth centuries see Raggio, *Faide e parentele.*

15. Dean, "Commune and Despot."

16. Varanini, "Aristocrazie e poteri," 166.

17. For a comprehensive account in English of the communal period see Jones, *Italian City-State.* For a more concise account see Hyde, *Society and Politics.*

18. For a useful discussion of the prevalence and problems of patrician claims of nobility see Grubb, "Patriziato, nobiltà, legittimitazione."
19. Castelnuovo, "L'identità politica delle nobiltà cittadine."
20. See Bartolomeo Cipolla, *De imperatore militum diligendo* (1453), discussed by Varanini, "Il giurista, il comune cittadino, la dominante." See also Lanfranchini, *Quaestio utrum praeferendus sit doctor an miles*, discussed by Mazzacane, "Stato e il dominio," 600 n. 75, and Giorgio Borelli, "'Doctor an miles'."
21. On this process see Jones, *Italian City-State*, 577.
22. Hyde, *Padua in the Age of Dante*, chap. 3.
23. Muir and Ruggiero, *Microhistory and the Lost Peoples*.
24. Burckhardt, *Civilization of the Renaissance*, title of pt. 2.
25. Chartier, "Fiction and Knowledge"; idem, *Cultural History*, introduction.
26. Te Brake, *Shaping History*. For an example of the importance of physical presence and effective authority see Appuhn, *Forest on the Sea*, 59, 73, 85, 108.
27. Gamberini, *Stato viscontea*, 11.
28. Lanza, *Firenze contro Milano*; Fubini, *Storiografia dell'umanesimo in Italia*; and Ianziti, *Humanistic Historiography under the Sforzas*. On the political accent in architectural language see Boucheron, "Architettura come linguaggio politico." On texts in architectural settings see Petrucci, *Writing the Dead*, esp. 73; and idem, *Public Lettering*, esp. chap. 2.
29. Chartier, "Fiction and Knowledge," 15.
30. Of course, textual and pictorial representations of good government were not unknown during the communal era: Tabacco, *Ideologie politiche*.
31. Della Misericordia, "Decidere e agire in comunità."
32. Gamberini, *Stato visconteo*, chaps. 1–3.
33. To quote the titles of Gamberini, *Città assediata*, and Brown, *In the Shadow of Florence*.
34. Bouwsma, "Venice and the Political Education."
35. Pocock, *Machiavellian Moment*; Wootton, "Ulysses Bound?"
36. Povolo, "Creation of Venetian Historiography."
37. Berengo, *Società veneta alla fine del Settecento*; Ventura, *Nobiltà e popolo*. Ventura's classic work has been critically assessed and placed in the context of subsequent historiography by Knapton, "'Nobiltà e popolo' e un trentennio di storiografia veneta."
38. Ferraro, *Family and Public Life in Brescia*, 4.
39. "[G]li amici dello stato rinascimentale." Law, "Un confronto fra due stati 'rinascimentali,'" 412.
40. Grubb, *Provincial Families of the Renaissance*, xi–xiii.
41. Varanini, "Venezia e l'entroterra"; Mallett, "Conquista della Terraferma"; Hay and Law, *Italy in the Age of the Renaissance*, 113–117; Cozzi and Knapton, *Repubblica di Venezia nell'età moderna*, 3–47.
42. *Patti con Brescia 1252–1339*.
43. Putelli, "Relazioni commerciali tra Venezia ed il bresciano."
44. On the ambitions of the Carrara see Kohl, *Padua under the Carrara*, esp. 328–336.

45. Mallett and Hale, *Military Organisation of a Renaissance State*, chap. 1 (quotation at 19).

46. On the question of 1381 and 1405 as turning points see Varanini, "Venezia e l'entroterra," 213.

47. Mallett and Hale, *Military Organisation of a Renaissance State*.

48. Varanini, "Venezia e l'entroterra," 216. Claudio Povolo has described the fifteenth-century *terraferma* as "una variegata e policentrica periferia" in his "Centro e periferia nella Repubblica di Venezia," 210. See also idem, *Intrigo dell'onore*, chap. 4. The "fluidità" of the system until 1454 is underlined by Viggiano, "Aspetti politici e giurisdizionali." On the "pletoricità del sistema polisinodale veneziano" as it pertained to the capital's magistracies see idem, *Governanti e governati*, 186.

49. I have tried thoughout this book to avoid using the terms "capital" and "state," since they have anachronistic connotations of modern statehood.

50. On the politics of granting benefices in the Veneto see Del Torre, "Stato regionale e benefici ecclesiastici."

51. The "coscienza giuridica dello Stato veneziano" is the formulation of Gaetano Cozzi in Cozzi and Knapton, *Repubblica di Venezia*, 221.

52. On the working of these bodies see Viggiano, *Governanti e governati*; Cozzi, "Politica del diritto nella Republica di Venezia," esp. 79–121; Caro Lopez, "Gli auditori nuovi," 261–316.

53. "[*Podestà* to execute justice] secundum eorum [i.e. Brescian] consuetudines et statuta dummodo sint secundum Deum et Iustitiam & honorum nostrum et communis Venetiarum et bonum statum ipsius civitatis & districtus bona fide." Ducal commission to the Brescian *podestà* Bertucio Contarini (1471), National Archives, London, PRO 30/25/104/1, p. 3. The fifty-one rubrics and nine folios in this commission had risen to 192 rubrics and sixty-six folios by the time Doge Andrea Gritti commissioned Vettore Barbarigo as *podestà* for Brescia in 1535: BL, additional MSS, 14,093.

54. Mazzacane, "Stato e il dominio."

55. Massimo, *Benedicti Maximi civis Brixiani*, title page. On this work and the circumstances of its composition see chapter 12 here.

56. Cozzi, "Politica del diritto nella Republica di Venezia," 98–100. Although not without local objections: see Zamperetti, *Piccoli principi*, 52 n. 18.

57. Zamperetti, *Piccoli principi*, 151 nn. 3–4, 152; Falcioni, "Malatesta, Pandolfo." See also Piasentini, "Relazioni tra Venezia e Pandolfo III Malatesta"; Rizzinelli, "Problemi giuridico-amministrativi"; and Zanelli, "Signoria di Pandolfo Malatesta."

58. Zamperetti, *Piccoli principi*, 149–153.

59. See Menniti Ippolito, "Dedizione di Brescia a Milano (1421) e a Venezia (1427)," 38; idem, "'Provedibitur sicut melius videbitur.'" A detailed account of Visconti rule is provided by Zanelli, *Brescia sotto la signoria*.

60. "Quia contra ventum mingere volui cruci suspendor." Capriolo, *Chronica de rebus Brixianorum*, fol. LIIv.

61. Manelmi, *Commentariolus de quibusdam gestis in bello Gallico*, 65; Barbaro, *Epistolario*, 2:375–376.

62. On representations of Brescia and other subject cities in the ducal palace see Franzoi, Pignatti, and Wolters, *Palazzo ducale di Venezia*, 271, 314, 317, 326, 329. On the myth of Brescia see chapter 2 here.

63. Romano, *Likeness of Venice*, 119, 124–128. However, John Law has argued that this imperial investiture was incomplete—Friuli, Verona, and Vicenza were omitted—and did not regularize matters: Law, "Verona and the Venetian State," 10–11.

64. Romano, *Likeness of Venice*, 158–159; Capriolo, *Chronica*, fol. LXVIr.

65. According to local tradition Venice was founded in 421 on the Feast of the Annunciation (25 Mar.).

66. ASC 491, 21 Apr. 1440, fol. 23r.

67. The Brescian experience in this respect was not unusual in the *terraferma:* see Rizzi, "Leontoclastia cambraica."

68. Rubinstein, "Italian Reactions to Terraferma Expansion."

69. Becichemo, *Panegyricus Leonardo Lauretano* sig. [B6v]. See also Law, "Venetian Mainland State in the Fifteenth Century," 157–161; and Grubb, *Firstborn of Venice*, 14–19. On Pesciatine submission to Florence in 1339 and Florentine *libertas* see Brown, *In the Shadow of Florence*, 17–20.

70. Sanudo, 24:656–659. For an English translation of this speech with commentary on Sanudo's views see idem, *Venice*, 15–16. Sanudo was always alert to sharp practice and trespassing on established competencies: in 1519 he criticized the Council of Ten for interfering with a matter—involving ducal approval of a sentence issued in favor of Brescian merchants by the city *podestà*—that properly belonged to the *avogadori di comun.* Idem, 27:420.

71. Contarini, *Commonwealth and Government of Venice*, 104.

72. Ibid., 147–148.

73. "Although they [i.e. Venetians] never allowed bloodshed, yet they fostered these discords [between Guelphs and Ghibellines in their subject cities] so that the citizens, taken up with their own dissensions, might never combine against them." Machiavelli, *Prince*, 67.

74. Hay and Law, *Italy in the Age of the Renaissance*, 116.

75. Law, "Venetian Mainland State in the Fifteenth Century," 172.

76. ASV, Senato terra, deliberazioni, reg. 10, fol. 29v (pencil foliation, 1 Dec. 1486).

77. ASV, Senato terra, deliberazioni, reg. 8, fol. 14r (pencil foliation, 2 July 1478).

78. For example, the Senate considered the request to the doge of the Brescian printer in Venice Paganino de Paganinis to print a Bible with glosses. His request was supported by the prior of San Michele da Murano, the Brescian Bernardino da Gadolo: ASV, Senato terra, deliberazioni, reg. 11, fol. 127r–v (pencil foliation, 20 Sept. 1492). This Latin Bible was printed under the name of Girolamo de' Paganini on 7 Nov. 1492: Borsa, "Attività dei tipografi di origine bresciana," 31.

79. ASV, Senato terra, deliberazioni, reg. 7, fols. 14v, 90v (pencil foliation). Exemption from tax was requested during one of Brescia's worst plague years: ASV, Senato terra, deliberazioni, reg. 8, fol. 46r (pencil foliation, 8 May 1479).

80. For example, in Mar. 1475 the Senate agreed to give the Brescian *podestà* the authority to ban and place a bounty on the head of the murderer of the doctor "Nicolai de Venetijs": ASV, Senato terra, deliberazioni, reg. 7, fol. 68v (pencil foliation). See also the Senate's reaction to an attack and robbery committed on Bartolomeo Capriolo: ASV, Senato terra, deliberazioni, reg. 8, fol. 27v (pencil foliation, 27 Oct. 1478); and ASV, Senato terra, deliberazioni, reg. 10, fol. 85r (pencil foliation, 26 Feb. 1487 [m.v. 1488]).

81. ASV, Senato terra, deliberazioni, reg. 10, fol. 99r (pencil foliation, 19 May 1488). It is not stated in the record why the *podestà* of Brescia required clarification on this occasion.

82. ASV, Senato terra, deliberazioni, reg. 7, fol. 92r (pencil foliation, 3 Oct. 1475).

83. ASV, Senato terra, deliberazioni, reg. 8, fol. 4r (pencil foliation, 27 Mar. 1478).

84. Viggiano, *Governanti e governati*, 147–177.

85. Ibid., 179–274; Knapton, "Consiglio dei X nel governo della Terraferma."

86. Mallett and Hale, *Military Organisation of a Renaissance State*, 163–169, 251–252; Grubb, *Firstborn of Venice*, 3–13.

87. Illuminating in this regard is Knapton, "Tribunali veneziani e proteste padovane," 151–170. See also Viggiano, *Governanti e governati*, 89–103.

88. Sanudo, 5:600. See also ASC 519, 12 Dec. 1503, fol. 78r.

89. Law, "Venetian Mainland State in the Fifteenth Century," 173–174.

90. Mannori, "Stato di Firenze e i suoi storici"; Hay and Law, *Italy in the Age of the Renaissance*, 117–119.

91. Lanaro Sartori, "Economia cittadina, flussi migratori e spazio urbano," 74; Beloch, *Storia della popolazione d'Italia*, 469–483; Pasero, "Dati statistici e notizie intorno al movimento della popolazione"; Medin, "Descrizione della città e terre bresciane."

92. Fragments of this decoration, depicting imaginary or unidentifiable townscapes, were uncovered in 1986: Falcioni, "Brescia." On the life of the court and the condition of the city under Malatesta see Zanelli, "Signoria di Pandolfo Malatesta"; Bonfiglio-Dosio, "Condizioni socio-economiche di Brescia"; eadem, "Vita a corte."

93. Bona, "Brescia: XV secolo," esp. 130–147.

94. The income from the *terraferma* in 1469 is outlined in Muir, *Mad Blood Stirring*, 62–65. The fiscal income for 1475–76 is outlined by Maria Ginatempo, "Spunti comparativi sulle trasformazioni della fiscalità," tabella 1, 216–217.

95. The map may be read in conjunction with the facing title page: a Roman monument surmounted by the shield of Brescia bearing a lion flanked by putti and flaming urns. The monument bears the inscription: "VRBIS'/'BRIXIAE'/ 'GRATISSIMAE'/'PATRIAE'/'MONVMENTVM'/'AETERNITATI'/ 'SACRVM'/'V[iro]. S[uo]. L[egavit]. M[onumentum]." Below this monument to Brescian strength stands a peacock symbolizing immortality—in this case, the immortal name and fame of the city. See Capriolo, *Chronica de rebus Brixianorum*. On cartographic constructions of political space see Cosgrove, "Mapping New Worlds."

96. Mallett, "Conquista della Terraferma," 214.
97. Grubb, "When Myths Lose Power."
98. See the bibliography in Chojnacki, "Identity and Ideology," 284–285 n. 8. Note also the "closure" of Padua's Greater Council in 1339 during the period of Venetian control: Kohl, *Padua under the Carrara*, 77.
99. Varanini, *Comuni cittadini*; Law, "Venice and the 'closing' of the Veronese Constitution"; Berengo, "Patriziato e nobiltà"; Lanaro Sartori, "'Essere famiglia di consiglio'"; eadem, *Oligarchia urbana nel Cinquecento veneto*.
100. A useful brief overview of the question, with key bibliographical references, is Cowan, *Marriage, Manners and Mobility*, 4–7.
101. Grubb, "Elite Citizens"; idem, "Venetian Patriciate."
102. The locus classicus of this interpretation of Venice's role is Ventura, *Nobiltà e popolo*. See also the discussion in Knapton, "'Nobiltà e popolo.'"
103. Geertz, *Local Knowledge*. See also Ditchfield, "'In search of local knowledge.'"
104. The single-authored work with broadest narrative scope remains Odorici, *Storie bresciane*.
105. Treccani degli Alfieri, *Storia di Brescia*. An alphabetically organized digest of the material in this work is the *Enciclopedia bresciana*.
106. Commenting on Pasero, "Dominio veneto," a recent historian of Brescia has described it as "un'opera che, seppure nel suo sforzo di esporre ogni problematica e nel consequente, inevitabile, carattere sintetico risenta dell'essere collocata in un'enciclopedia, resta la base di partenza necessaria per ogni ricerca sulla storia bresciana." Apostoli, "Scelte fiscali a Brescia," 349.
107. Ferraro, *Family and Public Life in Brescia*; Pegrari, *Metamorfosi di un'economia urbana*; Montanari, *Quelle terre di là dal Mincio*. Ferraro's work has been published in Italian translation as *Vita pubblica e privata a Brescia*.
108. Bayer, "Bergamo and Brescia." Gabriele Neher is completing a history of cultural life in Renaissance Brescia.
109. Scott, *Domination and the Arts of Resistance*.
110. On the historian as detective, hunter, or tracker see Ginzburg, "Clues: Roots of an Evidential Paradigm."

2. The Myths of Brescia

1. "Adì primo agosto venne el nostro Vescovo che fo el Cardinal Cornaro una dominica et fo acceptato cum grandissima pompa." Bartolomeo Palazzo, "Diario," 379.
2. For an account of Cardinal Francesco Corner's ceremonial entry in 1532 see Mercando, "Cronaca," 146–147; Sanudo, 56:474–476.
3. ASC 538, 19 May 1546, fols. 185v–186r. Cardinal Francesco Corner's ceremonial entry is mentioned in a marginal note relating to the procedures to be followed by the five councillors elected to make the arrangements for Andrea Corner. See also further deliberations and elections in relation to the entry in ibid., 31 May, 4 June, 16, 29 July 1546, fols. 189v, 191r–192r, 205v, 211v.

4. This account of the arches and their decorative schemes is based on the description in BQB, E.I.7, fols. 261r–271v (stamped foliation); and Nova, *Girolamo Romanino*, 334–335.

5. On the emergence of heresy in the city and region after ca. 1543, including the trial of a local noble for heresy in 1546, see Caponetto, *Protestant Reformation*, 178–181.

6. The sources for this program were probably Horace *Odes* 3.5; Livy 7.6.1–6; Cicero *Tusculan Disputations* 1.47.

7. "Uno theatro dentro uno vechio che salti, et il resto del populo alle muralie che difendono la città da i nimici che sono intorno." Quoted in Nova, *Girolamo Romanino*, 335.

8. "Pur essendo un programma piuttosto confuso e generico nelle sue allusioni," ibid. In his discussion Nova does not link the scenes to Brescian myth or history, and he omits the gods and goddesses entirely.

9. On the event as model and mirror see Handelman, *Models and Mirrors*, esp. chaps. 1, 6.

10. On the ambiguity of ritual and its complex relationship with political power see the lucid discussion of Brown, "Ritual and State-Building."

11. On the formation of narrative identity see Somers, "Narrative Constitution of Identity."

12. Hyde, *Society and Politics*, 83–93.

13. On the surviving medieval copies of statutes see Valentini, "Statuti di Brescia." On their conservation see ASC 505, 29 Oct., 2 Nov. 1475, fols. 153r, 157r.

14. ASC 507, 4 May 1482, fol. 8r.

15. *Statuta Brixiae* (1473), "De providendo super clavibus sanctarum crucium campi et auree flame."

16. ASC 505, 26 Apr. 1476, fol. 13v. Compare the distribution of copies of statutes in Verona after ca. 1450 examined by Varanini, "Statuti delle città," 47–48.

17. See ASC 1047; ASC 1079/A.

18. BQB, H.V.5.

19. Ibid; ASC 1523/A, fols. 22v–27r. A note at ibid., fol. 1r, reads: "Hic codex factus fuit in esequtione provisionis diei 22 augusti 1466." On the meaning and use of "sites of memory" see Nora, "Between Memory and History."

20. ASC 521, 23 Oct. 1508, fol. 6r–v.

21. An alphabetical list of men awarded *civilitas* by the Brescian council was also compiled from the council *provvisioni* in 1551 by the chancellor Pietro Suraga: ASC 1332–1334.

22. Sanudo, 15:280–282; ASC 527, 10 Nov. 1517, fol. 53r. The progress of work may be followed in ASC 530, 19 Oct. 1526, fol. 135r; ASC 532, 18 Mar. 1531, fol. 106v; ASC 533, 13 Sept. 1532, 15 July, 15 Nov. 1533, fols. 123r–v, 15r, 51v. Compare the reorganization of the archive in Parma in 1531 as it passed into papal hands: Arcangeli, *Gentiluomini di Lombardia*, 331–364.

23. On "scrivere la comunità" see Della Misericordia, "Decidere e agire in comunità."

24. For example, ASC 500, 19 Oct. 1463, fol. 61r.

25. ASC 509, 27 Apr. 1485, fol. 151v. The first edition of vernacular statutes in the *terraferma* were those of the Friuli printed at Udine in 1484. On the use of vernacular as an expression of authority and Latin as a defense of tradition in Venetian magistracies see Frassòn, "Tra volgare e latino."

26. ASC 505, 15 July 1474, fol. 155r.

27. For example, Captain Francesco Diedo: ASC 509, 25 Nov. 1485, fol. 18v

28. ASV, Senato terra, deliberazioni, reg. 10, fol. 99r (pencil foliation, 19 May 1488); ASC 513, 15 May 1492, fols. 132v–133r; ASV, Capi del consiglio dei dieci, misto, reg. 25, fol. 94v.

29. Hyde, *Padua in the Age of Dante*, 163, 286, 294–295.

30. Arnaldi and Capo, "Cronisti di Venezia e della Marca Trevigiana nel secolo XIV," esp. 286–287.

31. Zabbia, *Notai e la cronachistica cittadina nel Trecento*.

32. Fubini, *Storiografia dell'umanesimo in Italia*; idem, *Umanesimo italiano e i suoi storici*; Lazzarini, *Italia degli stati territoriali*, 5–27.

33. Cochrane, *Historians and Historiography in the Italian Renaissance*, 77–86.

34. ASC 507, 13 Oct. 1480, fol. 141v.

35. In general, see Schöpflin, "Functions of Myth."

36. Archetti, "Malvezzi, Giacomo."

37. Chapter 4 here.

38. "[T]emperatos, moderatosque mores." Aldo Manuzio, dedicatory epistle to Capriolo, in Pollux, *Vocabularii*, facing sig. aiir.

39. The manuscript of the first twelve books of Capriolo's chronicle is in Biblioteca Apostolica Vaticana, Vatican City, Ottobonensis lat. 2272. I have not seen this. The first printed edition is Capriolo, *Chronica de rebus Brixianorum*. The manuscript of books 13–14 is in BQB, C.II.24. For a complete Latin text of these books and the rest of the work see Capriolo, *Chronicorum de rebus Brixianorum*. A translation of all fourteen books is idem, *Dell'istorie della città di Brescia*, and is to be preferred to idem, *Aggiunta di due altri libri alle historie bresciane*, which is a much abridged translation.

40. Quotation from Odorici, *Storie bresciane*, 8:330. However, Capriolo is critical of Venetian monetary policy: Capriolo, *Chronica de rebus Brixianorum*, fols. LXIXr, LXIXv. Note the list of Capriolo's sources given in ibid., facing fol. Ir.

41. BQB, C.I.15. Some of Nassini's comments about his fellow Brescians have been printed, and I follow these transcriptions: Lechi, *Dimore bresciane*, 440, citing Malvezzi's "cronica" on betrayal of Brescia to Mastino della Scala of Verona by Maffe Chizzola; ibid., s.v. "Gosi," citing a family who came from a castle near Bagnolo, were made Brescian citizens in 1432 and were inscribed in the "libro del 1438"; ibid., 430, s.v. "Briggia," citing an inscribed stone; ibid., 440, s.v. "Gussagi," citing an inscribed stone over the door of the duomo.

42. "Opus Brixiae diligenter impressum per Arundum de Arundis hortatu et auspitio clarissimi D. D. Francisci Bragadini urbis et agri praetoris iusticia pietate et sapientia integerrimi." Capriolo, *Chronica de rebus Brixianorum*, fol. LXXIIIv (colophon).

43. Pusculo, "Oratio de laudibus Brixiae"; idem, *Elogio di Brescia;* Guerrini, "Umanista bagnolese."
44. Pasero, "Dominio veneto," 38; Caccia, "Cultura e letteratura," 501.
45. Busetto, "Concoreggio, Gabriele."
46. ASC 512, 25 June 1490, fol. 160v.
47. Their conjoined souls were celebrated in 1502 in Aldo Manuzio's dedicatory epistle to Capriolo in Pollux, *Vocabularii,* facing sig. aiir.
48. Clough, "Becichemo, Marino."
49. Santi, "Lazzaroni, Pietro"; Baroncelli, "Britannico, Giovanni."
50. ASC 504, 18 Jan. 1471; ASC 509, 14 Feb., 17 April 1486; ASC 510, 30 Aug. 1488.
51. His letter to Fedele is quoted in Capriolo, *Chronica de rebus Brixianorum,* fols. IIIIv–Vr.
52. Cereto, *De foro, et laudibus Brixiae,* II, IX–XI. Two sixteenth-century copies of this work are in BQB, C.I.7. miscellanea no. 2, fols. 17r–33v (stamped foliation); BQB, C.I.7. miscellanea no. 4, fols. 62r–82r (stamped foliation). Ludovico Cendrata of Verona alleged that in Brescia there was an "academy" of men and women: Capriolo, *Chronica de rebus Brixianorum,* fol IIIIv. See also ibid., fols. XIIr, LXXIIr [*recte* LXXIIIr] for Capriolo's praise of his fellow humanists. Laura Cereta's letters circulated among a group that met at the Franciscan monastery of Santa Chiara in Brescia: Cereta, *Collected Letters,* 176, 178.
53. Tamani, "Tipografia ebraica a Brescia"; Veneziani, "Stampa a Brescia e nel bresciano," 20–21.
54. Sandal, "Dal libro antico al libro moderno."
55. Figures and rankings taken from *The British Library Incunabula Short-title Catalogue,* www.bl.uk/catalogues/istc.
56. ASV, Senato terra, deliberazioni, reg. 14, fol. 112r (pencil foliation, 17 Oct. 1502). See Veneziani, "Stampa a Brescia e nel bresciano," 18.
57. Rhodes, "Career of Thomas Ferrandus," 544 (quotation), 547 (complaints), 548–549 (Lucretius). The printing of the *Iliad* for the benefit of other "studiosis" is mentioned by Capriolo, *Chronica de rebus Brixianorum,* fol. LXIXv.
58. Newett, *Canon Pietro Casola's Pilgrimage,* 118.
59. "Panegirico di Brescia," 249–250; Fiorentino Aldigheri, *Alla magnifica sua communità di Brexa,* sig. ar. See also Baroncelli, "Predicatore fiorentino del sec. XV," 36. According to Marin, Sanudo Brescia was called the "civitas Herculei" where the eponymous hero had lived: *Itinerario di Marin Sanuto,* 70. For a refutation of the tradition on the basis of archaeological detective work see Capriolo, *Chronica de rebus Brixianorum,* fol. IIr–v.
60. "Condidit hance urbem quis? Galli moenibus acti'/'Non: quia gallorum non habet haec rabiem:'/'An germanus atrox non credas: perfida non est.'/'Non cupit indomita crimina clade sequi:'/'Quid petis haec? Oculis percurras: moenia: campos.'/'Antra: lacus: sylvas: lugera: prata: domos'/'Invictum robur populi: violenta minervae'/'Pectora: belligeri tela: facesque: Dei:'/'Herculis hanc dices fondavit dextra: superbum'/'Hoc opus est: dextram quod decet Herculeam." Sasso, *Pamphili Saxi poetae lepidissimi epigrammatum libri quattuor,* sig. giiiiv. The Herculean motif reappears in several other poems in praise of Brescia in this collection.

61. *Leges brixianae* (1490); Capriolo, *Chronica de rebus Brixianorum*, title page. For coins minted in Brescia during 1406–8 with the lion and, possibly, a head of Hercules on them see Pialorsi, "Attività della zecca: 1406–1408," 144–146, 147.

62. On the decoration of the ceiling, destroyed by fire in 1575, see Wethey, *Paintings of Titian*, 87–89, figs. 66–68; and Frati, Gianfranceschi, and Robecchi, *Loggia di Brescia*, 2:211–239.

63. On Thracum and Trojan settlement see Capriolo, *Chronica de rebus Brixianorum*, fol. IIIr–v.

64. Sanudo, *Itinerario di Marin Sanuto*, 97; Fiorentino Aldigheri, *Alla magnifica sua communità di Brexa*, sig. ar; Vosonius, *Epigrammaton*, unpaginated.

65. Livy 5.35.1–4; Justin *Epitome* 20.5.8. Pliny and Ptolemy are cited by Capriolo, but he clearly preferred the authority of Livy: *Chronica de rebus Brixianorum*, fols. IIv, Vv.

66. Malvecius, *Chronicon Brixianum*, cols. 786–788.

67. Capriolo, *Chronica de rebus Brixianorum*, fols. IIv–IIIr. See also ibid., fols. Vv, XIXv. Toward the end of the fifteenth century the Milanese historian Bernardino Corio agreed that Brescia was "capo de Galli Cenomani." Corio, *Storia di Milano*, 2:1097.

68. Malvecius, *Chronicon Brixianum*, cols. 789, 792.

69. "Panegirico di Brescia," 252.

70. Pusculo, "Oratio de laudibus Brixiae," 6–7.

71. Capriolo, *Chronica de rebus Brixianorum*, fol. VIr–v. Note his discussion of Roman inscriptions found in Brescia in idem, *Helias Capreolus Francisco Arigoneo*, unpaginated.

72. King, *Death of the Child*, 69, 74–75.

73. Capriolo, *Chronica de rebus Brixianorum*, fol. VIr–v.

74. Malvecius, *Chronicon Brixianum*, col. 790.

75. Rabil, *Laura Cereta*, 103.

76. Capriolo, *Chronica de rebus Brixianorum*, fols. VIIr, VIIIr.

77. Livy 21.25.13–14, 55. 4, 32.30.1–13; Pusculo, "Oratio de laudibus Brixiae," 41; Fiorentino Aldigheri, *Alla magnifica sua communità di Brexa*, sig. av; Casato, *Ad Baptistam Zenum*, sigs. aiiv–aiiir. In ca. 1500 local humanist and poet Daniele Cereto wrote: "Quin etiam Galli qua tempestate feroces'/'Vastabant fines Itala terra tuos.'/'Roma parum cautis dum se se attolleret armis,'/'Illo Brixiacam tempore sensit opem.'/'Hic ubi Cannetum est, tunc horrida castra fuerunt,'/'Hic steterant acies, magnanimique Duces.'/'Tunc pia Romanas posita formidine vires'/'Diceris auxilio multiplicasse tuo." Cereto, *De foro, et laudibus Brixiae*, VII. See also Capriolo, *Chronica de rebus Brixianorum*, fol. Vv.

78. "Et hoc tempore Pandulfus Malatesta Pergami et Brixie efficitur dominus. Et post huius optimam dominationem Philippus Maria Brixie dominium accepit, a quo propter maximas rapinas, quia non dominus sed tirampnus [*sic*] pessimus erat, et propter alia crudelia cives defecerunt et ad illustrissimum optimum justissimumque venetorum dominium (se) transtulerunt, sub quo Brixia gloriosissima potentissima ditissima triumphat." "Panegirico di Brescia," 257.

79. Ibid., 258–259; Capriolo, *Chronica de rebus Brixianorum*, fols. LXIIv–LXIIIIv.

80. Solazio, "Prefazione storica," 138, 145. In 1485 Marcantonio Morosini, the Venetian *podestà* in Brescia, placed an inscription on a pilaster at the base of a new building (subsequently the *monte di pietà*) on the south side of the *piazza della loggia:* "SAGUNTINORUM ET'/'BRIXIANORUM'/'MIRANDA CONSTANTIA." In ca. 1499 Giovanni Stefano Buzzoni wrote: "Hoc tibi rara fides tribuit vulgata per orbem:'/'Moenibus evulsis pectora Marcus habet:'/'Magna Sagontinae fidei iam gloria cessit'/'Urbi brixiacae lumina cuncta meae." Vosonius, *Epigrammaton,* sig. br. See Capriolo, *Chronica de rebus Brixianorum,* fol. LXIIIv. See also King, *Death of the Child,* 71, 72, 74.

81. Pusculo's *L'assedio famoso, che patì Brescia da Nicolò Piccinino* is now lost. See Rossi, *Elogi historici de Bresciani,* 235; Cozzando, *Libraria bresciana,* 200.

82. Capriolo, *Chronica de rebus Brixianorum,* bk. 10.

83. In a speech of welcome for the visit of the Venetian cardinal Giovanni Battista Zeno to the city in 1489 the local humanist Giovanni Casato asserted that during that assault the women fought like viragos or amazons: Casato, *Ad Baptistam Zenum,* sig. aiiiv. See also Capriolo, *Chronica de rebus Brixianorum,* fols. LVIIv, LVIIIr–v, LIXr, LXv.

84. Biondo, *Roma ristaurata et Italia illustrata,* fol. 159v. Biondo is cited by Capriolo, *Chronica de rebus Brixianorum,* fol. LVIIr–v. See also Banterele, "Trasporto delle navi venete nel lago di Garda."

85. Chapter 4 here. The Venetian *podestà* in Brescia placed the following inscription on a pilaster at the base of a new building on *piazza della loggia:* "BRIXIA FIDEI BASIS'/'MCCCCXXXVIII'/'PESTE FAME BELLIS OPPRESSA." See also above, n. 80.

86. Casato, *Ad Baptistam Zenum,* sig. [avr]. The Brescian council, after some disagreement, rewarded Casato for his public oratory: ASC 514, 14 June, 1 Aug. 1493, fols. 94r, 110v; ASC 515, 28 Apr. 1495, fol. 154r; ASC 516, 22 Dec. 1498, fol. 141r.

87. Casato, *Ad Baptistam Zenum,* sig. [avv].

88. "Brixia qui dicit Veneto servire Leoni'/'Te: nescit: quid sint regna: nec imperium:'/'Non servit qui vult: servit servire coactus.'/'Qui servit: bello vincitur: aut emitur'/'Te ducibus Venetis non victa aut empta dedisti:'/'Non igitur serva es Brixia: sed socia." Sasso, *Pamphili Saxi poetae lepidissimi epigrammatum libri quattuor,* unpaginated; Capriolo, *Chronica de rebus Brixianorum,* fols. LXIIv–LXIVv.

89. "andandose a render a zente barbara [i.e. French], superba, avara e crudel, senza bota di bombarda; cavandose dil governo di tanto benigna e gratiosa Signoria, qual per 84 anni li havea governati non da subiti ma da proprii fioli, cavati da miseria e servitù, erano rustici senza urbanità veruna. *Defunctis patribus, surrexit prava juventus.*" Sanudo, 15:291.

90. Priuli, *Diarii,* 4:45–46.

91. As Taddeo Solazio put it in ca. 1480–93: "Qui [i.e. Faustino and Giovita] etiam miserantes Brixianorum civium calamitatem cum ipsa civitas a Nicolao Picinino non minus acri diutinoque bello quam fame pesteque premeretur,

armati muris insidentes maximo cum terrore ab hostibus visi fuere." Solazio, "Prefazione storica," 146.

92. This incident is not mentioned by the contemporary chronicler Cristoforo Soldo but does seem to originate in this period. See Soldo, *Cronaca*, 26 n. 1. The appearance of the saints to the enemy in the form of combatants is mentioned only very briefly in Capriolo, *Chronica de rebus Brixianorum*, fol. LXv. Capriolo gives much more attention to the "wonder" of the ships dragged overland to Lake Garda: ibid., fol. LXIr–v.

93. Amore, "Faustino e Giovita"; Cannata, "Iconografia."

94. Malvecius, *Chronicon Brixianum*, cols. 795–798. On their noble descent, see *Leggenda de Sancto Faustino e Jovita*, unpaginated; Ricci, *Passio sanctorum martyrum*, sig. a3r.

95. Rimoldi, "Calimero"; idem, "Apollonio"; Raggi, "Iconografia."

96. Solazio, "Prefazione storica," 146.

97. Capriolo, *De voluptate*, unpaginated.

98. Cereto, *De foro, et laudibus Brixiae*, I.

99. Malvecius, *Chronicon Brixianum*, cols. 797, 799. Marin Sanudo noted that it was between the gates of the Pille and Torre where the water from the miraculous fountain still ran that Faustino, Giovita, and Apollonio appeared at the time of Piccinino's bombardment of the city: Sanudo, *Itinerario di Marin Sanuto*, 70.

100. Chapter 6 here.

101. *Leggenda de Sancto Faustino e Jovita*; Ricci, *Passio Sanctorum martyrum*. In the same vein in Aug. 1505 Giovanni Battista Pontano of Brescia published a *Legenda de Sancto Honorio vescovo de Bressa* (untraced): Guerrini, "Miscellanea bresciana," 211.

102. "Anchora i[n] sanctimonia, per essere Brexia quasi un' altra Roma in tanto numero di martiri." Fiorentino Aldigheri, *Alla magnifica sua communità di Brexa*, sig. aiir.

103. Solazio, "Prefazione storica," 146; Rimoldi, "Anatalone."

104. "Brixia cives suos totque innumeros caelicolas summoque cum immortali deo assistentes venerando imitandoque gaudeat et exultet." Solazio, "Prefazione storica," 147.

105. "Panegirico di Brescia," 258–259.

106. "Verum dum de civitate ipsa idest de Brixiano populo cogito, saepe verbi illius, quod a sapiente quodam hispano viro, quiolim, ut scitis huc a summo Pontifice ad compescendas lites quasdam missus fuerat, dictum audivi mihi in mentem venit. Non monacos enim, inquit, tantum, sed populum ipsum Brixianum sibi religionis observantem videri." Pusculo, "Oratio de laudibus Brixiae," 39.

107. Solazio, "Prefazione storica," 147. On both crosses and associated objects see Panazza, *Tesoro delle sante croci*. See also the account of the crosses written ca. 1520 in ASC 1528, fols. 279v–280r; and ASC 1523/A, fols. 96v–98r (with the attestation of elderly Brescians).

108. Panazza, *Tesoro delle sante croci*, 7; Capriolo, *Chronica de rebus Brixianorum*, fols. XXVIIv–XXVIIIr. A verse account of Helen's discovery of the true cross was printed in Brescia ca. 1498 as *Invenzione della Croce*.

109. Solazio, "Prefazione storica," 147; "Ille Crucem moriens fidei monumenta reliquit:'/'Dicta fuit nostris *Aurea* Flamma prius.'/'Quam populus varios semper servavit ad usus:'/'Plurima namque illi vena salutis inest.'/'Quum volumus, toto decedunt nubila Coelo,'/'Quum libet, optata decidit imber aqua." Cereto, *De foro, et laudibus Brixiae,* IX. See also Chapter 5 here.

110. "Publica divitiis ornare palatia certant'/'Cultibus assiduis, muneribusque datis.'/'Non favor, aut studium vulgi, non cura senatus'/'Cessat; in officio Brixia tota pio.'/'Brixia magnipotens, nulli cessura sub armis,'/'Brixia praecipua conspicienda fide.'/'Tunc potuit Veneti vulgata potentia regni'/'Intima fortunae cernere corda tuae.'/'Quum male Nicoleos, jam captis undique muris'/'Pulsaret patriae moenia chara tuae.'/'Ille diu victor, massyli more Leonis'/'Quem stimulat rabies, & diuturna fames:'/'Agminibus medis hostili caede cruentus'/'Cingebat parvos obsidione Lares." Cereto, *De foro, et laudibus Brixiae,* VII. See also ibid., I, on the return of an age of gold, peace, and plenty under Saint Mark.

111. Quoted in Cistellini, "Vita religiosa," 399.

112. ASC 491, 21 Apr. 1440, fol. 23r; Capriolo, *Chronica de rebus Brixianorum,* fol. LXVIr.

113. Pusculo, "Oratio de laudibus Brixiae," 28, 29.

114. "Ut altera Corcyra videatur." Capriolo, *Chronica de rebus Brixianorum,* fol. IIIIv. See also "Panegirico di Brescia," 258–259; Cereto, *De foro, et laudibus Brixiae,* VIII. The Brescian poet Veronica Gambara wrote of her homeland in ca. 1532: "Natura, a te sol madre e pia nutrice,'/'ha fatto agli altri mille gravi offese'/'spogliandogli di quanto avean di buono'/'per farne a te cortese e largo dono." Gambara, *Rime,* 104.

115. "[N]on è altro a dire che spechio e luocho da contemplare i doni della natura, benché più tosto saria da dirla uno paradiso in terra e per la amenità del luogho e per copia optima de tutte cose necessarie al victo humano." Fiorentino Aldigheri, *Alla magnifica sua communità di Brexa,* sig. ar.

116. "Great and powerful Brescia triumphs under the sway of Mark." Sanudo, *Itinerario di Marin Sanuto,* 17, 70, 73.

117. Newett, *Canon Pietro Casola's Pilgrimage,* 119. Note "Nunc ubi constructa est Brixia bellipotens,'/'Haud incerta cano: magnis si crediturusque:'/'Livius hoc memorat primus in historia'/'Brixia sed nostris iam nomine dicta latinis'/'Magnipotens." Vosonius, *Epigrammaton,* unpaginated. Also note: "Pyramides tollat memphis: iactentur honores'/'Maxima quae magne templa decent triviae'/'Laudet arionias rupes parnasica sedes:'/'Punica cornigerum laudet harena Iovem:'/'Mirentur tumuli regis miracula cares:'/'Miretur sub se Brixia quicquid habet.'/'Pyramides: thermas: circos: delubra: colossos:'/'Rostra: palatinas tecta superba domos.'/'Omnia nam superant haec artem: credere posses'/'Vix oculis: urbs est Brixia quicquid habet'/'Mirari decet hanc: que tot miracula claudit'/'Nobilis haud uno munere nobilis est." Sasso, *Pamphili Saxi poetae lepidissimi epigrammatum libri quattuor,* unpaginated.

118. Wethey, *Paintings of Titian,* 88–89.

119. Grubb, *Firstborn of Venice,* 25.

120. A point made by Davidson, "'As Much for Its Culture as for Its Arms,'" 211–212.

3. Privilege, Power, and Politics

1. The text of the privileges is in Zanelli, *Delle condizioni interne di Brescia*, 207–222.
2. Law, "Verona and the Venetian State," 12–15.
3. Menniti Ippolito, "Dedizione di Brescia a Milano (1421) e a Venezia (1427)."
4. See Ginatempo, "Spunti comparativi sulle trasformazioni della fiscalità."
5. A point emphasized by Pegrari, *Metamorfosi di un'economia urbana*, 49.
6. "[E]viscerata, summersa et depopulata et miserabiliter cruciata, hactenus per tirannos." Quoted in Menniti Ippolito, "Dedizione di Brescia a Milano (1421) e a Venezia (1427)," 40–41.
7. In 1430 there were 1,230 heads of families listed in the tax census *(estimo)* as compared with 1,664 three decades earlier. See Pasero, "Dati statistici e notizie intorno al movimento della popolazione," 74–75.
8. "Quod S.a et Excell.a duc. dominatio Venetarium, que sua immensa clementia dignata fuit dictam comunitatem amplexari favore sincere caritatis aggregando cives et districtuales omnesque incolas Brixie in numero et consortio suorum fidelium subditorum et de servitude ad libertatem reducere sub alis expansis evangeliste gloriossisimi Sancti Marci divina gratia confovente." Zanelli, *Delle condizioni interne di Brescia*, 208 (clause I).
9. Ibid., 209 (clause III).
10. "Item, quoniam propter urbis afflictiones miserandas cives magne auctoritatis et incole notabiles quibus civitas florebat antiquitus diminuiti sunt in numero valde grandi propter impressiones guerrarum et tyrannorum persecutiones, dignetur prelibata dominatio, ut loca guasta et vacua repleantur et civitas per tempora restauretur, edicere et mandare quod cives sint et pro civibus habeantur, tractentur et reputentur quicumque fuerint creati et constituti cives per literas V. Ser. dominii aut per consilium generale comunis Brix," ibid., 211 (clause VI).
11. Montanari, *Quelle terre di là dal Mincio*, 40.
12. Ginatempo, "Spunti comparativi sulle trasformazioni della fiscalità," 198.
13. Zanelli, *Delle condizioni interne di Brescia*, 213–214.
14. Viggiano, *Governanti e governati*, 189–190.
15. Law, "Venetian Mainland State in the Fifteenth Century," 171.
16. On the potential for a conflict of maritime or commercial and *terraferma* cultures see Mallett, "Conquista della Terraferma," 214.
17. "Es tu vir prudentissime illustri loco excelsoque constitutus: quae res: ut plurimum in sicco scientiae iacentibus quid superbiae assert: sed tibi honestissimo humilitatis: clementiae vitae morumque & gravitatis multum attulit: quae res faciet ut non solum pretoris: sed etiam benignissimi: & optimi patris in hac nobilissima civitate: officium prestes: qui non admittit assentatores: non leves: non stultos virtutis comptemptores: Tollere discordias seditiones: quae solent maxime in propinquos & sanguine coniunctos oriri: iusticiae pietatisque est in benignissimo praetore: Concordiam tranquillitatem inducere summae bonitatis: & honestatis esse." Bornato, *Opusculum de laudibus matrimonii*, sigs. [bviiv–bviiir].
18. Sabellico, *De officio praetoris*, fols. 105r–108v.

19. In 1479 the council agreed to construct "una pulchra & digna arengeria" from which the *podestà* could issue condemnations in the piazza: ASC 506, 22 Oct. 1479, fol. 38r.

20. This judgment is based on a reading of the registers of proclamations ASC 1093 and 1094.

21. Frati, Gianfranceschi, and Robecchi, *Loggia di Brescia*, 1:26–27.

22. Ibid., 27–28; Zamboni, *Memorie intorno alle pubbliche fabbriche*, chap. 3. On the poor state of the *podestà*'s palace see the complaints in the requests for privileges made by Brescia to the Senate in 1517: ASV, Senato terra, deliberazioni, reg. 20, fol. 45r (pencil foliation, 27 Apr. 1517, with note: "Que fuerunt expedicta in Mense Junij").

23. The perpetrators of a violent and armed attack on Leonardo Martinengo were ordered to be exiled from Venetian territory by the Senate, but the rectors were impeded by a four months' Brescian statute of limitations. The Senate agreed by 104 votes to 6 (with 16 "non sincero") to instruct the rectors to ignore it: "Vadit pars quod scribatur dictis rectoribus quam non obstante statuto praedicto possint facere proclamari praedictos raptores in eo breviori termino qui ipsis videbitur et postea procedant secundum tenorem auctoritatis eis tributae ab hoc consilio." ASV, Senato terra, deliberazioni, reg. 23, fols. 85r–v, 105r (pencil foliation, 20 Feb. 1523 [m.v. 1524], 17 Mar. 1524). For the other cases see Viggiano, *Governanti e governati*, 71–73, 76–77.

24. On the evolution of rectorial administration see Viggiano, "Aspetti politici e giurisdizionali." Note the formal and informal limits imposed by the city on the power of the Viscontean *podestà* in Reggio at the end of the fourteenth century: Gamberini, *Città assediata*, 27–54.

25. Del Torre, *Venezia e la terraferma*, 223–224.

26. Beverley, "Venetian Ambassadors," app.

27. On military *provveditori* see Mallett and Hale, *Military Organisation of a Renaissance State*, 168–176.

28. Ibid., 204.

29. King, *Venetian Humanism*, 323–325, 340–341, 359–362, 366–368, 374–377, 379–381, 431–432.

30. Diedo, *Vita S. Rochi*; Oxford, Bodleian ms. Canon. Class. Lat. 261. On Bragadin and Capriolo see Chapter 2 here.

31. Del Torre, *Venezia e la terraferma*, 230.

32. "Et brexani spendevano voluntieri, sì per esser richi, qual per amar molto il lhoro podestà, per far bon rezimento et molto magnifico." Sanudo, 1:742. Correr's prudence and impartiality as *podestà* are praised in Planius, *Ad Catharinam Cyprorum reginam*, sigs. aiiiv–[aivr].

33. Ventura, "Bragadin, Francesco"; Sanudo, 25:35–36 (19 Oct. 1517).

34. Cozzi and Knapton, *Repubblica di Venezia*, 218–219.

35. ASC 513, 15, 22 May 1492, fols. 132v–133r, 136r; ASV, Capi del consiglio dei dieci, misto, reg. 25, fols. 129v–130r (pencil foliation). Domenico Malipiero recorded that Dandolo was punished "per haver fomentà le parti in Bressa, e ditto parole de deshonor contra la Comunità, a favor de Ghibelini; e fatto sindicato nel so palazzo a cinque Ghibelini de i cittadini, contra la voluntà de

Domenegho Trivisan K[avalier], Podestà: et è stà preso ch'esso sindicato sia depenà del tutto." Malipiero, "Annali veneti," 690.

36. ASC 489, 12 June 1439, fols. 211r–212r; ASC 492, 2 Mar. 1442, fols. 36v–37r; ASC 492, 10 Dec. 1448, fol. 190v; ASC 498, 1 June 1459, fol. 112v.

37. See the proclamation issued by the rectors on 18 Nov. 1460 in ASC 1092, fol. 43v.

38. ASV, Senato terra, deliberazioni, reg. 12, fol. 38v (pencil foliation, 14 Jan. 1493 [m.v. 1494]).

39. "Cum huic Consilio propositum fuisset contra illam scelestissimam personam, Que avisa est in publicis locis affligere buletina ignominiosa: & non mediocriter detrahentia honori: & dignitati Iustissimi: ac Integerrimi Magnifici Pretoris nostri, immo in vilipendium universae Civitatis nostrae." The council also condemned anyone who "famam violare contendit" in relation to the rectors' exercise of justice. The fine of 4,000 *lire planete* was agreed by 111 votes to 6: ASC 519, 2 Oct. 1503, fol. 50r–v. See also Del Torre, *Venezia e la terraferma*, 217–234.

40. Sanudo, 5:599–600.

41. For example, Nassino de Nassinis gave his report ("eleganter facta") on his mission in ASC 506, 8 July 1478, fol. 75r. See also ASC 519, 27 Jan. 1504, fol. 94v.

42. On appeals made in 1454 and 1482 see Viggiano, *Governanti e governati*, 97–98.

43. For details of the preparations of the delegations sent in 1458 and 1462 see Montanari, *Quelle terre di là dal Mincio*, 111–114.

44. On the resident ambassador see ASC 499, 3 Feb. 1461, fols. 7v–8r; ASC 515, 5 Aug., 10 Nov. 1496, fols. 117r–v, 135r; ASC 516, 18, 23 Sept. 1499, fols. 67v, 69v–70r. A house was requested in the deditions of 1428 and 1440. Its existence is testified by ASC 499, 25 July 1462, fol. 105r. On the proposal to construct a Brescian residence of twenty-two bedrooms near the Rialto in the parish of San Silvestro in Venice, see the discussions in ASC 505, 22, 24 Jan. 1474, fols. 94r–v, 97r; ASC 507, 6 Dec. 1482, fol. 53r. On the acquisition of a larger house, see ASC 521, 18, 19 Jan. 1507, fols. 93r–v, 94v–95r. The inventory of the house made in 1508 indicates fifteen rooms furnished with beds, tables, sideboards, and cooking and eating implements, as well as stores of food. A picture of the Virgin and Saints Faustino and Giovita hung in the house: ASC 1528, fols. 142v–145r.

45. ASV, Senato terra, deliberazioni, reg. 8, fol. 119v (pencil foliation, 9 Mar. 1481). The orator from Bergamo had also been kept waiting for an unspecified length of time. The Senate voted ninety-two votes to fifty-eight to expedite matters, a tally that may indicate some lack of enthusiasm to tackle *terraferma* affairs. See also Fasoli, "Nunzio permanente di Vicenza," where it is noted that the Vicentine nuncio was established in 1530 as a response to the number of appeals being made to Venice.

46. ASV, Capi del consiglio dei dieci, misto, reg. 25, fol. 119r (pencil foliation).

47. Asola and Salò were excepted from this ruling, which was passed by 111 votes to 34 (and one abstention). ASV, Senato terra, deliberazioni, reg. 20, fol.

34r (pencil foliation, 6 June 1517). The petitions on the communes of Lonato, Pontevico, Montechiari, Ghedi, and other parts of the Brescian territory were considered and approved by the Collegio rather than the Senate soon afterward: ibid., fols. 52v, 53r, 53v, 54r, 54v, 55r.

48. Dispatch to the Venetian Council of Ten quoted in Viggiano, *Governanti e governati*, 267 n. 138.

49. On the Brescian college of judges see Mistura, *Giudici e i loro collegi*, 7–73. See also Grubb, *Firstborn of Venice*, 56–62.

50. Cozzi, "Politica del diritto," esp. 79–121. See Chapter 4 here.

51. Suriano, *Relazione*, 6–7.

52. See Jones, *Italian City-State*; idem, "Economia e società," 185–372.

53. Da Lezze, *Catastico bresciano*, 2: 9.

54. The most succinct account of this process is Ferraro, "Proprietà terriera e potere nello Stato veneto."

55. Compare the complex network of relations between the Valtellina, Luganese, and Ossola Superiore and Milan studied by Della Misericordia, "'Coda' dei gentiluomini."

56. For example, in line with the concessions of 1440 the Brescians unsuccessfully petitioned the Venetian Senate for complete control of the Bresciano in 1454, 1483, 1484, and again in 1492: Zamperetti, *Piccoli principi*, 172 n. 57.

57. Parzani, "Territorio di Brescia."

58. Pasero, "Dominio veneto," 14, 28–29.

59. On fiscal inequity in the Padovano see Knapton, "Rapporti fiscali tra Venezia e la terraferma," 41–44.

60. These privileges and the deterioriation of the *contado* with respect to conditions in 1430 is noted in a letter from the Venetian rectors to the doge of 5 Feb. 1460 copied in ASC 1524, fols. 30v–31r.

61. Apostoli, "Scelte fiscali a Brescia." On the organization and growth of the Brescian "territorio" during the fifteenth century, see Parzani, "Territorio di Brescia"; idem, "Istituzioni del bresciano"; Rossini, "Continuità e trasformazioni"; and eadem, *Campagne bresciane*. On the territorial organizations that developed in the Veneto in the sixteenth and seventeenth centuries, see Zamperetti, "'Sinedri dolosi.'"

62. ASC 1092, fol. 159r (proclamation of 30 June 1492).

63. Chittolini, "Contadi e territori," 36.

64. "Allegantes ad ipsam oblationem non teneri, ob exemptionem: & separationem per nos [i.e. Venice] eis concessam." Doge Foscari to Brescian rectors, 16 Oct. 1436, in ASC 1523/A, fol. 36r. A similar problem was encountered in 1467: Zanelli, "Festa dell'Assunta," 8–9.

65. Rossini, *Campagne bresciane*, 50, 57.

66. The Senate upheld their objections: ASV, Senato terra, deliberazioni, reg. 11, fol. 122v (pencil foliation, 28 Aug. 1492).

67. ASV, Senato terra, deliberazioni, reg. 1, fols. 7r–8v (original foliation, 5 Jan. 1440 [m.v. 1441]); *Instituta Vallis Camonicae*.

68. The privileges granted by Venice on 9 Apr. 1440 are printed in Montanari, *Quelle terre di là dal Mincio*, app. 1. A letter of 1192 from Emperor Henry VI

to Brescia on this matter is printed in *Leges brixianae* (1490), sig. yzv. See also
Capriolo, *Chronica de rebus Brixianorum*, fol. XXXIv.

69. In Oct. 1503 Angelo Sanudo, the Venetian *provveditore* at Salò, passed to the
Brescian rectors a supplication from the Sabbia and Trompia valleys regarding
certain exemptions and privileges relating to the transport of wine granted by
the Brescian *podestà* in 1476. Sanudo argued in favor of the exemption, pointing out the scarcity in these valleys and also the loyalty of the inhabitants. The
Brescian rectors then passed the supplication and recommendation to the Venetian Senate for consideration. The Senate granted the request: ASV, Senato
terra, deliberazioni, reg. 14, fols. 200r–201r (pencil foliation, 30 Jan. 1503
[m.v. 1504]). See also a referral to Venice by the *provveditore* of Salò of a serious criminal matter: ibid., reg. 16, fol. 63r–v (pencil foliation, 13 Nov. 1508).
See also ASV, Senato terra, deliberazioni, reg. 9, fols. 117r (pencil foliation,
2 Nov. 1484), 118v, 119v (pencil foliation, 23 Nov. 1484). The activities of the
provveditore in Lonato during 1506–8 are recorded in a book of *provvisioni*
for those years in ASMa, Archivio Gonzaga, E.XLVIII.3, b. 1600.

70. Beverley, "Venetian Ambassadors," app.

71. *Statuta Ripariae Benacensis;* Capriolo, *Chronica de rebus Brixianorum*, fols.
XIIIv, LXXIIr [*recte* LXXIIIr]. Population figures for the vicariates in 1493 in
Medin, "Descrizione della città e terre bresciane," 682–683.

72. *Raccolta di privilegj*, 314, 350–352 (privileges of the Val Camonica granted in
1428 and 1448).

73. In general see Montanari, *Quelle terre di là dal Mincio*, 116–122. For instances of the failure to welcome Brescian officials see Pasero, "Dominio
veneto," 119 n. 1.

74. ASC 509, 9 June 1486, fol. 75r (arms of captain of the valleys and the Brescian
vicar at Pontevico slashed); ASC 510, 4 July 1488, fols. 70v–71r (defacement
of arms painted on the wall of the *podestà*'s palace at Lonato); ASC 514,
21 June 1493, fol. 95r–v (Benedetto Avogadro chased out of Orzinuovi).

75. Menniti Ippolito, "'Provedibitur sicut melius videbitur.'"

76. For example, in 1474 four orators from the Val Camonica bearing letters of
credential written by the captain of the valley explained to the special council
that some persons "querunt et tentant contra Iurisdictionem et auctoritatem
Capitanei Vallis prefate et consequenter huius Magnific[a]e comunitatis." ASC
505, 15 July 1474, fol. 155r. In 1486 "scelestissimis personis" dared "detur-
pare Insigne D. Iacobi de Advocatis Militis tunc capitanus Valliscamonic[a]e:
necnon Insigne Lancelloti de humeltatis vicarij pontifici." The special council
unanimously agreed to offer a 200 *lire planete* reward for an accusation or
notification of the guilty parties, and a further 600 *lire planete* when the malefactors were consigned to Brescian authority: ASC 509, 9 June 1486, fol. 75r.
Confirmed by the general council by eighty to four: ibid., fol. 76r.

77. Montanari, *Quelle terre di là dal Mincio*, 165–167.

78. For one example in 1463 see Viggiano, *Governanti e governati*, 211. On the political structures of the Riviera di Salò see Scotti, "Magnifica Patria nel '500."

79. On Brescian governance in Asola see Montanari, *Quelle terre di là dal Mincio*,
129–159.

80. Copy of petition presented to the Brescian chancellery by Jacopo Filippo and Ugolino da Asola on 14 Aug. 1441, in ASC 1523/A, fol. 42r.
81. ASV, Senato terra, deliberazioni, reg. 9, fols. 113r–114v (pencil foliation, 25 Oct. 1484).
82. ASV, Senato terra, deliberazioni, reg. 11, fols. 125v–126r (pencil foliation, 3 Sept. 1492). On the Brescian reaction to the Asolan delegation see ASC 515, 23 Apr. 1495, fol. 153r. See also the petition of the Brescian orators: ASV, Senato terra, deliberazioni, reg. 12, fols. 147v–148r (pencil foliation, 8 June 1496); and ibid., fol. 180v (pencil foliation, 14 Dec. 1496), where the decision of 1492 is confirmed.
83. ASC 515, 10, 25 June 1497, fols. 44v–45r, 49r–v; ASC 516, 12 June 1498, fol. 86v.
84. For example, a ducal letter of 1492 warned the *provveditore* in Asola against disobedience in trespassing on the jurisdiction of the Brescian *podestà* in Jewish matters, not only with respect to usury but also in mercantile affairs more generally: ASC 1079/A, ducal letter no. 134 (16 July 1492); copy in ASC 1525, fol. 103r; and text in Massetti, "Antisemitismo," 170–171. See also the ducal letter of 30 Apr. 1521 confirming Brescian jurisdiction in Asola, Lonato, and Orzinuovo in matter of arms, against the claims of the Venetian *provveditore*: ASC 1079/B, no. 193.
85. ASC 515, 3 Nov. 1496, fol. 131v.
86. Pasero, "Dominio veneto," 160 (on Salò); Montanari, *Quelle terre di là dal Mincio,* 134.
87. On the Viscontean period see Cengarle, *Immagine di potere e prassi di governo,* esp. 137 (no. 15), 138 (no. 19), 142 (no. 53). On the early Venetian period, see Zamperetti, *Piccoli principi,* esp. 155–162, 168–171.
88. Zamperetti, *Piccoli principi,* 160–166.
89. Ibid., 157–158.
90. The mausoleum (1503–16) commissioned by Francesco Martinengo di Padernello for his father and sculpted by Bernardino dalle Croci, with the possible contributions of Stefano Lamberti and Maffeo Olivieri, is now in the museum of Santa Giulia, Brescia. On Martinengo artistic commissions, see Nova, *Girolamo Romanino,* 229–231. Romanino also portrayed a member of the Gambara family in ca. 1522–24 (Allentown Art Museum, Allentown, Pa.). Portraits of members of the Martinengo clan by Alessandro Moretto and Bartolomeo Veneto dating to ca. 1540–46 are in the National Gallery, London.
91. Mallett and Hale, *Military Organisation of a Renaissance State,* 199; Melga, "Cronaca," 31–32.
92. Muraro, "Festa a Venezia." A comedy was recited in the house of Giulio Martinengo in Brescia in Oct. 1508: Bartolomeo Palazzo, "Diario," 258. Antonio Martinengo organized a party with a comedy by Angelo Beolco "Ruzante" in Jan. 1521: Sanudo, 29:536–537, with English translation in idem, *Venice,* 289–290.
93. Sanudo, 7:693.
94. According to Soldo, "Cronaca," 1–3.
95. Mallett and Hale, *Military Organization of a Renaissance State,* 252.

96. Sanudo, 4:754–755, 766.
97. For example, ASC 506, 16 Dec. 1479, fol. 65v; ASC 507, 28 June 1481, fols. 83v–84r. Brescian orators appeal to the Venetian Senate: ASV, Senato terra, deliberazioni, reg. 7, fol. 157r (pencil foliation, 17 Mar. 1477). On violence and insults against Venetian rectors generally see Del Torre, *Venezia e la terraferma*, 219–223.
98. ASC 519, 28 Dec. 1503, 15 Dec. 1504, fols. 85r, 18r–v; Sanudo, 5: 630, 658, 879, 998, 1037–1038.
99. The disposition of Venetian troops in the Bresciano in 1503 shows that Count Giovanni Francesco Gambara commanded 240 horsemen at Ghedi while Count Alvise Avogadro commanded the same force at Martinengo in the Bergamasco. Avogadro's troops were moved to the fortified outpost at Anfo in expectation of an imperial attack while the Brescia castle was well stocked with gunpowder. Sanudo, 4:833, 834, 846; ibid., 5:62–63; ibid., 7:282, 390.
100. Ibid., 6:63, 125. On troops commanded by Count Giovanni Francesco Gambara and Count Alvise Avogadro see ibid., 4:833, 834, 846; 5; 62–63; 7: 282, 390.
101. G. A. Baizoni to Lucrezia Gambara, Brescia, 6 Mar. 1506, cited in Pasero, *Francia, Spagna, Impero*, 20–21.

4. Forming an Urban Oligarchy

1. Pullan, "'Three Orders of Inhabitants.'"
2. Monti della Corte, *Famiglie del patriziato bresciano*.
3. Tedoldi, "Tra immigrazione e integrazione."
4. Gentile, "'Postquam malignitates temporum hec nobis dedere nomina'"; Zanetti, "Signorie (1313–1426)."
5. Chapter 11 here.
6. Versions of the list have been published in Guerrini, "'Libro d'oro' della nobiltà," and Lechi, *Dimore bresciane*, 423–459.
7. Lechi, *Dimore bresciane*, 427.
8. ASC 505, 18 Aug. 1474, fol. 5v.
9. "[V]orebbe nobilitar sé et chiamarsi dei Buschi, ma non è, è dei Orci, a quello ho sentito dire dal q. D. Jacomo mio Padre de mi Pandolfo Nassini, sono Gaitani, Ugoni et Buschi che fecero martirizar che fece i Santi Faustino et Jovita fratelli di Prignacchi, cittadini de Bressa et in questo è notato il tutto; qual Francesco si chiamava il Busca." Nassini quoted in Lechi, *Dimore bresciane*, 4:430. See also ibid., 439–440, 456.
10. "[E]t così si diventano ricchi, presto de poveri huomeni in altezza." Nassini quoted in ibid., 434.
11. Monti della Corte, "Il registro veneto dei nobili."
12. Ibid., 167, 255.
13. Ibid., 166.
14. Kirshner, "*Civitas sibi faciat civem*," 702.
15. Apostoli, "Scelte fiscali a Brescia."
16. Bonfiglio Dosio, "Criminalità ed emarginazione a Brescia," esp. 133 (homi-

cide), 139 (personal injury), 142–143 (insulting words), 163. See also eadem, "Società e ricchezza."

17. "[N]on sono de casa antica, veneno de Travajato t. b. Duoi di casa di Fasani sono picati ad uno salese [i.e. *salice*] ai Jorci novi sul canto della strada che vene a Bressa; la causa fu per portar vittovalia in Bressa all inimici della Il.ma Signoria di Venezia, et per questi sono fatti cittadini per tal causa et godono li beneficij della Città de Bressa." Nassini quoted in Lechi, *Dimore bresciane*, 438.

18. Ibid., 451.

19. "[E]t per detta parentela fu fatto del Concilio de Bressa, ma mi Pandolfo Nassino li ho visti vender Papero, et su la sua bottega averge de Razi todeschi et de candeleri et bazine et altre cose mercantili da vender. Questa Città va di mal in peggio, hanno tolti bastardi et filioli de monache, et homicidiari et botigari, sojari, confettori, barbieri, parolari et de assai altre generationi de artisti et anche de sodomiti, che sonno banditi per sodomia et di ladri, quali sono banditi, ma per sette et pratiche fanno ogni cosa." Nassini quoted in ibid., 453. On a case of sodomy committed by a clerical schoolmaster investigated by the bishop of Brescia in Mar. 1494, see Sanudo, 5:954–955.

20. Lechi, *Dimore bresciane*, 447.

21. Tedoldi, "Tra immigrazione e integrazione," 446, tabella 1; Pasero, "Dati statistici e notizie intorno al movimento della popolazione," 78–79.

22. Chojnacki, "Identity and Ideology"; Lanaro Sartori, *Oligarchia urbana nel Cinquecento veneto*.

23. As was noted in Chapter 1 the city was divided into four parts: San Faustino, with seven *quadre* (later reduced to six), San Giovanni with six, Sant' Alessandro with two, and Santo Stefano, which was divided into the *cittadella vecchia* and the *cittadella nuova*.

24. Grubb, *Firstborn of Venice*, 75–76.

25. The statutes of the first *quadra* of Sant' Alessandro are in BQB, L.III.10. The role of the elders of the *quadre* in criminal matters is outlined in *Statuta civitatis Brixiae* (1557), 160–161.

26. Ffoulkes, "Date of Vincenzo Foppa's Death."

27. Mistura, "Privilegi più speciali," 384–385.

28. Chapter 12 here.

29. BQB, C.I.3, fol. 95; ASC 484, 8 Jan. 1427, 8 Feb. 1428, fols. 1r, 81v–83r.

30. ASC 493, 24 Mar. 1445, fol. 110r; ASC 494, 6 Feb. 1446, 18 Jan. 1448, fols. 14r–v, 128r–v; ASC 495, 1, 5 Jan. 1449, fols. 1v–2r, 5r.

31. Montanari, *Quelle terre di là dal Mincio*, 75.

32. Romani, "Prestigio, potere."

33. Varanini, "Statuti delle città," esp. 22–50.

34. ASC 495, 8 Aug. 1449, fols. 81v–82r.

35. Montanari, *Quelle terre di là dal Mincio*, 75, 193–194.

36. ASC 1523/A, fols. 22v–27r. A note at ibid., fol. 1r, reads: "Hic codex factus fuit in esequtione provisionis diei 22 augusti 1466."

37. The "doctores" (of laws) involved with this revision were largely drawn from the "cives veteres": *Statuta Brixiae* (1473), fol. Iv.

38. ASV, Senato terra, deliberazioni, reg. 6, fol. 126v (pencil foliation, 11 Mar. 1471).

39. *Statuta Brixiae* (1473), "De consilio generali bonorum civium brixie et electione eorum."

40. ASC 505, 2 Nov. 1475, 31 May 1476, fols. 156v–157r, 29r–30v; and see ASC 509, 16 June 1485, fol. 165v.

41. *Statuta Brixiae* (1473), "De his qui non possunt habere officia." Clerics were also excluded from office and could not act as notaries. On the nature of *onera* and *factiones* see Cozzi and Knapton, *La Repubblica di Venezia*, 319–328.

42. "Quod aliquis non possit admitti ad officium Quadrae nisi habitaverit per X annos." BQB, L.III.10, unfoliated. These statutes for the first *quadra* of Sant' Alessandro are dated 1578–79 (with an addition of 1641) and copied out in the eighteenth century, but it is highly probable that they reflect the changes which occurred in the fifteenth century.

43. ASC 499, 22 Apr. 1461, fol. 26r–v.

44. *Statuta Brixiae* (1473), "Quod dominus potestate ut rector non possit petere Generalem absolutionem statutorum ad hoc ut regat ad arbitrium."

45. Ibid., "Quod anciani colegii notariorum brixie teneantur compellere notarios ad servandam statuta communis brixiensis."

46. ASC 509, 19 Dec. 1487, fol. 80v.

47. ASC 510, 21 June 1488, fol. 63r–v.

48. Ventura, *Nobiltà e popolo*, 109–110; Pasero, "Dominio veneto," 208; Zanelli, *Delle condizioni interne di Brescia*, 21–26.

49. ASC 509, 7 June 1485, fol. 163r, 31 Oct. 1485, fol. 12r, 31 Dec. 1485, fol. 32r, 7 Jan. 1486, fol. 33r, 25 Jan. 1486, fol. 40v, 9 Aug. 1486, fol. 87r, 21 Oct. 1486, fol. 97r, 28 Jan. 1487, fol. 81r, 21 Dec. 1487, fol. 81r.

50. Montanari, *Quelle terre di là dal Mincio*, 77.

51. ASC 510, 30 Aug., 5 Sept. 1488, fols. 98v, 99r (a unanimous vote in special council). See also ASC 511, 5, 11 Sept. 1488, fols. 15v–16r, 19r. The clause relating to inherited nobility was abrogated on 2 Nov. 1488—the distinction becoming purely personal and not transmissable.

52. ASC 514, 31 Dec. 1494, fol. 124v. Note the publication in Brescia in 1499 of De Sardis, *Tractatus de legitimatione*.

53. ASC 514, 30 Dec. 1494, fol. 122r. A second proposal in favor of Quarentino was defeated in the general council four years later: ASC 516, 23 Mar. 1498, fol. 50r.

54. ASC 510, 11 Sept. 1488, fol. 103r.

55. ASC 510, 29 Dec. 1488, fol. 36v. Adding those in possession of a noble title already, there were now three hundred new or old patrician families.

56. Compare the case of Verona where conciliar decisions were included in the statutory revision completed in 1450 in a form of "autoriforma continuata": Varanini, "Gli statuti delle città," 35.

57. ASC 510, 20 Nov. 1495, fols. 165r–166v.

58. Ferraro, *Family and Public Life in Brescia*, 60.

59. ASC 510, 26 Dec. 1496, fols. 167r–168r. On the ambiguous position of these men and for a suggestion that in 1488 they received a verbal promise that they might transfer citizenship to their sons in order to secure their votes see Montanari, *Quelle terre di là dal Mincio*, 78–79.

60. Chapter 12 here. In 1517 the ruling of 1488 was approved by the general council by fifty-three votes to eight with the amendment that the sons of those allowed to sit might be admitted: ASC 527, 17 July 1517, fol. 3r. See also the copies entered in ASC 510, 17 July 1517, fols. 168v–169r. See Ferraro, *Family and Public Life in Brescia*, 68–71; Romani, "Prestigio, potere," 118–124, and 125–130, app. 1.

61. Mistura, *Giudici e i loro collegi;* Guerrini, "Nobile collegio dei giudici di Brescia."

62. ASC 505, 22 Sept. 1475, fol. 145r–v.

63. ASC 510, 6 June, 24 Oct. 1488 (approved by ten votes to one), fols. 62r, 121r.

64. BQB, H.IV.5, fols. 41r, 42r.

65. This suggestion is made by Montanari, *Quelle terre di là dal Mincio,* 80.

66. ASC 513, 10 Oct., 6 Nov. 1491, fols. 60r, 71r; BQB, H.IV.5, fol. 42v.

67. ASC 513, 22 Dec. 1492, fol. 29v; ASC 514, 11 Jan. 1492 [m. v. 1493], fol. 38v (admission approved).

68. ASC 515, 30 Dec. 1495, fols. 48v–49r. He was later admitted after having shown that his grandfather took on Brescian honors and offices: ASC 516, 16 Mar. 1498, fol. 46v.

69. ASC 513, 5 Oct., 10 Nov. 1492, fols. 7v–8r, 19v.

70. ASC 513, 27 April 1492, fol. 129v. Members of this college were exempted from taxes and as a result were excluded from the general council and from office holding, much to the annoyance of some doctors. However, it was proclaimed that no doctor could practice in the city unless he was a member of the college: ASC 506, 5 Nov. 1479, fol. 47r.

71. Guerrini, *Cronotassi biobibliografica,* 15–16.

72. ASC 506, 8, 9, 10 Nov. 1479, fol. 55r.

73. Related to these concerns about a properly noble lifestyle may be the publication "in citadella vechia apresso al conte Piero da Gambara nela cita de Bressa" of Ruffo, *Arte de cognoscere la natura de cavalli,* colophon.

74. ASC 509, 27 Apr. 1485, fol. 151v. It is worth noting that when representatives of Brescia and the territorial organization (the *Territorio*) presented their lists of privileges to Venice in 1516 on the return to Venetian rule Sanudo noted that the latter did so in the vernacular: Sanudo, 23:587.

75. For several cases of blasphemy: ASC 506, 16 Mar. 1478, 14 July 1479, fols. 50v, 7v.

76. ASC 513, 29 Dec. 1492, fol. 35v. However, vicars and rectors in the Bresciano were prohibited from concubinage and gambling, as well as a number of other undignified activities in 1480: ASC 507, 14 June 1480, fols. 118r–119v. On 5 Mar. 1486 the episcopal vicar issued an edict against "aliquas mulieres suspectas" found in the homes of clergy without episcopal authority: "Cronaca ecclesiastica," 191.

77. ASC 526, 24 Apr. 1517, fol. 101v.

78. Chapters 7, 8, 12 here.

79. ASC 519, 28 Apr. 1503, fol. 174r.

80. ASC 519, 12 May 1503, fol. 7v.

81. ASC 515, 19 May 1495, fol. 160v.

82. This analysis is based on an examination of the applications recorded in the council *provvisioni*: ASC 503–521. An alphabetical list of those awarded *civilitas* can be found in ASC 1332–1334. This list drawn up in 1551 by the chancellor Pietro Suraga.

83. The decennial figures are 1420–30 (162), 1430–40 (290), 1440–50 (431), 1450–60 (284), 1460–67 (54). Tedoldi, "Tra immigrazione e integrazione," 446, tabella 1.

84. ASC 504, 18 Jan. 1471; ASC 505, 29 April, ASC 506, 1 Sept. 1479; ASC 509, 28 Jan., 1 Dec. 1475, 17 April 1476; ASC 510, 30 Aug. 1488; ASC 507, 21 Jan. 1480. The council rewarded a doctor for his work during the influenza and plague of 1477–79: ASC 506, 17 Aug. 1478, 10, 24 Sept. 1479, fols. 88r, 26v, 30v. On "civic doctors" who were compelled to offer free medical treatment to the poor in return for tax immunity and citizenship see Nutton, "Continuity or Rediscovery?" See also Palmer, "Physicians and the State."

85. ASC 510, 8, 17 Aug. 1488; ASC 513, 17 Feb. 1492.

86. ASC 516, 22, 23 Feb. 1499; Firpo, "Carmeliano, Pietro."

87. These figures are similar to a snapshot of immigration based on the 1459 *estimo* in which 47.3 percent of immigrants recorded there originated in the territory, 29.4 percent from Bergamo and the Bergamasco, 6.9 percent from the Cremonese and Cremasco, 9.7 percent from other Lombard towns, 5.2 percent from Mantua and the Mantovano, 0.8 percent from German lands, and 0.8 percent from the Veneto. Tedoldi, "Tra immigrazione e integrazione," 446 n. 33.

88. Grendler, *Schooling in Renaissance Italy,* chap. 1. Valgulio's complaints are discussed in Chapter 8 here.

89. In 1494 and 1498 the doge affirmed that there were five hundred rural applicants for citizenship. In 1508 citizenship was denied to those in rural occupations: Pasero, "Dati statistici e notizie intorno al movimento della popolazione," 81 n. 29.

90. ASC 517, 28 Feb. 1500, fol. 116v.

91. Lucchesi Ragni, "Affreschi di Floriano Ferramola," 107–111; Thomas, "Meeting of Two Worlds"; and Nova, *Girolamo Romanino,* 284–285.

92. Bettoni, "Aristocrazia senza corte." A marriage chest bearing the arms of the Sangervasio family and scenes attributed to Floriano Ferramola is illustrated in Panazza, "Pittura nella seconda metà," 996.

93. ASC 506, 23 May 1477, fol. 43r.

94. Lanfranchini, *Quaestio utrum praeferendus sit doctor an miles.* See also Mazzacane, "Stato e il dominio," 600 n. 75, and Borelli, "'Doctor an miles.'"

95. For the later period see Ferraro, *Family and Public Life in Brescia.*

5. Space, Ritual, and Identity

1. Sanudo, 1:741–743, 762–764, 766. See also Frati, Gianfranceschi, and Robecchi, *Loggia di Brescia,* 2:56–60.

2. S. Augustino to Nassino Nassini, Brescia, 5 Sept. 1497, in Sanudo, 1:763. See also Capriolo, *Chronica de rebus Brixianorum,* fols. LXXIv–LXXIIr [*recte* LXXIIv–LXXIIIr].

3. Lodovico Mantegna to Marquis Francesco Gonzaga, Val Camonica, 10 May 1497: ASMa, Archivio Gonzaga, E.XLVIII.2, b. 1599, filza LXVII, fol. 816r–v; Luzio, *Archivio Gonzaga di Mantova*, 2:239 n. 6.

4. Sanudo, 1:763; Zamboni, *Memorie intorno alle pubbliche fabbriche*, 131–133.

5. "Gaudent enim Patritii omnes: Plebei iubilant: puerique: ac puellae totam per urbem catervatim exultant. Aedium quoque parietes: ac ipsa urbis: quantacunque sunt moenia sublimitati tuae gestire videntur." Planius, *Ad Catharinam Cyprorum reginam*, sig. aiir–v.

6. "Quae omnia civitas nostra sic gessit ut animi sui promptitudine in venetos principes suos magis est significaret." Capriolo, *Chronica de rebus Brixianorum*, fol. LXXIIr [*recte* LXXIIIr].

7. Trexler, *Public Life*, 233–235. Compare Van den Neste, *Tournois, joûtes, pas d'armes*, 187–216. On Brescia see Frati, Gianfranceschi, and Robecchi, *Loggia di Brescia*, 1:172.

8. On the problem of linking ritual and society see Buc, *Dangers of Ritual*.

9. Melga, "Cronaca," 126.

10. Zamboni, *Memorie intorno alle pubbliche fabbriche*, 33.

11. Lucchesi Ragni, "Affreschi di Floriano Ferramola," 107–111; Thomas, "Meeting of Two Worlds."

12. ASV, Senato terra, deliberazioni, reg. 3, fol. 117v (pencil foliation, 4 June 1454).

13. Mallett and Hale, *Military Organisation of a Renaissance State*, 90, 132, 189.

14. On the Venetian influence over the physical appearance of towns see the essays—cited individually in the notes below—on Brescia, Bergamo, Verona, Vicenza, Padua, Treviso, and Feltre in Calabi, *Fabbriche, piazze, mercati*. See also Cozzi, "Ambiente veneziano, ambiente veneto."

15. An impression of Venetian expenditure on castellans and fortifications in the Bresciano is given by a statement of accounts in ASV, Senato terra, deliberazioni, reg. 3, fol. 171v (pencil foliation, 26 Aug. 1455). On Venetian concerns with the reconstruction and decorous condition of Brescian walls see, for example, the decision taken by the Senate on 30 May 1478, ASV, Senato terra, deliberazioni, reg. 8, fol. 10v.

16. Doge Moro to Brescian rectors, 26 June, 10 Aug. 1466, in ASC 1523/A, fols. 122r–v, 123r–v.

17. Priuli, *Diarii*, 4:46.

18. Soldo, *Cronaca*, 152–154.

19. Mallett and Hale, *Military Organisation of a Renaissance State*, 410; Pasero, "Dominio veneto," 168–169.

20. Boucheron, "Architettura come linguaggio politico." On the Viscontean citadel in Bergamo see Visioli, "Bergamo: XV–XVII secolo," 162, 178–181. On that of Verona see Law, "Cittadella."

21. "Et ut civitas hec vestra per truculentiam tyrannorum hactenus divisa et miserabiliter deformata per Beatis. Evangelistam Marcum et clementiam vestri ser. dominii omnimode uniatur et ad statum pristinum reducatur, ut sic unita flo-

reat et feliciter decoretur." The complaint is in the privileges conceded to Brescia by Venice in Jan. 1428 and printed in Zanelli, *Delle condizioni interne di Brescia,* 218 (clause XVI).

22. Mistura, "Privilegi più speciali," 383; Frati, Gianfranceschi, and Robecchi, *Loggia di Brescia,* 1:16–18.

23. Frati, Gianfranceschi, and Robecchi, *Loggia di Brescia,* 1: 82.

24. Ibid., 30–35. See the proclamations against various signs of disorder copied in ASC 1092 and 1093. See also ASC 1093, fol. 61r–v (proclamation of 27 Jan. 1526).

25. Frati, Gianfranceschi, and Robecchi, *Loggia di Brescia,* 1:passim.

26. Porfyriou, "Verona: XV–XVI secolo."

27. Zaggia, "Padova: XV–XVII secolo," 270–271; Moretti, "Vicenza: XV–XVII secolo," 238.

28. For example, at Feltre in 1524: Bona, "Feltre: XVI secolo," 339. A stone column topped with the winged lion, symbol of Saint Mark, erected in 1523, still stands in the center of Verona.

29. Frati, Gianfranceschi, and Robecchi, *Loggia di Brescia,* 1:39–40, 88–89, 123.

30. Ibid., 85.

31. ASC 533, 30 Oct. 1533, fol. 48r; Frati, Gianfranceschi, and Robecchi, *Loggia di Brescia,* 1:116; Zamboni, *Memorie intorno alle pubbliche fabbriche,* 39.

32. Sanudo, *Itinerario di Marin Sanuto,* 70–73.

33. Petrucci, *Public Lettering,* esp. chap. 2.

34. ASC 507, 13 Oct. 1480, fol. 141v.

35. Melga, "Cronaca," 122.

36. For fifteenth-century references to the constancy of Saguntines and the fidelity of Brescians see Chapter 2 here.

37. Joost-Gaugier, "Bartolomeo Colleoni as a Patron."

38. Probus, *Significatio litterarum antiquarum.* For Solazio's interests and links with Ferrarino, see his *Epistola* and "Prefazione storica."

39. Passamani, "Coscienza della romanità," 8–11. In 1499 Buzzoni dedicated a Latin verse to Mantegna: Vosonius, *Epigrammaton,* unpaginated.

40. Valentini, *Carlo Valgulio,* 19.

41. Sanudo, *Itinerario di Marin Sanuto,* 145. See also ibid., 7 ("Epigramma Pyladis ad lectorem"), 15, 17, 87. Two poems addressed to Sabellico by Boccardo are printed at the end of Sabellico, *De vetustate Aquileiensis patriae.*

42. Frati, Gianfranceschi, and Robecchi, *Loggia di Brescia,* 1:109–169.

43. Nevola, *Siena;* Howard, *Architectural History of Venice.*

44. Solazio, "Prefazione storica," 146.

45. Ibid, 147.

46. ASC 513, 23 Sept. 1491, fol. 56v.

47. De Voragine, *Golden Legend,* 1:178–179.

48. Paton, "'Una città faticosa,'" 122.

49. "De Justicia," in Bernardino da Feltre, *Sermoni,* 3:318–319.

50. Hind, *Early Italian Engraving,* pt. 2, vol. 5, 55–58, nos. 1–4; vol 6: plate 568.

51. Capriolo, *Chronica de rebus Brixianorum,* fol. IXv.

52. Ibid., fols. IXv–Xr. Malvezzi's discussion can be found in Malvecius, *Chronicon Brixianum*, cols. 793–794.

53. Capriolo, *Chronica de rebus Brixianorum*, fols. Xv–XIr, LXXXr–LXXXIv [*recte* LXXIr–LXXIv] (ca. 1492).

54. "Quod [*arietos* cancelled] figure sculpte in formam arietum . . . in ecclesiam Sanctum Petrum de Dom, quia representant memoriam idolatrie . . . deleantur et abradantur de muro parietum ambarum navis de ecclesie. Quod parietes postea de albentur debite & ornate. Item quod ale . . . fiant in volta de quadrello & bona calce, & ponantur seu laborentur in crosera alta ad debitam proportionem cum dictam navj per decorem ecclesiae dicte ad honorem & laudem omnipotentis dei & apostolicibus Petri & Pauli." ASC 497, 25 May 1456, fol. 117r.

55. Cereta to Paolo Zane, 22 Sept. 1485, in Cereta, *Collected Letters*, 46–48. An assault on the host is recorded in ASC 503, 23 May 1470, fol. 225v. A proclamation against "deturpantes" of the host in the duomo is copied in ASC 1092, fol. 88v (1 Feb. 1493).

56. "Cronaca ecclesiastica," 177–178; ASC 509, 15 June 1486; 2 Mar. 1487, fols. 77v, 129r.

57. ASC 506, 29 July 1478, fol. 81r–v. Marco Negro wrote in 1512: "Et di la oferta che ogni anno el dì di Nostra Dona de Avosto [*sic*] si faceva, la qual era zercha ducati 200, e fevano un massaro; ma questi volseno tal danari fosseno deputati a la fabricha dil Domo, nè mai li vescovi ha potuto veder la administration di tal danari, e la comunità li difendeva a non mostrar tal raxon." Sanudo, 15:300.

58. Zamboni, *Memorie intorno alle pubbliche fabbriche*, 108–109.

59. ASC 523, 13 Sept. 1511, fol. 104r; ASC 528, 19 Mar. 1520, fol. 40r–v.

60. My discussion here is much indebted to Vauchez, *Sainthood in the Later Middle Ages*.

61. Webb, *Patrons and Defenders*, 16.

62. Vauchez, "Patronage des saints," 75–77; Dickson, "115 Cults of the Saints."

63. Or, under imperial occupation in 1515, a two-headed eagle. See *Corpus nummorum italicorum*, 4:78–88; 8:135.

64. *Statuta Brixiae* (1473), "De dominis potestate et capitaneo Brixie." The same saints were present in the oath recorded some years later: *Leges brixianae* (1490).

65. The statutes of 1473 record Michael the Archangel, John the Baptist, Mary Magdalene, Faustino and Giovita, Apollonio, Blaise (conversion), Philaster, Nicholas of Tolentino, Laurence, Thomas Aquinas, Gregory, Honorius, Jerome, Nicholas, Anthony, Zeno, George, Agnes, Augustine, Mark, Urban, Lucy, Agatha, Eusebius, Catherine, Julia, Sebastian, Peter Martyr, Barnabas, Afra, Dominic, Roch, Florian, Francis, Clement, Savino and Cipriano, Martin, Salvator, Bernardino, and Ambrose. *Statuta Brixiae* (1473), "De feriis." The additions made by 1490 were Benedict, Anthony of Padua, Visit of Elizabeth to Mary, Alexander, and Saint John (beheaded).

66. See the rectorial proclamations in ASC 1092, fols. 2r (procession and oblation from the "piaza principal" to altar of San Sebastiano in the "ospedale grande,"

19 Jan. 1468), 3r (oblation and procession from "piaza granda" to church of Ss. Faustino and Giovita, 13 Feb. 1468), 6r (procession from the *piazza del duomo* to church of San Marco for homonymic feast day, 22 Apr. 1468), 9r (meeting at "loza" followed by oblation at altar of Ss. Savino and Cipriano), 14r (San Bartolomeo), 15r (Santa Maria delle Grazie), 16r (Santa Lucia), 112v (feast of San Giuseppe, 18 Mar. 1506); and ASC 1093, fols. 2r (San Giuseppe, 15 Mar. 1511), 3r (Carmelite church, 22 Mar. 1511), 5r (victory over the Venetians, 13 May 1511), 10v (altar of San Bernardino in church of San Francesco, n. d.), 130r (procession for the election of the pope, 31 Oct. 1534).

67. Doge Foscari to Brescian rectors, 16 Oct. 1436, in ASC 1523/A, fol. 36r; copy of petition presented to the Brescian chancellery by Jacopo Filippo and Ugolino da Asola on 14 Aug. 1441, in ASC 1523/A, fol. 42r; ASC 494, 16 Aug. 1446, fol. 39v. For similar cases of disobedience in late medieval Italy, see Chittolini, "Civic Religion and the Countryside," 76, 77–79.

68. In ca. 1475 the Brescian humanist Cristoforo Barzizza wrote a life of the Dominican Corradino Bornato (who was active in Brescia until 1418), which may have formed part of a campaign to promote his cult and initiate a process of canonization in Rome. Knowles Frazier, *Possible Lives*, 352–353 (as "Conradino Brixiensis").

69. De Sandre Gasparini, "Amministrazione pubblica dell'evento religioso," 201–217.

70. Goldthwaite, *Wealth and the Demand for Art*, 131–134 (Quotation at 131).

71. Malvecius, *Chronicon Brixianum*, cols. 797–798, 802.

72. ASC 497, 10, 18 Nov., 11, 18 Dec. 1455, fols. 77v, 81r, 86r–v, 88r; Corradino Palazzo, "Diario," 227; Capriolo, *Chronica de rebus Brixianorum*, fol. LXVIIIv.

73. ASC 497, 18 Dec. 1455, fol. 88r.

74. ASC 507, 12, 18 May 1481, fols. 67r, 71r.

75. "Cronaca ecclesiastica," 189; ASC 522, 30 Mar. 1509, fol. 55v.

76. Capriolo, *Chronica de rebus Brixianorum*, fol. XIIIv; Rimoldi, "Apollonio," col. 269 (giving the year of entombment as 1025). See the inventory of 9 Feb. 1475, ASC 1525, fol. 45r.

77. Inventory of 5 Jan. 1503, ASC 1528, fol. 68r.

78. ASC 522, 22 June, 26 July 1510, fols. 121r, 130r. It was later agreed to add a window to the chapel, ASC 522, 17 Dec. 1510, fol. 174v.

79. ASC 1528, fol. 172r.

80. ASC 497, 29 Jan., 6, 20 Feb. 1456, fols. 94v, 95v, 97v; Rimoldi, "Filastrio."

81. ASC 497, 20 Feb. 1456, fol. 97v.

82. Pusculo, "Oratio de laudibus Brixiae," 33.

83. The corpse was "repertum in altari S. Anatalonis in oratorio subteraneo sancti florianj translatum fuit cum sollem. processione et maximo populi applausi atque frequentia per Reverendissimum dominum Bartholomeum Maripetro Episcopum nostrum brixiensem et reconditum in quadam capsa repositum fuit in altari magno dicte ecclesie que capsa clausa fuit tribus Clavibus quarum una obsignata fuit R. domino episcopo Magnifico domini potestati una et tertia domino priori dicti loci." ASC 498, 28 Dec. 1458, fol. 83v.

84. Capriolo, *Chronica de rebus Brixianorum*, fol. LXXIr [*recte* LXXIIr]. Nodari, "Ottaziano"; idem, "Vigilio."
85. ASC 500, 12 Mar. 1464, fol. 85v. The plaque is now in the church of Sant' Afra, Brescia.
86. Simonelli, "Crisanto e Daria."
87. In 1488 the relics were placed in a marble urn and transferred to another altar by Galeazzo Fenaroli: Maccarinelli, *Glorie di Brescia*, 153 n. 260.
88. ASC 494, 8 Aug. 1449, fol. 81r; Capriolo, *Chronica de rebus Brixianorum*, fol. XXr–v. One episcopal chancellor was devoted to these saints and set up an altar in the duomo: Guerrini, "Cancelliere vescovile del quattrocento," 25–27. See also Desreumaux, "Savino e Cipriano."
89. Rimoldi, "Anatalone."
90. ASC 506, 21 Feb. 1478, fol. 43r; Nodari, "Paterio."
91. "[E] fu collocato ditto corpo sancto all'altar di la terza Capella de lo introito de la ditta Giesia [of Sant'Eufemia] versus montem, con grande solennitade de trumbe, cythare, e altri instrumenti musici, et con grandissima convocazione del synodo et chieresia." Melga, "Cronaca," 10–11. The sarcophagus is now in the city museum of Santa Giulia, Brescia.
92. BQB, C.I.15, fol. 27r (pencil foliation).
93. Masetti Zannini, "Silvino."
94. Inventory of relics in San Pietro Oliveto, 17 Feb. 1453, ASC 1523/A, fol. 88r; ASC 1528, fol. 131r; "Cronaca ecclesiastica," 195; ASC 497, 20 Feb. 1456, fol. 97v. Caraffa, "Evasio"; Camisani, "Deusdedit."
95. The sarcophagus bears the inscription: "Corpus adorandum est Titiani'/'Antistitis: ad quem confugit'/'in duris Brixia temporibus'/'M. D. V." Morassi, *Catalogo delle cose d'arte*, 135–136. See also Nodari, "Tiziano."
96. "Memorie tratte dall'archivio di padri del monasterio di Santo Clemente in Brescia," in BQB, E.I.11, fol. 125r.
97. ASB, Fondo di religione, San Giuseppe, b. 109, fols. 3v–4r.
98. Leonardelli, *"Pro bibliotheca erigenda,"* 70.
99. ASC 1525, fols. 66v–67r.
100. Melga, "Cronaca," 35–36. See also Capriolo, *Chronica de rebus Brixianorum*, fol. LXXv.
101. Sanudo, *Itinerario di Marin Sanuto*, 88–89; Capriolo, *Chronica de rebus Brixianorum*, fol. XIXr; Fappani, "Ercolano."
102. On anthropological approaches to ritual, see Bell, *Ritual*, chaps. 1–3. On festivities and their meaning in Brescia, see Ferri Piccaluga, "Tra liturgia e teatralità."
103. Trexler, *Public Life*, passim.
104. Muir, "Virgin on the Street Corner"; idem, *Civic Ritual in Renaissance Venice*.
105. On the *piazza della loggia* as a "piazza laica" see Frati, Gianfranceschi, and Robecchi, *Loggia di Brescia*, 1:41, 83.
106. Ibid., 97 n. 1.
107. De Sandre Gasparini, "Amministrazione pubblica dell'evento religioso," 205, 206.

108. James, "Ritual, Drama and Social Body"; Rubin, *Corpus Christi*, 243–271 (quotation at 266).

109. ASC 484, 28 May 1428, fol. 135v; ASC 485, 11 June 1432, fol. 276r; ASC 486, 28 May, 2 June 1433, fols. 50v–51v.

110. "Ad laudem Assumptionis Beat[a]e Mari[a]e semper virginis Iohannis Matthie Tyberini," in Tiberino, *In beatum Symonum*, unpaginated; "Versus in laudem Mariae Virginis," in Bernardino Bornato, *Opusculum de laudibus matrimonii*, sigs. [aviiv]–[aviiir].

111. The disruption of civic harmony in the form of changes of regime during the fourteenth and fifteenth centuries apparently did not interrupt the Assumption festivities: Zanelli, "Signoria di Pandolfo Malatesta," 131–132.

112. ASC 505, 21 July 1475, fol. 125v.

113. ASMa, Archivio Gonzaga, E.XLVIII.2, b. 1599, filza LXV, fol. 761r–v (Isabella d'Este Gonzaga's horses to compete in *palio* in 1495); ibid., filza LXVI, fol. 798r–v (Francesco Mocenigo, Brescian captain, explains to Marquis of Mantua in a letter dated 15 July 1496 that the council will decide on Monday whether to hold the *palio*).

114. "[The marquis] desiderar fosse prorogato [the *palio*] el zorno solito zorni 8 dapoi per esser a quel mede[si]mo tempo solito di corer nela cita sua di mantoa." The rectors invited the marquis—who intended to come with thirty horses and "forty mouths"—to choose the day of his coming and give them notice of it "per meglio decorar la festa." Brescian rectors to Francesco Gonzaga, Brescia, 4 Aug. 1490, in ASMa, Archivio Gonzaga, E.XLVIII.2, b. 1599, filza LX, fol. 647r–v.

115. ASMa, Archivio Gonzaga, E.XLVIII.2, b. 1599, filza LXV, fol. 762r–v. The expenses for the Marquis of Mantua's visit in 1491 when he lodged in the "hostaria del gambaro" are in ASV, Capi del consiglio dei dieci, lettere di rettori, b. 19, pezzo e.

116. A "cursu braviorum" was due to be held on the eve of the feast in 1480: ASC 23 July 1480, fol. 126r.

117. In her "Funeral Oration for an Ass" (ca. 1485) the Brescian humanist Laura Cereta has the orator recall that the ass "was the swiftest and speediest runner . . . Brescia is his witness: for there, under the rapt gaze of every spectator at the August games and with me urging him on, he won first prize in a race. Standing there with a fierce look, he was unable to stand still, but impatient for victory and exulting in his desire to triumph, this bold fellow took his stand against the barbarous and pugnacious horses." Cereta, *Collected Letters*, 192.

118. ASC 1092, fols. 11v (proclamation of 1471), 13r (proclamation of 14 Aug. 1467). In 1407 "panno celeste" cloth was given to the victorious prostitute: Zanelli, "Signoria di Pandolfo Malatesta," 140.

119. On the meanings of these races, which sometimes included Jews, see Shemek, "Circular Definitions"; and Trexler, "Correre la Terra."

120. In 1445 the races were described as "abominabile censentes, In solemnitate nostrae Gloriosissime Regine, qui est Virgo Verginum & stella stellarum, flos aromatum & pudicitie, Mater fillij di & sponsa di & hospita [one word illeg-

ible] facere spectacula fere libidinose & turpium mulierum quia sua coram ventris . . . quam quidam spectacula, originem havere a ritibus paganorum." ASC 493, 9 Aug. 1445, fol. 133r.

121. Zanelli, "Festa dell'Assunta," 12–15.

122. ASC 492, 11 Aug. 1442, fol. 115v.

123. "[Q]uod erat consuetudo bestialissam & Infernalis reperta per hostem antiquam contra honorem, lilium & decorem pudicitie & honestate nostre gloriose regime." ASC 493, 4 Aug. 1444, fol. 61r.

124. ASC 493, 9 Aug. 1445, fol. 133r; ASC 492, 20 Aug. 1442, fol. 119v.

125. ASC 495, 10 Aug. 1450, 9 Aug. 1451, fols. 156r, 229v.

126. ASC 499, 17 July 1461, fol. 45r; ASC 500, 26 July 1463, fol. 44v; Zanelli, "Festa dell'Assunta," 17–18.

127. An account of the oblations owed by each community in the territory during 1473–92 is in ASC 924. A large number of debts were not settled—if the failure to score a line through the account is any indication.

128. ASC 494, 16 Aug. 1446, fol. 39v. For similar cases of disobedience in late fourteenth- and early fifteenth-century Italy, see Chittolini, "Civic Religion and the Countryside," 76, 77–79.

129. Doge Foscari to Brescian rectors, 16 Oct. 1436, in ASC 1523A, fol. 36r.

130. For a similar case in 1467 see Zanelli, "Festa dell'Assunta," 8–9.

131. ASC 505, 12, 30 Aug. 1474, fols. 3v, 13v. See also ASC 506, 11 June 1477, fol. 49r.

132. ASC 509, 15 June 1486, fol. 77v (silver left by Bishop Domenico De' Domenichi for construction of the duomo to be used to construct the tabernacle); ASC 510, 27 June 1488, fol. 66r.

133. Panazza, *Tesoro delle sante croci*, 23; ASC 528, 20 Mar. 1520, 8, 15 Mar., 26 Apr. 1521, fols. 41r–42r, 155r, 158v, 10r.

134. For example, ASC 506, 16 Apr. 1477, 13 May 1478, fols. 27r, 67v; ASC 507, 19 July 1480, fol. 124v; ASC 509, 15 June 1486, 18 May 1487, fols. 77r, 21r; Melga, "Cronaca," 32–33; ASC 519, 20 Oct. 1503, fol. 55v. In ca. 1502 a local humanist wrote: "Ille Crucem moriens fidei monumenta reliquit [i.e. Naimo]:'/'Dicta fuit nostris *Aurea* Flamma prius.'/'Quam populus varios semper servavit ad usus:'/'Plurima namque illi vena salutis inest.'/'Quum volumus, toto decedunt nubila Coelo,'/'Quum libet, optata decidit imber aqua." Cereto, *De foro, et laudibus Brixiae*, IX.

135. Sanudo noted in 1483 that at the church of San Faustino and Giovita "è una + mirabelle, di miracolli piena; et quando le fontane è seche, si fa precesione et piove, et anche quando è gran pioza si stalla, et vien bon tempo." Sanudo, *Itinerario di Marin Sanuto*, 71.

136. ASC 503, 16 May 1468, fol. 144r; ASC 506, 16 Apr. 1477, fol. 27r.

137. "Cronaca ecclesiastica," 181.

138. ASC 497, 18 Dec. 1455, fol. 88r.

139. De Sandre Gasparini, "Amministrazione pubblica dell'evento religioso," 213.

140. Antonio Sanudo to Marin Sanudo, Brescia, 16 Jan. 1524: Sanudo, 35:341. See the copy of the proclamation of 9 Jan. 1524 in ASC 1093, fol. 48r.

141. Melga, "Cronaca," 24.

142. ASC 506, 9 Aug. 1479, fol. 18v.
143. Chapter 6 here.
144. Melga, "Cronaca," 41–42.
145. ASC 508, 6 July 1483, fol. 123v; and see Melga, "Cronaca," 44.
146. Guerrini, "Santuario delle grazie."
147. ASC 509, 23, 24, 31 May, 16 Nov. 1486, fols. 68v, 70v, 71v, 103r; ASC 510, 13 May 1488, fol. 50v. See also ASC 510, 29 Aug. 1488, fols. 92v–93v.
148. ASC 510, 13 May 1488, fol. 50v; ASC 526, 22 May 1517, fol. 113v. See also Zamboni, *Memorie intorno alle pubbliche fabbriche*, 131–133. Both Cardinal Andrea Corner and his predecessor Cardinal Francesco Corner made their ceremonial entry into the city as new bishops by the gate of San Nazaro. See Chapter 2 here.
149. Crouzet-Pavan, "*Sopra le acque salse*," 1:617–668.

6. Civic Religion and Reform

1. Parsons, *Perspectives on Civil Religion*.
2. Geertz, *Local Knowledge*; Ditchfield, "'In Search of Local Knowledge.'"
3. Chapters 7–9 here.
4. Chittolini, "Problema aperto."
5. For example, the *savi* of the Ten and the *savi* of the *terraferma* supported Cardinal Grimani's application for a vacant benefice at San Nazaro and Celso in Brescia: ASV, Senato terra, deliberazioni, reg. 12, fol. 134r (pencil foliation, 26 Mar. 1496). On Venice see Del Torre, "Stato regionale e benefici ecclesiastici." On Florence see Bizzocchi, "Chiesa e aristocrazia."
6. For example, the Brescian Virgilio Bornato travelled widely throughout Europe, including a visit to Edinburgh, between 1450 and 1460: Rivetti, "Di Virgilio Bornato (o Bornati)."
7. ASV, Senato terra, deliberazioni, reg. 16, fol. 71r (pencil foliation, 4 Dec. 1508). See Prodi, "Istituzioni ecclesiastiche."
8. For example, in 1504 following the death of his brother, Leonardo Valier was successfully nominated to the vacant parish of Sant' Andrea and Maria, in Pontevico by the Brescian bishop: ASV, Senato terra, deliberazioni, reg. 14, fol. 198v (pencil foliation, 19 Jan. 1503 [m.v. 1504]).
9. For example, the violent priest who attacked the supposed author of his downfall in a nocturnal raid: ASV, Senato terra, deliberazioni, reg. 15, fol. 17v (pencil foliation, 8 Mar. 1504).
10. ASV, Senato terra, deliberazioni, reg. 8, fol. 141r (pencil foliation, 16 Mar. 1482). Note also the concession made to Paolo Zane, bishop of Brescia, to award the lease of land in Roccafranca in the Bresciano (between Chiari and Orzinuovi) to Lorenzo Capriolo, ASV, Senato terra, deliberazioni, reg. 11, fol. 111v (pencil foliation, 14 May 1492). The college of canons of the cathedral in Brescia sold land to Count Giovanni Francesco Gambara: ASV, Senato terra, deliberazioni, reg. 12, fols. 19v–20r (pencil foliation, 10 Oct. 1493). Santa Giulia sought permission to dispose of lands in Mantuan and Milanese territory due to the inconvenient distance from them: ASV, Senato terra, de-

liberazioni, reg. 12, fol. 34r (pencil foliation, 3 Dec. 1493). The friars of San Fiorano sought permission to sell "unam domunculam cum uno modico terre": ASV, Senato terra, deliberazioni, reg. 13, fol. 70v (pencil foliation, 20 Feb. 1498 [m.v. 1499]). See also ASV, Senato terra, deliberazioni, reg. 15, fol. 20r (pencil foliation, 26 Mar. 1504).

11. Zanelli, *Delle condizioni interne di Brescia*, 216–217 (clause XV).

12. Mistura, "Privilegi più speciali," 392.

13. Zanelli, "Pietro del Monte," 46–54.

14. The almost unanimous senatorial decision to promote the candidacy of the prebend of Sant'Agata in Brescia via their orators in Florence (where a council of the church was being held) is recorded in ASV, Senato terra, deliberazioni, reg. 1, fol. 2r–v (original foliation, 16 Oct. 1440).

15. "[N]on est de numero nobilium licet sit de vulgo Venetiarum." Council provision quoted in Zanelli, "Pietro del Monte," 50 n. 2. See also the documents printed in ibid., 87–91.

16. On the ritual pillaging of episcopal or papal property as a rite of passage see Bologna Seminar, coordinated by Carlo Ginzburg, "Ritual Pillages." On these riots and the desire to possess the sacred see Bertelli, *King's Body*, 97–113.

17. ASC 493, 31 July 1445, fol. 131v; Pasero, "Dominio veneto," 82. Note a rectorial proclamation of 1466 against persons impeding or insulting the episcopal baldachin: ASC 1092, fol. 33v.

18. ASC 495, 8 Aug. 1449, fols. 81v–82r. An example of a request for the bishop's return and intervention in civic affairs is in ibid., 6 Nov. 1450, fol. 169r.

19. Compare the case of Bishop Pietro Donato of Padua: Holgate, "Paduan Culture."

20. Zanelli, "Pietro del Monte," 59–61.

21. Capriolo, *Chronica de rebus Brixianorum*, fol. LXIXr.

22. "Cronaca ecclesiastica," 174–177. On Domenichi see Ederer, *Humanism, Scholasticism*; King, *Venetian Humanism*, 363–365.

23. Ederer, *Humanism, Scholasticism*, 217–218.

24. "Cronaca ecclesiastica," 177–179.

25. Ederer, *Humanism, Scholasticism*, 18–19. On del Monte's interests see Rundle, "Renaissance Bishop and His Books"; idem, "Two Libraries."

26. "Cum ipso episcopatum nostram dignus sit: tam ob familie et progenitorum suorum antiquissimam in urbe nostram nobilitatem." ASC 505, 18 Aug. 1474, fol. 5v. When Domenichi died in 1478 the Brescian council agreed to ask Venice to intervene with the pope so that the new bishop not be designated "in co[m]mendam," since without a continually resident bishop scandals arose: ASC 506, 17 Feb. 1478, fol. 41v. This point was reiterated five years later: ASC 508, 23 June 1483, fol. 120v.

27. On Zane see King, *Venetian Humanism*, 446–447.

28. "Cronaca ecclesiastica," 189.

29. ASV, Senato terra, deliberazioni, reg. 10, fol. 47v (pencil foliation, 7 Apr. 1487). Zane may not have been entirely inactive as bishop at this time: he was at Cemmo in the Val Camonica undertaking "la visitatione generale per tutto la Diocese" on 12 Sept. 1486, according to a letter he addressed to Francesco

Gonzaga, Marquis of Mantua: ASMa, Archivio Gonzaga, E.XLVIII.2, b. 1599, filza LVI, fol. 564r–v.

30. ASV, Senato terra, deliberazioni, reg. 12, fol. 10v (pencil foliation, 6 June 1493).

31. ASC 514, 14 Sept., 2 Nov. 1493, fols. 122v–123r, 129r.

32. Indeed, it has been argued that in Venice "religious architecture . . . proved most receptive to ideas from mainland Italy" during the fifteenth century: Howard, *Architectural History of Venice*, 128. See also ibid., 75–87.

33. Fasoli, "Tra riforme e nuove fondazioni," esp. 433–434 (on Piacenza).

34. Zarri, "Aspetti dello sviluppo," 251.

35. Collett, *Italian Benedictine Scholars*.

36. Meneghin, *San Michele in Isola*; Bowd, *Reform before the Reformation*, esp. 62–69.

37. Chittolini, "Stati regionali e istituzioni ecclesiastiche," 173–177; Zarri, "Aspetti dello sviluppo"; Hay, *Church in Italy in the Fifteenth Century*, 60–61.

38. See, for example, "De vanitate mulierum," in Iacobus de Marchia, *Sermones dominicales*, 1:106–126.

39. On the reaction against funereal pomp in Florence after ca. 1480, see Strocchia, *Death and Ritual*, 210. See generally Weinstein, *Savonarola and Florence*. The veneration of Savonarola in Florence after 1498 is suggested by Polizzotto, *Elect Nation*.

40. ASC 503, 11 Nov. 1469, fol. 166v; ASC 505, 5, 18 Apr. 1476, fols. 6v, 10r; ASC 506, 24 Sept. 1479, fol. 29v; ASC 508, 29 Apr. 1483, fol. 100v; ASC 509, 8 Apr. 1485, fol. 144v; ASC 511, 8 May 1488, fol. 120r; ASC 513, 2 Aug. 1492, fol. 153r.

41. ASC 493, 26 Sept., 23 Oct. 1444, fols. 72v, 78v–79r.

42. Zanelli, "Predicatori a Brescia," 96–103, 132.

43. Soldo, *Cronaca*, 100–103.

44. The "[m]ira de Frate Joannes de Capistrano," as a marginal note puts it, are recorded in ASC 495, 25 Jan. 1451, fol. 182r.

45. On Sanson's patronage of artistic projects in Brescia see Begni Redona, "Committenza del Sansone"; Collareta, "Grande croce"; and Benetazzo, "Sumptuosissimis corali miniati."

46. "Panegirico di Brescia," 249–250, 258–259. The author may well be the Franciscan preacher mentioned in ASC 508, 29 Apr. 1483, fol. 100v.

47. Capriolo, *Chronica de rebus Brixianorum*, fol. LXXXv [*recte* LXXIv]; Mercando, *Laeticiae ac moeroris gaudii atque luctus agitatio*. A verse of welcome to Bernardino by Bartolomeo Mercando has been printed in Bernardino da Feltre, *Documenti vari*, 390–391.

48. ASC 514, 17 July 1494, fol. 56r; BQB, C.I.15, fol. 338v. The Brescian artist Vincenzo Foppa provided images of Christ's *pietà* with the saints Peter, Paul, John the Baptist, and Stephen for the chapel of the sacramental scuola in the duomo in 1501.

49. "Pro combustione cartarum, tabulariorum, librorum male lecture et multorum ornamentorum muliebrium fienda die dominica proxima super platea de domo ad persuasionem Reverendis patris dominum Francisci Bernardini . . . feltren-

sis ordinis minorum de observantia divini verbi predicatorum celeberimi. Captum fuit de balottis novem aff. et duobus negativis quod Johanni petro de benadusiis qui onus comburendarum . . . suscepit fiat buleta de ducatis duobus auri," ASC 514, 22 Aug. 1494, fol. 75r.

50. ASC 514, 21 July 1494, fol. 67r.

51. Fè D'Ostiani, *Di un codice laudario,* 49–51.

52. Capriolo, *Chronicorum de rebus Brixianorum,* cols. 129–131.

53. "Quod propter guerras preteritas funditus fuerunt combuste quamplures domucule secum tenentes que erant dicte ecclesie situate in dicta Civitate Brixie per modum q. dicta ecclesia nec fratres [i.e. Humiliati] unquam ex eis domibus alquam utilitatem perceperunt." ASV, Senato terra, deliberazioni, reg. 3, fol. 156v (pencil foliation, 13 May 1455); ASV, Senato terra, deliberazioni, reg. 4, fols. 33v–87r (pencil foliation, 28 Sept. 1458).

54. ASC 506, 30 Apr. 1477, fol. 33r; ASC 509, 23 Dec. 1485, 23 Feb., 3 Mar. 1486, fols. 29v, 50v, 51v.

55. ASC 491, 23 Mar. 1440, fol. 18v.

56. Frati, "Osservanti a Brescia," 437.

57. ASC 497, 24 May 1455, fol. 45r.

58. On the general chapter of the order, held over eight days in 1478 and consisting of several hundred Carmelites and eliciting numerous offerings, perhaps as much as 2,000 ducats in one estimation, which helped to accelerate the construction of the church of the Carmine under the auspices of the prior Angelo Capriolo see ASC 506, 10 Mar., 13 May 1478, fols. 49v, 67r; Corradino Palazzo, "Diario," 250; Melga, "Cronaca," 11. See also ASC 509, 22 Apr. 1485, fol. 150r (letters to the pope and cardinals in support of the maintenance of observance lately introduced at the Carmelite monastery approved by eighty votes to eleven) and 13, 17 Apr. 1486, fols. 58r–v, 60r (alms granted to Carmelites and Franciscans); ASC 1079/A, nos. 83, 86 (ducal letters relating to the dispute).

59. ASC 519, 23 May 1503, fols. 11v–12v.

60. The doughty nuns, who refused to enter the convent without sufficient support, were granted a mill by the Venetian Senate. ASV, Senato terra, deliberazioni, reg. 8, fol. 55v (pencil foliation, 30 July 1479).

61. Fasoli, "Tra riforme e nuove fondazioni," 433–434.

62. Frati, Gianfranceschi, and Robecchi, *Loggia di Brescia,* 1:113.

63. Ferri Piccaluga, "Economia, devozione e politica."

64. Corradino Palazzo, "Diario," 242; Sevesi, "Congregazione dei Capriolanti."

65. ASC 497, 13 May 1456, fol. 114v.

66. Frati, "Osservanti a Brescia," 437. On the saint's cult and iconography see Vauchez, "Rocco."

67. ASC 503, 6, 27 June, 4 July 1469, fols. 114v, 119r, 120r–v; Brescian council provisions quoted in Guerrini, *Cronache bresciane inedite,* 1:15n.

68. ASC 505, 4 Aug. 1474, fol. 1r; ASC 506, 3 Aug. 1478, fol. 83v; Brescian council provisions quoted in Guerrini, *Cronache bresciane inedite,* 1:17n.

69. ASC 506, 21 Aug. 1478, fol. 89r.

70. ASC 506, 12 Mar. 1479, fol. 106r.
71. Melga, "Cronaca," 28.
72. ASC 506, 23 Apr. 1479, fol. 111v.
73. ASC 508, 12 July 1484, fol. 79r.
74. ASC 509, 21 July 1486, fol. 86v.
75. ASC 509, 15 Sept. 1486, 28 Jan. 1487, fols. 94v, 121r–v. See also ASC 509, 29 Aug. 1488, fols. 92v–93v.
76. Diedo, *Vita S. Rochi*. In addition, a life of San Rocco is in Fiorentino Aldigheri, *Alla magnifica sua communità di Brexa*. See ASC 506, 16 Sept. 1479, fol. 28r (Diedo commended). In general, Marshall, "Manipulating the Sacred."
77. ASV, Senato terra, deliberazioni, reg. 3, fol. 167v (pencil foliation, 21 Aug. 1455). This was accomplished within a couple of years: ASV, Senato terra, deliberazioni, reg. 4, fol. 61v (pencil foliation, 23 Dec. 1457).
78. ASV, Senato terra, deliberazioni, reg. 3, fol. 191r (pencil foliation, 26 Jan. 1455 [m.v. 1456]).
79. ASV, Senato terra, deliberazioni, reg. 4, fols. 33v–35r (pencil foliation, 22 Mar. 1457).
80. ASV, Senato terra, deliberazioni, reg. 7, fol. 92r (pencil foliation, 3 Oct. 1475).
81. ASV, Senato terra, deliberazioni, reg. 10, fol. 187r (pencil foliation, 18 Dec. 1489).

7. Puritanism and the Social Order

1. In general, see Muzzarelli, *Pescatori di uomini*.
2. Brundage, "Sumptuary Laws and Prostitution."
3. Kovesi Killerby, *Sumptuary Law*, 87–88; Strocchia, *Death and Ritual*, 212.
4. Kovesi Killerby, *Sumptuary Law*, chap. 5.
5. Owen Hughes, "Distinguishing Signs," esp. 45–55.
6. "Et mulieres col petto discoperto, et juvenes quasi virilia ostendunt." Bernardino da Feltre, "De observatione festorum," in idem, *Sermoni*, 3:282. See also his "De amore proximi," in ibid., 15–16.
7. Ibid., 84. See also ibid., 85–86: "O Bressa, guarda che el bon tempo non te faza scavezar el collo e non te faza mal capitare! Oymè, quante differentie, discordie, partialità, rixe generatur, etiam inter consanguineos, propter ambitionem, pompas et vanitates."
8. Ibid., 121–131.
9. Bernardino da Feltre, "De conditionibus vie ad hoc ut sit idonea Christo parvulino nascituro," in ibid., 232.
10. On the rhetoric of the sermon see Mormando, *Preacher's Demons*.
11. Malvecius, *Chronicon Brixianum*, col. 793.
12. In his poem "Contra luxuriam" Bornato suggests that "Se occupa el mundo in altera scrocheza'/'Ne lo carnal piacer e bestialo'/'Quivi ponendo ogni sua prodeza'/'Inito spurco vicio: el mundo sale'/'Qua facilmente se intinge la coda'/'Et predicar contra: ogi non vale'/'Tanto e multiplicato questa

broda'/'Tanto crescuto hogi questo peccato'/'Che dentro se barchegia eli se noda'/'Piu volti el grando dio: nha movstrata [*sic*]'/'Singular vendeta: e gia fui submerse'/'Alquanti citade: di nobel stato'/'La characte del celo aperse'/'E labyssi per sti cose nephande'/'Rumper fece: e tutto el mundo submerse." Bornato, *Opusculum de laudibus matrimonii*, sig. [aviiir–v].

13. Having exhorted prudence as the best virtue for rulers, Codognelli draws attention to the vices and faults of the Brescians: "O perditam urbem. O civitatem desolatam. O patriam destitutam. O corda omni inclementia feritate barbarieque consepulta. Quis non mecum brixiae calamitatem iacturamque deploret?" *Oratio ad serenissimum venetorum principem Leonardum Lauredanum*, sig. biiir.

14. Capriolo, *De voluptate*, sig. aiiiiv; idem, *Chronica de rebus Brixianorum*, fol. XIr; idem, *Dell'istorie della città di Brescia*, 224.

15. Sanudo, 15:300.

16. Cereta, *Collected Letters*, 32, 33–34 (text slightly adapted). The *Lex Oppia* was introduced under the Roman republic in 215 BCE as a measure in time of war to restrict the use of gold and dye in dresses: ibid., 34 n. 39.

17. Ibid., 84–85.

18. Ibid., 84.

19. Ibid., 120.

20. Ibid., 39, 98, 132. Contrast Nicolosa Sanuti, who in ca. 1453 argued against sumptuary legislation in favor of the honor and virtue display could bring to a city, noting that women's virtues could be recognized through their dress: Kovesi Killerby, "'Heralds of a Well-instructed Mind.'"

21. Cereta, *Collected Letters*, 85.

22. Ibid., 34, 134–135.

23. Ibid., 36.

24. Ibid., 117–22 (quotation at 119). A comparable critique of worldly concerns and a preference for the rural world and a quiet life mark the ca. 1537 *stanze* of the Brescian poet Veronica Gambara that begin "Quando miro la terra, ornata e bella." See her *Rime*, 119–125.

25. "Non spectar la gran ruina,'/'hora mai fa' penitentia,'/'cossì far poi resistentia'/'al flagel chi ti è ordinato.'/'Piange, Bressa, el to peccato'/'se non voi haver supplicio." Civini (?), "Cominatione sopra la cità de Bressa," 694.

26. Cereta, *Collected Letters*, 85. However, Cereta goes on to state: "But those are disasters that come from heaven, not from our women's arms." Cereta's letters are mentioned with approval by Capriolo, *Chronica de rebus Brixianorum*, fol. LXXXr (at the same time as events of ca. 1490).

27. Ibid., 161–164, 169–175. The influence of Pliny the Elder can be detected here, as elsewhere in her letters.

28. Bernardino da Feltre, *Sermoni*, 1:284–285.

29. Cereta, *Collected Letters*, 46–48 (corrected).

30. Figures from Kovesi Killerby, *Sumptuary Law*, 34, and see ibid., table 2.1.

31. ASV, Senato terra, deliberazioni, reg. 7, fols. 133r–134r (pencil foliation, 28 Sept. 1476); ASC 506, 16, 17, 18 Apr. 1477, fols. 27r, 28v, 29r; Bistort,

Magistrato alle pompe, 48–49, 352–366. See also ibid., 125–129, on Venetian legislation regulating clothing in 1503–5 that may have affected Brescian conciliar decrees of 1503 and 1505, although I have not been able to establish a direct connection.

32. For example, see ASC 506, 10 June, 8 July 1478, fols. 71r, 75r.
33. For example, see the copy of a decision taken by the Ten on 26 Mar. 1506 "contra li zugadori," with exception of "i zuogi de Schachi, archo, Balestra & Balla," in ASC 1528, fols. 105v–106r. The *podestà* described his proceedings against gamblers in a letter to the heads of the Ten on 6 Oct. 1501: ASV, Capi del consiglio dei dieci, lettere di rettori, b. 19, no. 25. On the Ten and blasphemers see Povolo, *Intrigo dell'onore*, 122.
34. ASC 492, 7, 13 Mar. 1442, fols. 36r, 38r.
35. "Cum memoratum fuisset in hac civitate varios habitus & vestes per cives nostros portari cum aliquali ignominia nostra nominis quam Brixiani: ac cum ostentationem aliqualis levitatis eorum q. ipsas vestes & Inhonestos habitus defferunt: et huic non mediocri Inconvenienti providendum sit pro bonis moribus & civili habitu conservandis." ASC 514, 15 Sept. 1497, fol. 71v.
36. "[U]t omnipotens et misericors Dominus peccata nostra non respiciat sed pro ineffabili misericordia et clementia sua flagella haec a nobis auferat." ASC 520, 23, 28 Apr. 1505, fols. 62r–63v, 64v.
37. ASC 506, 23 May 1477, fol. 43r; ASC 515, 23, 28 Dec. 1495, fols. 45r–v, 48r; ASC 516, 26 Apr. 1499, fol. 15v; ASC 519, 16 Jan. 1503, fol. 133r–v; ASC 1092, fol. 101v (rectorial proclamation about feasts dated 20 Jan. 1503).
38. ASC 506, 23 May 1477, fol. 43r.
39. "[P]er le qual le facultà di nostri Citadini se extrema, le persone per la superchia carga se deforma e debilita: assidue dissensioni in le familie se zenera ed la Città nostra rendese infamia." ASC 519, 28 Apr. 1503, fol. 172v. This formula was repeated two years later: ASC 520, 23 Apr. 1505, fol. 62r.
40. Chapter 8 here.
41. A penalty of 25 *lire planete* and one month's imprisonment was threatened: ASC 497, 13 July 1457, fol. 29v.
42. ASC 515, 23, 28 Dec. 1495, fols. 45r–v, 48r.
43. Later amended to one year for parents, wife, or children, and agreed unanimously: ASC 519, 12 May 1503, fol. 7v. It was not proposed on 23 Apr. 1505, but on 27 Sept. 1509 the Venetian diarist Marin Sanudo noted news of "una crida fata a Brexa che niun non porti barba si non di zorni 12, in pena grandissima, exceptuando quelli hanno legitimo coroto." Sanudo, 9:192.
44. Cavallo, *Artisans of the Body*, 39, 40, 42, 54–56; Bartlett, "Symbolic Meanings of Hair"; Constable, "Introduction," esp. 53, 66–67, 87, 102, 109.
45. The special council rejected a proposal to limit dowries to 150 in gold (probably ducats rather than *scudi*) by eight votes to six, but it agreed to propose that the general council elect five citizens to investigate the matter: ASC 515, 29 Apr. 1496, fol. 87r. On the delegation to Orsini see ASC 520, 1 Nov. 1506, fol. 68v. The scale of wedding festivities for the Capriolo and Martinengo in ca. 1502 is indicated by Capriolo, *Chronicorum de rebus Brixianorum*, col. 132.

46. "Et comedbant equos et asinos et infirmitate seu fame morientes & canes, lupos, & mures, & omnia oltra et incogita & alij fame periunt. Et alij, ut assertum fuit per dominum prepositum S. Agate, bonum religiosum deliberaverunt veneno interficere medietatem filiorum ex impotentia, & deffectum victualium & summa calamitate & egestate. Heu Brixiam tam magnipotens, super quantas ceteras urbis uberissima victualium ad quod venisti. . . . Tolle tuas divitias, tolle palatia, tolle daurata tuarum ornamenta. Induebatis purpura & bisso ferarij & fetagrarij, caligarij atque lanifices induebant uxores veluto cremesino, panno damasco & scarlato finissimo earum manice vexillis amplissimis, suffulte pellibus bavij aut martar, quam solis regibus conveniunt & perlarum in capitibus earum corone splendat gemis plene. . . . Ad eo fuisse ego videre [. . .] caigariorum portare balza de panno aura & vestes richamatas de perle, auro, argento, & perito mirifice contextus heu pudor judicia." ASC 491, 2 Mar. 1440, fol. 16r. In 1458 it was suggested that during the siege of the city in 1438–40 the inhabitants ate grass and roots, horses, mules, and asses. They were even forced to use dried dogs, cats, and mice in their cooking: Pusculo, "Oratio de laudibus Brixiae," 12.
47. "[D]ichiarando che in lo numero de le persone mecaniche compreso se intenda ogniuno che incapace sia de le dignità nostre, *dummodo* el non sia incapace *respectu exceptionis vel artis militaris.*" ASC 519, 28 Apr. 1503, fols. 172v–174r.
48. Cassa, *Funerali, pompe e conviti*, 96–97.
49. Omitted in legislation passed on 23 Apr. 1505.
50. Omitted in legislation passed on 23 Apr. 1505. On the Brescian house and its interior, see Bettoni, "Aristocrazia senza corte." On the significance of household furnishings in Renaissance Venice, see Allerston, "Consuming Problems." In general, see Ajmar-Wollheim and Dennis, *At Home in Renaissance Italy*.
51. ASC 506, 23 May 1477, fol. 41v.
52. ASC 516, 26 Apr. 1499, fol. 15v.
53. ASC 506, 23 May 1477, fol. 44r.
54. Sanudo, *Itinerario di Marin Sanuto*, 70.
55. "De antiano eligendo, et eius officio." BQB, L.III.10, unfoliated.
56. Otis, *Prostitution in Medieval Society*, 12.
57. Brundage, "Prostitution in Medieval Canon Law."
58. Quoted in Shahar, *Fourth Estate*, 206.
59. Otis, *Prostitution in Medieval Society*, 23.
60. Le Goff, *Time, Work and Culture*, 60–62.
61. Rossiaud, *Prostitution mèdiévale*, 91.
62. In general, see the essays in Hanawalt, *Women and Work*. On the predominance of immigrants in criminal condemnations in Brescia during 1411–17 see Bonfiglio Dosio, "Criminalità ed emarginazione," esp. 133 (homicide), 139 (personal injury), 141 (Caterina, a German prostitute), 142–143 (insulting words), 160 n. 215 ("Nanna figlia del fu Francesco de Prata meretrice.")
63. Trexler, "Prostitution florentine." This article was published in English translation: idem, "Florentine Prostitution." On the problem of sodomy in Florence and the institution of the office of "honesty," see Rocke, *Forbidden Friendships*.

64. ASC 504, 29 Nov. 1471, fol. 14v. Note also Bornato, *Opusculum de laudibus matrimonii*, and also Carlo Valgulio's translation of Plutarch: "Praecepta connubialia," in idem, *Moralia Plutarchi*, sigs. pv–[q4v].

65. "Ali quali cossi elletti debia esser sato sacramento di over cum ogni dilligentia, solicitudine e vigilantia cerchar, pensar e operar di far contraer tutti quelli matrimoni saranno possibeli cossi nella sua quadra come per tutta la Cità de Bressa." ASC 506, 23 May 1477, fol. 43v.

66. On 24 Mar. 1485 the *podestà* Marcantonio Morosini "fece impiccar per le cane di la gola una puttana da bordello chiamata *la Moretta*" of twenty-eight years of age who had stolen from her clients. Melga, "Cronaca," 127.

67. On contemporary prohibitions against masks in Ferrara see Gundersheimer, "Crime and Punishment in Ferrara," 121–122n. 43.

68. ASC 502, 20 June 1466, fol. 116r–v.

69. "Quot et quanta inconvenientia tam contra deum, quam contrabonos mores quottidie sequantur: permittendo quod maschare fiant: Maiora quod in dies sequi possent: si fieri patentur: tam periculo publico quam privato." ASC 507, 28 Feb. 1481, fol. 46r.

70. See Brundage, "Sumptuary Laws and Prostitution."

71. ASC 505, 7 June 1476, fol. 36v.

72. ASC 506, 10 Mar. 1478, fol. 50r, with marginal annotation on publication.

73. "[A] ciò per questo mezzo sia cognosciuto le donne honeste de le dishoneste." ASC 519, 28 Apr. 1503, fol. 174r. This exemption was omitted from the clauses proposed on 23 Apr. 1505.

74. On gendered space see Romano, "Gender and the Urban Geography." See also Ghirardo, "Topography of Prostitution."

75. For example, see the complaint to the council made by Antonio Capriolo against the incursions of the "postribulum" on his property and the need to provide for "honesta via." ASC 495, 29 July 1449, fol. 78v. Capriolo was involved in drawing up the extensive sumptuary legislation issued in 1477.

76. *Statuta Brixiae* (1473), "Statuta criminalia," "De meretricibus expellendis," no. 211. This applied to unofficial brothels rather than to the official brothel.

77. "De antiano eligendo, et eius officio." BQB, L.III.10, unfoliated.

78. A young girl "alla finestra mai non facia posa": *Costume delle donne*, unpaginated.

79. Martines, *Strong Words*, 174–175.

80. ASC 505, 7 June 1476, fols. 36–37r. The proclamation of the *podestà* outlining these injunctions is dated 12 June 1476 and is copied in ASC 1092, fols. 67v–68v.

81. A chronicler noted that the poor were confined to the "postribulo, ciouè in una casa di quello, acciò non havessero andar vagabondi per la Cittade e imbrattar questo e quel altro." They were almost killed by a fire in the building: Melga, "Cronaca," 24–25.

82. Proclamation of 9 Nov. 1483 in ASC 1092, fols. 79v–80r.

83. In Feb. 1492 five citizens were appointed to look into and correct or reform sumptuary laws of May 1477. See ASC 513, 10 Feb. 1492, fol. 100r; Zanelli, "Predicatori a Brescia," 117 n. 4; and Cassa, *Funerali, pompe e conviti*, 82. In

Feb. 1508 some citizens were appointed to look at all the existing statutes on superfluous clothing: ibid., 107–108. The injunctions against superfluous clothing were proclaimed once again in 1533: ASC 1093, fols. 118v–119v.

84. ASC 528, 28 Mar., 24 May 1520, fols. 46v–47r (referring to decision of 24 Mar. 1519), fol. 70r.

85. Frati, "Osservanti a Brescia," 438 n. 12, 441 n. 14.

8. A Funerary Fracas

1. See the rectorial proclamation in ASC 1092, fols. 108v–109r (30 June 1505). Some of the rubrics in question are printed in the Dominican attack on the statute: *Qu[a]estio*, sig. av. They are provided in their entirety in the report of an episcopal commission in July 1507: ASC 1528, fol. 134r–v. Finally, they appear with minor variations in *Statuta Brixie* (1508), "Statuta potestatis," rubric 34.

2. Vovelle, *Mort et l'occident*, 142–146.

3. Ariès, *Hour of Our Death*, 165.

4. Strocchia, "Death Rites," 121. See also eadem, *Death and Ritual;* and Terpstra, *Art of Executing Well.*

5. As one anonymous author, possibly Elia Capriolo, puts it: "But according to popular rumor you own farms, houses and many other articles of property. You reap abundant supplies each year and take a share of harvests, vintages and everything, the fruit and produce belonging to everybody in the abundant territory of Brescia" ([Capriolo?], *Defensio*, sig. Aiiv).

6. On shameful and unmanly grieving see King, *Death of the Child*, 136–142.

7. A table illustrating the range and number of Italian sumptuary concerns between 1200 and 1500 is provided in Kovesi Killerby, *Sumptuary Law*, 38.

8. Ibid., 71–76, 80–81, 89.

9. Ibid., 101–102, 106 (quotation), 107; Pezzana, *Storia della città di Parma*, 239, 239–240 n. 3.

10. Valgulio, *Statutum*, sig. Ar. All further references to this work are cited in text with the title and signature number. All translations of the three pamphlets are by J. Donald Cullington.

11. "Ad resecandas superfluas expensas, que in funeribus Mortuorum in hac civitate fiunt." See above, n. 1, and ASC 520, 28 June 1505, fol. 92r, with a clarification and amplification on 26 Aug. 1505, fol. 108r, asserting that this provision was not for the prohibition of almsgiving "sed pro honore commodo et utilitate civitatis et civium nostrorum et propria servandi." Accordingly, members of the council who transgressed would be deprived of membership. The clauses on "scola" and the poor did not make it into the final statute, although they were initially approved by nine votes to one. The accounts of the dispute by Cassa, *Funerali, pompe e conviti*, 42–48; Sandal, "Autonomie municipali e libertà ecclesiastica"; and Kovesi Killerby, *Sumptuary Law*, 107–108, should be supplemented by this archival material and the following discussion.

12. ASC 506, 23 May 1477, fol. 44r; ASC 515, 2 Nov. 1495, fol. 28r; and the rectorial proclamation of 7 Nov. 1495 in ASC 1092, fol. 91v. See also Cassa, *Funerali, pompe e conviti*, 36–41. The council later agreed that every citizen,

of whatever condition, ought to rent mourning clothes from the *monte di pietà* bank to save expense and avoid burdening the heirs of the deceased: ASC 529, 27 June 1524, fol. 66r–v; ASC 530, 9 May 1525, fol. 99r.

13. [Capriolo?], *Defensio*, sig. Aviv. All further references to this work are cited in text with the title and signature number. The bishop was del Monte, according to *Qu[a]estio*, sig. Ciir–v. However, if the statute is that of 1473, the bishop in question was Domenico De' Domenichi.

14. It was claimed that thirty thousand Brescians died of the influenza known as the "mal di mazucho" in 1477–78. See Melga, "Cronaca," 15–17. Melga notes that at that time Brescians did not attend funerals for fear of contagion, and that the Dominicans were exceptional among the religious orders for continuing to bury the dead: ibid., 21–22. Of course, this exceptional service may have been motivated by Dominican greed as much as by charity. In addition, Melga may not have been impartial: he acted as notary on behalf of the Dominicans before the episcopal commission investigating the funerary statute in 1507. ASC 1528, fol. 133r–v (pencil foliation).

15. See the rubrics printed under "Statuta domini potestatis," in *Statuta Brixiae* (1473), "Generalis rubrica de funeribus mortuorum"; and *Leges Brixianae* (1490), sig. [aviir–v], no. 34.

16. See *Qu[a]estio*, title page. The resort to publication was not unprecedented— see the polemical work of a Lateran canon regular published in Brescia in 1502: Maffeo, *Apologia*. Note also the polemically inspired lives of Augustine and Monica by Agostino Novi and published in Brescia in 1511: Ticinensis, *Elucidarium Christianarum religionum*.

17. A copy of their letter to the pope, dated 1 Feb. 1507, is in ASC 1528, fol. 122v (pencil foliation).

18. This is noted in ASC 1528, 4 Feb. 1507, fol. 122v (pencil foliation). They met on 13 Feb. 1507 and again on 10 June 1507: ASC 1528, fols. 123v, 133r (pencil foliation).

19. The proposal is recorded in ASC 520, 7 Apr. 1506, fol. 17r, where it is noted: "Tamen quia multi cives nostri dicunt eis conscientiam factam fuisse per nonnullos religiosos asserentes dictum statutum esse contra libertatem ecclesiasticam & recusare velle eos absolvere." The vote was ten to one in favor of the proposal. The decision to appoint "quinque boni docti sincerique cives" to ascertain whether the statute is "validum & bonum" and "non contra libertatem ecclesiasticam" was agreed by the general council by forty-eight votes to thirty-eight: ASC 521, 23 Feb. 1507, fol. 109v. Five men were duly elected: ASC 521, 11 Mar. 1507, fols. 113v–114r.

20. ASC 521, 7 Apr. 1507, fol. 123r, where the committee's work is praised ("copiosa ac eleganti relatione facta per sp[ecia]les quinque cives nostros"), and approved by seventy-six votes to eight.

21. ASC 521, 15 May 1507, fol. 138r, where the decision of 28 June 1505 is approved by sixty-six votes to thirty-six, and the decision of 26 Aug. 1505 by sixty-six votes to twenty-two.

22. ASC 1528, 21 July 1507, fols. 132v–135r (pencil foliation), quotation at fol. 133r.

23. ASC 521, 3 Aug. 1507, fol. 12r–v, where it is noted that the bishop, following apostolic briefs, has recently confirmed the validity of the statute and has asserted that the Dominican appeal to the pope was made "verbis ignominiosis contra honorem & dignitatem" of the archbishop, his vicar-general, and the city. Approved by eighty-seven votes to ten.

24. The *oblatio* concerning the Dominican friar is in ASC 1528, 9 Oct. 1508, fol. 141r (pencil foliation). The ducal letter of support to the rectors of Brescia dated 9 Oct. 1508 is in ASB, Ospedale, San Domenico, b. 62, filza 12.

25. ASC 521, 23 Oct. 1508, fol. 6r–v. Approved by seven votes to four.

26. The anonymous humanist author mockingly describes the Dominican book as "the work of many months and of all the brothers of that order who had any reputation among them for learning" ([Capriolo?] *Defensio*, sig. Aiir).

27. *Qu[a]estio* sig. divr: "Nam videntes se non posse ligare clericos directe, per indirectum poenam apposuerunt in fraudem."

28. Ibid., sig. er.

29. Ibid., sig. biir–v. Vulgate passages cited are Tob. 4:7, 11, 17; Luke 7:12, 11:41; Dan. 4:24; Heb. 13:16; Ecclus. 3:33; Prov. 22:9.

30. *Qu[a]estio*, sig. Aiir: "We note that laypeople—even devout ones—have been given no power over churches and church members, laypeople who still have the obligation to obey, not the authority to command; and any statute that they make on their own initiative and that also impinges on the convenience and favorable treatment of churches has no standing unless it has been approved by the Church," X 1.2.10, in Richter and Friedberg, *Corpus iuris canonici*, 2:12–14.

31. *Qu[a]estio*, sig. aiir–v: "Since laypeople, however devout, have been given no power to deal with church property—for to them falls the need to obey, not the dignity of command—it irks us when love grows so cold in some of them that by their ordinances (or rather inventions) they fearlessly attack the immunity of church freedom, which not merely holy fathers but even secular princes have buttressed with many privileges. This they do not only by their unlawful presumption in alienating fiefs and other church possessions and in appropriating jurisdictions but also in regard to death disbursements, and other things, too, that are seen as adjuncts of spiritual authority. Wishing, therefore, to look after the security of churches in these matters and to guard against such great troubles, with the sacred council's approval we rule that ordinances of this kind and claims to fiefs or other church goods, taken up without the formal consent of ecclesiastics and achieved by a lay power's ordinance, do not hold, since it cannot be called an ordinance—rather, an act of defiance or destruction, as well an appropriation of jurisdictions. Those responsible for these things must be coerced by the Church's censure." X 3.13.12, in Richter and Friedberg, *Corpus iuris canonici*, 2:516; Tanner, *Decrees of the Ecumenical Councils*, 1:254.

32. *Qu[a]estio*, sigs. aivv (quoting the second sentence only), biiir (quoting the first sentence only): "Animae defunctorum quatuor modis solvuntur, aut oblationibus sacerdotum, aut precibus sanctorum, aut karorum elemosinis, aut ieiunio cognatorum. Curatio vero funeris, conditio sepulturae, pompa exequi-

arum, magis sunt vivorum solatia quam subsidia mortuorum. Si aliquid prod-
est inpio sepultura preciosa, oberit pio vilis aut nulla. Nec ideo tamen
contempnenda sunt corpora et abicienda defunctorum, maximeque iustorum.
Ubi et illud salubriter discitur, quanta possit esse remuneratio pro elemosinis,
quas viventibus et sentientibus exhibemus si neque hoc apud Deum perit, quod
examinis hominum membris offitii diligentia persolvitur." X 13.2.22, in Richter and Friedberg, *Corpus iuris canonici,* 1:728. Much of this discourse derives
from Augustine's *De cura pro mortuis gerenda* (*Patrologia Latina,* 40:591–
610), written as a reply to Paulinus of Nola: see Trout, *Paulinus of Nola,*
245–247.

33. *Qu[a]estio,* sigs. divv; bivr–v.

34. The anonymous author condemns Thomas Aquinas's "captious syllogisms"
([Capriolo?], *Defensio,* sig. Aiir); and attacks "the hair-splitting of tub-thumpers"
(sig. Aiiiv).

35. "De mandato: & sumptu. R[ei]. P[ublicae]. Brixianae impressa.'/'Et per reverendissimum dominum Archiepiscopum Episcopi Brixiensis locumtenentem
Generalem visa & probata." (ibid., colophon).

36. Christ enjoined his disciples: "Freely ye have received, freely give" (Matt. 10:8).

37. Testaments containing bequests, requests, and endowments to the Dominican
convent of San Domenico survive in ASB, Ospedale, San Domenico, bb. 11
and 12. There are two peaks in the numbers of wills, which coincide with the
years of highest mortality: 1478 and 1505 (twelve and six, respectively).

38. A typical name used (especially for the judge) in Roman legal formulae:
Borkowski, *Roman Law,* 75–76.

39. *Qu[a]estio,* sig. diiiv. Compare Aristotle *Politics* 1252a7–16, where the states-
man *(politikos)* is contrasted with the ruler of a kingdom *(monarkhos)* or of a
household *(oikonomikos)* or of a group of slaves *(despotês).*

40. "Carolus Valgulius civis noster in utraque lingua eminentiss." Capriolo, *Helias Capreolus Francisco Arigoneo,* unpaginated.

41. On the vacancies in those parishes that arose on his death, see ASV, Senato
terra, deliberazioni, reg. 19, fol. 159r (pencil foliation, 21 Feb. 1516 [m.v.
1517).

42. "Verum enim vero cum *Carolus Valgulius* civis noster, & stemmate, & virtute
praeclarus, multa fortunae commoda & ornamenta sprevisset, ut sacratissi-
mae philosophiae expeditior, quietusque magis vacaret, quo nihil gratius, ni-
hilque magis homini expetendum seculo censuit." Capriolo, *Chronicorum de
rebus Brixianorum,* bk 13, col. 136.

43. Bartolomeo Palazzo, "Diario," 301. The Brescian *podestà*'s report of Valgulio's murder was noted in Venice on 21 Feb. 1517: Sanudo, 23:596. The senatorial instruction to the *podestà* to send the perpetrator into exile was agreed
by 160 votes to 4 (1 abstention) in ASV, Senato terra, deliberazioni, reg. 19,
fol. 158r–v (pencil foliation, 21 Feb. 1516 [m.v. 1517). See also Pasero, "Dominio veneto," 308–309.

44. Valentini, *Carlo Valgulio,* 14–15.

45. A similar emphasis on true inner virtue rather than worldly honors can be
found in the letters of Laura Cereta: see eadem, *Collected Letters,* 106, 168.

46. There is a breakdown of the Brescian population by occupation based on the tax estimates of 1388, 1416, and 1454 in Pegrari, *Metamorfosi di un'economia urbana*, 224–227, tabella I.1.

47. "Generosity" *(generositas)* and "nobility" *(nobilitas)* were classical and Renaissance synonyms. However, the recipients of this liberality were most often friends and clients of political and social significance rather than the truly needy. On notions of charity and noble munificence as gifts see Zemon Davis, *Gift in Sixteenth-century France*, esp. chaps. 1–2.

48. On this, see Henderson, *Piety and Charity*; and, for some Bolognese cases, Terpstra, "Death and Dying."

49. Cohn, *Cult of Remembrance and the Black Death*, 122–133; McClure, "Art of Mourning"; and idem, *Sorrow and Consolation*.

50. For example, the testament of the Brescian noble Sandrino quo. Giacomo de Cucchi, dated 27 Sept. 1477, requests at least 144 religious to accompany the body to burial in the convent of San Domenico: ASB, Ospedale, San Domenico, b. 11, no. 114.

51. After ca. 1400, wild mourning figures appear on tombs, in contrast to an early medieval disdain for violent and uncontrolled gesticulation, especially in mourning, which was often attributed to pagans, Jews, devils, and sinners. This Stoic moderation only gradually gave way to the "new emotionalism" of late medieval art (especially evident in depictions of the Lamentation over Christ and the Entombment). On this and the "expressive tendencies" in fourteenth- and fifteenth-century art see Barasch, *Gestures of Despair*.

52. Strocchia, *Death and Ritual*, 61–63, 201–205, 210–212, 225, 232.

53. Erasmus, "Funeral," 772–773.

54. Schraven, "Giovanni Battista Borghese's Funeral," 23–28. See also Hiesinger, "Fregoso Monument." On the marked rise in the number of elaborate funerals in Madrid after 1561 for the purpose of "impressing God and neighbor," see Eire, *From Madrid to Purgatory*, chap. 4.

55. Zemon Davis, *Gift in Sixteenth-century France*, chap. 7.

56. Luther, *Babylonian Captivity*, 25–36; and idem, *Misuse of the Mass*, 203. See also idem, *Treatise on the New Testament*, esp. 93–94, 96.

57. Quoted in Ozment, *Reformation in the Cities*, 112–113.

58. Quoted in Marshall, *Beliefs and the Dead*, 55. See also ibid., 56–64.

59. Koslofsky, *Reformation of the Dead*, chaps. 3, 4; and Houlbrooke, *Death, Religion, and the Family*, chap. 9, esp. 270–271.

60. Chapter 12 here. Emilio Emigli's translation of Erasmus's *Enchiridion* appeared in Brescia in April 1531 with his verses on penitence and death appended to it.

61. Augustine *De Civitate Dei* 1.12. This passage was also used by sixteenth-century English evangelicals in their attacks on the doctrine of purgatory and the organization of communion. See Marshall, *Beliefs and the Dead*, 52, 144–145, 150, 268.

62. Cited in Eire, *From Madrid to Purgatory*, 123.

63. Baron, "Franciscan Poverty," 1, 7 (Petrarch quoted).

64. Petrarch *De Remediis* 2.119. For an English translation see Petrarch, *Petrarch's*

Remedies, 3:302. Compare Petrarch's description of the death as the great leveler in *Triumphus mortis* 1: "U' sono or le ricchezze? U' son gli onori?'/'e le gemme e gli scettri e le corone,'/'e le mitre e i purpurei colori?'/'Miser chi speme in cosa mortal pone'/'(ma chi non ve la pone?), e se si trova'/'alla fine ingannato è ben ragione": idem *Rime e trionfi* 558, lines 82–87.

65. Petrarch *De Remediis* 2.132; idem, *Petrarch's Remedies*, 335.
66. Petrarch *De Remediis*, 2.122.
67. Baron, "Franciscan Poverty," 33.
68. Ibid., 22. See also McManamon, *Funeral Oratory*.
69. Becichemo, *Panegyricus Leonardo Lauretano*, sigs. xiiir–yiir. Britannico, *Sermones funebres vulgares* was published in Brescia in 1495, 1498, 1500, 1505, and 1508.
70. Panofsky, *Tomb Sculpture*, 67; Petrucci, *Writing the Dead*.
71. Panofsky, *Tomb Sculpture*, 75; Bowd, *Vainglorious Death*, frontispiece.
72. The mausoleum commissioned by Francesco Martinengo di Padernello for his father and sculpted by Bernardino dalle Croci, possibly with contributions from Stefano Lamberti and Maffeo Olivieri, is now in the city museum of Santa Giulia, Brescia. See Lucchesi Ragni, Gianfranceschi, and Mondini, *Coro delle monache*, 84; Morassi, *Catalogo delle cose d'arte*, 339–349.
73. D'Amico, *Renaissance Humanism*, 230–231. Compare Murphy, "Worldly Reform."
74. Giustiniani and Querini, "Libellus ad Leonem Decem," col. 699. See also the note drafted by Querini in relation to this proposal held in Sacro Eremo Tuscolano, Frascati, cod. F II A, fols. 348r–349r, printed in Jedin, "Vincenzo Quirini und Pietro Bembo," 165–166, and discussed in Bowd, *Reform before the Reformation*, 165–179.
75. D'Amico, *Renaissance Humanism*, 41–44.
76. Diane Owen Hughes has argued that after public female laments at funerals, which encouraged vendetta, were outlawed, memorialization "became male and patrilineal" and realized through permanent tombs rather than fleeting gestures. See her "Mourning Rites." For an illuminating discussion of the impact of spoken and written forms of language see Ong, *Orality and Literacy*.
77. The foregoing argument is a modification of my position in Bowd, *Vainglorious Death*, lxviii.
78. The debate on the significance of regionality and autonomy in Renaissance Italy has been outlined by Fasano Guarini, "Center and Periphery."
79. See the suggestive remarks in Neher, "Moretto and the Congregation."
80. Isaacs, "States in Tuscany and Veneto," 302, 303.

9. Jewish Life

1. [Capriolo?], *Defensio*, sig. Aiir.
2. Bonfil, *Jewish Life*, 101–123.
3. On Jews in Renaissance Italy see ibid.; Shulvass, *Jews in the World*; Wittmayer Baron, *Social and Religious History*, 220–296; Milano, *Storia degli ebrei*; and Roth, *History of the Jews*. On Jews in Venice and the Venetian *terraferma* see

Varanini and Mueller, *Ebrei nella terraferma;* Davis and Ravid, *Jews of Early Modern Venice;* Varanini, "Appunti per la storia del prestito"; Jacoby, "Juifs à Venise"; and Pullan, *Rich and Poor in Renaissance Venice,* 431–475. On Jews in Brescia or the Bresciano see Massetti, "Antisemitismo"; Bontempi, *Ferro e la stella,* esp. 14–18, 27–64, 193–201; Gamba, *Ebrei a Brescia;* and Glissenti, *Ebrei nel Bresciano.*

4. Mueller, "*Status* degli ebrei," 17. On exemplary and moralizing sermons in fifteenth-century Italy see Mormando, *Preacher's Demons.*

5. "Qui tanquam vere columne fidei nostrae, & vera ecclesiae luminaria Iudeos tanquam publicam luem ac ignem intestinum non modo à civitatibus se ab omnium Christianorum frequentia arcendos & repellendos penitus esse consulebant cum Iudei ipsi non modo omnem ex civitatibus sostantiam exhauriunt: Verum etiam mentes hominum tanquam publica pestis erroribus scismatibus heresibus," ASC 498, 15, 17 April 1458, fol. 27v.

6. Mueller, "Imperialismo monetario veneziano," 287. For these changes and the incredulous Brescian reaction see Capriolo, *Chronica de rebus Brixianorum,* fols. LXIXr, LXIXv.

7. ASV, Senato terra, deliberazioni, reg. 3, fol. 158r (pencil foliation, 31 May 1455); ASV, Senato terra, deliberazioni, reg. 4, fols. 79v (pencil foliation, 29 July 1458), 81r (pencil foliation, 1 Aug. 1458).

8. ASC 492, 20 Oct. 1441, fol. 104r. In 1408 the Veronese invited German Jews into their city for the same reason: Pullan, *Rich and Poor in Renaissance Venice,* 445.

9. ASC 493, 21 Aug., 23, 26 Oct., 1444, 12, 14, 27 Apr., 28 May 1445, fols. 65r, 78v–79r, 80r, 112r, 120v; ASC 496, 7, 10 Jan., 18 Feb. 1452 (mentioning threat of excommunication and fear of committing a sin); Zanelli, "Predicatori a Brescia," 130–131.

10. Grubb, *Firstborn of Venice,* 28–35, 105–106; Mueller, "*Status* degli ebrei," 14–15, 23–24. For the Council of Ten's supervision of the Veronese Jews see Varanini, "Comune di Verona," esp. 286–287.

11. Venice responded in 1428: "Fiat ut petitur." Menniti Ippolito, "Dedizione di Brescia a Milano (1421) e a Venezia (1427)," 42–43. See also ASV, Senato terra, deliberazioni, reg. 20, fol. 45r (pencil foliation, 27 Apr. 1517, with a note that "Que fuerunt expedicta in Mense Junij").

12. Pusculo, *Duo libri Symonidos,* sigs. aiiiv–aiiiir. Translated by J. Donald Cullington. Pusculo's presence in the Brescian council is noted, for example, in ASC 514, 12 May 1493, fol. 80r.

13. ASC 1525, 23 Feb. 1463 [m.v. 1464], fol. 23r-v. The text of Bessarion's letter printed in Bessarion, *Kardinal Bessarion,* 3:529–530.

14. Rovigo, "Aspetti della presenza ebraica a Verona," 132–133.

15. In 1462 Michele da Milano and Giacomo della Marca, known for their hostility to Jews, preached in the city. At the end of Mar. the doge asked his *podestà* in Brescia to protect Jews in Orzinuovi, Gavardo, Iseo, and Gottolengo who were being attacked from the pulpit. Massetti, "Antisemitismo," 160.

16. Ibid., 161.

17. Jacoby, "Juifs à Venise," 205.

18. "[C]um sint contra legem dei, et honorem Christiani nominis: et contra bonum reipublice." ASC 499, 4 Jan. 1462, fol. 69v.

19. ASC 500, 3 Mar. 1463, fol. 12r; ASC 502, 21 Nov. 1466, fol. 169r–v.

20. ASC 503, 6 June 1469, fol. 115r.

21. ASC 503, 22 Sept. 1469, fols. 146v–147v.

22. ASC 503, 2 Nov. 1469, fols. 161v–162r.

23. ASC 504, 25 Oct. 1473, fol. 61r.

24. ASC 505, 30 Dec. 1473, fols. 86v–87r. Among the statutes reformed by the commune and published in 1473 was "De stochis et usuris prohibendis," in *Statuta Brixiae* (1473), no. CCXXVIIII, fols. 95v–96v. This was reformed by ducal letter in response to Brescian petition on 11 Apr. 1475: ASC 1079/A, ducal letter no. 47; printed in *Leges Brixianae* (1490), "Statuta civilia," no. 233. See also ASC 1525, fol. 48r.

25. ASC 505, 23 Jan. 1475, fol. 53v; ASC 506, 7 Feb. 1478, fol. 35r.

26. ASC 1525, 30 Mar. 1478, 27 Aug., 25 Oct. 1479, fols. 56r–v, 59v–60r.

27. ASC 506, 16 Dec. 1479, fol. 65v; ASC 1525, 8 Apr. 1480, fol. 61r.

28. ASC 1525, 19 Apr. 1480, fol. 61r.

29. ASC 507, 28 July 1480, fol. 127r.

30. ASC 513, 18 Feb., 27 May 1491, fols. 120r, 11r; ASC 514, 24 May, 3 June 1494, fols. 17v, 19r. In 1503 alms of 30 *lire planete* were granted as a dowry to Jewish convert Zentilina: ASC 519, 27 July 1503, fol. 35r–v.

31. ASC 513, 18 Feb. 1491, fol. 120r; Corradino Palazzo, "Diario," 255.

32. Britannico, *Sermones funebres*, sigs. Kiiiv–[Kviir].

33. I have not seen the *Adhortatio Philippi ad quendam Theodosium Iudaeum ut Christi religionem relicta Iudaeorum*, published in Brescia by Giovanni Antonio Bresciano on 15 Oct. 1508. However, I consulted the text printed in Giovanni Pierio Valeriano's edition of Lactantius, *Divina opera*, fols. CLVIIIIv–CLXv. Note also Marochitano, *Tractatus Rabby Samuelis*.

34. ASC 1525, 22 Jan. 1479, fol. 60r. On the imposition of this sign by Venice see ASV, Senato terra, deliberazioni, reg. 12, fol. 135r (pencil foliation, 26 Mar. 1496); Jacoby, "Juifs à Venise," 174–175, and 175 n. 50.

35. ASC 1079/A, ducal letter no. 74 (4 July 1483).

36. ASB, Cancelleria pretoria, atti, reg. 20, fol. 270r.

37. 18 May 1438, quoted in Massetti, "Antisemitismo," 157–158; ASC 1092, fol. 153r (proclamation of 7 Sept. 1494).

38. *Statuta Brixiae* (1473), "Statuta criminalia," "De iudeo aduleerante cum cristiana et converso," no. LXXIIII.

39. Martinengo di Erbusco, "Della congiura de' Bresciani," 80. The "fonte vocato Iudaeorum" in the *contrada* of Sant' Agata was mentioned in 1498: Pasero, *Francia, Spagna, Impero*, 203 n. 81. On synagogues see ASC 1092, fol. 153v (undated proclamation, but probably late fifteenth century).

40. On the "epoca d'oro dell'ebraismo bresciano, tra il 1490 e il 1512" see Bontempi, *Ferro e la stella*, xxxv. On the *jeshivà* in 1508 see ibid., 92. The Jewish presence in Brescia at this time is noted in Simonsohn, *Jews in the Duchy of Milan*, 2:912, 943, 944.

41. Bontempi, *Ferro e la stella*, xxviii–xxxiii; Tamani, "Tipografia ebraica a Brescia"; Gengaro, Leoni, and Villa, *Codici decorati e miniati*, 47–50, plates 21–48; and Perani, "Bibbia ebraica Soncino."

42. Guerrini, *Celebre famiglia lombarda*, 202–205.

43. Meneghin, *Monti di pietà*, 55–115. Until 1470 the Scuola del Santissimo Sacramento e Immacolata Concezione lent money at interest to the needy: Pasero, "Dominio veneto," 199 n. 2.

44. Simonsohn, *Jews in the Duchy of Milan*, 1:46–48, 105, 151, 155–157. In 1447 a contract was drawn up between Vivianus and his partners and the commune of Gottolengo to lend money at the rate of 30 percent per annum: ibid., 35–36. See also Gamba, *Ebrei a Brescia*, and Massetti, "Antisemitismo," 157–173. Articles were drawn up between the community of Padenghe, on Lake Garda, and a certain Moses to lend money at 20 percent and 40 percent in Dec. 1460. These were revoked by the Senate as "excessiva, et inhonestissima" the following year: ASV, Senato terra, deliberazioni, reg. 4, fol. 174r (pencil foliation, 30 June 1461).

45. Massetti, "Antisemitismo," 157–173.

46. Toaff, *Pasque di sangue*, 74–75.

47. Simonsohn, *Jews in the Duchy of Milan*, 1: 433.

48. ASC 1525, 2 Apr. 1481, fol. 65r.

49. ASC 507, 26 Oct. 1481, fol. 116r; ASC 507, 23 June 1486, fol. 79r.

50. ASB, Cancelleria pretoria, atti, reg. 20, fols. 160r–170v, 182r–v.

51. ASB, Cancelleria pretoria, atti, reg. 20, fols. 161r–164r; Gamba, *Ebrei a Brescia*, 24–31. Compare the lists of pawns, often of very high value, in Toaff, "'Banchieri' cristiani," 284. See also the lists from Nuremberg (1483–99) and Regensburg (1519) in Toch, "Jüdische Geldhandel," 306–309; Matzel and Riecke, "Pfandregister."

52. ASB, Cancelleria pretoria, atti, reg. 19, fol. 73r.

53. ASB, Cancelleria pretoria, atti, reg. 15, fol. 35v, "Pro Rizardo, & Jacob Iudeis," 12 May 1466; ibid., reg. 17, fol. 13r, 10 Dec. 1473; ibid., reg. 20, fol. 170v, 30 Oct. 1488. A Jew called Mandolino and a priest at San Zeno, near Brescia, were involved in a counterfeiting operation in 1499: Brescian rectors to the Ten, 6 Feb. 1499, in ASV, Capi del consiglio dei dieci, lettere di rettori, b. 19, nos. 1–2.

54. For example, Salò (1449) and Palazzolo (1461): Masetti, "Antisemitismo," 159, 160.

55. Ibid., 163.

56. Pullan, *Rich and Poor in Renaissance Brescia*, 456.

57. ASB, Cancelleria Pretoria, atti, reg. 17, fol. 13r, 10 Dec. 1473.

58. ASB, Cancelleria Pretoria, atti, reg. 20, fol. 169r–170v.

59. ASC 1528, fol. 62v.

60. Masetti, "Antisemitismo," 173. A ducal letter of 1492 warned the *provveditore* in Asola against disobedience in trespassing on the jurisdiction of the Brescian *podestà* in Jewish matters, not only with respect to usury but also in mercantile affairs more generally: ASC 1079/A, ducal letter no. 134 (16 July 1492); ASC 1525, fol. 103r; and Masetti, "Antisemitismo," 170–171.

61. ASV, Senato terra, deliberazioni, reg. 13, fol. 30v (pencil foliation, 31 Dec. 1497). The Brescians had called for an end to the residence and activities of Jews in the city within four months, and even those allowed to live over five miles out of the city were not to be permitted to lend money.

62. Masetti, "Antisemitismo," 160; ASC 505, 13, 23 Jan. 1475, fols. 52r, 53v.

63. Simonsohn, *Jews in the Duchy of Milan*, 1:677; ASMa, Archivio Gonzaga, E.XVIII.2, b. 1599, filza LXII, fol. 679r–v.

64. Pasero, "Dominio veneto," 166.

65. The Brescian humanist texts about this case are considered in more detail in Bowd and Cullington, *"On Everyone's Lips."*

66. For what follows in this section I am indebted to Po-chia Hsia, *Trent 1475;* Rogger and Bellabarba, *Principe vescovo Johannes Hinderbach.*

67. Po-chia Hsia, *Myth of Ritual Murder.*

68. "Fo la novella di Giudei da Trento": Corradino Palazzo, "Diario," 227 (noted by the Brescian Palazzo before he left for a pilgrimage to Rome on 19 Apr. 1475). In general, see Esposito, "Culto del 'beato' Simonino."

69. Po-chia Hsia, *Trent 1475*, 52. A list of the miracles, probably provided by Hinderbach, is printed in Tiberino, *Hystoria completa de passione.* The first three miracles, including the restoration of sight to a partially blind man, are described in Pusculo, *Duo libri Symonidos*, sigs. dr–diir.

70. Hinderbach, *Epistola*, unpaginated.

71. Tiberino, *Hystoria completa de passione*, unpaginated.

72. Kristeller, "Alleged Ritual Murder"; Esposito, "Stereotipo dell'omicidio rituale"; Meserve, "News from Negroponte"; Quondam, "Parte del volgare"; Bowd and Cullington, *"On Everyone's Lips,"* app. 1.

73. Hinderbach, *Epistola*, unpaginated.

74. Zovenzoni, *Carmen ad Gabrielem*, unpaginated. Translated by J. Donald Cullington.

75. Calfurnio, *Mors et apotheosis Simonis;* Pusculo, *Duo libri Symonidos;* idem, "Ubertini Pusculi Brixiensis Simonidos," Biblioteca Palatina, Parma, MS Parmense 1583, fols. 55r–86v, and Österreichische Nationalbibliothek, Vienna, Codex Vindobonensis Palatinus, new ser. 12,822.

76. For example, see "Cronaca di anonimo veronese," 308–309.

77. Katz, *Jew in the Art*, chap. 5.

78. "Scripsit summus pontifex omnibus dominis et petentatibus breve, per quod Declarat & Iubet sub pena excomunicationis ut puer ille qui Tridenti ab Judeis Interfectus dicitur pingi non finatur, neque ill res ab scriptoribus Imprimi, aut a predicatoribus diffamari Instigarique vulgus contra Judeos, ab ecclesia tolleratos, In testimonium veritatis Dominice passionis." ASB, Cancelleria pretoria, atti, reg. 18, fols. 46v–47r. A copy of the papal brief dated 10 Oct. 1475 ("Licet inter causas") was included with the ducal letter: ibid., fol. 47r–v.

79. A *cerretano* was a peddler who recited or sang vernacular ballads, often concerning dramatic events, before crowds in public square in Italian cities. These peddlers also sold copies of the ballads alongside their other goods: Meserve, "News from Negroponte," 454.

80. "[C]he non dobia penzere ne far penzere in carto, in muro, ne altramente, ne

vendere imagine alguna da Martyro ne beato, ne predicar per zaratani, ne per modo de versi, overo epistole scrivere, ne scritte vendere, de quello Fantolino appellato Simono et Morto per le mane de li zudei, ne la cita de Trento." ASB, Cancelleria pretoria, atti, reg. 18, fol. 47v. English text (adapted) in Baron, *Social and Religious History*, 286.

81. Corradino Palazzo, "Diario," 246 (entry for 13 Apr. 1476); Capriolo, *Chronica de rebus Brixianorum*, fol. LXXIXv.

82. Rigaux, "Immagine di Simone di Trento"; eadem, "Antijudaïsme par l'image"; Ferri Piccaluga, "Economia, devozione e politica"; eadem, "Iconografia francescana"; eadem, "Ebrei nell'iconografia lombarda"; Massetti, "Culto di Simonino a Brescia." All of these essays are illustrated, but some of the woodcut and engraved images are also reproduced in Schreckenberg, *Jews in Christian Art*, 277–280.

83. For example, Zovenzoni's daughter Bartolomea was saved from death when he made a vow to Simon. See his verse "Obductis tenebris occulos iam morte propinqua," printed at the end of Calfurnio, *Mors et apotheosis Simonis*. Giovanni de Salis noted the many miracles taking place in the Bresciano in a letter to Hinderbach dated at Brescia on 10 July 1480 and printed in Esposito and Quaglioni, *Processi contro gli ebrei*, 1:451–452.

84. Bartolomeo Palazzo, "Diario," 302. See also a visit made by a Vicentine in 1479 noted in Grubb, *Provincial Families of the Renaissance*, 193, 195–197.

85. In ca. 1530 Pandolfo Nassini wrote of "uno Ms. Zoan di Sale Dottore il quale fu Podestà della Città di Trento, il quale Ms. Zoan fu al tempo che era Podestà che fece morire li zudei li quali feno morire lo beato Simone, quale è anche in detta Città di Trento." Quoted in Lechi, *Dimore bresciane*, 4:452.

86. Ducal letters of 24 Apr., 17 July, and 5 Nov. 1475 in ASB, Cancelleria pretoria, atti, reg. 18, fols. 19v, 32v–33r, 46v–47r; ducal letters of 14 May, 18 Aug. 1476, 22 Aug. 1477 in ibid., reg. 19, fols. 16r, 16v, 64v–65r, 143v, 143v–144r, 144r–v, 241r.

87. Tiberino, *Relatio*, unpaginated. Translated by J. Donald Cullington.

88. Toaff, *Pasque di sangue*, 74–75. Po-chia Hsia, *Trent 1475*, 91, 97, 98.

89. Toaff, *Pasque di sangue*, 76.

90. De' Giudici, *Apologia Iudaeorum*, 19, 133.

91. Pasero, "Dominio veneto," 174 n. 8.

92. Esposito, "Culto del 'beato' Simonino," 440–441, and 440 n. 57, 441 n. 61. The Brescian council granted 50 *lire planete* to Sanson toward the expenses of holding the meeting in the city: ASC 505, 4 Jan. 1476, fol. 193v.

93. "[N]on cessant [i.e. preachers] in suis predicationibus abhominari Judeos subditos nostros quos volumus habitare posse in omnibus terris et locis nostris, salvos et securos." ASB, Cancelleria pretoria, atti, reg. 19, fol. 143v (ducal letter of 2 Apr. 1476).

94. ASB, Cancelleria pretoria, atti, reg. 19, fol. 241r (ducal letter of 22 Aug. 1477).

95. ASB, Cancelleria pretoria, atti, reg. 19, fols. 16r, 64v–65r, 143v–144r, 144r–144v (ducal letters of 14 May, 18 Aug. 1476). See also Zanelli, "Predicatori a Brescia," 111; Glissenti, *Ebrei nel Bresciano*, 9–11.

96. ASC 507, 23 June 1486, fol. 79r. On Cremona as the center of Jewry in Lom-

bardy see Wittmayer Baron, *Social and Religious History,* 283–284. Census proposals in ASC 512, 4 June 1490, fol. 58r; ASC 514, 27 Sept. 1493, fol. 125r.

97. Montanari, "Monti di pietà."
98. ASC 512, 7 Aug. 1489, fol. 111v.
99. ASC 512, 28 Aug. 1489, fol. 124v. The rules are printed by Zanelli, "Predicatori a Brescia," 138–142. They were approved by the Venetian Senate in Sept. 1490: ASV, Senato terra, deliberazioni, reg. 11, fols. 26r–27v (pencil foliation, 13 Sept. 1490). The ducal letter of approval is copied in ASC 1525, fols. 96v–97v.
100. Cistellini, "Vita religiosa," 422–423.
101. Meneghin, *Bernardino da Feltre,* 517.
102. ASC 513, 13 June 1493, fol. 93r.
103. ASC 529, 27 June 1524, fol. 66r–v; ASC 530, 9 May 1525, fol. 99r.
104. For example, see ASC 512, 4 June 1490, fol. 58r; ASC 513, 27 May 1491, fol. 11r; ASC 514, 30 June 1494, fols. 69v–70r; ASC 516, 5 Feb. 1498, fol. 31r. The Venetian authorities, perhaps mindful of the new *monte di pietà,* supported the calls for expulsion in 1492: ASC 1079, no. 131 (ducal letter dated 22 May 1492), and see ASC 1525, 30 June 1492, fol. 103r.
105. ASC 514, 18 Apr. 1494, fol. 27r; Zanelli, "Predicatori a Brescia," 142–143.
106. Pullan, *Rich and Poor in Renaissance Venice,* 450–475.
107. The ducal warning is printed in part in Bonfil, *Jewish Life,* 52–53. In Aug. 1492 the council unanimously agreed to invite Bernardino da Feltre to preach in Brescia at Advent and at Lent the following year: ASC 513, 2 Aug. 1492, fol. 153r. Another invitation was issued the following year: ASC 514, 22, 24 Aug. 1493, fol. 115r.
108. Bernardino da Feltre, *Sermoni,* vol. 3, passim; Meneghin, *Bernardino da Feltre,* 504–520.
109. ASC 514, 10 July 1494, fols. 54v–55r. On this occasion 2,300 ducats were collected: Meneghin, *Bernardino da Feltre,* 517.
110. Zanelli, "Predicatori a Brescia," 129 n. 1.
111. Varanini, "Comune di Verona."
112. Sanudo, 19:125.
113. For example, Capriolo, *Chronica de rebus Brixianorum,* fol. LXXXv (*recte* LXXIv).
114. ASC 505, 7 June 1476, fols. 36r–37r, printed in Zanelli, "Predicatori a Brescia," 136–137; ASC 506, 10 Mar. 1478, fol. 50r, printed in Zanelli, "Predicatori a Brescia," 137–138.
115. "Aliud invenit remedium Brixia, erexit videlicet sacrum pietatis montem per quem pauperibus et egenis pecunie mutuo gratuito erogantur; sede non obstante liberari non potuimus ab hac peste, sed auctius et in dies augetur numerus huius perfide gentis, ita ut iam sit repleta civitas, quia cum ab aliis christianissimis regibus et dominis expellantur huc refugiunt, ita ut per urbem undique obstrepat et christianorum aures obtundat ebreus sermo, ubique sinagoge congregatur, xerofagia celebrantur et iam christiani clarius ebreorum cerimonias quam suas intelligant, et quamvis iudeos ecclesia tolleret chris-

tiane, non eo tamen modo decrevit tollerari prout Brixie fit; deberet enim ut publice meretrices, que etiam tollerantur, ob eorum spurcitiam in lupanari habitant, ita et hi ebrei ob eorum foedissimam vitam in aliquo foedissimo loco a christianis separati vivere." Massetti, "Antisemitismo," 172; English translation in Owen Hughes, "Distinguishing Signs," 29. Compare ASC 502, 21 Nov. 1466, fol. 169r–v; ASC 1525, 9 Feb. 1477, fol. 56. Note also the proximity of the "damno ebreorum" to the "inaudita epidemiae" in a council provision: ASC 506, 16 Dec. 1479, fol. 65v.

10. Witches

1. Kieckhefer, *European Witch Trials*, 123, 132; Giorgetta, "Pestalozzi accusato," available at the website of Paolo Portone: paoloportone.it/giorgetta1/giorgietta1.htm; and idem, "Documenti sull' inquisizione."

2. Previous studies of witchcraft in the area include "Atti del convegno eretici e streghe"; Lorenzi, *Sante, medichesse e streghe*; Tortelli, "Inquisizione e stregoneria a Brescia"; Bernadelli Curuz, *Streghe Bresciane*; Del Col, "Organizzazione, composizione e giurisdizione," 250–259; and Odorici, *Streghe di Valtellina*. See also Burke, "Witchcraft and Magic."

3. Medin, "Descrizione della città e terre bresciane," 678–679; Lanaro Sartori, "Economia cittadina, flussi migratori e spazio urbano," 74; and the *relazione* of Pietro Tron, former *podestà* in Brescia, as reported in Sanudo, 29:334.

4. "Est locus in agri nostri finibus, id est Vallis Monicae summitate, qui ineptis hominibus, lamiisque semper abundavit, cujus incolarum multos nunc uxores invicem permutavisse relatum est: & qui hebetiorem dabat, addebat & capram, ut non minoris capra ab accipiente, quam alteri nobilior traditae uxoris conditio aestimari videretur. Quod tamen nefandum fertur amotum, ibi fundata divi *Francisci* sacra religione." Capriolo, *Chronicorum de rebus Brixianorum*, col. 131.

5. Giuseppe "da Orzinuovi" to Ludovico Querini, 1 Aug. 1518, in Sanudo, 25:602.

6. Cereta, *Collected Letters*, 54, 60–61. In her "Funeral Oration for an Ass" Cereta gave the miller and the shepherd a rustic Latin style: ibid., 180–181, 191 n. 15; Rabil, *Laura Cereta*, 118–134.

7. Trevor-Roper, *European Witch-Craze*, 29, 32, 38.

8. Borst, "Origins of the Witch-Craze," 310.

9. Putelli, *Intorno al castello di Breno*, 408.

10. Ferri Piccaluga, "Economia, devozione e politica"; Pullan, *Rich and Poor in Renaissance Venice*, 202.

11. In 1485 the inquisitor of Como shaved and burned forty-two witches in Bormio (at the head of the Valtellina near the pass to Trent) following the burning of a Jew and communal sponsorship of a Franciscan preacher: Giorgetta, "Processi di stregoneria a Bormio," available at the website of Paolo Portone: www.paoloportone.it/giorgetta2/giorgetta2.htm.

12. For example, works by the Milanese Dominican Girolamo Visconti, *Opusculum de striis, videlicet an strie sint velud heretice iudicande* (ca. 1460), and

Lamiarum sive striarum opusculum (ca. 1460), both published in Milan in 1490; Giordano (Jordanes) da Bergamo, *Quaestio de strigis* (ca. 1470); Vincenzo Diedo, *Apologia contra quaestionem de lamiis fratris Samuelis Cassinis* (Pavia, after 1500); and Bernardo Ratengo of Como, *De strigiis* (ca. 1510).

13. "De sortilegiis," in Iacobus de Marchia, *Sermones dominicales*, 1:419–435.

14. On the formation of the European witch see Cohn, *Europe's Inner Demons*; Kieckhefer, *European Witch Trials*; and Ginzburg, *Ecstasies*.

15. Martín de Arles quoted in Martin, *Witchcraft and the Inquisition*, 124. On the link between superstition and heresy see ibid., 74 n. 149.

16. Thomas Aquinas, *Summa theologiae*, pt. 2 (second pt.), qq. 92–96.

17. On "superstition" as a broadly defined "catch-all label" in fifteenth-century Italy see Paton, "'To the fire, to the fire!'" 15. See also eadem, "Preaching Friars," 272–281; and eadem, *Preaching Friars*.

18. On demonic theory and the defence of natural and supernatural aspects of Christian theology see Stephens, *Demon Lovers*.

19. Zanelli, "Predicatori a Brescia," 113–114; Bynum, *Wonderful Blood*, 120–125.

20. ASC 496, 16, 19 Aug., 6 Sept. 1454, fols. 222v, 224r–v, 227v; ASC 497, 6 Feb., 4 May, 3 Dec. 1455, 19 Feb. 1457, fols. 6v, 34r, 84r, 197r–v; ASC 498, 11 Jan. 1458, fol. 3v.

21. Scribner, "Cosmic Order and Daily Life"; idem, "Ritual and Popular Belief."

22. Gentilcore, *From Bishop to Witch.*

23. Ruggiero, *Binding Passions*; Jacobson Schutte, *Aspiring Saints.*

24. Pucci, *Oratio*, sig. Cv.

25. Giustiniani and Querini, "Libellus ad Leonem Decem," cols. 670, 674–688. See also Giustiniani to his sister Lucia, Camaldoli, 14 Sept. 1511, warning against the use of certain words to effect cures: Sacro Eremo Tuscolano, Frascati, Cod. F +, fols. 181r–191r.

26. Contarini, *Office of a Bishop*, 105–109, 129–133. The bishop is warned against practising "superstitious disciplines such as magic and skill at divination, whether from the stars or from anything of that sort," ibid., 83.

27. Giustiniani and Querini, "Libellus ad Leonem Decem," cols. 674–676; Contarini, *Office of a Bishop*, 131.

28. On clerical necromancy see Kieckhefer, *Magic in the Middle Ages*, 151–175.

29. A woman interrogated in 1518 confessed that demons had appeared to her at the sabbat in the guise of monks: Sanudo, 25:639–640.

30. Hansen, *Quellen und Untersuchungen*, 472, 19–20.

31. ASC 514, 10 Dec. 1494, fol. 112v; ASC 521, 23 Oct. 1508, fol. 6r–v.

32. "Cronaca ecclesiastica," 185–187.

33. The description of Stefano's sentencing is taken from a contemporary copy of a report on this case by the inquisitor to the archdeacon and the episcopal vicar: BQB, H.V.7, fols. 133r–134v.

34. "Cronaca ecclesiastica," 183–185.

35. See Grubb, *Firstborn of Venice*, 28–35, 105–106.

36. Labalme, "Sodomy and Venetian Justice," 238–239.

37. ASC 496, 16, 19 Aug. 1454, fols. 222v, 224r–v.

38. "[U]t fiat super tali officio, honesta utilis, & Justa provisio." ASC 496, 6 Sept. 1454, fol. 227v.
39. The council granted 38 *lire planete* and 8 *soldi* to be spent on wood. ASC 497, 6 Feb., 4 May 1455, fols. 6v, 34r.
40. ASC 497, 19 Feb. 1457, fol. 197r–v.
41. ASC 498, 11 Jan. 1458, fol. 3v.
42. "[I]llis crudelissimis carceribus." ASC 497, 3 Dec. 1455, 19 Feb. 1457, fols. 84r, 197v (quotation). The man in question may have been "dominum Johanem de Soltia" on whose behalf the Venetian Senate agreed to ask the Venetian cardinals to supplicate the pope for clemency: ASV, Senato terra, deliberazioni, reg. 4, fol. 66r (pencil foliation, 18 Feb. 1457 [m.v. 1458]).
43. "[L]onga fuit differentia, que multis respectibus tolenda est." The Senate agreed to write to Rome to ask for an end to the matter: ASV, Senato terra, deliberazioni, reg. 4, fol. 82r (pencil foliation, 4 Aug. 1458).
44. Doge to Brescian rectors, Venice, 10 Dec. 1485, in Odorici, *Streghe di Valtellina*, 125–126. A version is in ASV, Senato terra, deliberazioni, reg. 9, fol. 164r–v (pencil foliation, 9 Dec. 1485). See also ASV, Capi del consiglio dei dieci, lettere, filza 5, no. 10; and Sanudo, 26:32–33.
45. Odorici, *Streghe di Valtellina*, 128–130.
46. Ibid., 129; Bernardelli Curuz, *Streghe Bresciane*, 52. Zane was at Cemmo in the Val Camonica undertaking "la visitatione generale per tutto la Diocese" on 12 Sept. 1486, according to a letter he addressed to Francesco Gonzaga, Marquis of Mantua: ASMa, Archivio Gonzaga, E.XLVIII.2, b. 1599, filza LVI, fol. 564r–v.
47. Odorici, *Streghe di Valtellina*, 130–133.
48. ASC 516, 26 Mar. 1499, fol. 1r.
49. The clerics misused the holy oil to perpetrate "ignominiosas superstitiones et scelera." Sanudo, 2:1204–1208. Much of the same material was copied by Sanudo into his diary nineteen years later at the time of a new outbreak of witch-hunting: ibid., 26:34–37.
50. Ibid., 26:34, and 2:1207–1208.
51. Chapter 8 here. For the texts, see Bowd, *Vainglorious Death*.
52. An allusion to Acts 4:34–37.
53. [Capriolo?], *Defensio*, sig. Avr. Translated by J. Donald Cullington.
54. "Pro quadam muliere dicta mora ex mallefitio incarcerata captum fuit nemine discentiete quod debeat relaxari de carcere expensis communis nostri et expellatur e civitate et agro brixiano ex quo bannita fuit propter mallefitium." ASC 522, 14 Dec. 1510, fol. 173v.
55. ASV, consiglio dei dieci, misto, reg. 44, fols. 63r–64r, 69r, 85r–v (pencil foliation); Santo ufficio, processi, b. 160; ASC 1552, fols. 1v–2r; Sanudo, 25:537–538, 541, 545–548, 572–575, 585, 586–588, 602–608, 609–610, 632–650; 26:23, 29–32, 32–37, 55–56, 95, 396, 411–412, 436; 28:144, 273, 287; 29:65, 211, 465, 506–507, 544; 30:13, 15, 44, 103; 31:353. For English translations of some of this material, with a commentary, see Sanudo, *Venice*, 402–412. The relevant material in ASV, Consiglio dei dieci, misto, reg. 42 and 43 was unavailable to me for consultation, but is discussed in Del Col, "Organizzazione, composizione e giurisdizione," 250–259.

56. Sanudo, 25:187–190. A detailed analysis of this phenomenon is in Niccoli, "Re dei morti," and eadem, *Prophecy and People,* chap. 3.
57. Sanudo, 27:591.
58. "Et per questo non posamo pensar altramente che el sia una mala setta in questa valle diabolica . . . 'fina che non lassano star le strie et strioni non sarà mai di altro.'" Ibid., 29:173–176.
59. Sier Carlo Miani, castellan of Breno, to Sier Marin Zorzi, 24 Jun. 1518, in 25:545–548.
60. Tamburini, "Suppliche per i casi di stregoneria," 639–643.
61. "[E] cognosso veramente che vado corporalemente et che non me insonio [*sic*]." Sanudo, 25:632–650. This material is printed in "Processi di streghe."
62. Giuseppe "da Orzinuovi" to Lodovico Querini, 1 Aug. 1518, Sanudo, 25:602–608. The courier is mentioned, along with the chancellor "missier Pasino," in a letter written by an eyewitness to the interrogations and burnings: Dr Alessandro Pompeio to Giovanni Giustiniani, Brescia, 28 July 1518, ibid., 574–575.
63. Ibid., 575.
64. Ibid., 548. This doctor of laws naturally turned to the *Decretum* (compiled by Gratian ca. 1140), *causa* 26, *quaestio* 5 for the text of the Canon *Episcopi,* which condemned as illusory the belief that one could ride out at night with the goddess Diana; to the canon law collection of Dionysius Exiguus (ca. 500); to the commentary of St Thomas Aquinas to Book IV, distinction 34 of Peter Lombard's *Sentences* where he noted that many did not think demons existed outside the imagination of ignorant, uneducated people; and to an unspecified passage of Augustine (probably *De civitate Dei* 7.21) where he asserted that God did not permit to demons any supernatural power.
65. Sanudo, 25:588.
66. Ibid., 26:55–56. The priest's case is also mentioned at ibid., 29–32.
67. Quoted in Tavuzzi, *Renaissance Inquisitors,* 194–195.
68. ASC 527, 21 Oct. 1519, fol. 117r–v.
69. Sanudo, 30:13. Tron's opposition is reported in ibid., 26:411; 29:211, 465, 506–507.
70. ASV, Consiglio di dieci, misto, registro 44, fol. 8r (pencil foliation).
71. Del Col, "Organizzazione, composizione e giurisdizione," 258–259.
72. Odorici, *Streghe di Valtellina,* 91–116; Girolamo Aleandro cited by Martin, *Witchcraft and the Inquisition,* 15.
73. Gaeta, *Nunziature di Venezia,* 1:77, 97, 141, 155, 221. On Querini's absence from Venice in 1533 and his differences with the government see Sanudo, 57:289, 302, 353; 58: 171, 387, 677.
74. Indeed, the title of Bernardino of Siena's fifteenth-century treatise on witchcraft and superstition is *De idolatriae cultu.* See Mormando, *Preacher's Demons,* 82.
75. Bowd, *Vainglorious Death,* 29, 53, 71.
76. Martin, *Witchcraft and the Inquisition,* esp. chap. 5.
77. Ibid., 207–213.
78. Sanudo, 41:196.

11. Disloyal Brescia

1. Abulafia, *French Descent.*
2. Gilbert, "Venice in the Crisis."
3. Arcangeli, "Appunti su guelfi e ghibellini."
4. For Machiavelli's views in this respect see Cervelli, *Machiavelli e la crisi dello stato.* On the fiscal regime in Padua and its contribution to the Paduan revolt in 1509 see Knapton, "Rapporti fiscali tra Venezia e la terraferma." On Verona see Varanini, "Terraferma al tempo della crisi." On the loyalty of Treviso see Del Torre, *Trevigiano nei secoli XV e XVI.*
5. Massimo, *Benedicti Maximi civis Brixiani.*
6. Suriano, *Relazione* (1525), 6–7.
7. "Et quella cossa di mortuarii far uno statuto contra la libertà eccclesiasticha [*sic*], e tuor el viver a li poveri religiosi; e perchè li frati di San Domenico li diceva non potevano far et erano scomunicati, i volse cazarli de la terra." Sanudo, 15:300.
8. Ibid., 7:282.
9. What follows is indebted to Pasero, *Francia, Spagna, Impero;* and Frati et al., *Sacco di Brescia.*
10. Sanudo, 7:690, 742.
11. "El nostro capitanio, conte di Pitigliano, non val o, è vechio e non à cuor, tutti crida, *tamen* si convien haver pacientia." Ibid., 8:548.
12. Ibid., 134, 227, 233, 247–249, 249–250, 256 (quotation).
13. Ibid., 260, 264, 265–266, 289–290, 294–295.
14. Pasero, *Francia, Spagna, Impero,* 19, 32, 38.
15. Ibid., 48, 266–267.
16. Sanudo, 8:393. However, it has been suggested that the transfer of episcopal feudal territories to Vittore Martinengo in Nov. 1509 may have been attempt to save them from French appropriation: Pasero, *Francia, Spagna, Impero,* 85.
17. ASC 522, 18, 22 Sept. 1509, fols. 32v–38r; Pasero, *Francia, Spagna, Impero,* 103; Zanelli, *Delle condizioni interne di Brescia,* 34–38.
18. A delegation to Venice on this matter was led by the doctor and knight Giovanni Franceso de Milis, provoking outrage in the Brescian council: ASC 513, 22 May 1492, fol. 136r. Three citizens were also elected subsequently to look into the actions of "nonnullos malos cives" who continually detracted from the dignity and honor of the city and infringed its privileges and statutes, especially in the matter of Orzinuovi: ASC 513, 27 July 1492, fol. 150r.
19. Pasero, *Francia, Spagna, Impero,* 111–116, 159.
20. ASC 1528, fols. 151r–155v.
21. On attacks on Jews as a form of ritual pillaging of property in a rite of passage see Bologna Seminar, coordinated by Carlo Ginzburg, "Ritual Pillages," 28.
22. Sanudo, 8:300, 302, 305; "Cronaca di anonimo autore," 141; Capriolo, *Chronicorum de rebus Brixianorum,* cols. 139, 142.
23. Sanudo, 8:300, 302, 305.
24. See ASC 1528, fols. 151r–155v, and the roughly contemporary copy of the *capitula* in ASB, Archivio Gambara, b. 218.

25. ASC 522, 27 July 1509, 26 Sept. 1510, fols. 18v, 153v; ASC 1528, fols. 156v–157r, edict of Louis XII dated 16 July 1509; ibid., fol. 180v, decree proclaimed on 5 Oct. 1510 calling on citizens who borrowed money from Jews before they were sacked "al tempo de la mutatione dil stado de brixia" must inform the chancellor of Brescia of the pledges they gave and the money they received in return; ibid., fols. 192r, 194r–v, edicts of Louis XII dated 13 Mar., 5 Apr. 1511, in favor of the Jews. In 1514 Jews were found to be living in Brescia against the ordinances and provisions of the city, and it was proposed that they be expelled: ASC 524, 11 July 1514, fol. 117v.

26. "*Tamen* ahora senza bota di spada et senza colpo de alteraria et senza morte de hommo in uno momento senza rispecto se havea rebellato ali sui tantto gratissimi Signori." Priuli, *Diarii,* 4:46.

27. "Fo ben alcuni per ignorantia, altri per fragilità pecorno; li terzi pecorno per propria malitia." Sanudo, 15:292.

28. In 1504 the Venetian heads of the Council of Ten asserted that Brescia, above all other cities of the Venetian *terraferma,* "è meglio fornita" with grain: ASV, Capi del consiglio dei dieci, lettere, filza 4bis, pezzo no. 449. The *capitano* of Brescia in 1506 reported that the city was "richissima terra et fidelissima, *maxime* il populo": Sanudo, 6:508.

29. Mallett and Hale, *Military Organisation of a Renaissance State,* 410.

30. Pasero, *Francia, Spagna, Impero,* 87.

31. Capriolo, *Chronicorum de rebus Brixianorum,* col. 140.

32. Sanudo, 8:302–303, 305.

33. "[E]ssendo poi la città di Brescia male trattata et universalmente malcontenta per le insolentie, strussioni et violentie, che continuamente facevano li soldati de' Francesi sì nella città come nello territorio," Martinengo di Erbusco, "Della congiura de' Bresciani," 68, 72; Casari, "De exterminio Brixianae," 38.

34. On this case and examples of the defacement or removal of other Venetian winged lions see Rizzi, "Leontoclastia cambraica."

35. "Va di bona voja San Marco, che tu sarà signor di Milan." Sanudo, 8:316, 416 (quotation). Sanudo recorded a report of a similar incident in Bergamo: ibid., 448.

36. Ibid., 416, 338; 9:9–10, 327, 416; 10:28, 187, 291. During 1510–19 over 130 families entered the General Council, as compared with forty-one during 1499–1509 and twenty-two during 1487–98: Romani, "Prestigio, potere," 118, tabella II.

37. Pasero, *Francia, Spagna, Impero,* 97–100.

38. ASC 522, 27 Dec. 1509, 17–18 Sept. 1510, fols. 60v–61r, 149r, 150r; ASC 523, 4 July 1511, fol. 78r.

39. A sense of popular unease may lie behind the unusual proclamation of 3 Apr. 1511: "Per consolation del populo domenicha proxima che vene da po desinare sotta la loza grande se cavara le duodecime novamente imborsate, et ogniun prega che la ge venga bona." ASC 1093, fol. 4r.

40. Pasero, *Francia, Spagna, Impero,* 108–109.

41. Sanudo, 11:185–186.

42. Bartolomeo Palazzo, "Diario," 269.

43. Sanudo, 11:340–341; 12:377.
44. Ibid., 13:413, 416.
45. Ibid., 437, 488, 491.
46. Ibid., 442–444.
47. The Senate voted 136 in favor of and 48 against the exchange of a French captive for Gritti. However, this outcome may not be related to Gritti's unpopularity, as a similar vote is recorded in another case on the same day: ASV, Senato terra, deliberazioni, reg. 18, fols. 18v, 19r (pencil foliation, 30 Mar. 1512).
48. "[N]el qual tempo per suo mal governo fo sachezata, per non havere provisto a quello fazeva busogno per la venuta deli inimici che herano franciosi, che certo se havesse fatto parte del debito una cum quelli dela cita de Bressa, al mio parer le cose non se saria intervenuti come interveneno." BQB, C.I.15, fol. 263r (pencil foliation).
49. Muir, *Ritual in Early Modern Europe,* 107. On violence and carnival see Le Roy Ladurie, *Carnival.*
50. Compare the Udine carnival massacre of 1511: Muir, *Mad Blood Stirring.*
51. Sanudo 13:491, 494–495, 496, 497–498
52. Bembo, *Historiae Venetae,* fols. 193v–197r.
53. Sanudo 13:508, 509, 514–518, 519, 513, 522, 523, 528.
54. "Cosí per le mani de' franzesi, da' quali si gloriavano i bresciani essere discesi, cadde in tanto sterminio quella città, non inferiore di nobiltá e di degnitá ad alcuna altra di Lombardia, ma di ricchezze, eccettuato Milano, superiore a tutte l'altre." Guicciardini, *Storia d'Italia,* 3:170.
55. Zemon Davis, "Rites of Violence." Compare accounts of the sack of Rome in 1527: Sanudo, 45:167–168, 435–437; Sanudo, *Venice,* 182–186.
56. Sanudo, 15:287–303.
57. "[U]rtate sti poltroni come valenti homeni che seti e amazateli come cani." Ibid., 288 (emphasis in the original).
58. "Come ha terminato scriver stando in caxa, in aspectation de le cosse che spera, sentendo assa' bone nove dil felicissimo campo di la sacro sancta Liga, qual prospera fugando questi perfidi barbari francesi nimici de Dio e de la humana generation, sitibondi del sangue humano, gente senza leze e senza fede, gente da non esser reputada nel numero de' cristiani." Ibid., 287–288.
59. Ibid., 280–282. See also Pasero, *Francia, Spagna, Impero,* 239–240. It was later agreed to construct an "archivio": ASC 527, 10 Nov. 1517, fol. 53r.
60. Pandolfo Nassini later claimed that Cristoforo de Guainari had suffered an arson attack during the sack of 1512 and "fu detto che furono hebrei che lo bruseno." Nassini quoted in Lechi, *Dimore bresciane,* 4:440.
61. "In questo tempo, era fuzito Zuan Hironimo suo nepote nel Duomo, dove crudelmente fu morto con zercha 60 altri, fra li quali fu alcuni preti, perchè quelli barbari non perdonavano a niuno, e fra questa perfida generationi era zudei sitibondi del sangue cristiano, dice lui." Sanudo, 15:288.
62. Ibid., 289–290, 298.
63. "Non si trova galine ne li nostri monasteri: li più di loro sono mendicanti e viveno di elemosina, e *tamen* convengono far le spexe a questi poltroni; e il

Roy si fa chiamar Christianissimo e comporta questo; ma è avarissimo, crudelissimo e injustissimo fautor di ladri e ribaldi e di zudei." Ibid., 293.

64. "Lì in Brexa al presente è vasconi e scozesi. El governador monsignor di Obignì è scocexe, è barbaro senza leze e senza boni costumi, cussì è tutti scozesi." Ibid., 296.

65. "Dice bisogneria un mexe di tempo a scriver, e maxime madama Alda ha facto più guera a la Signoria che si havesse auto contra 1000 cavalli; mai non feva altro che scriver e far pratiche, etc." Ibid., 15:292. See also ibid., 14:9, 288.

66. Ibid., 5:511, 599–600, 631. Negro was also subject to an investigation in 1477 when discrepancies were discovered in his records of the munitions in the city: ASV, Capi del consiglio dei dieci, lettere di rettori, b. 19, pezzi a–d.

67. Sanudo, 15:291; ASC 519, 12 Dec. 1503, fol. 78r.

68. "Li rincresse dil danno di la Signoria e da alcuni boni servidori, ben pochi. Ma al presente adorano essa Signoria e chiamanla grandi e picoli dì e note che la venga a socorere la povera Brexa desolata e desfata, che non ha più faza de citade, et era in tanta altura e morbedeza che come mosche che se aniega nel lacte e nel miel cussì se hanno anegato nel bon tempo." Sanudo, 15:291.

69. *Defunctis patribus, surrexit prava juventus.*" Ibid. (emphasis in the original).

70. Casari, "De exterminio Brixianae," 45.

71. The comparison with Troy was made in Sanudo, 13:511. Negro compares the sack to that of Rome by the Goths: quoted in ibid., 15:298.

72. Casari, "De exterminio Brixianae," 43. A document in the cathedral archive outlines the losses suffered there during the sack: Putelli, "[Documenti sul sacco di Brescia]," 283–284.

73. Casari, "De exterminio Brixianae," 46, 49, 50.

74. Begni Redona, *Alessandro Bonvicino Il Moretto,* 252–256; Neher, "Moretto and Romanino," 75–77.

75. Rosand, *Myths of Venice.*

76. "[U]rbs [i.e. Brescia] imperterrita pectus'/'defendit clypeo propria quem Mulciber illi'/'materia in tales resonis fornacibus usus'/'fecerat, insistit contra prima agmina taelo'/'infestans," Aruscone, "Battaglia di Brescia," 439.

77. "Patria alta cadit cum sanguine multo'/'innumeras fundens animas deiectaque passim'/'nobilitas cum plebe perit," Ibid., 440.

78. About a dozen of these are reprinted in Frati et al., *Sacco di Brescia,* 1/2: 370–445.

79. "Si ritrovorno stesi per el paese'/'Cinquanta millia era il numer tale'/'Tra Francesi e Todeschi e anchor zudei'/'Che soprazonse il zorno e farisei." *Libro o vero cronicha,* canto 9, sig. [Giiiir].

80. "[N]on fu terra in simil stato mai:'/'li corpi son per le strade e sentieri,'/'sol si crida sacco, ferro e moia:'/'immaginar to poi l'anticha Troia." "Rotta e presa fatta a Bresa," 394.

81. "Historia delle guerre," 402. Survivors of the fall of Negroponte and prisoners of the Turks and their families were supported by the Brescian council: ASC 504, 22 Feb. 1470 [m.v. 1471], 12 July 1471, 7 Apr. 1473, fols. 41v, 81r, 5r; ASC 505, 21 July 1475, 21 June 1476, fols. 125v, 39r; and possibly ASC 506,

1 May 1478, fol. 62v, and ASC 507, 14 Dec. 1481, fol. 125r. See Meserve, "News from Negroponte."

82. "[A]qua boglicta dai balcon travasa'/'le donne bresane e saxi che gli avanza'/'a dosso a quei che cridan: 'Franza, Franza!'" "Rotta e presa fatta a Bresa," 394. See also the eyewitness account in Coccinius, *De bellis italicis*, 215.

83. *Vera nova de Bressa*; "Lassamo costor e dicemo un poco'/'Che in cittadella comincio a cridare'/'Franza, Franza perchera in quel loco'/'Francesi ascosti shebbeno a trovare." *Libro o vero cronicha*, canto 9, sig. [Giiiiv].

84. "Quanto si dolse de la patria el Grito'/'che ha tante gente perse, e le megliore:'/'Quando—diceva—da te mi fui partito,'/'Venetia, promettisti a tutte l'hore'/'de artelaria e gente haver fornito:'/'contra mia voia cadeste in questo errore;'/'pur se le promise havesse atese'/'son certo seria stato ale defese." "Rotta e presa fatta a Bresa," 395.

85. "Nemico al ciel et a natura anchora'/'el primo fondator che dette initio'/'a te, Venetia; quanto meglio alhora'/'nel mar s'havesse dato a precipitio,'/'poi che fundata fusti a la mal hora'/'et protendevi al scieme humano exitio,'/'como s'è visto già nel tempo vecchio;'/'et ora Bresa a tuto il mondo è specchio." Ibid., 391. Also note the verse dated 26 Jan. 1516 inscribed in a copy of Capriolo's chronicle: "Divitiis concors si BRIXIA creverat olim,'/'Et populo, & donis fortunae erat omnibus aucta.'/'Nil mirum, si nunc, quia discors lapsa, flagellum'/'Sentit, & *Italiae* reliquis haec urbibus una'/'Fit speculum, quales pariat discordia fructus." Quoted in Capriolo, *Chronicorum de rebus Brixianorum*, unpaginated (following index).

86. "Lamento che fa el principo di Venetia 1509," 366; "Historia nova della ruina de Venetiani."

87. "Vui vedeti come Bressa'/'e Bologna con Ravenna'/'han patito tanta pena,'/'par ch'el ciel molto ne langue;'/'vostre terre e vostro sangue'/'è stà sparso in ogni loco,'/'vostre case a fiamma e foco'/'tanti straci e tanti affani,'/'su valenti Taliani." "Berzelleta in laude de tutta l'Italia," 373.

88. Niccoli, *Prophecy and People*, 28, 46–47. See also Minnich, "Prophecy and the Fifth Lateran Council."

89. "Di bressa pur vedendo il tristo auguria'/'el sangue sparto cum mortal tormento'/'la penna tolsi inmman cum molta furia,'/'cum carte e inchiostro comenzai dar dentro,'/'recognoscando la celeste curia'/'esser sdegnata di tal falimento,'/'e tienti certa che cum voce netta'/'quel sangue iusto a Dio chiama vendetta." "Historia nova della ruina de Venetiani," 370–371.

90. Sanudo, 11:264.

91. Capriolo, *Chronicorum de rebus Brixianorum*, col. 142.

92. Sanudo, 12:614.

93. Martinengo di Villachiara, *Segni e prodigi spaventosi apparsi in Lombardia*. This work and the ghostly battles is reports are analyzed in Niccoli, "Re dei morti," and eadem, *Prophecy and People*, chap. 3.

94. I owe this phrase to Richard Mackenney.

95. Sanudo, 12:614 (Sanudo added the comment "e non credo").

96. Ibid., 14:516–517. A weeping figure ("ymagine") of Christ crucified in the duomo became the focal point for miraculous cures in June 1501: "A Brexa, a

dì 11 zugno, achadete, che la ymagine dil Crucifixo del domo *emisit lacrimas e subsequenter* continua certi miracoli, *sanat claudos et aliis gravissimis morbis vexatos.*" Ibid., 4:65 (emphasis in the original). The appearance of an image of Christ in the duomo on 11 May 1500 noted in BQB, C.I.15, fol. 238v. See also Capriolo, *Chronica de rebus Brixianorum*, fols. LXXIIv–LXXIIIr.

97. BQB, C.I.15, fols. 67v–68r (pencil foliation).
98. Cistellini, *Figure della riforma pretridentina*, 160, 166.
99. Pasero, *Francia, Spagna, Impero*, 240.
100. On Giovanni Maria and his prints see Serafini, "Giovanni Maria da Brescia"; Hind, *Early Italian Engraving*, pt. 2, 5:55–58, nos. 1–4; 6: plates 567–571; Zucker, *Illustrated Bartsch*, 25:305–313, nos. 2510.001–2510.004; and idem, "Early Italian Engravings."
101. Kirshner, "Capriolo, Angelo."
102. For example, Capriolo, *Chronica de rebus Brixianorum*, fol. LXXIv [recte, LXXIIv].
103. Capriolo, *De confirmatione Christianae fidei.*
104. See Trumbower, *Rescue for the Dead*, chap. 8. On Foppa's image of the same subject see Lucchesi Ragni, "Vincenzo Foppa."
105. ASC 512, 29 Oct. 1490, fol. 184r. Chapter 5 here.
106. On the Carmelite invention of tradition see Jotischky, *Carmelites and Antiquity.*
107. Guerrini, "Umanisti bresciani minori," 94–95.
108. Bartolomeo Palazzo, "Diario," 266.
109. Pasero, *Francia, Spagna, Impero*, 258 n. 151; Giansante, "Capriolo, Elia," 218.
110. I owe this point to the detective work of Leofranc Holford-Strevens, who writes: "The inscription begins with the Greek for 'years' in the genitive plural, which is the correct formula for ages, not dates. Then follows what might have been taken for IV but for the breathings, which appear to indicate that they are Greek letters, used for numerals in the Mileto-Alexandrian system, iota for 10 and upsilon for 400; in the next line there are two chis, each 600, and another upsilon, making a total of 2010. This is odd, but so would interpretation as IV. XV. X be; for even if we pretended that the last two meant 1510, what would IV contribute? This does not seem to make much sense; much simpler are the last two lines, which are the Attic numerals for 254: two H (HEKATON in Attic spelling) for 200, a pi (pente) enclosing a delta (deka) for 50, and four verticals. We call these numerals Attic, because they remained in official use at Athens till 88 BC, though they were the older Greek system in general; they are also found as stichometrical notations in e.g. manuscripts of Demosthenes. Unlike the Mileto-Alexandian numerals, they are never used for ordinals; but that is probably a detail unknown to the contemporaries of Bro. Giovanni Maria, Carmelite of Brescia, though it would match the initial etwn. If we add all the figures together, we arrive at a total of 2264, which would be the year from the foundation of Rome down to 20 April," e-mail to the author, 5 May 2008.

111. Jotischky, *Carmelites and Antiquity,* 203–205, 298.
112. Arthur Hind noted that this image is a copy, in reverse, after Mantegna's engraving of the Virgin and Child: Hind, *Early Italian Engraving,* 5:58, no. 3; 10, no. 1, in ibid., 6: plate 486. See also Lightbown, *Mantegna,* 489–490, no. 207.
113. Meiss, *Painting in Florence and Siena,* chap. 6.
114. The impact of the events of 1512 on the poetry of Veronica Gambara, who addressed several sonnets to the Virgin and may have been an eyewitness to the sack, is considered in Dionisotti, "Elia Capriolo e Veronica Gàmbara."

12. Venice and the Recovery of Power

1. See the supplication of his brother to the Council of Ten in June 1517: ASV, Consiglio dei dieci, parti miste, filza 39, no. 201.
2. Sanudo, 14:472, 488, 573.
3. Pasero, *Francia, Spagna, Impero,* 318. See also ibid., 331–332.
4. ASC 525, 20 Jan. 1515, fol. 19r.
5. Sanudo, 15:319, 341; 16: 65
6. Ibid., 16: 159, 379.
7. ASC 524, 3 Apr., 7 June 1514, fols. 105r, 110r.
8. ASC 524, 5 Apr. 1513, fol. 48v.
9. ASC 524, 23 Feb., 15, 18 Apr., 7, 16 Aug., 30 Sept., 18 Oct., 8 Nov. 1513, 16 June, 31 July 1514, fols. 34v, 53v, 55r, 77v, 79r, 85r, 86v, 89v, 114r, 120r–v; ASC 525, 26 Jan. 1515, fol. 22r. On the need for all corporations to meet to give the usual offering on the altar of San Bernardino in the church of San Francesco for the protection of the city, see ASC 1093, fol. 10r.
10. ASC 524, 7 Sept., 6 Oct. 1514, fols. 126r, 127v; ASC 525, 23 May, 27 July 1515, fols. 59r, 89r.
11. ASC 524, 5 Jan. 1513, 10 Apr., 10, 16 June 1514, fols. 15v, 108r, 113r, 114v; ASC 525, 16 Mar. 1515, fol. 31r; ASC 526, 12 Aug. 1516, fol. 19r.
12. Sanudo, 21:439 ("in Brexa è carestia grande di ogni cossa"), 497; 22:30, 99.
13. ASV, Senato secreta, deliberazioni, reg. 47, fols. 25v–26v.
14. Sanudo, 22:241, 245.
15. "[C]he mai fu el più bel veder: alcune composte el viso, alcune destropade, a le qual fo dato, per quelli dil campo nostro e di francesi, grandissimi stridori." Ibid., 249.
16. ASC 526, 4 Sept. 1516, fol. 24r.
17. "[S]ub felicissima exoptatisimaque umbra ac Justissimo principatu Illustrisima." ASC 526, 15, 16 May 1517, fols. 108r–v, 109v–110r.
18. Trevisan to heads of Ten, Brescia, 12 June 1516, in ASV, Capi del consiglio dei dieci, lettere di rettori, b. 19, no. 69.
19. Trevisan to heads of Ten, Brescia, 20 June 1516 "hora 4 noctis," in ASV, Capi del consiglio dei dieci, lettere di rettori, b. 19, no. 71.
20. Trevisan to heads of Ten, Brescia, 29 Sept. 1516, in ASV, Capi del consiglio dei dieci, lettere di rettori, b. 19, no. 73.
21. The council's feelings in these matters are noted in Trevisan's letters of 29 Sept.

and 11 Nov. 1516, in ASV, Capi del consiglio dei dieci, lettere di rettori, b. 19, nos. 73, 75.

22. Sanudo, 23:303–304, 316–317, 575. This was the largest amount demanded of any of the *terraferma* cities.

23. Ibid., 575.

24. ASV, Senato terra, deliberazioni, reg. 20, fols. 42v–46r (petitions), fols. 46r–49r (responses) (pencil foliation, 27 Apr. 1517, with a note that "Que fuerunt expedicta in Mense Junij").

25. "[M]axime potestaria Salodij & Asulae." ASV, Senato terra, deliberazioni, reg. 20, fol. 42v.

26. See ASV, Senato terra, deliberazioni, reg. 20, fols. 49r–50r (petitions), fol. 50r–v (responses); Sanudo, 23:587; 24: 432. The *Territorio* was conceded a house in Venice: ibid., 24:334–335.

27. The petitions of the Val Camonica, Val Trompia, and Val Sabbia are in ASV, Senato terra, deliberazioni, reg. 20, fols. 55v–56r, 56v–57r (pencil foliation, 17, 30 June 1517). For Salò see ASV, Senato secreta, deliberazioni, reg. 47, fols. 107v–110v (pencil foliation). The Venetians agreed to the request to bar Jews lending money in the Riviera and, like Brescia and the *Territorio*, conceded a house in the city. For a discussion of relations between Venice and the Brescian Riviera del Garda during the later sixteenth century see Scotti, "'Magnifica patria.'"

28. Sanudo, 24:190–192.

29. ASV, Senato terra, deliberazioni, reg. 20, fol. 46v.

30. ASV, Senato terra, deliberazioni, reg. 20, fol. 47r.

31. Sanudo, 24:334–335; BQB, H.IV.5, fols. 72v–73r.

32. "[N]on toleseno li diti capitoli, dicendo la so' fedeltà non lo meritava, e quello haveano patito dil sacho fato." Sanudo, 24:191, 210–211, 212–213, 217–218, 334–335.

33. ASC 526, 20 May 1517, fol. 105r.

34. Sanudo, 27:432–433, 507, 544; 28:567, 587, 591, 592, 641, 661; 30:56–57.

35. Mistura, "Privilegi più speciali," 402.

36. "[M]olte difficulta promosse da questi citadini con infinite altercatione per le faction diverse et rabiose discordie qual sono tra loro . . . con la gratia del signor Dio havemo talmente quietati li animi de questi citadini." Marco Foscari and Lorenzo Ariani to heads of Ten, Brescia, 24 May 1517, in ASV, Capi del consiglio dei dieci, lettere di rettori, b. 19, no. 83.

37. I have consulted Massimo, *Benedicti Maximi civis Brixiani*, and the abridged Italian translation: idem, "De concordia Brixianorum."

38. Massimo, "De concordia Brixianorum," 700.

39. Ventura, *Nobiltà e popolo*, 269–273.

40. "[N]ihil dubito quin toto animo ac studio in eam rationem incumbatis ut senatus seu consilium Brixiae civitatis, quod in paucos divites et fere omnes affinitatibus et cognationibus atque necessitudinibus inter se coniunctos, qui soli honoribus et utilitatibus publicis fruuntur, restrictum est, maiore numero civium amplificetur ut utilitas reipublicae sit communior et latius in cives pateat," Massimo, "De concordia Brixianorum," 698.

41. "Non dico si quis sit rusticitatem generis adhuc olens: iumentario patre natus etsi inflato collo et adipe tumenti ventre et ebriosa facie per urbem forumque incedat ac si forenses aliquas litteras habeat quibus ad suscitandas lites manifeste iniustas et iustas in longum protrahendas perturbandamque omnino iustitiam quaestus gratia, cuius est avidissimus, utatur, talem hominem non modo non esse in senatum ascribendum, sed in ultimas terras exterminandum esse censeo," Ibid., 700–701.

42. BQB, C.I.15, fol. 311. However, given Nassini's lineage it is highly unlikely he was sympathetic to Massimo's cause, and this may be a characteristic piece of malicious gossip.

43. Lanaro Sartori, *Oligarchia urbana nel Cinquecento veneto*, 43–52.

44. Ventura, *Nobiltà e popolo*, 271. The suggestion that a conciliar decision of 1518 marked the widening of access to the councils is made by Zanelli, *Condizioni interne di Brescia*, 40, 41–42. This supposition has been corrected by Ventura, *Nobiltà e popolo*, 273 n. 199.

45. On the rate of admission of new citizens to the council see Romani, "Prestigio, potere," 118, tabella II. Bernardo Malvezzi proposed to exclude those involved in manual work, or whose fathers were involved in manual work, from admission to the council: ASC 531, 2 Jan. 1528, fol. 116r.

46. "Intellecto quod Benedictus de Maximis instinctu ut creditur quorumdam malorum et seditiosorum civium iam multo tempore ausu quodam temerario et perniciosissimo tentat et querit subvertere ordinem antiqui et optimi regiminis, dati per Illustrissimam dominum nostrum, et ponere ac facere novum, et perniciosum modum regiminis in civitate nostram contra antiquissimam consuetudinem contra formam privilegiorum statutorum provisionum et ordinum presente civitatis nostrae et contra ipsius quietum, et pacificum statum ac tranquillum vivere, cui inconvenienti pessimo, et perniciosissimi exempli cum omnino obviandum sit, et omnis studio providendum pro honore, et bono civitatis nostrae quod antiquum regimen datum per Illustrissimum dominum nostrum consernetur, tum esset ut consulatur quieto, et pacifico statui civitatis nostrae, et omnes seditionem causae succidantur," ASC 526, 5, 6 June 1517, fols. 122r, 122v–123r.

47. ASC 526, 18 June 1517, fols. 129v–130r.

48. "[U]n modesto lanaiolo rovinato dalla guerra." Ventura, *Nobiltà e popolo*, 263–265. Daniele Montanari has also detected "la fertile mano" of Valgulio behind Massimo's pamphlet: Montanari, *Quelle terre di là dal Mincio*, 46, 84 (mistakenly identified as "Cesare Valgulio").

49. "[U]n vero manifesto del partito antiaristocratico": Ventura, *Nobiltà e popolo*, 267. On Valgulio's murder see Bartolomeo Palazzo, "Diario," 301. The Brescian *podestà*'s report of Valgulio's murder was noted in Venice on 21 Feb. 1517: Sanudo, 23:596. The senatorial instruction to the *podestà* to send the perpetrator into exile was agreed by 160 votes to 4 (1 abstention) in ASV, Senato terra, deliberazioni, reg. 19, fol. 158r–v (pencil foliation, 21 Feb. 1516 [m.v. 1517]). The Brescian council's decision to ask the rectors to petition Venice for aid in bringing justice to those who attacked Brescian citizens is in ASC

526, 7 Apr. 1517, fol. 96r–v. See also Pasero, "Dominio veneto," 308–309; and Valentini, *Carlo Valgulio,* 14–15.

50. Del Torre, *Venezia e la terraferma,* 21 n. 14, 24.

51. Ibid., 28.

52. ASV, Senato terra, deliberazioni, reg. 20, fol. 50v.

53. Romani, "Prestigio, potere," 118, tabella II.

54. Del Torre, *Venezia e la terraferma,* 29.

55. Sanudo, 23:169–170; 24:75. The *spianata* and the compensation offered to the displaced religious is outlined in instructions to Andrea Trevisan in ASV, Senato terra, deliberazioni, reg. 19, fol. 108r (pencil foliation, 18 July 1516).

56. Sanudo, 15:117 (skirmishes at San Fiorano); 22:14 (troops at San Rocco), 366, 368.

57. Ibid., 24:701–702; 25:11, 88.

58. "Per fortifichar la terra nostra, ne domandate mo' licentia al Papa? havemo fato butar zoso chiesie a Padoa, Treviso e Brexa, non si dimandò licentia al Papa." Ibid., 29:298. Chapter 10 here.

59. See Frati, Gianfranceschi, and Robecchi, *Loggia di Brescia,* 2:145–149.

60. ASC 528, 28 Mar. 1520, 27 Apr. 1521, fols. 46r–v, 48v–49r (tax plan approved eighty-one votes to three), fol. 12r.

61. For example, see the accounts for this period in ASB, Fondo di religione, San Giuseppe, b. 109.

62. On the expansion of San Giuseppe see ASB, Fondo di religione, San Giuseppe, b. 109, and ASC 528, 16 Mar., 6 May 1521, fols. 159r–v, 14v. See also Frati, "Osservanti a Brescia," 438.

63. Bayer, "Brescia after the League of Cambrai," chap. 4 (quotation at 224).

64. Guerrini, "Santuario delle Grazie." On the new realism and religiosity in Brescian painting see Guazzoni, *Moretto.*

65. Mazzonis, "Female Idea of Religious Perfection"; and idem, *Spirituality, Gender, and the Self,* esp. 80–86, 146–153.

66. ASC 528, 15 Mar., 27 Apr. 1521, fols. 158r–v, 11v–12r. Cistellini, *Figure della riforma pretridentina,* 69–103, 230–240. The rules of the Oratory of Divine Love are printed in ibid., 277–282.

67. ASC 523, 4 July 1511, fols. 77v–78r; ASC 524, 3 Apr. 1514, fol. 105v. The usual offerings were made again that year on the feast of the Assumption: ASC 524, 29 July 1514, fol. 120r.

68. ASC 524, 7 Aug. 1513, fol. 77v. Four years later it was agreed to place an image ("imago") or statue of San Rocco and a "capsa pro recipiendis elemosinis pro fabrica dicti Sancti Rochi" in the church of San Giuseppe, and to pay 12 ducats per annum to the "Guardiano" of the church to say a daily mass for San Rocco because the church and monastery of San Rocco outside the gate of San Giovanni had been destroyed by Venetian forces: ASC 526, 1 Apr. 1517, fol. 94r.

69. ASC 524, 14 Mar., 3 Apr. 1514, fols. 104r, 105r.

70. ASC 522, 30 Mar., 27 Apr., 14 May 1509, fols. 55v, 64v–65r, 73r.

71. ASC 522, 26 July 1509, fol. 18r; ASC 526, 9 Apr. 1517, fols. 97v–98r.

72. ASC 526, 17 Apr. 1517, fol. 98v.
73. ASC 527, 30 Nov. 1519, fol. 142r–v; ASC 528, 6, 20 Mar. 1520, 8, 15 Mar. 1521, fols. 30v–31r, 41v–42r, 155r, 158v.
74. ASC 528, 3 Mar. 1520, fol. 29v. Bishop Mattia Ugoni sought 100 *lire planete* from the *fabrice* of the duomo for these improvements and for a standard ("vexillum").
75. "Hec tibi mota facit soles crux mira serenos ac eadem largas Brixia mittit aquas." Begni Redona, *Alessandro Bonvicino il Moretto*, 116–121; Guazzoni, *Moretto*, 15, 26–27.
76. ASC 528, 27 Mar. 1520, 1 Mar. 1521, fols. 44v, 153v. The "Processus pro Crucibus Campi et Auri flammae" may date to this period: ASC 1528, fols. 279v–280r.
77. "L'iconografia civile dei santi Faustino e Giovita." Guazzoni, *Moretto*, chap. 2 (title).
78. Bayer, "Bergamo and Brescia," 310. See also Begni Redona, *Alessandro Bonvicino il Moretto*, 86–91; Guazzoni, *Moretto*, 15; Peroni, "Architettura e la scultura," 727.
79. Amore, "Faustino e Giovita"; Cannata, "Iconografia." Note Romanino's representation of the saints in sacerdotal guise in his painting of the communion of Sant' Apollonio in Santa Maria in Calchera, Brescia (ca. 1516–20): ibid., cols. 271–272 (plate).
80. *Leggenda de sancto Faustino e Jovita*; Ricci, *Passio sanctorum martyrum Faustini & Jovite Brixiensium*. Vincenzo Foppa's image of the saints for the "pala dei Mercanti" (ca. 1505–10, Brescia, Pinacoteca Tosio Martinengo) depicts them in ecclesiastical dress.
81. ASV, Senato terra, deliberazioni, reg. 16, fols. 130v–131r (pencil foliation, 29 June 1509).
82. Cistellini, *Figure della riforma pretridentina*, 58–67, 213–230, 241–243.
83. Giuliani, "Genesi e primo secolo di vita."
84. ASC 526, 9 Dec. 1516, fols. 51r–v.
85. The preamble runs: "Et si decet eos quibus rerum publicum cura tradita est solicitos et diligentes esse in omnibus spectantibus eorum offitio, maxime eos laborare et accuratos essere convenit in hijs quam laudem et gloriam omnipotentis dei, morum modestiam et vite honestatem concernunt, et ad obviandum ne scelera et peccata comittantur, et illa precipue propter que iusticia Dei ad flagelandos varijs calamitatibus mortales provocatur. Et cum inter omnia peccata propter quam ira Dei venit super peccatore perniciosissima sint religiosiarum personarum peccata, maxime si impunita remaneant," ASC 526, 2 July 1517, fols. 135v–136r; ASC 527, 23 Nov. 1519, fols. 134v–135r; ASC 528, 30 June 1520, fol. 80r–v; ASC 1079/B, no. 183, ducal letter dated 29 June 1519; Sanudo, 27:636.
86. ASC 528, 12 May 1520, fol. 65v. The proposal was narrowly rejected.
87. ASC 525, 27 Mar., 13, 27 Apr. 1515, fols. 33r–v, 39v, 49r; ASC 1093, fols. 11r–13r. Note the attack on games in the ca. 1502 *Barzelletta nuova*.
88. Frati, "Osservanti a Brescia," 438 n. 12, 441 n. 14. On prostitution in Brescia see Chapter 7 here.

89. ASC 526, 9 Dec. 1516, fol. 50v, 51v; ASC 1093, fols. 18v–20 (proclamation of 20 Dec. 1516). On the tax and processions employed to satisfy the debts of the *monte* and to restore it see ASC 526, 18 Mar. 1517, fols. 84v–85r; ASC 1093, fol. 28v (proclamation of 5 Apr. 1520). The proposal for investigatory citizens in each *quadra* was reiterated in ASC 528, 9 Apr. 1521, fol. 3r–v.

90. Sanudo, 24:361–362. Note also ibid., 25:63.

91. "Brexa è terra richissima, tutti vestono seda, e cussì le donne. La terra piena di botege, non par sia mai stà sacho." Ibid., 29:335. Here I follow the recent English version of the text, which is based on the original manuscript and corrects the figure of thirty thousand given for the city's population in the Italian edition of Sanudo's diaries: Sanudo, *Venice*, 103, 103 n. 138.

92. Sanudo, 46:612; idem, *Venice*, 327.

93. Pasero, "Dati statistici e notizie intorno al movimento della popolazione," 87.

94. Sanudo, 29:171–172, 194, 200, 259–260. For other murders or scores settled in the postwar period see ASV, Senato terra, deliberazioni, reg. 19, fols. 106r, 127r (pencil foliation, 3 July, 8 Oct. 1516); ASV, Senato terra, deliberazioni, reg. 19, reg. 20, fols. 26v–27r (pencil foliation, 14 May 1517).

95. "Certi boletini cum parolle scandalose et diffamatorie." ASC 1093, fol. 30r. See also ibid., fol. 133r–v. On the posting of defamatory notices and other signs of hostility toward the rectors after ca. 1520 see Montanari, *Quelle terre di là dal Mincio*, 46–48.

96. In 1524 Clement VII wrote to the nuncio in Venice condemning heresy in the Bresciano. A subsequent proclamation against the "rebelli de la religion Christiana et del divino culto" who were blaspheming against God, the Virgin, and the saints during the night is in ASC 1093, fols. 67v–68r (2 June 1527). Verses and notices attacking the cross of *orifiamma* were also in circulation in 1527 and again in 1542. In 1528 the council elected three citizens to punish and expel heretics, and a Carmelite preacher was expelled for heresy. See Cistellini, "Vita religiosa," 447–450; Caponetto, *Protestant Reformation*, 175–181.

97. Camillo "Contin" (little count) Martinengo, son of Count Vittore Martinengo da Barco, kidnapped the ten-year-old daughter of Girolamo Capriolo in Apr. 1518, for which crime he was banned from Veronese territory for five years: Sanudo, 25:368, 417, 420, 493, 495–496, 522; 27:509. On the case of the murderous Lupatino brothers in Dec. 1520 see 29:446. The entries relating to the former case have now been published, with commentary, in Sanudo, *Venice*, 132–135.

98. Sanudo, 27:530; ASV, Senato terra, deliberazioni, reg. 19, fol. 151r–v (pencil foliation, 30 Dec. 1516).

99. On the count of Lodrone and his strong-arm tactics in Bagolino in 1520 prompting Venetian intervention see Sanudo, 29:55–56, 67, 68, 137. On the confirmation and restitution to the heirs of Pietro Avogadro of income and possessions granted by Venice in recognition of his service and loyalty, with some limits placed on exemption from taxes to avoid "contentione," see ASV, Senato terra, deliberazioni, reg. 20, fols. 41v–42r (pencil foliation, 29 June 1517).

100. Sanudo, 31:128–129.
101. On the intensification of relations between Venetian magistracies and the *terraferma* after ca. 1520 see Viggiano, *Governanti e governati*, 285–290.
102. Rossini, *Campagne bresciane*, esp. chaps. 2–4.
103. The broader context is provided in Ginatempo, "Spunti comparativi sulle trasformazioni della fiscalità."
104. Zanelli, "Devozione di Brescia a Venezia," 66–77.
105. Zamperetti, *Piccoli principi*, 299–306.
106. For a summary account of these problems based on rectorial reports see Borelli, "Brescia tra recessione e decadenza."
107. Ferraro, *Family and Public Life in Brescia*, chap. 7; eadem, "Oligarchs, Protesters, and the Republic of Venice."

Conclusion

1. Note, for example, the oration by the printer Tommaso Ferrandus in praise of the Marquis of Mantua on the occasion of his marriage in 1490 that was published in Brescia. The influence of Mantuan style on Brescian decoration is suggested by Thomas, "Meeting of Two Worlds," 1:6–7, 36. This point deserves further study.
2. Knapton, "Territorio vicentino."
3. It may be significant that the records of the appeals considered by the *Quarantia civil nuova* between 1499 and 1505 reveal that 40 percent of cases emanated from nearby Padovano and Trevigiano, while two-thirds of letters sent to *auditori novi* during 1473–74 (when records exist) were expedited to the same places, and half of ducal letters sent out of Venice in relation to sentences of the *Cancelleria inferiore* went to these areas: Knapton, "Tribunali veneziani e proteste padovane," 155–156, 161.
4. Priuli, *Diarii*, 4:239.
5. A number of papers touched on this theme at a conference organized by Simon Oakes at St John's College, Oxford, in March 2008: "Venice and the League of Cambrai: Politics, Art, Architecture." For a flattering Venetian view of Bergamo in 1516 see Michiel, *Agri et urbis Bergomatis descriptio.* See also Davidson, "'As Much for Its Culture as for Its Arms.'"
6. Zen, *Relazione*, 38.
7. "[U]n linguaggio politico comune." Viggiano, *Governanti e governati*, 120.
8. As in the case of French and Spanish efforts to delineate a boundary in the Pyrenees explored by Sahlins, *Boundaries.*

Bibliography

Manuscript Sources

Archivio di Stato, Brescia

Archivio Gambara, b. 218, Miscellaneous material relating to Gambara family, ca. 1500–ca. 1700.

ASC 146 "Archivio civico. Inventario mazzi e documenti."

ASC 484–533 "Provvisioni del Consiglio Cittadino" (1426–1533).

ASC 538 "Provvisioni del Consiglio Cittadino" (1545–1546).

ASC 924 "Partitarie. Oblazioni e spese per S. Ma[ria] del Duomo anno 1473–1492."

ASC 1047 "Statuti del 1429."

ASC 1056 "Statuti dei paratici" (copies of fourteenth- and fifteenth-century guild statutes drafted in ca. 1520, with additions to ca. 1575).

ASC 1079/A "Ducali" (ducal letters nos. 1–100).

ASC 1079/B "Ducali" (ducal letters nos. 101–220).

ASC 1092 Proclamations of Venetian rectors and foreign governors, 1468–1511.

ASC 1093 Proclamations of Venetian rectors and foreign governors, 1511–1545.

ASC 1332 "Cittadinanze accordate: Indice alfabetico" (alphabetical index of grants of *civilitas*, 1421–1550).

ASC 1333 "Cittadini creati: Indice alfabetico" (alphabetical index of grants of *civilitas*, 1421–1633).

ASC 1334 "Cittadini creati: Indice alfabetico" (alphabetical index of grants of *civilitas*, 1421–1633).

ASC 1523/A (Copies of ducal letters, inventories, sentences, and other material, twelfth to sixteenth centuries).

ASC 1524 (Copies of privileges, concessions, statutes, and letters to and from rectors, ca. 1300–ca. 1560).

ASC 1525 (Register of diverse material, 1339–1499).

ASC 1528 (Register of diverse material, 1400–1520).

Cancelleria pretoria, atti, registri 15, 17, 18, 19, 20.
Fondo di religione, San Giuseppe, b. 109.
Ospedale, San Domenico, bb. 11, 12, 62, 89.

Biblioteca Queriniana, Brescia

C.I.3 Ottavio Rossi, "Annali di Brescia dall'anno 1030 al 1530."
C.I.7 Daniele Cereto (sixteenth-century copy of poems).
C.I.15 "Registro di molte cose seguite scritte da Do. Pandolfo Nassini nob. di Bressa," ca. 1520–44.
C.II.24 Elia Capriolo, "Chronica de Rebus Brixianorum," bk. 13, autograph (?) copy, ca. 1505.
E.I.7 "Serie e fatte dei 62 vescovi di Brescia estratti da Costanzo Maria Zinelli dal MSS autografe delle storie bresciane d'Ottavio Rossi." ca. 1780.
E.I.11 "Monasteri Bresciani."
H.IV.5 "Repertorium statutorum et Provisionum Collegj [of Judges]" (copy of ca. 1788).
H.V.5 "Codice di privilegi concessi alla città, alle famiglie e al territorio di Brescia," ca. 1472.
H.V.7 Inquisitorial report to archdeacon and episcopal vicar, 1480.
L.III.10 "Statuta Primae Quadrae Sancti Alexandri Civitatis Brixiae. Anno post soevissimam, ac memorabilem pestem Brixia. Cura Basilij Cirimbelli MDLXX-VII ac LXXVIIII. Tertio Massrij. Ne peririrent restarata [*sic*]." (1578)

Archivio del Duomo, Archivio Capitolare, Brescia

Parte 1, b. 7, "Varia ordinamenta pro Ecclesia Brixiae ac Constitutiones Sinodales pro Clero Brixiensi ab anno Domini MCCCCLXVI." (Missing from the archive in Nov. 2004).

Sacro Eremo Tuscolano, Frascati

Papers and correspondence of Tommaso Giustiniani and Vincenzo Querini, ca. 1500–1528:
Cod. F II A
Cod. F +

British Library, London

Additional MSS, 14,093 Ducal commission to Vettore Barbarigo as *podestà* for Brescia, 3 July 1535.

National Archives, London

PRO 30/25/104/1 Ducal commission to Bertucio Contarini as *podestà* for Brescia, 16 Sept. 1471.

Archivio di Stato, Mantua

Material relating to Brescian affairs ca. 1330–ca. 1730, including letters from Brescian rectors, members of the Martinengo clan, Bartolomeo Colleoni, the bishop, and other ecclesiastics:
Archivio Gonzaga, E.XLVIII.2, b. 1599.
Archivio Gonzaga, E.XLVIII.3, b. 1600.

Bodleian Library, Oxford MS. Canon. Class. Lat. 261 (Valerius Maximus. *Memorabilia*. Written out by Taddeo Solazio and dedicated to *podestà* Giovanni Moro and *capitano* Francesco Diedo in 1479) Accessed online at www.bodley.ox.ac.uk.

Parma, Biblioteca Palatina

MS Parmense 1583, fols. 55r–86v "Ubertini Pusculi Brixiensis Simonidos," ca. 1481.

Archivio di Stato, Venice

Capi del consiglio dei dieci, lettere, filze 4bis, 5.
Capi del consiglio dei dieci, lettere di rettori, b. 19 (Brescia, 1477–1533).
Capi del consiglio dei dieci, misto, registri 25, 42, 44.
Consiglio dei dieci, parti miste, filze 38–40.
Santo ufficio, processi, b. 160.
Senato secreta, deliberazioni, registro 47.
Senato terra, deliberazioni, registri 1–23 (microfilm).

Österreichische Nationalbibliothek, Vienna

Codex Vindobonensis Palatinus, new ser. 12,822 "Ubertini Pusculi Brixienesis Simonidos," ca. 1481 (microfilm).

Primary Printed Sources

The locations of copies of rare or unique editions of fifteenth- and sixteenth-century works consulted are given.

Aruscone, Ambrogio. "La battaglia di Brescia." In *Il sacco di Brescia: Testimonianze, cronache, diari, atti del processo e memorie storiche della "presa memoranda et crudele" della città nel 1512.* Ed. Vasco Frati, Ida Gianfranceschi, Françoise Bonali Fiquet, Irene Perini Bianchi, Franco Robecchi, and Rosa Zilioli Faden, vol. 1/pt. 2:437–444. Brescia: Grafo, 1990.

Barbaro, Francesco. *Epistolario.* Ed. Claudio Griggio. 2 vols. Florence: Olschki, 1991–99.

Barzelletta nuova qual tratta del gioco, del qual ne viene insuportabili vitii, a chi seguita ditto stile gionge a increpabili morte. N. p., n d. [Brescia? Bernardino Misinta? ca. 1502?] [Biblioteca Palatina, Parma, Inc. Parm. 893/4].

Becichemo, Marino. *Panegyricus Leonardo Lauretano. Centuria epistolicarum quaestionum.* N. p., n. d. [Brescia: Angelo Britannico, 1505?] [BL, G.9007].

Bembo, Pietro. *Historiae Venetae libri XII.* Venice: Apud Aldi filios, 1551.

Bernardino da Feltre. *Documenti vari intorno al b. Bernardino Tomitano da Feltre.* Ed. Vittorino Meneghin. Studi e testi francescani 35. Rome: Edizioni francescane, 1966.

———. *Sermoni del beato Bernardino Tomitano da Feltre nella redazione di fra Bernardino Bulgarino da Brescia minore osservante.* Ed. P. Carlo Varischi da Milano. 3 vols. Milan: Renon, 1964.

"Berzelleta in laude de tutta l'Italia 1512." In *Il sacco di Brescia: Testimonianze, cronache, diari, atti del processo e memorie storiche della "presa memoranda et crudele" della città nel 1512.* Ed. Vasco Frati, Ida Gianfranceschi, Françoise Bonali Fiquet, Irene Perini Bianchi, Franco Robecchi, and Rosa Zilioli Faden, vol. 1/pt. 2:372–373. Brescia: Grafo, 1990.

Bessarion, Cardinal. *Kardinal Bessarion als Theologe, Humanist und Staatsmann: Funde und Forschungen.* Ed. Ludwig Mohler. 3 vols. Quellen und Forschungen aus dem Gebiete der Geschichte 20, 22, 24. Paderborn: Neudruck der Ausgabe, 1923–42.

Biondo, Flavio. *Roma ristaurata et Italia illustrata.* Trans. Lucio Fauno. Venice: Michele Tramezzino il vecchio, 1543.

Bornato, Bernardino. *Opusculum de laudibus matrimonii . . . Et de immortalitate animae.* Brescia: Bernardino Misinta, 20 Sept.–1 Oct. 1501 [BQB, Cinq. E.76].

Bowd, Stephen, and J. Donald Cullington, eds. *"On Everyone's Lips": Humanists, Jews, and the Tale of Simon of Trent.* Trans. J. Donald Cullington. Tempe, Ariz.: Medieval and Renaissance Texts and Series, forthcoming.

Britannico, Gregorio. *Sermones funebres vulgares litteraliterque pronunciandi. Item sermones nuptiales pulcherrimi . . .* Venice: Per Manfredo de Bono de Monte ferrato, 10 Feb. 1508 [National Library of Scotland, SBA.84].

Calfurnio, Giovanni. *Mors et apotheosis Simonis infantis novi martiris; Elegia Calphurnii poetae Brix[iensis] ad Franciscum Tronum, patricium Venetum clarissimum et Mecoenatem suum; Ad librum.* Trent: Giovanni Leonardo Longo, ca. 1481 [BL, IA.51138].

Capriolo, Elia. *Aggiunta di due altri libri alle historie bresciane d'Elia Capriolo scritti in latino dal medesimo autore ad istanza di Monsig. Altobello vescovo di Pola.* Trans. Giacomo Maria Rossi. Brescia: Francesco Tebaldino, 1630.

———. *Chronica de rebus Brixianorum.* Brescia: Arundo de' Arundi, n. d. [ca. 1505] [BL, 662.g.13 (1)].

———. *Chronicorum de rebus Brixianorum libri quatuordecim,* in *Thesaurus antiquitatum et historiarum Italiae . . .* Ed. J. G. Graevius, vol. 9. pt. 7. Leiden: Petrus Vander, 1723.

———. *De confirmatione Christianae fidei.* Brescia: Bernardino Misinta, 31 May 1497 [BQB, Inc.F.VII.28m2].

———. *Dell'istorie della città di Brescia.* Venice: Agostino Savioli and Agostino Camporese, 1744.

———. *De voluptate libellus; De nimio vivendi affectu ad amicos lucubratio.* N. p., n. d. [Brescia: Bernardino Misinta, ca. 1500] [John Rylands University Library, Manchester, R9236.1].

———. *Helias Capreolus Francisco Arigoneo equiti doctissimo sal.* N.p., n.d. [Brescia: Angelo and/or Iacopo Britannico, after 4 Sept. 1503] [BQB, E.115.m.3].

[Capriolo, Elia?]. *Defensio populi Brixiani rei violatae ecclesiasticae libertatis ob decretum ab eo factum de ambitione et sumptibus funerum minuendis, accusantibus fratribus Sancti Dominici.* N. p. [Venice?], n. d. [1506?]. Translated as "A Defense of the Brescians' Statute for Reducing the Rivalry and the Expenses of Funerals." In *Vainglorious Death: A Funerary Fracas in Renaissance Brescia,* ed. Stephen Bowd, trans. J. Donald Cullington, 1–87. Tempe, Ariz.: Medieval and Renaissance Texts and Series, 2006.

Casari, Innocenzo. "De exterminio Brixianae civitatis libellus." In *Il sacco di Brescia: Testimonianze, cronache, diari, atti del processo e memorie storiche della "presa memoranda et crudele" della città nel 1512*. Ed. Vasco Frati, Ida Gianfranceschi, Françoise Bonali Fiquet, Irene Perini Bianchi, Franco Robecchi, and Rosa Zilioli Faden, vol. 1/pt. 1:36–52. Brescia: Grafo, 1989.

Casato, Giovanni. *Ioannis Casati iure consulti civis Brixie ad Baptistam Zenum patricium Venetum reverendissimum. d. d. cardinalem Sancte Marie in Porticu pro senatu & populo Brixiano oratio*. Brescia: Bernardino Misinta, 15 July 1494 [BQB, Lechi.140.m2].

Cereta, Laura. *Collected Letters of a Renaissance Feminist*. Ed. and trans. Diana Robin. The Other Voice in Early Modern Europe. Chicago: University of Chicago Press, 1997.

Cereto, Daniele. *De foro, et laudibus Brixiae ad magnificum Ludovicum Martinengum libellus*. Ed. B. Zamboni. Brescia: Pietro Vescovi, 1778.

[Civini, Marco?]. "Cominatione sopra la cità de Bressa." In *Il sacco di Brescia: Testimonianze, cronache, diari, atti del processo e memorie storiche della "presa memoranda et crudele" della città nel 1512*. Ed. Vasco Frati, Ida Gianfranceschi, Françoise Bonali Fiquet, Irene Perini Bianchi, Franco Robecchi, and Rosa Zilioli Faden, 2:693–694. Brescia: Grafo, 1990.

Coccinius, Michael. *De bellis Italicis liber unus*. In Coriolano Cippico, *De Petri Mocenici imperatoris gestis*; Conrad Wenger, *De bello inter Sigismundum archistrategum Austriae & Venetos libellus*. Basel: Per Robertum Winter, 1544.

Codognelli, Martino. *Oratio ad serenissimum Venetorum principem Leonardum Lauredanum in commendationem magnifici Andreae Lauredani*. Venice: [Bernardino Vitali?], 1504.

Contarini, Gasparo. *The Commonwealth and Government of Venice* . . . Trans. Lewis Lewkenor. London: John Windet for Edmund Mattes, 1599. The English Experience 101. Facsimile. Amsterdam: Theatrum Orbis Terrarum'/'New York: Da Capo Press, 1969.

———. *The Office of a Bishop* (De officio viri boni et probi episcopi). Trans. and ed. John Patrick Donnelly. Milwaukee: Marquette University Press, 2002.

Corio, Bernardino. *Storia di Milano*. Ed. Anna Morisi Guerra. 2 vols. Turin: UTET, 1978.

El costume delle donne incomenzando dala pueritia per fin al maritar: La via el modo che se debbe tenere acostumarle e amaistrarle secondo la condition el grado suo; Et similmente de i fanciulli; Et e uno spechio che ogni persona doverebbe haverlo: & maxime quelli che hanno figlie & figlioli over aspettano di haverne; Con un capitolo de la trentatre cose che conviene alla donna a esser bella . . . Venice: Paolo Danza, n. d. [1525?].

Cozzando, Leonardo. *Libraria bresciana prima, e seconda parte nuovamente aperta*. Brescia: Gio. Maria Rizzardi, 1694.

"Cronaca di anonimo autore (1508–1511)." In *Le cronache bresciane inedite dei secoli XV–XIX*. Ed. Paolo Guerrini, 1:136–146. Brescia: Brixia Sacra, 1922.

"Cronaca di anonimo veronese, 1446–1488." In *Monumenti storici pubblicati dalla r. deputazione veneta di storia patria*, ser. 3, vol. 4, *Cronache e diarii*. Ed. Giovanni Soranzo. Venice, 1915.

"Una cronaca ecclesiastica degli anni 1466–1484 e un sinodo sconosciuto del 1467." In *Le cronache bresciane inedite dei secoli XV–XIX*. Ed. Paolo Guerrini, 1:169–202. Brescia: Brixia Sacra, 1922.

Da Lezze, Giovanni. *Il catastico bresciano di Giovanni Da Lezze (1609–10)*. Ed. Carlo Pasero. 3 vols. Studi Queriniani 3. Brescia: F. Apollonio, 1969–73.

Defensio populi Brixiani rei violatae ecclesiasticae libertatis ob decretum ab eo factum de ambitione et sumptibus funerum minuendis, accusantibus fratribus Sancti Dominici. N. p., n. d. [Venice? Giorgio de' Rusconi? 1506?] [BL, 662.g.13.2].

De' Giudici, Battista. *Apologia Iudaeorum; Invectiva contra Platinum: Propaganda antiebraica e polemiche di curia durante il pontificato di Sisto IV (1471–1484)*, ed. and trans. Diego Quaglioni. Rome: Gestisa, 1987.

De Sardis, Ludovicus. *Tractatus de legitimatione*. Brescia: Angelo Britannico, 14 Mar. 1499 [BL, IC.31173].

De Voragine, Jacobus. *The Golden Legend: Readings on the Saints*. Trans. William Granger Ryan. 2 vols. Princeton: Princeton University Press, 1993.

Diedo, Francesco. *Vita S. Rochi*. N. p., n. d. [Milan? Simon Magniagus? after 1 June 1479] [BQB, 910.E.16].

Erasmus, Desiderius. "The Funeral." In *Collected Works of Erasmus*, vol. 40, *Colloquies*. Trans. Craig R. Thompson, 763–795. Toronto: Toronto University Press, 1997.

Fiorentino Aldigheri [*sic*], Paolo [Paolo Attavanti]. *Alla magnifica sua communità di Brexa salute*. Brescia: Bartholomaeus Vercellensis, n. d. [1481?] [BQB, Inc. G.VI.23].

Gaeta, Franco, ed. *Nunziature di Venezia*. Vol. 1, *1533–1535*. Vol. 2, *1536–1542*. Fonti per la storia d'Italia 32, 45. Rome: Istituto storico italiano per l'età moderna e contemporanea, 1958.

Gambara, Veronica. *Rime*. Ed. Alan Bullock. Florence and Perth: Leo S. Olschki and University of Western Australia Press, 1995.

Giustiniani, Tommaso, and Vincenzo Querini, "Libellus ad Leonem Decem." In *Annales Camaldulenses ordinis Sancti Benedicti quibus plura interseruntur tum ceteras Italico-monasticas res, tum historiam ecclesiasticam remque diplomaticam illustrantia*. Ed. J. B. Mittarelli and A. Costadoni, vol. 9, cols. 613–719. Venice, 1755–72. Facsimile. Farnborough England: Gregg, 1970.

Guerrini, Paolo, ed. *Le cronache bresciane inedite dei secoli XV–XIX*. Brescia: Brixia Sacra, 1922.

Guicciardini, Francesco. *Storia d'Italia*. Ed. Costantino Panigada. 5 vols. Bari: Laterza, 1929.

Hinderbach, Johannes. *Epistola Raphaeli Zovenzonio*. In Giovanni Mattia Tiberino, *Relatio de Simone puero tridentino, Miraculum*. Venice: Gabriele di Pietro, n. d. [after 30 Apr. 1475] [BL, IA.19916].

"Historia nova della ruina de Venetiani. Et una barzeletta de Bressa 1512." In *Il sacco di Brescia: Testimonianze, cronache, diari, atti del processo e memorie storiche della "presa memoranda et crudele" della città nel 1512.* Ed. Vasco Frati, Ida Gianfranceschi, Françoise Bonali Fiquet, Irene Perini Bianchi, Franco Robecchi, and Rosa Zilioli Faden, vol. 1/pt. 2:370–371. Brescia: Grafo, 1990.

Iacobus de Marchia, *Sermones dominicales.* Ed. Renato Lioi. 3 vols. Ancona: Biblioteca Francescana, 1978.

Instituta Vallis Camonicae. Ed. Iacopo Armani. Brescia: [Angelo and/or Iacopo Britannico] per Pietro Pedretti da Grevo, 1 Sept. 1498 [BQB, G.II.7].

Justin, *Epitome of the Philippic History of Pompeius Trogus.* Trans. J. C. Yardley. Atlanta: Scholars Press, 1994.

Lactantius, *Divina opera Lactantii Firmiani & aliorum supradictorum.* Ed. Giovanni Pierio Valeriano. Venice: Ioannis Tacuinus, 3 Jan. 1502 [m.v. 1503] [BL, 3623.cc.1].

"Lamento che fa el principo di Venetia 1509." In *Il sacco di Brescia: Testimonianze, cronache, diari, atti del processo e memorie storiche della "presa memoranda et crudele" della città nel 1512.* Ed. Vasco Frati, Ida Gianfranceschi, Françoise Bonali Fiquet, Irene Perini Bianchi, Franco Robecchi, and Rosa Zilioli Faden, vol. 1/pt. 2:365–366. Brescia: Grafo, 1990.

Lanfranchini, Cristoforo. *Quaestio utrum praeferendus sit doctor an miles.* Brescia: Angelo Britannico, 8 July 1497 [BQB, Lechi.127].

Leges Brixianae. Brescia: Iacopo Britannico, 8 Dec. 1490 [BL, IB.31134].

Leggenda de sancto Faustino e Jovita. Brescia: Battista Farfengo, 5 June 1490 [BQB, D.VI.14].

Libro o vero cronicha di tutte le guerre de Italia incomenzando dal millequatrocento nonantaquatro fin al millecinquecento decedoto. Venice: n. p., 1522 [BL, 11422.c.25].

Luther, Martin. *The Babylonian Captivity of the Church* (1520). In *Luther's Works,* ed. Helmut T. Lehman, vol. 36, *Word and Sacrament II,* ed. Abdel Ross Wentz, 25–36. Philadelphia: Muhlenberg Press, 1959.

———. *The Misuse of the Mass* (1521). In *Luther's Works,* ed. Helmut T. Lehman, vol. 36, *Word and Sacrament II.* Ed. Abdel Ross Wentz, 127–230. Philadelphia: Muhlenberg Press, 1959.

———. *A Treatise on the New Testament, That Is, The Holy Mass* (1520). In *Luther's Works,* ed. Helmut T. Lehman, vol. 35, *Word and Sacrament I,* ed. E. Theodore Bachman, 75–111. Philadelphia: Muhlenberg Press, 1960.

Machiavelli, Niccolò. *The Prince.* Trans. George Bull. London: Penguin Books, 1961.

Maffeo, Celso. *Apologia d. Caelsi Maphei Veronensis canonici regularis contra librum fratris Ambrosii de Chora: ordinis fratrum heremitarum: in quo nititur probare ipsos fratres heremitanos institutos fuisse ab Aug.ino et fuisse tempore Aug. ante canonicos regulares: & contra sermones ad heremitas mendacissime Aug. attributos. Directa reverendissimis cardinalibus Neapolitano Ulisbonensi Senensi. et S. Georgii. dominis suis observandissimis.* Brescia: Bernardino Misinta, 18 Mar. 1502 [BL, 1477.aaa.4].

Malipiero, Domenico. "Annali veneti dall'anno 1457 al 1500 del senatore Domenico Malipiero ordinati e abbreviati dal senatore Francesco Longo." *Archivio Storico Italiano,* ser. 1, 7.1–2 (1843–44).

Malvecius, Jacobus. *Chronicon Brixianum ab origine urbis ad annum MCCCXXXII.* In *Rerum Italicarum scriptores.* Ed. L. A. Muratori, vol. 14, cols. 776–1004. Milan: Ex typografia societatis palatinae in regia curia, 1729.

Manelmi, Evangelista. *Commentariolus de quibusdam gestis in bello Gallico . . . seu de obsidione Brixiae.* Ed. Giannandrea Astezati. Brescia: Giovanni Maria Rizzardi, 1728.

Marochitano, Samuel. *Tractatus rabby Samuelis, errorem iudeorum indicans.* Brescia: Per Damiano and Iacopo Filippo, 1535 [BL, 4034.b.28].

Martinengo di Erbusco, Gian Giacomo. "Della congiura de' Bresciani per sottrarre la patria alla francese dominazione." In *Il sacco di Brescia: Testimonianze, cronache, diari, atti del processo e memorie storiche della "presa memoranda et crudele" della città nel 1512.* Ed. Vasco Frati, Ida Gianfranceschi, Françoise Bonali Fiquet, Irene Perini Bianchi, Franco Robecchi, and Rosa Zilioli Faden, vol. 1/pt. 1:61–118. Brescia: Grafo, 1989.

Martinengo di Villachiara, Bartolomeo. *Segni e prodigi spaventosi apparsi in Lombardia nel confino de Trevì e Rivolta Seccha: Quali appareno doi o tre volte al zorno a combattere in ordenanza e con ferissime artelarie viste visibilmente per el magnifico Bartolameo da Villa Chiara et molti altri huomini degni de fede.* N. p., n. d. [ca. 1510] [BL, C.20.c.22.58].

Massimo, Benedetto [Pseud. Carlo Valgulio?]. *Benedicti Maximi civis Brixiani vetustissima familia Romana Maximorum oriundi de forma rei publice Brixianae constituenda qua discordiae civiles tollantur ad serenissimum princepem Leonardum Lauredanum et magnanimum Andream Griti provisorem generalem et clarissimos ac optimos rectores Brixiae urbis Franciscum Faletrium in administranda justitia imaginem dei et Petrum Marcellum.* N. p., n. d. [Brescia: Giovanni Antonio Bresciano, ca. 1516–17] [BQB, 5.H.VII.26.m.9].

———. "De concordia Brixianorum." In *Il sacco di Brescia: Testimonianze, cronache, diari, atti del processo e memorie storiche della "presa memoranda et crudele" della città nel 1512.* Ed. Vasco Frati, Ida Gianfranceschi, Françoise Bonali Fiquet, Irene Perini Bianchi, Franco Robecchi, and Rosa Zilioli Faden, 2:695–704. Brescia: Grafo, 1990.

Melga, Jacopo. "Cronaca (1471–1487)." In *Le cronache bresciane inedite dei secoli XV–XIX.* Ed. Paolo Guerrini, 1:4–135. Brescia: Brixia Sacra, 1922.

Mercando, Bartolomeo. *Laeticiae ac moeroris gaudii atque luctus agitatio.* Brescia: Battista Farfengo, 6 Dec. 1497 [Facsimile in BQB, 910.E.15].

Mercando, Tomaso [*sic*]. "Cronaca (1532–1546)." In *Le cronache bresciane inedite dei secoli XV–XIX,* ed. Paolo Guerrini, 1:146–168. Brescia: Brixia Sacra, 1922.

Michiel, Marcantonio. *M. Antonii Michaelis P. V. agri et urbis Bergomatis descriptio ann. MDXVI*/*Descrizione della città di Bergamo e suo territorio di Marcantonio Michele patrizio veneto nell'anno 1516.* In *Bergamo 1516: Città e territorio nella "Descriptio" di Marcantonio Michiel,* Trans. P. M. Francesco Piatti. Ed. Maria Luisa Scalvini and Gian Piero Calza. 48–73. Padua: Centro grafico editoriale, 1983.

Newett, M. Margaret, ed. and trans. *Canon Pietro Casola's Pilgrimage to Jerusalem in the Year 1494.* Publications of the University of Manchester Historical Series 5. Manchester: Manchester University Press, 1907.

Palazzo, Bartolomeo. "Diario di Bartolomeo Palazzo (1502–1548)." In *Le cronache bresciane inedite dei secoli XV–XIX.* Ed. Paolo Guerrini, 1:256–386. Brescia: Brixia Sacra, 1922.

Palazzo, Corradino. "Cronaca di Corradino Palazzo (1399–1473)." In *Le cronache bresciane inedite dei secoli XV–XIX,* Ed. Paolo Guerrini, 1:212–225. Brescia: Brixia Sacra, 1922.

———. "Diario di Corradino Palazzo (1404–1495)." In *Le cronache bresciane inedite dei secoli XV–XIX,* Ed. Paolo Guerrini, 1:225–256. Brescia: Brixia Sacra, 1922.

"Il panegirico di Brescia di un anonimo umanista francescano dell'anno 1483." In *Le cronache bresciane inedite dei secoli XV–XIX,* Ed. Paolo Guerrini, 2:244–259. Brescia: Brixia Sacra, 1927.

I patti con Brescia 1252–1339. Ed. Luca Sandini. Venice: Il cardo, 1991.

Petrarch, Francesco. *Petrarch's Remedies for Fortune Fair and Foul: A Modern English Translation of "De remediis utriusque Fortune," with a Commentary by Conrad H. Rawski.* 5 vols. Bloomington: Indiana University Press, 1991

Planius, Johannes Baptista [Giovanni Battista Appiani]. *Ad Catharinam Cyprorum reginam pro senatu populoque Brixiano oratio.* N. p., n. d. [Brescia: Angelo Britannico, after 6 Sept. 1497] [BL, IA.31161].

Plutarch, *Moralia Plutarchi traducta.* Trans. Giovanni Calfurnio, Carlo Valgulio, et al. Venice: Per Bernardinum Venetum Vitalis, ca. 1505 [BL, 1481.c.17].

Pollux, Julius. *Pollucis vocabularii index in latinum tralatus, ut vel graece nescientibus nota sint, quae a Polluce tractantur.* Venice: Aldus Manutius, Apr. 1502.

Priuli, Girolamo. *I diarii di Girolamo Priuli [AA. 1499–1512].* Ed. Arturo Segrè and Roberto Cessi. In *Rerum Italicarum Scriptores,* vol. 24, pt. 3, fasc. 262, 276, 290, 298–299, 310, 314, 326, 333, 342. Bologna: Nicola Zanichelli, 1933–1941.

Probus, Marcus Valerius. *Significatio litterarum antiquarum Valerii Probi et Fr. Michaelis Regien. Carmelitae divae Mariae.* Ed. Michele Ferrarino. [Brescia]: Boninus de Boninis, de Ragusia, 27 Oct. 1486 [BL, C.5.a.3].

Pucci, Antonio. *Oratio habita per reverendum patrem dominum Antonium Pucciu[bus] camere apostolice clericum: in nona sacrosancti Lateranensium concilii sessione. Tertio Nones Maii. M. d. xiiii.* N. p., n. d. [Rome? Marcello Silber? 1514?].

Pusculo, Ubertino. *Duo libri Symonidos: De iudaeorum perfidia . . .* Ed. Johannes Kurtz von Eberspach. Augsburg: Johannes Ot[h]mar, 11 Apr. 1511.

———. *Elogio di Brescia.* Trans. Enrico Bisanti. Monumenta Brixiae historica 17. Brescia: Ateneo di scienze lettere ed arti, 2002.

———. "Oratio de laudibus Brixiae." In *Le cronache bresciane inedite dei secoli XV–XIX,* ed. Paolo Guerrini, 2:1–44. Brescia: Brixia Sacra, 1927.

Qu[a]estio an infrascripta statuta super mortuariis sint contra ecclesiasticam libertatem. San Domenico, Brescia: Angelo Britannico, 1 Apr. 1506 [BL, C.118.c.26; BQB Cinq. DD.10.m1]. Translated as "An Enquiry as to Whether the Statutes about Death Disbursements Quoted Below Go against Church Freedom," in *Vainglorious Death: A Funerary Fracas in Renaissance Brescia*, ed. Stephen Bowd, trans. J. Donald Cullington, 153–233 (Tempe, Ariz.: Medieval and Renaissance Texts and Series, 2006).

Raccolta di privilegj, ducali, giudizi, terminazioni, e decreti pubblicii sopra varie materie giurisdizionali, civili, criminali, ed economiche, concernanti la città, e provincia di Brescia. Brescia: Gianbattista Bossino, 1732.

Ricci, Giacomo. *Passio sanctorum martyrum Faustini & Jovite Brixiensium.* Brescia: Giovanni Antonio Bresciano, 1511 [BQB, Cinq.E.96].

Richter E. L., and E. Friedberg, eds. *Corpus iuris canonici.* 2 vols. Leipzig: Tauchnitz, 1879–81.

Rossi, Ottavio. *Elogi historici de Bresciani illustri.* Brescia: Bartolomeo Fontana, 1620.

"La rotta e presa fatta a Bresa per li francesi 1512." In *Il sacco di Brescia: Testimonianze, cronache, diari, atti del processo e memorie storiche della "presa memoranda et crudele" della città nel 1512.* Ed. Vasco Frati, Ida Gianfranceschi, Françoise Bonali Fiquet, Irene Perini Bianchi, Franco Robecchi, and Rosa Zilioli Faden, vol. 1/pt. 2:390–395. Brescia: Grafo, 1990.

Ruffo, Giordano. *Arte de cognoscere la natura de cavalli & quelli regere & governar e lor infirmitade cognoscere e liberare lo qual vulgarmente se chiama arte de mareschalchi.* Ed. and trans. Gabriele Bruno. Brescia: Tommaso Ferrando, Aug. 1491 [BL, IA.31020].

Sabellico, Marcantonio. *De officio praetoris.* In Marcantonio Sabellico, *Opera*, fols. 105r–108v. Venice: Albertino de Lisona, 24 Dec. 1502 [BQB, 4.D.II.25].

———. *De vetustate Aquileiensis patriae carmina: Elegiae XIII in natalem diem divae Virginis Mariae.* [Padua]: Antonius de Avinione, n. d. [ca. 1480–83] [BL, IA.22607].

Sanudo, Marin. *I diarii di Marino Sanuto.* Ed. Rinaldo Fulin, Federico Stefani, Nicolò Barozzi, Guglielmo Berchet, and Marco Allegri. 58 vols. Venice: Fratelli Visentini, 1879–1903. Facsimile. Bologna: Forni, 1969–70.

———. *Itinerario di Marin Sanuto per la terraferma veneziana nell'anno MCCCCLXXXIII.* Ed. Rawdon Brown. Padua: Tipografia del Seminario, 1847.

———. *Venice, Città Excelentissima: Selections from the Renaissance Diaries of Marin Sanudo.* Trans. Linda L. Carroll. Ed. Patricia H. Labalme and Laura Sanguineti White. Baltimore: Johns Hopkins University Press, 2008.

Sasso, Panfilo. *Pamphili Saxi poetae lepidissimi epigrammatum libri quattuor; Distichorum libri Duo; De Bello Gallico, De laudibus Veronae; Elegiarum liber unus.* Brescia: Bernardino Misinta for Angelo Britannico, 6 July 1499 [BQB, Lechi.98].

Solazio, Taddeo. *Epistola Albertino Corrigio.* N. p., n. d. [Brescia: Boninus de Boninis, ca. 1486–91].

———. "La prefazione storica di Taddeo Solazio alla prima raccolta archaeologica di iscrizioni bresciane." In *Le cronache bresciane inedite dei secoli XV–XIX*, ed. Paolo Guerrini, 2:133–152. Brescia: Brixia Sacra, 1927.

Soldo, Cristoforo. "Cronaca (brano inedito—1469)." In *Le cronache bresciane inedite dei secoli XV–XIX*, ed. Paolo Guerrini, 1:1–3. Brescia: Brixia Sacra, 1922.

———. *La cronaca di Cristoforo da Soldo*. Ed. Giuseppe Brizzolara. In *Rerum Italicarum Scriptores*, 21, pt. 3, fasc. 312, 331, 347. Bologna: Nicola Zanichelli, 1938–42.

Statuta Brixiae. Brescia: Tommaso Ferrando, 21 May–29 June 1473 [BL, IB.31013].

Statuta Brixie. N. p. [Brescia:] Angelo Britannico, 1508.

Statuta civitatis Brixiae: Cum reformationibus alias aeditis, necnon cum aliquibus decretis illustriss. du. do. Vene. superadditis. Brescia: Damiano Turliano, 1557.

Statuta Ripariae Benacensis. Ed. Johannes Stephanus Vosonius. Portese: Bartholomaeus de Zanis, for Angelo Cozzali, 20 Aug. 1490 [BL, IB.35701].

Suriano, Antonio. *Relazione*. In *Relazioni dei rettori veneti in terraferma*. Ed. A. Tagliaferri, vol. 11, *Podestaria e capitanato di Brescia*, 5–7. Milan: Giuffrè, 1978.

Tanner, N. P., ed. *Decrees of the Ecumenical Councils*. 2 vols. London and Washington, D.C.: Sheed and Ward and Georgetown University Press, 1990.

Tiberino, Giovanni Mattia. *Hystoria completa de passione et obitu pueri Simonis*. [Albrecht Kunne for] Hermann Schindeleyp: Trent, 9 Feb. 1476 [BL, IA.51126].

———. *In beatum Symonum novum sanctissimae passionis Christi lumen & martirem epigrama*. Trent: Giovanni Leonardo Longo, 5 Sept. 1482 [BL, IA.51136].

———. *Relatio de Simone puero Tridentino; Miraculum*. Venice: Gabriele di Pietro, n. d. [after 30 Apr. 1475] [BL, IA.19916].

Ticinensis, Aug.inus [Agostino Novi]. *Elucidarium Christianarum religionum*. Brescia: Angelo Britannico, 5 Nov. 1511 [Cambridge University Library, Norton d.128].

La vera nova de Bressa de punto in punto come andata novamente impressa. N. p., n. d. [ca. 1512] [BL, C.20.c.22.17].

Valgulio, Carlo. *Statutum Brixianorum de sumptibus funerum optima ratione nullum facere discrimen fortunae inter cives. Nec esse honores: qui vulgo putantur*. Brescia: Io. Antonius de Gandino dictus de Caegulis, apud portam Sancti Stephani, 10 February 1509. Translated as "That the Brescians' Statute about Funeral Expenditure with Perfect Logic Makes No Distinction of Rank among Citizens, and That What Are Commonly Regarded as Honors Are Not So," in *Vainglorious Death: A Funerary Fracas in Renaissance Brescia*, ed. Stephen Bowd, trans. J. Donald Cullington, 89–143. Tempe, Ariz.: Medieval and Renaissance Texts and Series, 2006.

Vosonius, Johannes Stephanus [Giovanni Stefano Buzzoni]. *Epigrammaton liber primus*. Brescia: Battista Farfengo, n. d. [ca. 1499] [Facsimile copy, BQB, 910.E.13].

Zen, Catterino. *Relazione*. In *Relazioni dei rettori veneti in terraferma*, ed. A. Tagliaferri, vol. 11, *Podestaria e capitanato di Brescia*, 37–45. Milan: Giuffrè, 1978.

Zovenzoni, Raffaele. *Carmen ad Gabrielem Petri*. In Giovanni Mattia Tiberino, *Relatio de Simone puero Tridentino; Miraculum*. Venice: Gabriele di Pietro, n. d. [after 30 Apr. 1475] [BL, IA.19916].

Secondary Sources

Abulafia, David, ed. *The French Descent into Renaissance Italy 1494–95: Antecedents and Effects.* Aldershot, England: Ashgate, 1995.

Ajmar-Wollheim, Marta, and Flora Dennis, eds. *At Home in Renaissance Italy: Art and Life in the Italian House, 1400–1600.* New Haven: Yale University Press, 1998.

Allerston, Patricia. "Consuming Problems: Worldly Goods in Renaissance Venice." Chapter 1 of *The Material Renaissance.* Ed. Michelle O'Malley and Evelyn Welch. Manchester: Manchester University Press, 2007.

Amore, Agostino. "Faustino e Giovita." *BS,* vol. 5, cols. 483–485.

Apostoli, Andrea. "Scelte fiscali a Brescia all'inizio del periodo veneto." In *Politiche finanziarie e fiscali nell'Italia settentrionale (secoli XIII–XV).* Ed. Patrizia Mainoni, 345–407. Milan: Unicopli, 2001.

Appuhn, Karl. *A Forest on the Sea: Environmental Expertise in Renaissance Venice.* Baltimore: Johns Hopkins University Press, 2009.

Arcangeli, L. "Appunti su guelfi e ghibellini in Lombardia nelle guerre d'Italia (1494–1530)." In *Guelfi e ghibellini nell'Italia del Rinascimento.* Ed. Marco Gentile, 391–472. Rome: Viella, 2005.

———. *Gentiluomini di Lombardia: Ricerche sull'aristocrazia padana nel Rinascimento.* Milan: Unicopli, 2003.

Archetti, G. "Malvezzi, Giacomo." *DBI,* 68:316–318.

Ariès, Philippe. *The Hour of Our Death.* Trans. H. Weaver. Harmondsworth, England: Penguin, 1981.

Arnaldi, G., and L. Capo. "I cronisti di Venezia e della Marca trevigiana nel secolo XIV." In *Storia della cultura veneta.* Ed. G. Arnaldi and M. Pastore Stocchi, vol. 2, *Il Trecento.* Ed. Girolamo Arnaldi, 272–337. Vicenza: Neri Pozza, 1976.

"Atti del convegno eretici e streghe: Quando e come; Cemmo, 6 marzo 1999." Special issue of *Synopsis: Quaderno di approfondimenti storici* 1 (2000).

Banterele, Gabriele. "Il trasporto delle navi venete nel lago di Garda (1439) nella testimonianza degli umanisti veronesi." In *Il primo dominio veneziano a Verona (1405–1509): Atti del Convegno tenuto a Verona il 16–17 settembre 1988,* 191–202. Verona: Grafiche Fiorini, 1991.

Barasch, Moshe. *Gestures of Despair in Medieval and Early Renaissance Art.* New York: New York University Press, 1976.

Baron, Hans. "Franciscan Poverty and Civic Wealth as Factors in the Rise of Humanistic Thought." *Speculum* 13 (1938): 1–37.

Baroncelli, Ugo. "Britannico, Giovanni." *DBI,* 14:342–343.

———. "Un predicatore fiorentino del sec. XV: Paolo Attavanti e il suo panegirico di Brescia." In *Studi in onore di Luigi Fossati,* 33–39. Brescia: Geroldi, 1974.

Bartlett, Robert. "Symbolic Meanings of Hair in the Middle Ages." *Transactions of the Royal Historical Society,* 6th ser., 4 (1994): 43–60.

Bayer, Andrea. "Bergamo and Brescia." Chapter 7 of *Venice and the Veneto,* ed. Peter Humfrey. Cambridge: Cambridge University Press, 2007.

———. "Brescia after the League of Cambrai: Moretto, Romanino and the Arts." Ph.D. diss., Princeton University, 1991.

Begni Redona, Pier Virgilio. *Alessandro Bonvicino Il Moretto da Brescia*. Brescia: La scuola, 1988.

———. "La committenza del Sansone: L'ancona per la pala del Romanino e il coro ligneo in San Francesco." In *Frate Francesco Sansone "de Brixia" ministro generale OFMConv (1414–1499): Un mecenate francescano del Rinascimento*. Ed. Giovanna Baldissin Molli, 109–123. Padua: Centro studi Antoniani, 2000.

Bell, Catherine. *Ritual: Perspectives and Dimensions*. Oxford: Oxford University Press, 1997.

Beloch, Karl Julius. *Storia della popolazione d'Italia*. Ed. Eugenio Sonnino. With an introduction by Lorenzo del Pianta. Società Italiana di Demografia Storica. Florence: Le lettere, 1994.

Benetazzo, Michele. "I sumptuosissimis corali miniati voluti dal Sansone per la chiesa di San Francesco di Brescia." In *Frate Francesco Sansone "de Brixia" ministro generale OFMConv (1414–1499): Un mecenate francescano del Rinascimento*, ed. Giovanna Baldissin Molli, 141–170. Padua: Centro studi Antoniani, 2000.

Berengo, Marino. "Patriziato e nobiltà: Il caso veronese." *Rivista Storica Italiana* 87 (1975): 493–517.

———. *La società veneta alla fine del Settecento*. Florence: G. C. Sansoni, 1956.

Bernadelli Curuz, Maurizio. *Streghe Bresciane: Confessioni, persecuzioni e roghi fra il XV e il XVI secolo*. Desenzano: Ermione, 1988.

Bertelli, Sergio. *The King's Body: Sacred Rituals of Power in Medieval and Early Modern Europe*. Trans. R. Burr Litchfield. University Park: Pennsylvania State University Press, 2001.

Bettoni, Barbara. "Aristocrazia senza corte: Interni domestici a Brescia nel corso del XVIo e XVIIo secolo." *Journal de la Renaissance* 4 (2006): 9–23.

Beverley, Tessa. "Venetian Ambassadors, 1454–1494: An Italian Elite." Ph.D. diss., University of Warwick, 1999.

Bibliotheca sanctorum. 12 vols. Rome: Città nuova editrice, 1961–70.

Bistort, G. *Il magistrato alle pompe nella republica di Venezia*. Venice, 1912. Facsimile. Bologna: Forni, 1969.

Bizzocchi, Roberto. "Chiesa e aristocrazia della Firenze del Quattrocento." *Archivio Storico Italiano* 142 (1984): 191–282.

Bologna Seminar, coordinated by Carlo Ginzburg. "Ritual Pillages: A Preface to Research in Progress." In *Microhistory and the Lost Peoples of Europe*, trans. Eren Branch, ed. Edward Muir and Guido Ruggiero, 20–41. Baltimore: Johns Hopkins University Press, 1991.

Bona, Andrea. "Brescia: XV secolo; Acque e mercati nella formazione del nuovo centro urbano." In *Fabbriche, piazze, mercati: La città italiana nel Rinascimento*. Ed. Donatella Calabi, 130–158. Rome: Officina, 1997.

———. "Feltre: XVI secolo: La ricostruzione della 'plathea magna' nella prima metà del Cinquecento." In *Fabbriche, piazze, mercati: La città italiana nel Rinascimento*, ed. Donatella Calabi, 327–353. Rome: Officina, 1997.

Bonfiglio Dosio, Giorgetta. "Condizioni socio-economiche di Brescia e del suo distretto." In *La signoria di Pandolfo III Malatesti a Brescia, Bergamo e Lecco*, ed. Giorgetta Bonfiglio Dosio and Anna Falcioni, 109–136. Rimini: Bruno Ghigi, 2000

———. "Criminalità ed emarginazione a Brescia nel primo Quattrocento." *Archivio Storico Italiano* 136 (1978): 113–164.

———. "Società e ricchezza Brescia in epoca malatestiana sulla scorta dell'estimo del 1416." In *Le signorie dei Malatesti: Storia, società, cultura; Atti giornata di studi malatestiani di Brescia* 2, 1–78. Rimini: Bruno Ghigi, 1989.

———. "La vita a corte." In *La signoria di Pandolfo III Malatesti a Brescia, Bergamo e Lecco*, ed. Giorgetta Bonfiglio Dosio and Anna Falcioni, 155–173. Rimini: Bruno Ghigi, 2000.

Bonfiglio Dosio, Giorgetta, and Anna Falcioni, eds. *La signoria di Pandolfo III Malatesti a Brescia, Bergamo e Lecco.* Rimini: Bruno Ghigi, 2000.

Bonfil, Robert. *Jewish Life in Renaissance Italy.* Trans. Anthony Oldcorn. Berkeley: University of California Press, 1994.

Bontempi, Franco. *Il ferro e la stella: Presenza ebraica a Brescia durante il Rinascimento.* Boario Terme: Gianico-La cittadina, 1994.

Borelli, Giorgio. "Brescia tra recessione e decadenza (1630–1766)." *Rivista Storica Italiana* 71 (1987): 587–596.

———. "'Doctor an miles': Aspetti della ideologia nobiliare nell'opera del giurista Cristoforo Lanfranchini." In *Il primo dominio veneziano a Verona (1405–1509): Atti del Convegno tenuto a Verona il 16–17 settembre 1988*, 53–71. Verona: Grafiche Fiorini, 1991.

———, ed. *Un lago, una civiltà: Il Garda.* 2 vols. Verona: Grafiche Fiorini, 1983.

Borkowski, A. *Roman Law.* 2nd ed. London: Blackstone Press, 1997.

Borsa, Gedeon. "L'attività dei tipografi di origine bresciana al di fuori del territorio bresciano, fino al 1512." In *I primordi della stampa a Brescia 1472–1511: Atti del convegno internazionale (Brescia, 6–8 giugno 1984)*, ed. Ennio Sandal, 25–59. Padua: Editrice Antenore, 1986.

Borst, Arno. "The Origins of the Witch-craze in the Alps." In *New Perspectives on Witchcraft, Magic and Demonology*, ed. Brian P. Levack, vol. 2, *Witchcraft in Continental Europe*, 299–320. New York: Routledge, 2001.

Boucheron, Patrick. "L'architettura come linguaggio politico: Cenni sul caso lombardo nel secolo XV." In *Linguaggi politici nell'Italia del Rinascimento: Atti del convegno Pisa, 9–11 novembre 2006*, ed. Andrea Gamberini and Giuseppe Petralia, 3–53. Rome: Viella, 2007.

Bouwsma, William J. "Venice and the Political Education of Europe." In *Renaissance Venice*, ed. J. R. Hale, 445–465. London: Faber and Faber, 1973.

Bowd, Stephen D. *Reform before the Reformation: Vincenzo Querini and the Religious Renaissance in Italy.* Studies in Medieval and Reformation Thought 87. Leiden: Brill, 2002.

———, ed. *Vainglorious Death: A Funerary Fracas in Renaissance Brescia.* Trans. J. Donald Cullington. Tempe: Arizona Center for Medieval and Renaissance Studies, 2006.

Brown, Andrew. "Ritual and State-Building: Ceremonies in Late Medieval Bruges." In *Symbolic Communication in Late Medieval Towns*, ed. J. van Leeuwen, 1–28. Leuven: Leuven University Press, 2006.

Brown, Judith C. *In the Shadow of Florence: Provincial Society in Renaissance Pescia*. Oxford: Oxford University Press, 1982.

Brundage, James. "Prostitution in Medieval Canon Law." *Signs* 1 (1976): 825–845.

———. "Sumptuary Laws and Prostitution in Late Medieval Italy." *Journal of Medieval History* 13 (1987): 343–355.

Buc, Philippe. *The Dangers of Ritual: Between Early Medieval Texts and Social Scientific Theory*. Princeton: Princeton University Press, 2001.

Burckhardt, Jacob. *The Civilization of the Renaissance in Italy: An Essay*. Trans. S. G. C. Middlemore. 4th rev. ed. London: Phaidon, 1951.

Burke, Peter. "Witchcraft and Magic in Renaissance Italy: Gianfrancesco Pico and His *Strix*." In *The Damned Art: Essays in the Literature of Witchcraft*, ed. S. Anglo, 32–52. London: Routledge, 1977.

Busetto, G. "Concoreggio, Gabriele." *DBI*, 27:743–746.

Bynum, Caroline Walker. *Wonderful Blood: Theology and Practice in Late Medieval Northern Germany and Beyond*. Philadelphia: University of Pennsylvania Press, 2007.

Caccia, E. "Cultura e letteratura nei secoli XV e XVI." In *Storia di Brescia*, ed. Giovanni Treccani degli Alfieri, vol. 2, *La dominazione veneta (1426–1575)*, 477–535. Brescia: Morcelliana, 1963.

Calabi, Donatella, ed. *Fabbriche, piazze, mercati: La città italiana nel Rinascimento*. Rome: Officina, 1997.

Camisani, Enrico. "Deusdedit." *BS*, vol. 4, col. 590.

Cannata, Pietro. "Iconografia." *BS*, vol. 5, cols. 485–492.

Capelli, Adriano, ed. *Manuali Hoepli: Lexicon abbreviaturarum; Dizionario di abbreviature latine ed italiane usate nelle carte e codici specialmente del medioevo riprodotte con oltre 14000 segni incisi*. 6th ed. Milan: Ulríco Hoeplí, 1985.

Caponetto, Salvatore. *The Protestant Reformation in Sixteenth-century Italy*. Trans. Anne C. Tedeschi and John Tedeschi. Sixteenth Century Essays and Studies 43. Kirksville, Mo.: Thomas Jefferson University Press, 1999.

Caraffa, Filippo. "Evasio." *BS*, vol. 5, col. 375.

Caro Lopez, Ceferino. "Gli auditori nuovi e il dominio di terraferma." In *Stato, società e giustizia nella repubblica Veneta (sec. XV–XVIII)*, ed. Gaetano Cozzi, 261–316. Rome: Jouvence, 1980.

Cassa, A. *Funerali, pompe e conviti: Escursione nel vecchio archivio municipale*. Brescia: Stabilimento Unione Tipografica Bresciana, 1887.

Castelnuovo, G. "L'identità politica delle nobiltà cittadine (inizio XIII–inizio XVI secolo)." In *Le aristocrazie dai signori rurali al patriziato*, ed. R. Bordone, G. Castelnuovo, and G. M. Varanini, 195–244. Rome: Laterza, 2004.

Cavallo, Sandra. *Artisans of the Body in Early Modern Italy: Identities, Families and Masculinities*. Manchester: Manchester University Press, 2007.

Cengarle, F. *Immagine di potere e prassi di governo: La politica feudale di Filippo Maria Visconti*. Rome: Viella, 2006.

Cervelli, Innocenzo. *Machiavelli e la crisi dello stato Veneziano*. Naples: Guida, 1974.

Chartier, Roger. *Cultural History: Between Practices and Representations.* Trans. Lydia G. Cochrane. Oxford: Polity, 1988.

———. "Fiction and Knowledge." In Chartier, *Edge of the Cliff: History, Language, and Practices.* Trans. Lydia G. Cochrane, 13–27. Baltimore: Johns Hopkins University Press, 1997.

Chittolini, Giorgio. "Alcune considerazioni sulla storia politico-istituzionale del tardo medioevo: alle origine degli 'stati regionali.'" *Annali dell'Istituto Storico Italo-germanico in Trento* 2 (1976): 20–45.

———. *Città, comunità e feudi negli stati dell'Italia centrosettentrionale (secoli XIV–XVI).* Milan: Unicopli, 1996.

———. "Civic Religion and the Countryside in Late Medieval Italy." In *City and Countryside in Late Medieval and Renaissance Italy: Essays Presented to Philip Jones,* ed. Trevor Dean and Chris Wickham, 69–80. London: Hambledon Press, 1990.

———. "Contadi e territori: Qualche considerazione." *Studi Bresciani* 12 (1983): 35–48.

———. *La crisi degli ordinamenti comunali e le origini dello stato del Rinascimento.* Bologna: Il Mulino, 1979.

———. *La formazione dello stato regionale e le istituzioni del contado.* Turin: Einaudi, 1979.

———. "Il 'privato,' il 'pubblico,' lo Stato." In *Origini dello Stato: Processi di formazione statale in Italia fra medioevo ed età moderna,* ed. Giorgio Chittolini, Anthony Molho, and Pierangelo Schiera, 553–589. Bologna: Il Mulino, 1994.

———. "Un problema aperto: La crisi della proprietà ecclesiastica fra quattro e cinquecento; Locazioni novennali, spese di migliorie ed investiture perpetue nella pianura lombarda." *Rivista Storica Italiana* 85 (1973): 353–393.

———. "Stati regionali e istituzioni ecclesiastiche nell'Italia centrosettentrionale del Quattrocento." In *Storia d'Italia,* ed. Giorgio Chittolini and Giovanni Miccoli. *Annali,* 9. *La Chiesa e il potere politico dal medioevo all'età contemporanea,* 147–193. Turin: Einaudi, 1986.

———. "Le terre separate nel ducato di Milano in età sforzesca." In *Milano nell'età di Lodovico il Moro: Atti del convegno internazionale 28 febbraio–4 marzo 1983,* 2:115–146. Milan: Comune di Milano. Archivio Storico Civico e Biblioteca Trivulziano, 1983.

Chittolini, Giorgio, Anthony Molho, and Pierangelo Schiera, eds. *Origini dello Stato: Processi di formazione statale in Italia fra medioevo ed età moderna.* Bologna: Il Mulino, 1994.

Chojnacki, Stanley. "Identity and Ideology in Renaissance Venice." In *Venice Reconsidered: The History and Civilization of an Italian City-State, 1297–1797,* ed. John Martin and Dennis Romano, 263–294. Baltimore: Johns Hopkins University Press, 2000.

Cistellini, Antonio. *Figure della riforma pretridentina: Stefana Quinzani, Angela Merici, Laura Mignani, Bartolomeo Stella, Francesco Cabrini, Francesco Santabona.* Brescia: Morcelliana, 1948.

————. "La vita religiosa nei secoli XV e XVI." In *Storia di Brescia*, ed. Giovanni Treccani degli Alfieri, vol. 2, *La dominazione veneta (1426–1575)*, 397–473. Brescia: Morcelliana, 1963.

Clough, C. H. "Becichemo, Marino." *DBI*, 7:511–515.

Cochrane, Eric. *Historians and Historiography in the Italian Renaissance*. Chicago: University of Chicago Press, 1981.

Cohn, Norman. *Europe's Inner Demons: An Enquiry Inspired by the Great Witch-Hunt*. London: Heinemann, 1975.

Cohn, Jr., Samuel K. *The Cult of Remembrance and the Black Death: Six Renaissance Cities in Central Italy*. Baltimore: Johns Hopkins University Press, 1992.

Collareta, Marco. "La grande croce di Gian Francesco dalle Croci." In *Frate Francesco Sansone "de Brixia": Ministro generale OFMConv (1414–1499); Un mecenate francescano del Rinascimento*, ed. Giovanna Baldissin Molli, 124–139. Padua: Centro studi Antoniani, 2000.

Collett, Barry. *Italian Benedictine Scholars and the Reformation: The Congregation of Santa Giustina in Padua*. Oxford: Clarendon Press, 1985.

Constable, Giles. "Introduction." In *Apologiae duae: Gozechini epistola ad Walcherum. Burchardi ut videtur, abbatis Bellevallis apologia de barbis*, ed. R. B. C. Huygens, Turnhoult: Brepols, 1985.

Corpus nummorum italicorum: primo tentativo di un catalogo generale delle monete medievali e moderne coniate in Italia o da Italiani in altri paesi. 20 vols. Rome: R. Accademia dei lincei, 1910–1971.

Cosgrove, Denis. "Mapping New Worlds: Culture and Cartography in Sixteenth-Century Venice." *Imago Mundi* 44 (1992): 65–89.

Cowan, Alexander. *Marriage, Manners and Mobility in Early Modern Venice*. Aldershot, England: Ashgate, 2007.

Cozzi, Gaetano. "Ambiente veneziano, ambiente veneto: Governanti e governati nel dominio di qua dal Mincio nei secoli XV–XVIII." In *Storia della cultura veneta*, ed. G. Arnaldi and M. Pastore Stocchi, vol. 4, pt. 2, *Il Seicento*, 495–539. Vicenza: Neri Pozza, 1984.

————. "Considerazioni sull'amministrazione della giustizia nella repubblica di Venezia (secc. XV–XVI)." In *Florence and Venice: Comparisons and Relations; Acts of two Conferences at Villa I Tatti in 1976–1977; Organized by Sergio Bertelli, Nicolai Rubinstein, and Craig Hugh Smyth*, vol. 2, *Cinquecento*, ed. Christine Smith, with Salvatore I. Camporeale, 101–133. Florence: La Nuova Italia Editrice, 1980.

————. "La politica del diritto nella Republica di Venezia." In *Stato, società e giustizia nella repubblica Veneta (sec. XV–XVIII)*, ed. Gaetano Cozzi, 17–151. Rome: Jouvence, 1980.

Cozzi, Gaetano, and M. Knapton. *La repubblica di Venezia nell'età moderna*. Vol. 1. *Dalla guerra di Chioggia al 1517*. Turin: UTET, 1986.

Crouzet-Pavan, Elisabeth. *"Sopra le acque salse": Espaces, pouvoir et société à Venise à la fin du moyen âge*. 2 vols. Nuovi studi storici 14. Rome: École française de Rome and Istituto storico italiano per il medio evo, 1992.

D'Amico, John F. *Renaissance Humanism in Papal Rome: Humanists and Church-men on the Eve of the Reformation.* Baltimore: Johns Hopkins University Press, 1983.

Davidson, Nicholas. "'As Much for Its Culture as for Its Arms': The Cultural Relations of Venice and Its Dependent Cities, 1400–1700." In *Mediterranean Urban Culture, 1400–1700,* ed. Alexander Cowan, 197–214. Exeter: University of Exeter Press, 2000.

Davis, Natalie Zemon. *The Gift in Sixteenth-Century France.* Oxford: Oxford University Press, 2000.

———. "The Rites of Violence: Religious Riot in Sixteenth-century France." *Past and Present* 59 (1973): 51–91.

Davis, Robert C., and Benjamin Ravid, eds. *The Jews of Early Modern Venice.* Baltimore: Johns Hopkins University Press, 2001.

Dean, Trevor. "Commune and Despot: The Commune of Ferrara under Este Rule, 1300–1450." In *City and Countryside in Late Medieval and Renaissance Italy: Essays presented to Philip Jones,* ed. Trevor Dean and Chris Wickham, chap. 13. London: Hambledon Press, 1990.

Del Col, Andrea. "Organizzazione, composizione e giurisdizione dei tribunali dell'Inquisizione romana nella repubblica di Venezia (1500–1550)." *Critica Storica* 25 (1988): 244–294.

Della Misericordia, Massimo. "La 'coda' dei gentiluomini: Fazioni, mediazione politica, clientelismo nello stato territoriale; il caso della montagna lombarda durante il dominio sforzesco (XV secolo)." In *Guelfi e ghibellini nell'Italia del Rinascimento,* ed. Marco Gentile, 275–389. Rome: Viella, 2005.

———. "Decidere e agire in comunità nel XV secolo (un aspetto del dibattito politico nel dominio sforzesco)." In *Linguaggi politici nell'Italia del Rinascimento: Atti del convegno Pisa, 9–11 novembre 2006,* ed. Andrea Gamberini and Giuseppe Petralia, 291–378. Rome: Viella, 2007.

———. *La disciplina contrattata: Vescovi e vassalli tra Como e le Alpi nel tardo Medioevo.* Milan: Unicopli, 2000.

Del Torre, Giuseppe. "Stato regionale e benefici ecclesiastici: vescovadi e canonicati nella terraferma veneziana all'inizio dell'età moderna." *Atti dell'Istituto Veneto di Scienze, Lettere ed Arti* 151 (1992–93): 1171–1236.

———. *Il Trevigiano nei secoli XV e XVI: L'assetto amministrativo e il sistema fiscale.* Venice: Il Cardo and Fondazione Benetton, 1990.

———. *Venezia e la terraferma dopo la guerra di Cambrai: Fiscalità e amministrazione (1515–1530).* Milan: Franco Angeli, 1986.

De Sandre Gasparini, Giuseppina. "L'amministrazione pubblica dell'evento religioso: Qualche esempio della terraferma veneta del secolo XV." In *La religion civique à l'époque médiévale et moderne (Chrétienté et Islam): Actes du colloque organisé per le centre de recherche "Histoire sociale et culturelle de l'occident. XIIe–XVIIIe siècle" de l'université de Paris X. Nanterre et l'Institut universitaire de France (Nanterre, 21–23 juin 1993),* 201–217. Rome: École Française de Rome, 1995.

Desreumaux, Roger. "Savino e Cipriano." *BS,* vol. 11, cols. 704–705.

Dickson, Gary. "The 115 Cults of the Saints in Later Medieval and Renaissance

Perugia: A Demographic Overview of a Civic Pantheon." *Renaissance Studies* 12 (1998): 6–25.

Dionisotti, Carlo. "Elia Capriolo e Veronica Gàmbara." In *Veronica Gambara e la poesia del suo tempo nell'Italia settentrionale: Atti del Convegno (Brescia-Correggio, 17–19 ottobre 1985)*, ed. Cesare Bozzetti, Pietro Gibellini, and Ennio Sandal, 13–21. Florence: Olschki, 1989.

Ditchfield, Simon. "'In Search of Local Knowledge': Rewriting Early Modern Italian Religious History." *Cristianesimo nella Storia* 19 (1998): 255–296.

Dizionario biografico degli Italiani. Rome: Istituto della enciclopedia italiana, 1960–.

Ederer, Martin F. *Humanism, Scholasticism, and the Theology and Preaching of Domenico de' Domenichi in the Italian Renaissance*. Lewiston, Me.: Edwin Mellen Press, 2003.

Eire, Carlos M. N. *From Madrid to Purgatory: The Art and Craft of Dying in Sixteenth-century Spain*. Cambridge: Cambridge University Press, 1995.

Elliott, J. H. "A Europe of Composite Monarchies." *Past and Present* 137 (1992): 48–71.

Enciclopedia Bresciana. 20 vols. Brescia: Edizioni "La voce del popolo," n. d.–2001.

Esposito, Anna. "Il culto del 'beato' Simonino e la sua prima diffusione in Italia." In *Il principe vescovo Johannes Hinderbach (1465–1486) fra tardo Medioevo e umanesimo: Atti del convegno promosso dalla biblioteca comunale di Trento (2–6 ottobre 1989)*, ed. Iginio Rogger and Marco Bellabarba, 429–443. Bologna: Edizioni dehoniane, 1992.

———. "Lo stereotipo dell'omicidio rituale nei processi tridentini e il culto del 'beato' Simone." In *Processi contro gli ebrei di Trento (1475–1478)*, vol 1, *I processi del 1475*, ed. Anna Esposito and Diego Quaglioni, 53–95. Padua: CEDAM, 1990.

Esposito, Anna, and Diego Quaglioni, eds. *Processi contro gli ebrei di Trento (1475–1478)*. Padua: CEDAM, 1990.

Falcioni, Anna. "Brescia." In *Gentile da Fabriano: Studi e ricerche*, ed. Andrea De Marchi, Laura Laureati, and Lorenza Mochi Onori, 116–120. Milan: Electa, 2006.

———. "Malatesta, Pandolfo." *DBI*, 68:90–95.

Fappani, Antonio. "Ercolano." *BS*, vol. 4: cols. 1301–1302.

Fasano Guarini, E. "Center and Periphery." In *The Origins of the State in Italy, 1300–1600*, ed. Julius Kirshner, chap. 4. Chicago: University of Chicago Press, 1996.

———. *Potere e società negli stati regionali del '500 e '600*. Bologna: Il Mulino, 1978.

Fasoli, Gina. "Nascità di un mito." In *Studi storici in onore di Gioacchino Volpe per il suo 80 compleanno*, 1:445–479. Florence: Sansoni, 1958.

———. "Il nunzio permanente di Vicenza a Venezia nel secolo XVI." *Archivio Veneto*, 5th ser., 17 (1935): 90–178.

Fasoli, Sara. "Tra riforme e nuove fondazioni: L'osservanza domenicana nel ducato di Milano." *Nuova Rivista Storica* 76 (1992): 416–494.

Fè D'Ostiani, L., ed. *Di un codice laudario Bresciano-Vaticano*. Brescia: Querini-ana, 1893.

Ferraro, Joanne M. *Family and Public Life in Brescia, 1580–1650: The Founda-tions of Power in the Venetian State*. Cambridge: Cambridge University Press, 1993. Translated by Laura Novati as *Vita pubblica e privata a Brescia (1580–1650): I fondamenti del potere nella repubblica di Venezia* (Brescia: Edizioni Morcelliana, 1998).

———. "Oligarchs, Protesters, and the Republic of Venice: The 'Revolution of the Discontents' in Brescia, 1644–1645." *Journal of Modern History* 60 (1988): 627–653.

———. "Proprietà terriera e potere nello stato veneto: La nobiltà bresciana del '400–'500." In *Dentro lo "stado italico": Venezia e la terraferma fra Quattro e Seicento*, ed. G. Cracco and M. Knapton, 159–182. Trent: Gruppo Culturale Civis-Biblioteca Cappuccini, 1984.

Ferri Piccaluga, Gabriella. "Ebrei nell'iconografia lombarda del '400." In Ferri Pic-caluga, *Il confine del nord: Microstoria in Vallecamonica per una storia d'Europa*, 305–334. Valcamonica: BIM, 1989.

———. "Economia, devozione e politica: Immagini di francescani, amadeiti ed ebrei nel secolo XV." In *Il Francescanesimo in Lombardia: Storia e arte*, 107–122. Milan: Silvana, 1983.

———. "Iconografia francescana in Vallecamonica." In Ferri Piccaluga, *Il confine del nord: Microstoria in Vallecamonica per una storia d'Europa*, 255–275. Valcamonica: BIM, 1989.

———. "Tra liturgia e teatralità: Consuetudini sociali immagini dal medioevo al controriforma." In Ferri Piccaluga, *Il confine del nord: Microstoria in Valle-camonica per una storia d'Europa*, 137–164. Valcamonica: BIM, 1989.

Ffoulkes, C. Jocelyn. "The Date of Vincenzo Foppa's Death: Gleanings from the Archives of S. Alessandro at Brescia." *Burlington Magazine for Connoisseurs* 1.1 (1903): 103–121.

Finlay, Robert. "The Foundation of the Ghetto: Venice, the Jews, and the War of the League of Cambrai." *Proceedings of the American Philosophical Society* 126.2 (1982): 140–154.

———. "Venice, the Po Expedition, and the End of the League of Cambrai, 1509–1510." In Finlay, *Venice Besieged: Politics and Diplomacy in the Italian Wars, 1494–1534*, chap. 6. Aldershot, England: Ashgate, 2008.

Firpo, M. "Carmeliano, Pietro." *DBI*, 20:410–413.

Franzoi, Umberto, Terisio Pignatti, and Wolfgang Wolters. *Il palazzo ducale di Venezia*. Treviso: Canova, 1990.

Frassòn, Paolo. "Tra volgare e latino: Aspetti della ricerca di un propria identità da parte di magistrature e cancelleria a Venezia (Secc. XV–XVI)." In *Stato, soci-età e giustizia nella repubblica Veneta (sec. XV–XVIII)*, ed. Gaetano Cozzi, 577–615. Rome: Jouvence, 1980.

Frati, Vasco. "Gli osservanti a Brescia e la fondazione dl convento di S. Giuseppe." In *Il Francescanesimo in Lombardia: storia e arte*, 436–448. Milan: Silvana, 1983.

Frati, Vasco, Ida Gianfranceschi, Françoise Bonali Fiquet, Irene Perini Bianchi, Franco Robecchi, and Rosa Zilioli Faden, eds. *Il sacco di Brescia: Testimoni-*

anze, cronache, diari, atti del processo e memorie storiche della "presa memoranda et crudele" della città nel 1512. 2 vols. in 3 pts. Brescia: Grafo, 1989.

Frati, Vasco, Ida Gianfranceschi, and Franco Robecchi, *La loggia di Brescia e la sua piazza: Evoluzione di un fulcro urbano nella storia di mezzo millennio.* 3 vols. Brescia: Grafo, 1993–95.

Frazier, Alison Knowles. *Possible Lives: Authors and Saints in Renaissance Italy.* New York: Columbia University Press, 2005.

Fubini, Riccardo. *Storiografia dell'umanesimo in Italia da Leonardo Bruni ad Annio da Viterbo.* Rome: Edizioni della storia e letteratura, 2003.

Gamba, Aldo. *Gli ebrei a Brescia nei secoli XV–XVI: Appunti per uno studio storico.* Brescia: Il maglio, 1938.

Gamberini, Andrea. *La città assediata: Poteri e identità; Politiche a Reggio in età viscontea.* Rome: Viella, 2003.

———. *Lo stato viscontea: Linguaggi politici e dinamiche costituzionali.* Milan: Franco Angeli, 2005.

Geertz, Clifford. "Deep Play: Notes on the Balinese Cockfight." In Geertz, *The Interpretation of Cultures,* 412–453. London: Hutchinson, 1973.

———. *Local Knowledge: Further Essays in Interpretative Anthropology.* New York: Basic Books, 1983.

Gengaro, Maria Luisa, Francesca Leoni, and Gemma Villa. *Codici decorati e miniati dell'Ambrosiana ebraici e greci.* Milan: Casa editrice Ceschina, 1957.

Gentilcore, David. *From Bishop to Witch: The System of the Sacred in Early Modern Terra d'Otranto.* Manchester: Manchester University Press, 1992.

Gentile, Marco. *Terra e poteri: Parma e il Parmense nel ducato viscontea all'inizio del Quattrocento.* Milan: Unicopli, 2001.

———. "Postquam malignitates temporum hec nobis dedere nomina . . . : Fazioni, idiomi politici e practiche di governo nella tarda età viscontea." In *Guelfi e ghibellini nell'Italia del Rinascimento,* ed. M. Gentile, 249–274. Rome: Viella, 2005.

Ghirardo, Diane Yvonne. "The Topography of Prostitution in Renaissance Ferrara." *Journal of the Society of Architectural Historians* 60.4 (2001): 402–431.

Giansante, M. "Capriolo, Elia." *DBI,* 19:218–219.

Gilbert, Felix. "Venice in the Crisis of the League of Cambrai." Chap. 10 of *Renaissance Venice,* ed. John R. Hale. London: Faber and Faber, 1973.

Ginatempo, Maria. "Spunti comparativi sulle trasformazioni della fiscalità nell'Italia post-comunale." In *Politiche finanziarie e fiscali nell'Italia settentrionale (secoli XIII–XV),* ed. Patrizia Mainoni, 125–220. Milan: Unicopli, 2001.

Ginzburg, Carlo. "Clues: Roots of an Evidential Paradigm." In Ginzburg, *Clues, Myths, and the Historical Method.* Trans. John Tedeschi and Anne ca. Tedeschi, 96–125. Baltimore: Johns Hopkins University Press, 1989.

———. *Ecstasies: Deciphering the Witches' Sabbath.* Trans. Raymond Rosenthal. Ed. Gregory Elliot. London: Hutchinson, 1989.

Giorgetta, Giovanni. "Documenti sull' inquisizione a Morbegno nella prima metà del secolo XV." *Bollettino della Società Storica Valtellinese* 33 (1980): 59–83.

———. "Un pestalozzi accusato di stregoneria." *Clavenna: Bollettino del Centro di Studi Storici Valciavennaschi* 20 (1981): 58–72, www.paoloportone.it/giorgetta1/giorgetta1.htm

————. "Processi di stregoneria a Bormio tra il 1483 ed il 1486." *Bollettino della Società Storica Valtellinese* 36 (1983): 153–167, www.paoloportone.it/giorgetta2/giorgetta2.htm

Giuliani, I. "Genesi e primo secolo di vita del magistrato sopra monasteri, Venezia, 1519–1620." *Le Venezie Francescane: Rivista Storica Artistica Letteraria Illustrata* 28 (1961): 42–68, 106–169.

Glissenti, Fabio. *Gli ebrei nel Bresciano al tempo della dominazione veneta: Nuove ricerche e studi; Saggio storico letto all' Ateneo di Brescia il 9 marzo 1890.* Brescia: F. Apollonio, 1891.

Gnaga, Arnaldo. *Vocabolario topografico toponomastico della provincia di Brescia.* Brescia: P. L. Orfani, 1937; Facsimile edn., 1981.

Goldthwaite, Richard A. *Wealth and the Demand for Art in Italy, 1300–1600.* Baltimore: Johns Hopkins University Press, 1993.

Gossman, Lionel. *Basel in the Age of Burckhardt: A Study in Unseasonable Ideas.* Chicago: University of Chicago Press, 2000.

Grendler, Paul F. *Schooling in Renaissance Italy: Literacy and Learning, 1300–1600.* Baltimore: Johns Hopkins University Press, 1989.

Grubb, James S. "Elite Citizens." Chap. 10 of *Venice Reconsidered: The History and Civilization of an Italian City-State, 1297–1797,* ed. John Martin and Dennis Romano. Baltimore: Johns Hopkins University Press, 2000.

————. *Firstborn of Venice: Vicenza in the Renaissance State.* Baltimore: Johns Hopkins University Press, 1988.

————. "Patriziato, nobiltà, legittimazione: con particolare riguardo al Veneto." In *Istituzioni, società e potere nella marca trevigiana e veronese (secoli XIII–XIV) sulle tracce di G. B. Verci: Atti del convegno, Treviso, 25–27 Settembre 1986,* ed. Gherardo Ortalli and Michael Knapton, 235–251. Rome: Istituto storico italiano per il medio evo, 1988.

————. *Provincial Families of the Renaissance: Private and Public Life in the Veneto.* Baltimore: Johns Hopkins University Press, 1996.

————. "The Venetian Patriciate: The View from Below." Paper presented at the fifty-fourth annual meeting of the Renaissance Society of America, Chicago, 3–5 Apr. 2008.

————. "When Myths Lose Power: Four Decades of Venetian Historiography." *Journal of Modern History* 58 (1986): 43–94.

Guazzoni, V. *Moretto: Il tema sacro.* Brescia: Grafo, 1981.

Guerrini, Paolo. "Un cancelliere vescovile del quattrocento." *Brixia Sacra* 6 (1915): 18–29.

————. *Una celebre famiglia lombarda: I conti di Martinengo; Studi e ricerche genealogiche.* Brescia: Geroldi, 1930.

————. *Cronotassi biobibliografica dei cardinali, arcivescovi e abbati regolari di origine bresciana dal secolo IX al tempo presente.* Brescia: Scuola tipografica opera pavoniana, 1958.

————. "Il 'libro d'oro' della nobiltà bresciana nel cinquecento." *Rivista del Collegio Araldico (Rivista Araldica)* 17 (1919): 196–201, 231–237, 272–276, 319–322; 26 (1928): 467–473.

————. "Miscellanea bresciana." *Memorie Storiche della Diocesi di Brescia* 1 (1953).

————. "Il nobile collegio dei giudici di Brescia e la sua matricola dal 1342 al 1796." *Rivista Araldica* 24 (1926): 485–493.

————. "Il Santuario delle grazie." *Brixia Sacra* 2 (1911): 249–281.

————. "Un umanista bagnolese prigioniero dei Turchi a Constantinopoli e a Rodi." *Brixia Sacra* 6 (1915): 261–271.

————. "Umanisti bresciani minori." *Memorie Storiche della Diocesi di Brescia* 27 (1960): 86–95.

————, ed. *Le cronache bresciane inedite dei secoli XV–XIX.* 5 vols. Brescia: Brixia Sacra, 1922–32.

Gundersheimer, Werner L. "Crime and Punishment in Ferrara, 1440–1500." Chap. 5 of *Violence and Civil Disorder in Italian Cities, 1200–1500,* ed. Lauro Martines. Berkeley: University of California Press, 1972.

Hanawalt, Barbara A., ed. *Women and Work in Preindustrial Europe.* Bloomington: Indiana University Press, 1986.

Handelman, Don. *Models and Mirrors: Towards an Anthropology of Public Events.* Cambridge: Cambridge University Press, 1990.

Hansen, Joseph. *Quellen und Untersuchungen zur Geschichte des Hexenwahns und der Hexenverfolgung im Mittelalter: Mit einer Untersuchung der Geschichte des Wortes Hexe von Johannes Franck.* Bonn: C. Georgi, 1901.

Hay, Denys. *The Church in Italy in the Fifteenth Century: The Birkbeck Lectures, 1971.* Rev. ed. Cambridge: Cambridge University Press, 1979.

Hay, Denys, and John Law. *Italy in the Age of the Renaissance, 1380–1530.* London: Longman, 1989.

Henderson, John. *Piety and Charity in Late Medieval Florence.* Oxford: Clarendon Press, 1994.

Hiesinger, Kathryn B. "The Fregoso Monument: A Study in Sixteenth-century Tomb Monuments and Catholic Reform." *Burlington Magazine* 118 (1976): 283–293.

Hind, Arthur M. *Early Italian Engraving: A Critical Catalogue with Complete Reproduction of All the Prints Described.* 7 vols. London: B. Quaritch, 1938–48.

Holgate, Ian. "Paduan Culture in Venetian Care: The Patronage of Bishop Pietro Donato (Padua 1428–47)." *Renaissance Studies* 16.1 (2002): 1–23.

Hornblower, Simon, and Antony Spawforth, eds. *The Oxford Classical Dictionary.* 3rd ed. Oxford: Clarendon Press, 1996.

Houlbrooke, Ralph. *Death, Religion, and the Family in England, 1480–1750.* Oxford: Clarendon Press, 1998.

Howard, Deborah. *The Architectural History of Venice.* New Haven: Yale University Press, 2002.

Hyde, J. K. *Padua in the Age of Dante.* Manchester: Manchester University Press, 1966.

————. *Society and Politics in Medieval Italy: The Evolution of the Civil Life, 1000–1350.* London: Macmillan, 1973.

Ianziti, Gary. *Humanistic Historiography under the Sforzas: Politics and Propaganda in Fifteenth-century Milan.* Oxford: Clarendon Press, 1988.

Isaacs, Ann Katherine. "States in Tuscany and Veneto." In *Resistance, Representation, and Community*, ed. Peter Blickle, 291–304. Cambridge: Cambridge University Press, 1997.

Jacobson Schutte, Anne. *Aspiring Saints: Pretense of Holiness, Inquisition, and Gender in the Republic of Venice, 1618–1750*. Baltimore: Johns Hopkins University Press, 2001.

Jacoby, David. "Les juifs à Venise du XIVe au milieu du XVIe siècle." In *Venezia: Centro di mediazione tra oriente e occidente (secoli XV–XVI); aspetti e problemi*, ed. Hans-Georg Beck, Manoussos Manoussacas, and Agostino Pertusi, 163–216. Florence: Olschki, 1977.

James, Mervyn. "Ritual, Drama and Social Body in the Late Medieval English Town." *Past and Present* 98 (1983): 3–29.

Jedin, Hubert. "Vincenzo Quirini und Pietro Bembo." In Jedin, *Kirche des Glaubens—Kirche der Geschichte: Ausgewählte Aufsätze und Vorträge*, 1:153–166. Freiburg im Breisgau: Herder, 1966.

Jones, Philip. "Economia e società nell'Italia medievale: La leggenda della borghesia." In *Storia d'Italia: Annali, 1. Dal feudalesimo al capitalismo*, 185–372. Turin: Einaudi, 1978.

———. *The Italian City-State: From Commune to Signoria*. Oxford: Clarendon Press, 1997.

Joost-Gaugier, Christiane L. "Bartolomeo Colleoni as a Patron of Art and Architecture: The Palazzo Colleoni in Brescia." *Arte Lombarda*, new ser. 84/85 (1988): 61–72.

Jotischky, Andrew. *The Carmelites and Antiquity: Mendicants and Their Pasts in the Middle Ages*. Oxford: Oxford University Press, 2002.

Katz, Dana E. *The Jew in the Art of the Italian Renaissance*. Philadelphia: University of Pennsylvania Press, 2008.

Kieckhefer, Richard. *European Witch Trials: Their Foundations in Popular and Learned Culture, 1300–1500*. Berkeley: University of California Press, 1976.

———. *Magic in the Middle Ages*. Cambridge: Cambridge University Press, 1989.

King, Margaret L. *The Death of the Child Valerio Marcello*. Chicago: University of Chicago Press, 1994.

———. *Venetian Humanism in an Age of Patrician Dominance*. Princeton: Princeton University Press, 1986.

Kirshner, Julius. "Capriolo, Angelo." *DBI* 19:217–218.

———. "*Civitas sibi faciat civem*: Bartolus of Sassoferrato's Doctrine on the Making of a Citizen." *Speculum* 48 (1973): 694–713.

———, ed. *The Origins of the State in Italy, 1300–1600*. Chicago: University of Chicago Press, 1996.

Knapton, M. "Il consiglio dei dieci nel governo della terraferma: un'ipotesi interpretativa per il secondo '400." In *Atti del convegno Venezia e la terraferma attraverso le relazioni dei rettori: Trieste 23–24 ottobre 1980*, 235–260. Milan: Giuffrè, 1981.

———. "'Nobiltà e popolo' e un trentennio di storiografia veneta." *Nuova Rivista Storica* 82 (1998): 167–192.

―――. "I rapporti fiscali tra Venezia e la terraferma: Il caso padovano nel secondo '400." *Archivio Veneto*, 5th ser., 117 (1981): 5–65.

―――. "Il Territorio vicentino nello stato veneto dell '500 e primo '600: Nuovi equilibri politici e fiscali." In *Dentro lo "stado italico": Venezia e la terraferma fra Quattro e Seicento*, ed. G. Cracco and M. Knapton, 33–115. Trent: Gruppo Culturale Civis-Biblioteca Cappuccini, 1984.

―――. "Tribunali veneziani e proteste padovane nel secondo Quattrocento." In *Studi veneti offerti a Gaetano Cozzi*, ed. Gino Benzoni, Marino Berengo, Gherardo Ortalli, and Giovanni Scarabello, 151–170. Vicenza: Il cardo, 1992.

Kohl, Benjamin G. *Padua under the Carrara, 1318–1405*. Baltimore: Johns Hopkins University Press, 1998.

Koslofsky, Craig M. *The Reformation of the Dead: Death and Ritual in Early Modern Germany, 1450–1700*. Basingstoke, England: Macmillan, 2000.

Kovesi Killerby, Catherine. "'Heralds of a Well-instructed Mind': Nicolosa Sanuti's Defence of Women and Their Clothes." *Renaissance Studies* 13.3 (1999): 255–282.

―――. *Sumptuary Law in Italy 1200–1500*. Oxford: Clarendon Press, 2002.

Kristeller, Paul Oskar. "The Alleged Ritual Murder of Simon of Trent (1475) and Its Literary Repercussions: A Bibliographical Study." *Proceedings of the American Academy for Jewish Research* 59 (1993): 103–135.

Labalme, Patricia H. "Sodomy and Venetian Justice in the Renaissance." *Tijdschrift voor rechtsgeschiedenis¹/¹Revue d'histoire du droit¹/¹Legal History Review* 52 (1984): 217–254.

Lanaro Sartori, Paola. "Economia cittadina, flussi migratori e spazio urbano in terraferma veneta tra basso medioevo ed età moderna." In *La città italiana e i luoghi degli stranieri XIV–XVIII secolo*, ed. Donatella Calabi and Paola Lanaro, 63–81. Rome: Laterza, 1998.

―――. "L'esenzione fiscale a Verona nel '400 e nel '500: Un momento di scontro tra ceto dirigente e ceti subalterni." In *Il sistema fiscale veneto*, ed. G. Borelli, P. Lanoro, and F. Vecchiato, 189–215. Verona: Libreria universitario editrice, 1982.

―――. "'Essere famiglia di consiglio': Social Closure and Economic Change in the Veronese Patriciate of the Sixteenth Century." *Renaissance Studies* 8.4 (1994): 428–438.

―――. *Un'oligarchia urbana nel Cinquecento veneto: Istituzioni, economia, società*. Turin: G. Giappichelli, 1992.

Lanza, G. *Firenze contro Milano: Gli intellettuali fiorentini nelle guerre con i Visconti (1390–1440)*. Anzio: De Rubeis, 1991.

Law, John E. "Un confronto fra due stati 'rinascimentali': Venezia e il dominio sforzesco." Chap. 2 of Law, *Venice and the Veneto in the Early Renaissance*. Aldershot, England: Ashgate, 2000.

―――. "The Cittadella of Verona." Chap. 15 of Law, *Venice and the Veneto in the Early Renaissance*. Aldershot, England: Ashgate, 2000.

―――. "The Venetian Mainland State in the Fifteenth Century." *Transactions of the Royal Historical Society*, 6th ser., 2 (1992): 153–174.

―――. "Venice and the 'Closing' of the Veronese Constitution in 1405." *Studi Veneziani*, new ser., 1 (1977): 69–103.

————. *Venice and the Veneto in the Early Renaissance.* Aldershot, England: Ashgate, 2000.

————. "Verona and the Venetian State in the Fifteenth Century." Chap. 10 of Law, *Venice and the Veneto in the Early Renaissance,* Aldershot, England: Ashgate, 2000.

Lazzarini, Isabella. *L'Italia degli stati territoriali: secoli XIII–XV.* Rome: Laterza, 2003.

Lechi, Fausto. *Le dimore bresciane in cinque secoli di storia.* 8 vols. Brescia: Edizioni di storia bresciana, 1973–1983.

Le Goff, Jacques. *Time, Work and Culture in the Middle Ages.* Trans. Arthur Goldhammer. Chicago: University of Chicago Press, 1980.

Leonardelli, Fabrizio. *"Pro bibliotheca erigenda": Manoscritti e incunaboli del vescovo di Trento Iohanne Hinderbach (1465–1486).* Trent: Comune di Trento—biblioteca comunale, 1989.

Le Roy Ladurie, Emmanuel. *Carnival: A People's Uprising at Romans, 1579–1580.* Trans. Mary Feeney. London: Scolar Press, 1980.

Lightbown, Ronald W. *Mantegna, with a Complete Catalogue of the Paintings, Drawings and Prints.* Oxford: Phaidon, 1986.

Lorenzi, Roberto Andrea, ed. *Sante, medichesse e streghe nell' arco alpino: Atti del convegno promossa dall'Università popolare di Val Camonica—Sebino, 24–25 aprile 1993.* Bolzano: Praxis, 1994.

Lucchesi Ragni, Elena. "Gli affreschi di Floriano Ferramola nel salone di palazzo Calini." In *La loggia di Brescia e la sua piazza: Evoluzione di un fulcro urbano nella storia di mezzo millennio,* ed. Vasco Frati, Ida Gianfranceschi, and Franco Robecchi, vol. 2, *La costruzione del palazzo (1492–1574): Dalla cultura Bramantesca agli interventi di Sansovino, Palladio e Tiziano,* 107–111. Brescia: Grafo, 1995.

————. "Vincenzo Foppa e la *figura Trayani imperatoris.*" In *La Loggia di Brescia e la sua piazza: Evoluzione di un fulcro urbano nella storia di mezzo millennio,* ed. Vasco Frati, Ida Gianfranceschi, and Franco Robecchi, vol 2, *Dall'apertura della piazza alla posa della prima pietra del palazzo della Loggia (1433–1492),* 251–260. Brescia: Grafo, 1993.

Lucchesi Ragni, Elena, Ida Gianfranceschi, and Maurizio Mondini, eds. *Il coro delle monache: Cori e corali.* Milan: Skira, 2003.

Lupo, Giulio. "Platea Magna Communis Brixiae: 1433–1509." Dottorato di ricerca in storia dell'architettura. Instituto universitario di architettura di Venezia, 1987.

Luzio, Alessandro. *L'archivio Gonzaga di Mantova: La corrispondenza familiare, amministrativa e diplomatici dei Gonzaga.* Verona: A. Mondadori, 1922.

McClure, George W., "The Art of Mourning: Autobiographical Writings on the Loss of a Son in Italian Humanist Thought (1400–1461)." *Renaissance Quarterly* 39 (1986): 440–475.

————. *Sorrow and Consolation in Italian Humanism.* Princeton: Princeton University Press, 1990.

McManamon, John M. *Funeral Oratory and the Cultural Ideals of Italian Humanism.* Chapel Hill: University of North Carolina Press, 1989.

Maccarinelli, Francesco. *Le glorie di Brescia, 1747–1751.* Ed. Camillo Boselli. Supplemented to the "Commentari dell'Ateneo di Brescia per il 1959." Brescia: Geroldi, 1959.

Mallett, Michael E. "La conquista della terraferma." In *Storia di Venezia dalle origini alla caduta della serenissima,* ed. Alberto Tenenti and Ugo Tucci, vol. 4, *Il Rinascimento: Politica e cultura,* 181–244. Rome: Istituto dell'enciclopedia italiana, 1996.

Mallett, Michael E., and J. R. Hale. *The Military Organisation of a Renaissance State: Venice c. 1400 to 1617.* Cambridge: Cambridge University Press, 1984.

Mannori, L. "Lo stato di Firenze e i suoi storici." *Società e Storia* 76 (1997): 401–415.

Marshall, Louise. "Manipulating the Sacred: Image and Plague in Renaissance Italy." *Renaissance Quarterly* 47 (1994): 485–532.

Marshall, Peter. *Beliefs and the Dead in Reformation England.* Oxford: Oxford University Press, 2002.

Martin, Ruth. *Witchcraft and the Inquisition in Venice, 1550–1650.* Oxford: Blackwell, 1989.

Martines, Lauro. *Strong Words: Writing and the Social Strain in the Italian Renaissance.* Baltimore: Johns Hopkins University Press, 2001.

Marubbi, Mario. *Vincenzo Civerchio: Contributo alla cultura figurativa cremasca nel primo Cinquecento.* Milan: Il vaglio cultura arte, 1986.

Massetti, Gianfranco. "Antisemitismo e presenza ebraica a Brescia nel Quattrocento." *Studi Trentini di Scienze Storiche* 74.2 (1995): 125–178.

———. "Il culto di Simonino a Brescia e l'affresco di Santa Maria Rotonda a Pian Camuno." *Ateneo Veneto,* 3rd ser., 190.2/1 (2003): 67–79.

Masetti Zannini, Antonio. "Silvino." *BS,* vol. 11, cols. 1087–1088.

Matzel, Klaus, and Jörg Riecke, eds. "Das Pfandregister der Regensburger Juden vom Jahre 1519." *Zeitschrift für Bayerische Landesgeschichte* 51 (1988): 767–806.

Mazzacane, Aldo. "Lo stato e il dominio nei giuristi veneti durante il 'secolo della terraferma.'" In *Storia della cultura veneta,* ed. G. Arnaldi and M. Pastore Stocchi, vol. 3, pt. 1, *Dal primo Quattrocento al concilio di Trento,* 577–650. Vicenza: Neri Pozza, 1980.

Mazzonis, Querciolo. "A Female Idea of Religious Perfection: Angela Merici and the Company of St Ursula (1535–40)." *Renaissance Studies* 18 (2004): 391–411.

———. *Spirituality, Gender, and the Self in Renaissance Italy: Angela Merici and the Company of St Ursula (1474–1540).* Washington, D.C.: Catholic University of America Press, 2007.

Medin, A. "Descrizione della città e terre bresciane nel 1493." *Archivio Storico Lombardo,* 2nd ser., 3 (1886): 676–686.

Meiss, Millard. *Painting in Florence and Siena after the Black Death.* Princeton: Princeton University Press, 1951.

Meneghin, Vittorino. *Bernardino da Feltre e i monti di pietà.* Vicenza: LIEF, 1974.

———. *I monti di pietà in Italia dal 1462 al 1562.* Vicenza: LIEF, 1986.

———. *San Michele in Isola di Venezia.* 2 vols. Venice: Stamperia di Venezia, 1962.

Menniti Ippolito, A. "La dedizione di Brescia a Milano (1421) e a Venezia (1427): Città suddite e distretto nello stato regionale." In *Stato, società e giustizia nella Repubblica veneta (secoli XV–XVIII)*, ed. G. Cozzi, 19–58. Rome: Jouvence, 1985.

———. "'Providibitur sicut melius videbitur': Milano e Venezia nel bresciano nel primo '400." *Studi Veneziani*, new ser., 8 (1984): 37–76.

Meserve, Margaret. "News from Negroponte: Politics, Popular Opinion, and Information Exchange in the First Decade of the Italian Press." *Renaissance Quarterly* 59 (2006): 440–480.

Milano, Attilio. *Storia degli ebrei in Italia*. 2nd ed. Turin: Einaudi, 1992.

Minnich, Nelson H. "Prophecy and the Fifth Lateran Council (1512–1517)." Chap. 4 of *Prophetic Rome in the High Renaissance Period: Essays*, ed. Marjorie Reeves. Oxford: Clarendon Press, 1992.

Mistura, Raffaele. *I giudici e i loro collegi: Ricerche sul territorio veneto*. Padua: CEDAM, 1986.

———. "Dei privilegi più speciali concessi dalla serenissima alla Brescia." In *Studi in onore di Ugo Gualazzini*, 2:377–407. Milan: Giuffrè, 1981.

Mitchell, Bonner. *The Majesty of State: Triumphal Progresses of Foreign Sovereigns in Renaissance Italy (1494–1600)*. Florence: Olschki, 1986.

Montanari, Daniele. "I monti di pietà del territorio bresciano (secoli XV–XIX)." In *Per il quinto centenario del monte di pietà a Brescia (1489–1989)*, ed. Daniele Montanari and Roberto Navarrini, 1:231–270. Travagliato-Brescia: Officina grafica artigiana, 1989.

———. *Quelle terre di là dal Mincio: Brescia e il contado in età veneta*. Brescia: Grafo, 2005.

Monti della Corte, Alessandro Augusto. *Le famiglie del patriziato Bresciano*. Brescia: Fratelli Geroldi, 1960.

———. "Il registro veneto dei nobili estimati nel territorio bresciano tra il 1426 e il 1498: 'Cives agrestes habitantes in villis Brixiane qui appellantur nobiles'; (Archivio di stato di Brescia fondo territoriale ex Veneto—mazzo 256)." *Commentari dell'Ateneo di Brescia* 159 (1960): 165–274.

Morassi, Antonio, ed. *Catalogo delle cose d'arte e di antichità d'Italia: Brescia*. Rome: Libreria dello Stato, 1939.

Moretti, Silvia. "Vicenza: XV–XVII secolo: Tra volontà di riscatto e 'normalizzazione.'" In *Fabbriche, piazze, mercati: La città italiana nel Rinascimento*, ed. Donatella Calabi, 224–254. Rome: Officina, 1997.

Mormando, Franco. *The Preacher's Demons: Bernardino of Siena and the Social Underworld of Early Renaissance Italy*. Chicago: University of Chicago Press, 1999.

Mueller, Reinhold C. "L'imperialismo monetario veneziano nel Quattrocento." *Società e Storia* 8 (1980): 277–297.

———. "Lo *status* degli ebrei nella terraferma veneta del Quattrocento: tra politica, religione, cultura ed economia; Saggio introduttivo." In *Ebrei nella terraferma veneta del Quattrocento*, ed. G. M. Varanini and R. Mueller, 1–21. Florence: Florence University Press, 2005.

Muir, Edward. *Civic Ritual in Renaissance Venice*. Princeton: Princeton University Press, 1981.

————. *Mad Blood Stirring: Vendette and Factions in Friuli during the Renaissance.* Baltimore: Johns Hopkins University Press 1993.

————. *Ritual in Early Modern Europe.* Cambridge: Cambridge University Press, 1997.

————. "The Virgin on the Street Corner: The Place of the Sacred in Italian Cities." In *Religion and Culture in the Renaissance and Reformation,* ed. Steven Ozment, 25–40. Kirksville, Mo.: Sixteenth Century Essays and Studies, 1989.

Muir, Edward, and Guido Ruggiero, eds. *Microhistory and the Lost Peoples of Europe.* Trans. Eren Branch. Baltimore: Johns Hopkins University Press, 1991.

Muraro, Maria Teresa. "La festa a Venezia e le sue manifestazioni rappresentative: Le compagnie della calza e le *momarie.*" In *Storia della cultura veneta,* ed. Girolamo Arnaldi and Manlio Pastore Stocchi, vol. 3, *Dal primo quattrocento al Consilio di Trento,* 315–341. Vicenza: Neri Pozza, 1981.

Murphy, P. V. "A Worldly Reform: Honor and Pastoral Practice in the Career of Cardinal Ercole Gonzaga (1505–63)." *Sixteenth Century Journal* 31 (2000): 399–418.

Muzzarelli, Maria Giuseppina. *Pescatori di uomini: Predicatori e piazze alla fine del Medioevo.* Bologna: Il Mulino, 2005.

Neher, Gabriele. "Moretto and Romanino: Religious Painting in Brescia 1510–1550; Identity in the Shadow of *la Serenissima.*" Ph.D. diss., University of Warwick, 2000.

————. "Moretto and the Congregation of S. Giorgio in Alga 1540–1550: Fashioning a Visual Identity of a Religious Congregation." In *Fashioning Identities in Renaissance Art,* ed. Mary Rogers, 131–148. Aldershot, England: Ashgate, 2000.

Nevola, Fabrizio. *Siena: Constructing the Renaissance City.* New Haven: Yale University Press, 2008.

Niccoli, Ottavia. *Prophecy and People in Renaissance Italy.* Trans. Lydia G. Cochrane. Princeton: Princeton University Press, 1990.

————. "I re dei morti sul campo di Agnadello." *Quaderni Storici* 51 (1982): 929–958.

Niero, Antonio. "Culto dei santi militari nel veneto." In *Armi e cultura nel bresciano, 1420–1870,* 225–272. Brescia: Ateneo di Brescia, 1981.

Nodari, Alberto. "Ottaziano." *BS,* vol. 9, cols. 1314–1315.

————. "Paterio." *BS,* vol. 10, cols. 374–376.

————. "Tiziano." *BS,* vol. 12, cols. 507–508.

————. "Vigilio." *BS,* vol. 12, cols. 1085–1086.

Nora, Pierre. "Between Memory and History: *Les lieux de mémoire.*" *Representations* 26 (1989): 7–25.

Nova, Alessandro. *Girolamo Romanino.* Turin: Umberto Allemandi, 1994.

Nutton, Vivian. "Continuity or Rediscovery? The City Physician in Classical Antiquity and Medieval Italy." In *The Town and State Physician in Europe from the Middle Ages to the Enlightenment,* ed. Andrew W. Russell, 9–46. Wolfenbüttel: Herzog August Bibliothek, 1981.

Odorici, Federico. *Storie bresciane dai primi tempi sino all'età nostra.* 11 vols. Brescia: Pietro di Lor Gilberti, 1853–65.

———. *Le streghe di Valtellina e la santa inquisizione con documenti inediti del secolo XVI.* Milan, 1862.

O'Malley, John W. *Giles of Viterbo on Church and Reform.* Leiden: Brill, 1968.

Ong, Walter J. *Orality and Literacy: The Technologizing of the Word.* London: Methuen, 1982.

Otis, Leah Lydia. *Prostitution in Medieval Society: The History of an Urban Institution in Languedoc.* Chicago: University of Chicago Press, 1985.

Owen Hughes, Diane. "Distinguishing Signs: Ear-rings, Jews and Franciscan Rhetoric in the Italian Renaissance City." *Past and Present* 112 (1986): 3–59.

———. "Mourning Rites, Memory, and Civilization in Premodern Italy." In *Riti e rituali nelle società medievali,* ed. Jacques Chiffoleau, Lauro Martines, and Agostino Paravicini Bagliani, 23–38. Spoleto: Centro italiano di studi sull'alto medioevo, 1994.

Ozment, Steven E. *The Reformation in the Cities: The Appeal of Protestantism to Sixteenth-century Germany and Switzerland.* New Haven: Yale University Press, 1975.

Palmer, Richard. "Physicians and the State in Post-medieval Italy." In *The Town and State Physician in Europe from the Middle Ages to the Enlightenment,* ed. Andrew W. Russell, 47–61. Wolfenbüttel: Herzog August Bibliothek, 1981.

Panazza, Gaetano. "La pittura nella seconda metà del Quattrocento." In *Storia di Brescia,* ed. Giovanni Treccani degli Alfieri, vol. 2, *La dominazione veneta (1426–1575),* 949–1010. Brescia: Morcelliana, 1963.

———. *Il tesoro delle sante croci nel duomo vecchio di Brescia.* Brescia: Compagnia dei custodi delle sante croci, cattedrale di Brescia, 2000.

Panofsky, Erwin. *Tomb Sculpture: Four Lectures on Its Changing Aspects from Ancient Egypt to Bernini,* ed. H. W. Janson. London: Phaidon, 1992.

Parsons, Gerald. *Perspectives on Civil Religion.* Aldershot, England: Ashgate, 2002.

Parzani, Diego. "Istituzioni del bresciano durante la dominazione veneziana." *Civiltà Bresciana* 6.4 (1997): 3–20.

———. "Il territorio di Brescia intorno alla metà del quattrocento." *Studi Bresciani* 12 (1983): 51–75.

Pasero, Carlo. "Dati statistici e notizie intorno al movimento della popolazione bresciana durante il dominio veneto (1426–1797)." *Archivio Storico Lombardo,* 9th ser., 1 (1961): 71–97.

———. "Il dominio veneto fino all'incendio della loggia (1426–1575)." In *Storia di Brescia,* ed. Giovanni Treccani degli Alfieri, vol. 2, *La dominazione veneta (1426–1575),* 3–396. Brescia: Morcelliana, 1963.

———. *Francia, Spagna, Impero a Brescia, 1509–1516.* Brescia: Geroldi, 1958.

Passamani, Bruno. "La coscienza della romanità e gli studi antiquari tra umanesimo e neoclassicismo." In *Brescia Romana: Materiali per un museo.* 2:5–17. Brescia: Grafo, 1979.

Paton, Bernadette. "'Una città faticosa': Dominican Preaching and the Defence of the Republic in Late Medieval Siena." In *City and Countryside in Late Medieval and Renaissance Italy: Essays Presented to Philip Jones,* ed. Trevor Dean and Chris Wickham, 109–123. London: Hambledon, 1990.

————. *Preaching Friars and the Civic Ethos: Siena, 1380–1480.* London: Centre for Medieval Studies, Queen Mary and Westfield College, University of London, 1992.

————. "Preaching Friars and the Civic Ethos: Siena, 1380–1480." Ph.D. diss., University of Oxford, 1986. Microfilm.

————. "'To the Fire, to the Fire! Let Us Burn a Little Incense to God': Bernardino, Preaching Friars and *Maleficio* in Late Medieval Siena." In *No Gods Except Me: Orthodoxy and Religious Practice in Europe, 1200–1600,* ed. Charles Zika, 7–36. Parkville: University of Melbourne History Department, 1991.

Pegrari, M. *Le metamorfosi di un'economia urbana tra medioevo ed età moderna: Il caso di Brescia.* Brescia: Grafo, 2001.

Perani, Mauro. "La Bibbia ebraica Soncino di Brescia del 1494: Un esempio di continuità fra manoscritto e icunabolo." In *Gli ebrei a Castel Goffredo, con un studio sulla Bibbia Soncino di Brescia del 1494,* ed. Perani, 141–151. Florence: Giuntina, 1998.

Peroni, Adriano. "L'architettura e la scultura nei secoli XV e XVI." In *Storia di Brescia,* ed. Giovanni Treccani degli Alfieri, vol. 2, *La dominazione veneta (1426–1575),* 619–887. Brescia: Morcelliana, 1963.

Petrucci, Armando. *Public Lettering: Script, Power, and Culture.* Trans. Linda Lappin. Chicago: Chicago University Press, 1993.

————. *Writing the Dead: Death and Writing Strategies in the Western Tradition.* Trans. Michael Sullivan. Stanford: Stanford University Press, 1998.

Pezzana, Angelo. *Storia della città di Parma,* vol. 2, *1401–1449.* Parma: Dalla ducale tipografia, 1842.

Pialorsi, Vincenzo. "L'attività della zecca: 1406–1408." In *La signoria di Pandolfo III Malatesti a Brescia, Bergamo e Lecco,* ed. Giorgetta Bonfiglio-Dosio and Anna Falcioni, 137–153. Rimini: Bruno Ghigi Editore, 2000.

Piasentini, Stefano. "Le relazioni tra Venezia e Pandolfo III Malatesta nelle fonti veneziane (1404–21)." In *La signoria di Pandolfo III Malatesti a Brescia, Bergamo e Lecco,* ed. Giorgetta Bonfiglio-Dosio and Anna Falcioni, 175–216. Rimini: Bruno Ghigi Editore, 2000.

Po-chia Hsia, R. *The Myth of Ritual Murder: Jews and Magic in Reformation Germany.* New Haven: Yale University Press, 1988.

————. *Trent 1475: Stories of a Ritual Murder Trial.* New Haven: Yale University Press, 1992.

Pocock, J. G. A. *The Machiavellian Moment: Florentine Political Thought and the Atlantic Republican Tradition.* Princeton: Princeton University Press, 1975.

Polizzotto, Lorenzo. *The Elect Nation: The Savonarolan Movement in Florence, 1494–1545.* Oxford: Clarendon Press, 1994.

Porfyriou, Heleni. "Verona: XV–XVI secolo: Da 'virtù civile' a 'decoro pubblico.'" In *Fabbriche, piazze, mercati: La città italiana nel Rinascimento,* ed. Donatella Calabi, 189–223. Rome: Officina, 1997.

Povolo, Claudio. "Centro e periferia nella Repubblica di Venezia: Un profilo." In *Origini dello Stato: Processi di formazione statale in Italia fra medioevo ed età moderna,* ed. Giorgio Chittolini, Anthony Molho, and Pierangelo Schiera, 207–221. Bologna: Il Mulino, 1994.

————. "The Creation of Venetian Historiography." In *Venice Reconsidered: The History and Civilization of an Italian City-State, 1297–1797*, ed. John Martin and Dennis Romano, 491–519. Baltimore: Johns Hopkins University Press, 2000.

————. *Intrigo dell'onore: Potere e istituzioni nella repubblica di Venezia tra cinque e seicento*. Verona: Cierre, 1997.

"Processi di streghe." *Archivio Storico Lombardo* 6 (1889): 625–645.

Prodi, Paolo. "Istituzioni ecclesiastiche e mondo nobiliare." In *Patriziati e aristocrazie nobiliari*, ed. C. Mozzarelli and Pierangelo Schiera, 64–77. Trent: Libera università degli studi di Trento, 1978.

Pullan, Brian. *Rich and Poor in Renaissance Venice: The Social Institutions of a Catholic State, to 1620*. Oxford: Blackwell, 1971.

————. "'Three Orders of Inhabitants': Social Hierarchies in the Republic of Venice." In *Orders and Hierarchies in Late Medieval and Renaissance Europe*, ed. Jeffrey Denton, 147–168. Houndmills, England: Macmillan, 1999.

Putelli, Salvo Romolo. "[Documenti sul sacco di Brescia]." In *Il sacco di Brescia: Testimonianze, cronache, diari, atti del processo e memorie storiche della "presa memoranda et crudele" della città nel 1512*, ed. Vasco Frati, Ida Gianfranceschi, Françoise Bonali Fiquet, Irene Perini Bianchi, Franco Robecchi, and Rosa Zilioli Faden, vol. 1/pt. 1: 283–286. Brescia: Grafo, 1989.

————. *Intorno al castello di Breno: Storia di Valle Camonica, Lago d'Iseo e vicinanze da Federico Barbarossa a s. Carlo Borromeo*. Breno: Associazione "Pro Valle Camonica" editrice, 1915.

————. "Relazioni commerciali tra Venezia ed il bresciano nei secoli XIII e XIV." *Nuovo Archivio Veneto*, new ser., 30 (1915): 297–318.

Quondam, A. "La parte del volgare." In *I primordi della stampa a Brescia, 1472–1511: Atti del convegno internazionale (Brescia, 6–8 giugno 1984)*, ed. Ennio Sandal, 139–205. Padua: Editrice Antenore, 1986.

Rabil, Albert, Jr. *Laura Cereta: Quattrocento Humanist*. Binghamton, NY: Medieval and Renaissance Texts and Studies, 1981.

Raggi, Angelo Maria. "Iconografia." *BS*, vol. 2, cols. 269–275.

Raggio, Osvaldo. *Faide e parentele: Lo stato genovese visto dalla Fontanabuona*. Turin: Einaudi, 1990.

Rhodes, Dennis E. "The Career of Thomas Ferrandus of Brescia." *Bulletin of the John Rylands University Library of Manchester* 67.1 (1984): 544–559.

Rigaux, D. "Antijudaïsme par l'image: L'iconographie de Simon de Trente (+ 1475) dans la région de Brescia." In *Politique et religion dans le judaïsme ancien et médiéval: Interventions au colloque des 8 et 9 décembre 1987, organisé par le Centre d'études juives de l'université Paris–IV Sorbonne*, ed. D. Tollet, 309–318. Paris: Desclée, 1989.

————. "L'immagine di Simone di Trento nell'arco alpino per il secolo XV: Un tipo iconografico?" In *Il principe vescovo Johannes Hinderbach (1465–1486) fra tardo Medioevo e Umanesimo: Atti del convegno promosso dalla biblioteca comunale di Trento (2–6 ottobre 1989)*, ed. Iginio Rogger and Marco Bellabarba, 485–496. Bologna: Edizioni dehoniane, 1992.

Rimoldi, Antonio. "Anatalone." *BS*, vol. 1, cols. 1073–1074.

―――. "Apollonio." *BS*, vol. 2, col. 269.

―――. "Calimero." *BS*, vol. 3, cols. 670–672.

―――. "Filastrio." *BS*, vol. 5, cols. 684–685.

Rivetti, L. "Di Virgilio Bornato (o Bornati) viaggiatore bresciano del secolo XV." *Archivio Storico Italiano*, 5th ser., 33 (1904): 156–171.

Rizzi, Alberto. "Leontoclastia cambraica." In *Storia dell'arte marciana: Sculture, tesoro, arazzi. Atti del Convegno internazionale di studi Venezia, 11–14 ottobre 1994*, ed. Renato Polacco, 21–33. Venice: Marsilio, 1997.

Rizzinelli, Vincenzo. "I problemi giuridico-amministrativi: Aspetti del dominio scaligero, viscontea e malatestiano." In *Brescia nell'età delle signorie*, 97–108. Brescia: Grafo, 1984.

Rocke, Michael. *Forbidden Friendships: Homosexuality and Male Culture in Renaissance Florence*. Oxford: Oxford University Press, 1998.

Rogger, Iginio, and Marco Bellabarba, eds. *Il principe vescovo Johannes Hinderbach (1465–1486) fra tardo Medioevo e Umanesimo: Atti del convegno promosso dalla biblioteca comunale di Trento (2–6 ottobre 1989)*. Bologna: Edizioni dehoniane, 1992.

Romani, Marzio A. "Prestigio, potere e ricchezza nella Brescia di Agostino Gallo (prime indagini)." In *Agostino Gallo nella cultura del Cinquecento: Atti del convegno. Brescia, 23–24 ottobre 1987*, ed. Maurizio Pegrari, 109–133. Brescia: Edizioni del Moretto, 1988.

Romano, Dennis. "Gender and the Urban Geography of Renaissance Venice." *Journal of Social History* 23.2 (1989): 339–353.

―――. *The Likeness of Venice: A Life of Doge Francesco Foscari, 1373–1457*. New Haven: Yale University Press, 2007.

Rosand, David. *Myths of Venice: The Figuration of a State*. Chapel Hill: University of North Carolina Press, 2001.

Rossiaud, Jacques. *La Prostitution médiévale*. Paris: Flammarion, 1988.

Rossini, Alessandra. *Le campagne bresciane nel Cinquecento: Territorio, fisco, società*. Milan: Franco Angeli, 1994.

―――― "Continuità e trasformazioni nei rapporti tra la città di Brescia e il contado." *Civiltà Bresciana* 6.4 (Dec. 1997): 21–32.

Roth, Cecil. *The History of the Jews of Italy*. Philadelphia: Jewish Publication Society of America, 1946/5706.

Rubin, Miri. *Corpus Christi: The Eucharist in Late Medieval Culture*. Cambridge: Cambridge University Press, 1991.

Rubinstein, Nicolai. "Italian Reactions to Terraferma Expansion in the Fifteenth Century." In *Renaissance Venice*, ed. J. R. Hale, 197–217. London: Faber and Faber, 1973.

Ruggiero, Guido. *Binding Passions: Tales of Marriage, Magic, and Power at the End of the Renaissance*. Oxford: Oxford University Press, 1993.

Rundle, David. "A Renaissance Bishop and His Books: A Preliminary Survey of the Manuscript Collection of Pietro del Monte (c. 1400–57)." *Papers of the British School at Rome* 69 (2001): 245–272.

―――. "The Two Libraries: Humanists' Ideals and Ecclesiastics' Practice in the Book-collecting of Paul II and His Contemporaries." In *Humanisme et église en Italie et en France méridionale (XVe siècle—milieu du XVIe siècle)*, ed. Patrick Gilli, 167–185. Rome: École française de Rome, 2004.

Saggi, Ludovico. *La congregazione mantovana dei Carmelitani sino alla morte del B. Battista Spagnoli (1516)*. Rome: Institutum Carmelitanum, 1954.

Sahlins, Peter. *Boundaries: The Making of France and Spain in the Pyreneees.* Berkeley: University of California Press, 1989.

Sandal, Ennio. "Autonomie municipali e libertà ecclesiastica: Un episodio di intolleranza a Brescia nel primo Cinquecento." *Commentari dell'Ateneo di Brescia* 187 (1988): 375–383.

———. "Dal libro antico al libro moderno: Premesse e materiali per una indagine; Brescia, 1472–1550; una verifica esemplare." In *I primordi della stampa a Brescia, 1472–1511: Atti del convegno internazionale (Brescia, 6–8 giugno 1984)*, ed. Sandal, 227–307. Padua: Editrice Antenore, 1986.

Santi, F. "Lazzaroni, Pietro." *DBI*, 64:243–245.

Scalvini, Maria Luisa, and Gian Piero Calza, eds. *Bergamo 1516: Città e territorio nella "Descriptio" di Marcantonio Michiel.* Padua: Centro grafico editoriale, 1983.

Schöpflin, George. "The Functions of Myth and a Taxonomy of Myths." In *Myths and Nationhood*, ed. Geoffrey Hosking and George Schöpflin, 19–36. London: Hurst, 1997.

Schraven, M. "Giovanni Battista Borghese's Funeral 'Apparato' of 1610 in S. Maria Maggiore, Rome." *Burlington Magazine* 143 (2001): 23–28.

Schreckenberg, Heinz. *The Jews in Christian Art: An Illustrated History.* Trans. John Bowden. London: SCM Press, 1996.

Scott, James ca. *Domination and the Arts of Resistance: Hidden Transcripts.* New Haven: Yale University Press, 1990.

Scotti, G. "La 'magnifica patria' nel '500 (disegno storico delle istituzioni)." *Studi Veneziani* 11 (1969): 243–324.

Scribner, R. W. "Cosmic Order and Daily Life: Sacred and Secular in Pre-industrial German Society." In Scribner, *Popular Culture and Popular Movements in Reformation Germany*, 1–16. London: Hambledon, 1987.

———. "Ritual and Popular Belief in Catholic Germany at the Time of the Reformation." In Scribner, *Popular Culture and Popular Movements in Reformation Germany*, 17–47. London: Hambledon, 1987.

Serafini, A. "Giovanni Maria da Brescia." *DBI* 56:347–351.

Sevesi, Paolo M. "La congregazione dei Capriolanti e le origini della provincia dei frati minori della regolare osservanza di Brescia." *Archivum Franciscanum Historicum* 7 (1914): 108–121.

Shahar, Shulamith. *The Fourth Estate: A History of Women in the Middle Ages.* London: Routledge, 1991.

Shemek, Deanna. "Circular Definitions: Configuring Gender in Italian Renaissance Festival." *Renaissance Quarterly* 48.1 (1995): 1–40.

Shulvass, Moses A. *The Jews in the World of the Renaissance.* Trans. Elvin I. Kose. Leiden: Brill, 1973.

Simonelli, Prospero. "Crisanto e Daria." *BS*, vol. 4, cols. 300–305.

Simonsohn, Shlomo, ed. *The Jews in the Duchy of Milan.* 4 vols. Jerusalem: Israel Academy of Sciences and Humanities, 1982–86.

Somaini, F. "Processi costitutivi, dinamiche politiche e strutture istituzionali dello stato viscontea-sforzesco." In *Storia d'Italia*, ed. Giuseppe Galasso, vol. 6, *Comuni e signorie nell'Italia settentrionale: La Lombardia*, 681–782. Turin: UTET, 1998.

Somers Margaret R. "The Narrative Constitution of Identity: A Relational and Network Approach." *Theory and Society* 23.5 (1994): 605–649.

Stephens, Walter. *Demon Lovers: Witchcraft, Sex and the Crisis of Belief.* Chicago: University of Chicago Press, 2002.

Strocchia, Sharon T. *Death and Ritual in Renaissance Florence.* Baltimore: Johns Hopkins University Press, 1992.

——. "Death Rites and the Ritual Family in Renaissance Florence." In *Life and Death in Fifteenth-century Florence*, ed. Marcel Tetel, Ronald G. Witt, and Rona Goffen. Durham, N.C.: Duke University Press, 1989.

Tabacco, G. *Le ideologie politiche del medioevo.* Turin: Einaudi, 2000.

Tamani, Giuliano. "La tipografia ebraica a Brescia e a Barco nel sec. XV." In *I primordi della stampa a Brescia, 1472–1511: Atti del convegno internazionale (Brescia, 6–8 giugno 1984)*, ed. Ennio Sandal, 61–80. Padua: Editrice Antenore, 1986.

Tamburini, Filippo. "Suppliche per i casi di stregoneria diabolica nei registri della Penitenzieria e conflitti inquisitoriali (sec. XV–XVI)." *Critica Storica* 23.4 (1986): 605–659.

Tavuzzi, Michael. *Renaissance Inquisitors: Dominican Inquisitors and Inquisitorial Districts in Northern Italy, 1474–1527.* Leiden: Brill, 2007.

Te Brake, Wayne. *Shaping History: Ordinary People in European Politics, 1500–1700.* Berkeley: University of California Press, 1998.

Tedoldi, Leonida. "Tra immigrazione e integrazione sociale: La cittadinanza 'creata' a Brescia in età veneta (secc. XVI–XVIII)." *Società e Storia* 93 (2001): 439–462.

Terpstra, Nicholas, ed. *The Art of Executing Well: Rituals of Execution in Renaissance Italy.* Kirksville, Mo.: Truman State University Press, 2008.

——. "Death and Dying in Renaissance Confraternities." In *Crossing the Boundaries: Christian Piety and the Arts in Italian Medieval and Renaissance Confraternities*, ed. K. Eisenblicher, 179–200. Kalamazoo: Medieval Institute Publications, Western Michigan University, 1991.

Thomas, Anne Elisabeth. "The Meetting of Two Worlds: The Classical and the Secular in Floriano Ferramola's Fresco Cycle in Palazzo Calini, Brescia." MA diss., Courtauld Institute of Art, 2 vols. 1999.

Toaff, Ariel. "'Banchieri' cristiani e 'prestatori' ebrei?" In *Storia d'Italia: Annali, 11. Gli ebrei in Italia; Dall'alto Medioevale all'età dei ghetti*, ed. Corrado Vivanti, 267–287. Turin: Einaudi, 1996.

——. *Pasque di sangue: Ebrei d'Europa e omicidi rituali.* Bologna: Il Mulino, 2007.

Toch, Michael. "Der jüdische Geldhandel in der Wirtschaft des Deutschen Spätmittelalters: Nürnberg, 1350–1499." *Blätter für deutsche Landesgeschichte* 117 (1981): 283–310.

Tortelli, Giorgio. "Inquisizione e stregoneria a Brescia e nelle valli: La difficile convivenza fra autorità laiche e religiose nei primi decenni del XVI secolo." In *Scritti in onore di Gaetano Panazza*, 259–268. Brescia: Geroldi, 1994.

Treccani degli Alfieri, Giovanni, ed. *Storia di Brescia*. 4 vols. Brescia: Morcelliana, 1961–64.

Trevor-Roper, H. R. *The European Witch-craze of the Sixteenth and Seventeenth Centuries*. London: Penguin, 1988.

Trexler, Richard C. "Correre la Terra: Collective Insults in the Late Middle Ages." *Mélanges de l'École française de Rome* 96 (1984): 845–902.

⸺. "Florentine Prostitution in the Fifteenth Century: Patrons and Clients." In Trexler, *Dependence in Context in Renaissance Florence*, 373–414. Binghamton, NY: Medieval and Renaissance Texts and Studies, 1994.

⸺. "La Prostitution Florentine au Xe siecle: Patronages et clientèles." *Annales: E. S. C.* 36 (1981): 983–1015.

⸺. *Public Life in Renaissance Florence*. Ithaca: Cornell University Press, 1991.

Trout, D. E. *Paulinus of Nola: Life, Letters, and Poems*. Berkeley: University of California Press, 1999.

Trumbower, Jeffrey A. *Rescue for the Dead: The Posthumous Salvation of Non-Christians in Early Christianity*. Oxford: Oxford University Press, 2001.

Valentini, Andrea. *Carlo Valgulio: Letterato bresciano del XV secolo*. Brescia: A. Luzzago, 1903.

⸺. "Gli statuti di Brescia dei secoli XII al XV illustrati e documenti inediti." *Nuovo Archivio Veneto* 15 (1898): 5–98, 370–391.

Van den Neste, Evelyne. *Tournois, joûtes, pas d'armes dans les villes de Flandre à la fin du Moyen Age (1300–1486)*. Paris: Écoles des chartes, 1996.

Varanini, Gian Maria. "Appunti per la storia del prestito e dell'insediamento ebraico a Verona nel Quattrocento: Problemi e linee di ricerca." In *Gli ebrei e Venezia secoli XIV–XVIII: Atti del Convegno internazionale organizzato dall'Istituto di storia della società e dello stato veneziano della Fondazione Giorgio Cini, Venezia, Isola di San Giorgio Maggiore 5–10 giugno 1983*, ed. Gaetano Cozzi, 615–628. Milan: Edizioni Comunità, 1987.

⸺. "Aristocrazie e poteri nell'Italia centro-settentrionale dalla crisi comunale alle guerre d'Italia." In *Le aristocrazie dai signori rurali al patriziato*, ed. R. Bordone, G. Castelnuovo, and G. M. Varanini, 121–194. Rome: Laterza, 2004.

⸺. "Il comune di Verona, Venezia e gli ebrei nel Quattrocento: Problemi e linee di ricerca." In Varanini, *Comuni cittadini e stato regionale: Ricerche sulla terraferma veneta nel Quattrocento*, 279–293. Verona: Libreria editrice universitaria, 1992.

⸺. *Comuni cittadini e stato regionale: Ricerche sulla terraferma veneta nel Quattrocento*. Verona: Libreria editrice universitaria, 1992.

⸺. "Il giurista, il comune cittadino, la dominante: Bartolomeo Cipolla legato del comune di Verona a Venezia (1447–1463)." In Varanini, *Comuni cittadini e stato regionale: Ricerche sulla terraferma veneta nel Quattrocento*, 361–384. Verona: Libreria editrice universitaria, 1992.

⸺. "Gli statuti delle città della terraferma veneta dall'età signorile alle riforme quattrocentesche." In Varanini, *Comuni cittadini e stato regionale: Ricerche sulla terraferma veneta nel Quattrocento,* 3–56. Verona: Libreria editrice universitaria, 1992.

———. "La terraferma al tempo della crisi della Lega di Cambrai: Proposte per una rilettura del 'caso' veronese (1519 [*sic*]–1517)." In Varanini, *Comuni cittadini e stato regionale: Ricerche sulla terraferma veneta nel Quattrocento,* 397–435. Verona: Libreria editrice universitaria, 1992.

———. "Venezia e l'entroterra (1300 circa-1420)." In *Storia di Venezia dalle origini alla caduta della serenissima,* ed. G. Arnaldi, G. Cracco, and A. Tenenti, vol 3, *La formazione dell stato patrizio,* 159–236. Rome: Istituto dell'enciclopedia italiana, 1997.

Varanini, Gian Maria, and R. Mueller, eds. *Ebrei nella terraferma veneta del Quattrocento.* Florence: Florence University Press, 2005.

Veneziani, Paolo. "La Stampa a Brescia e nel bresciano 1472–1511." In *I primordi della Stampa a Brescia, 1472–1511. Atti del convegno internazionale (Brescia, 6–8, giugno 1984),* ed. Ennio Sandal, 1–23. Padua: Antenore, 1986.

Vauchez, André. "Patronage des saints et religion civique dans l'Italie communale à la fin du moyen âge." In *Patronage and Public in the Trecento: Proceedings of the St Lambrecht Symposium, Abtei St Lambrecht, Styria, 16–19 July 1984,* ed. V. Moleta, 59–80. Florence: Olschki, 1986.

———. "Rocco." *BS,* vol. 11, cols. 264–273.

———. *Sainthood in the Later Middle Ages.* Trans. Jean Birrell. 2nd ed. Cambridge: Cambridge University Press, 1997.

Ventura, Angelo. "Bragadin, Francesco." *DBI,* 13:672–674

———. *Nobiltà e popolo nella società veneta del '400 e '500.* Rome: Laterza, 1964.

Viggiano, Alfredo. "Aspetti politici e giurisdizionali dell'attività dei rettori veneziani nell *stato da terra* del Quattrocento." *Società e Storia* 65 (1994): 473–505.

———. *Governanti e governati: Legittimità del potere ed esercizio dell'autorità sovrana nello Stato veneto della prima età moderna.* Treviso: Fondazione Benetton'/'Edizioni Canova, 1993.

Visioli, Monica. "Bergamo: XV–XVII secolo; Organizzazione e trasformazione degli spazi urbani." In *Fabbriche, piazze, mercati: La città italiana nel Rinascimento,* ed. Donatella Calabi, 159–188. Rome: Officina, 1997.

Vovelle, Michel. *La mort et l'occident de 1300 à nos jours.* Paris: Gallimard, 1983.

Webb, Diana. *Patrons and Defenders: The Saints in the Italian City-States.* London: Tauris, 1996.

Weinstein, Donald. *Savonarola and Florence: Prophecy and Patriotism in the Renaissance.* Princeton: Princeton University Press, 1970.

Wethey, Harold E. *The Paintings of Titian: Complete Edition.* Vol. 3. *The Mythological and Historical Paintings.* London: Phaidon, 1975.

Wittmayer Baron, Salo. *A Social and Religious History of the Jews: Late Middle Ages and Era of European Expansion, 1200–1650.* Vol. 10. *On the Empire's Periphery.* New York Philadelphia: Columbia University Press and Jewish Publication Society of America, 1965/5726.

Wootton, David. "Ulysses Bound? Venice and the Idea of Liberty from Howell to Hume." In *Republicanism, Liberty, and Commercial Society, 1649–1776,* ed. David Wootton, 341–367, 473–477. Stanford: Stanford University Press, 1994.

Zabbia, M. *I notai e la cronachistica cittadina nel Trecento*. Rome: Istituto storico italiano per il medio evo, 1999.

Zaggia, Stefano. "Padova: XV–XVII secolo: Trasformazione e continuità negli spazi urbani centrali." In *Fabbriche, piazze, mercati: La città italiana nel Rinascimento*, ed. Donatella Calabi, 255–293. Rome: Officina, 1997.

Zamboni, Baldassarre. *Memorie intorno alle pubbliche fabbriche più insigni della città di Brescia*. Brescia: Pietro Vescovi, 1778.

Zamperetti, Sergio. *I piccoli principi: Signorie locali, feudi e comunità soggette nello Stato regionale veneto dall'espansione territoriale ai primi decenni del '600*. Venice: Il cardo, 1991.

——. "'I sinedri dolosi': Note sulla formazione e lo sviluppo dei corpi territoriali nello Stato regionale veneto tra '500 e '600." *Rivista Storica Italiana* 99 (1987): 51–101.

Zanelli, Agostino. *Brescia sotto la signoria di Filippo Maria Visconti (1421–1426)*. Turin: Fratelli Bocca, 1892. Extracted from *Rivista Storica Italiana* 9.3 (1892): 395–451.

——. *Delle condizioni interne di Brescia dal 1426 al 1644 e del moto della borghesia contro la nobiltà nel 1644*. Brescia: Tipografia editrice, 1898.

——. "La devozione di Brescia a Venezia e il principio della sua decadenza economica nel secolo XVI." *Archivio Storico Lombardo*, 4th ser., 17 (1912): 23–100.

——. "La festa dell'Assunta in Brescia nel medio evo." *Archivio Storico Italiano*, 5th ser., 9 (1892): 1–30.

——. "Pietro del Monte." *Archivio Storico Lombardo*, 4th ser., 7 (1907): 317–78; 8 (1908): 46–115.

——. "Predicatori a Brescia nel quattrocento." *Archivio Storico Lombardo*, 3rd ser., 15 (1901): 83–144.

——. "La signoria di Pandolfo Malatesta in Brescia secondo i registri dell'archivio Malatestiano di Fano." *Archivio Storico Lombardo*, 6th ser., 58 (1931): 126–141.

Zanetti, Ginevra. "Le signorie (1313–1426)." In *Storia di Brescia*, ed. Giovanni Treccani degli Alfieri, vol. 1, *Dalle origini alla caduta della signoria viscontea*, 823–876. Brescia: Morcelliana, 1963.

Zarri, Gabriella. "Aspetti dello sviluppo degli ordini religiosi in Italia tra Quattro e Cinquecento: Studi e problemi." In *Strutture ecclesiastiche in Italia e in Germania prima della Riforma*, ed. Paolo Prodi and Peter Johanek, 207–257. Bologna: Il Mulino, 1984.

Zucker, Mark J. "Early Italian Engravings for Religious Orders." *Zeitschrift für Kuntsgeschichte* 56.3 (1993): 366–384.

——. *The Illustrated Bartsch*, vol. 25, (*Commentary*): *Early Italian Masters*. New York: Abaris Books, 1984.

Index

Elisha, 209
Elizabeth, Saint, and feast of visit to Mary,
    266n65
Enoch, 211
Epictetus, 149
Epicureanism, 121, 186
Erasmo da Narni, 15
Erasmus, Desiderius, 149, 284n60
Estimo. See Taxation
Evasio, Sant', 96
Eymeric, Nicolau, 179

Fabius Maximus, Quintus, 219
Façade decoration, 123
Factions, 23, 218–219, 227. *See also* Feuds
Faenza, 137
Faita clan, 74
Faith: image of, 27, 28; virtue of, 147, 155
Falier, Francesco *(podestà)*, 14, 219
Famine, 124–125, 139, 143, 185
Fasani clan, 68
Fasting, 123
Faustino, San, 15, 27; descended from
    Scipio Africanus, 38; miraculous
    appearance of, 41, 94, 200–201; life and
    works of, 41; transfer of body of, 42,
    102; images of, 88, 92, 94–95, 225–226;
    sites associated with, 93–94, 102;
    discovery of body of, 94; processions for,
    98; square of, 129. *See also* Giovita, San
Feasts, 123, 124, 186, 201
Fedele, Cassandra, 36
Federici clan, 61, 175, 202, 233
Feliciano, Felice, 89
Feltre, 52
Fenaroli, Ventura di Giorgio, 75, 214
Fenaroli clan, 74
Feroldi, Giacomo, 75
Ferramola, Floriano: decorates Calini
    palace, 77, 84–85, 86; decorates organ
    shutters in duomo, 225; decorates
    marriage chest, 263n92
Ferrandus, Tommaso, 37, 308n1
Ferrara, 99, 160, 164
Ferrarino, Michele, 89
Ferraro, Joanne, 26
Feuds, 62–63, 70, 108, 112, 118, 226. *See
    also* Factions
Fifth Lateran Council, 178, 208
Filipin de Ramoligo, 165
*Five Saints with a Vision of the Virgin and
    Child in Glory* (Giovanni Maria da
    Brescia), 209–213

Flood, 102, 185
Flora (goddess), 29
Folch de Cardona, Ramòn, 214, 215
Foppa, Vincenzo, 90, 211, 273n48, 306n80
Fortifications, 86–87, 215, 222, 234
Fortune, indifference to, 152
Foscari, Doge Francesco: 15, 87
Foscari, Marco *(podestà)*, 87, 227
Foscarini, Ludovico *(provveditore)*, 52,
    52–53
Fountains, 41, 43, 102, 124, 226
Fourth Lateran Council, 141
Francis, Saint, 93, 266n65. *See also*
    Franciscans
Franciscans, 42, 103, 107, 113, 114, 138,
    170, 222; of San Francesco della Vigna,
    111, 114; and poverty, 152; praised, 155;
    and Val Camonica, 174, 176; superstition
    of, 179. *See also* Amadeites; Bernardino
    da Feltre; Capriolanti; Francis, Saint;
    Monte di pietà; Preaching; Sanson,
    Francesco
Frederick III, emperor, 62
French: occupation, 198–202, 214; and
    Jews, 205, 206, 207. *See also* League of
    Cambrai; Louis XII; Sack of Brescia
    (1512)
Frigerio, Francesco, 162
Friuli, 169
Funerals: in Brescia, 23–24, 123, 197;
    increasing size of, 135–137, 139, 148;
    social function of, 136–137; in England,
    150; orations at, 152. *See also* Tombs

Gabbiano, 61
Gadolo, Bernardino, 243n78
Gaetano da Thiene, 223
Gambara, Alda, 203, 206
Gambara, Count Giovanni Francesco, 62,
    203, 259nn99, 100, 271n10
Gambara, Count Niccolò, 63, 199
Gambara, Ludovico, 75
Gambara, Veronica, 203, 252n114,
    276n24, 302n114
Gambara clan, 61, 66, 164, 199,
    202
Gambara vicariate, 57, 59, 61
Gambling, 108, 122, 262n76
Gaming, 100, 220, 227
Garda, lake, 15, 89, 91, 97
Gaspare da Rivedessa, 185
Gates, 18. *See also* Bruciata gate; San
    Giovanni; San Nazaro

Harvard University Press is a member of Green Press Initiative
(greenpressinitiative.org), a nonprofit organization working to
help publishers and printers increase their use of recycled paper
and decrease their use of fiber derived from endangered forests.
This book was printed on recycled paper containing 30%
post-consumer waste and processed chlorine free.